BOULDER COUNTY

An Illustrated History

Thomas J. Noel & Dan W. Corson

First Edition

All inquiries should be addressed to Heritage Media Corp.

ISBN: 1-886483-26-4

Library of Congress
Card Catalog Number: 98-073493

Author: Thomas J. Noel & Dan W. Corson

Publisher: C.E. Parks

Editor-in-Chief: Lori M. Parks

VP/National Sales Manager: Ray Spagnuolo

VP/Corporate Development: Bart Barica

CFO: Randall Peterson

Production Manager: Deborah Sherwood

Managing Editor: Betsy Baxter Blondin

Art Director: Gina Mancini

Production Staff: Jason Atzert, Jeff Caton, Sean Gates, Brad Hartman, Dave Hermstead, Jay Kennedy, John Leyva, Barry Miller, Susie Passons, Norm Pruitt, Chris Rivera, Steve Trainor

Project Editor: Renee Kim

Coordinating Editors: Betsy Lelja, Elizabeth Lex, Sara Rufner, Adriane Wessels, John Woodward

Regional Sales Manager: Jill DeLeary

Profile Writers: Dennis Bloomquist, Lorraine Campbell, Phil Carson, Bridget Cook, Elizabeth Ellis, Therese Eminian-Schoen, Sarah Massey-Warren, Ihla Nation, Allison Rainey, Kerri Shea

Administration Manager: Ellen Ruby

Administration: Juan Diaz, Emily Knopp, Majka Penner Scott Reid, Patrick Rucker, Cory Sottek

Project Coordinators: Megan Bennett, Judy Pinson

Published by

Heritage Media Corp.

6354 Corte del Abeto, Suite B

Carlsbad, California 92009

www.heritagemedia.com

Printed by Heritage Media Corp. in the United States of America
Published in cooperation with Historic Boulder Inc.

Photos on page 2, 5, 6 and 8 by Ron Ruhoff
page 5 photo by Tom Noel

this book is dedicated to

Sharyn, Laura-Claire & Bailey Corson and Gracie, Ned & Sam Noel

table of *contents*

PART I

Acknowledgments 8

One
The Shining Mountains 12

Two
Boulder City's Birth & Boosterism 24

Three
Boulder Blossoms 40

Four
Mountain Towns 58

Five
Longmont 80

Six
Louisville, Lafayette & the Coal Towns 96

Seven
Sodbuster Communities 116

Eight
Planning Ahead 132

Nine
Preserving Boulder County 150

Ten
Into the 21st Century 170

Continued...

table of contents

PART 2

Partners in Boulder

Building a Greater Boulder 188

Business & Finance 204

Manufacturing & Distribution 216

Marketplace 224

Professional Services 258

Quality of Life 272

Technology 292

index

Bibliography 300

Index 307

Partners Index 312

acknowledgments

All over Boulder County we found people who made this book possible and made it a joy. In Broomfield, we were educated by Depot Museum Director Peggy Atkinson, Arne Carlson, Elaine Davis, City Manager George DiCiero, Terrie Hospers, Jim Long, Shawn Stark and Terri Thompson. They helped us try to tell the story of that boom town about to become Colorado's first new county since 1913. In Canfield, we were treated to a tour and photos with pioneer grande dame Dr. Sarah Wise and received help from Erie Town Planner Debra Bachelder.

Gold Hill, the county's oldest mining camp, has hospitable and spirited human resources who shared much with us, especially their concern about keeping Gold Hill the way it is. Thank you Jeff Cambelie, Chellee Courtney, Edith Eilender, Barbara and Frank Finn, Hugh Moore, Joseph Stepanek and Lynne Walter.

In Lafayette, Elizabeth and James Hutchison gave us a terrific tour of the Lafayette Miner's Museum and shared stories and photos. Dr. Steven Mehls, who has done much to preserve the town, gave us a tour of Lafayette's treasures. A tip of the hat as well to Dana Coffield, Douglas Conarroe, City Administrator Gary Klaphake, Susan Koster, Josephine Najera, Andy Proctor and Planning Director Bonnie Starr.

In Longmont, Dale Bernard, executive director of the St. Vrain Historical Society, gave us a grand tour of the Callahan and Hover estates and generously allowed us to revel in the society's resources. Longmont has one of Colorado's finest municipal museums. It is run by Kent Brown, and Cathey M. Dunn provided terrific knowledge and guidance to the museum's photo collection. Thanks also to Longmonters Commander Craig Earhart, Paula Fitzgerald, Councilman Ron Gallegos, Harriette Grigsby, City Planner Andrea Mimnaugh, Betty Anne Newby, Brian O'Hanlon. Silvia Pettem, Bea Ramos, City Planner Brad Schol, Edwina Salazar Waldrip, Michael Woodruff and Mayor Leona Stoecker.

Don Ross showed us around Louisville and arranged for copies from the crackerjack photo archives of the Louisville Historical Commission. Thanks also to Louisvillians Eugene, Nadine and Virginia Caranci, Carolyn Conarroe, Bill Convery, Jay Fell, Eric Hartronft, Donna Hudgel, Gina Liscum, City Planners Meredyth Muth and Manjeet Ranu, Steve Rowe, Cassandra Volpe, Paul Weissman and Judy and Luther Wilson.

Lyons' grande dame of preservation, LaVern Johnson, lived up to her reputation, giving us a tour, a look inside the Lyons Red Sandstone Schoolhouse Museum, a walk through Sandstone Park and copies of Lyons' photos and documents. Rarely does one town owe so much to one person. Thanks also to Town Clerk Terry Andrews and Fred Shelton. Niwot's Anne Dyni is another wonder who has done prodigious work to research, write and preserve Boulder County's agricultural heritage. In Meeker Park, Lillian Trevarton, who lovingly saved her family's ranch, was most gracious as was Marjorie Cinnamon, who led us through Hygiene's Dunkard Church.

For information on Nederland and Caribou, we are indebted to Town Trustee Scott Bruntjen, Glenna Carline, Alisa Lewis, Betsy Phillips and Tom Hendricks, who treated us to a tour of his working gold mine. A. L. Fisher and June Howard taught us about Sunshine, while Marti Anderson helped with Salina. Wall Street miner and author Delores "Dee" Bailey shared her memories and photos. Dan Kupfner shared his thoughts and knowledge of Superior, while Rev. Stephen Bird and Hugh McGinty saved us in Valmont. In Ward, we learned from Tom Ward, former Mayor Jill Sturdevant, Town Clerk Deb Johnson-Evangelista and various congenial, informative bartenders at the Mill Site Inn.

In the City of Boulder we received help from so many people that we must apologize for anyone we've overlooked in the course of this two-year-long project. Historic Boulder, Inc. originally proposed this book and made it run smoothly thanks to Myrna Ashley, Kathryn Barth, Doug Conarroe, Marilee DeGoede, Executive Director Alan Hafer, Gerry Haedrich, Sarah Massey-Warren, Mildred Nilon, Executive Director Sandy Priester, Naomi Ware, Jo Wright and Rebecca

Waugh, who provided tours and her exemplary preservation plans for sites countywide.

Boulder's human landmarks Mary Axe, Al Bartlett, John Buechner, Betty Chronic, Margaret Coel, Paul Danish, Joyce Davies, Leslie Durgin, Tom Eldridge, Margaret Hansen, Tom Meier, Laurence Paddock, Rob Pudim, Janet Roberts, Dorothy Rupert, Jack Smith, Ricky Weiser and Ruth Wright were more than kind.

We could not have done this without Leslie Aaholm, Margaret Bartlett Anderson, Matthew Appelbaum, G. Paul Bailey, Vincent Beach, City Planner Brent Bean, Gary Berg, City Attorney Alan Boles, Cindy Brown, Libby Brown, Eric Butler, Beverly Carrigan, Open Space Director Jim Crain, William Cramer, Nancy Dayton, City Attorney Joseph N. de Raismes III, Parks Director Chris Dropinski, Woody Eaton, Richard Epstein, Ann FitzSimmons, County Planner Pete Fogg, Donna Gartenmann, City Attorney Rosemary Gearhart, Kurt Gerstle, Wendy Gordon, Kent Groninger, Phyllis Gunn, Joel Haertling, City Planner Jean Hagen, Richard Harris, Barrie Hartman, Jane Henry, Norris Hermsmeyer, Michael Holleran, Julie Husband, James Johnson, William Branham Jones, Kathy Keller, Neil King, County Open Space Planner Rich Koopman, City Planner Gary Kretschmer, County Planner Camilla Laughlin, City Clerk Alisa Lewis, Jeff Limerick, Eric Lombardi, "Dick" Lyman, Russell MacCachran, Harold Malde, Jack Mann, Joe Mantione, James Marsden, Eric Mason, City Planner Ruth McHeyser, Robert McKelvey, Sara Michl, Charles Moore, Bernie Morson, Chris Mueller, Quigg Newton, Mary Ann Nitchie, David Norcross, Betty O'Lear, City Planner Susan Osborne, Cynthia Owsley, City Planning Director Peter Pollock, City Human Services Director Susan Purdy, City Planner Lara Ramsey, City Public Works Director David Rhodes, City Planner Susan Richstone, Allan B. Rogers, Jr., June Sampson, Pete Saucier, Christopher Shears, City Parks Planner Maureen Spitzer, Caryn Stinson, Dave Sutherland, Carol Taylor, Ray Tuomey, Richard Varnes, Delani Wheeler, Diane Williamson, Butch Wilson and Jim and Nurit Wolf.

At CU-Boulder, campus architect William R. Deno and William Arndt helped us, as did Bob Nero, Kay Oltmans and Darrell Wells.

Photographers and photo collectors James Baca, Ed and Nancy Bathke, Robert L. Brown, Mary Sullivan, Mary Anne Stevens, Peter Pollock and Nurit Wolf provided illustrations. Liz Clancy of the Denver Museum of Natural History dug deep into the museum's vast photo archives as did the late Dick Conn of the Denver Art Museum.

Librarians Jody Corruccini, Wendy Hall and Mary Jo Reitsema at Boulder's wonderful Carnegie Branch Library for Local History were indispensable as was the University of Colorado's archives at Norlin Library. The Boulder Historical Society gave us a great Harbeck House tour and allowed use of its fabulous photo collection.

Eleanor Gehres, manager of the Western History Department of the Denver Public Library, and her fine staff, especially photo librarians Jennifer Thom and Lori Swingle, produced many new Boulder County photos. Across the street at the Colorado Historical Society we were blessed to work with photo curator Eric Paddock and librarians Rebecca Lintz and Deborah Neiswonger. On the third floor, State Archaeologist Susan Collins and the staff of the Office of Archaeology and Historic Preservation shared their awesome files.

Research papers by CU-Denver students Scott Allen, Patricia L. Austin, Susan Bodak, Robert Bouche, Michael Clark, Jonathan Gettings. J. Linden Hagans, Martha Ripley, Doris Schwab, Ron D. Sladek and Don Walker were also helpful, not to mention John O'Dell's 1999 master's thesis on Middle Boulder Creek. Thanks also to Chas Moore, Quigg Newton, Noel Semple and Rike Wootten.

Some wonderful people worked on many different parts of this project, lending us editorial reviews, tours, expertise, documents and photos. Authors are blessed by the likes of Dale Bernard, Bill Bessesen, Rosemary Fetter, Steve Leonard, Laurence Paddock, Silvia Pettem. Peter Pollock, Jack Smith, Mike Smith, and Rebecca Waugh.

Lastly and most importantly, our families supported this time-consuming endeavor. Thanks to Sharyn, Laura-Claire and Bailey Corson and Jim, Chris, Gracie, Ned, Sam and Vi Noel. ◆

ALLEN'S PARK
ORE MILL
CONTINENTAL DIVIDE
(SNOWY RANGE OF ROCKY MOUNTAINS)
GOLD AND SILVER
MINING
MIDDLE FORK
SOUTH FORK OF
JAMES CREEK
WARD-STRUGGLER MINES
WARD
COLUMBIA VEIN
LULU B
UTICA
MORNING STAR
SUPERIOR
MOUNTAIN CHIEF
GREY EAGLE
AMERICAN STAR
NUGGET
WAND
BIG FIVE MINES
FRANCIS
BRAINERD MINES
COLD SPRING
PRUSSIAN
SLIDE
GOLD H
SUMMERVILLE
DUNCAN
RED LION
PUZZLER
GOLDEN SLIPPER
WARD-ROSE MINES
LUCKY STAR
WALL STREET
GOWANDA
MILWAUKEE
YUKON G.M.-M. COS MINES
SUNSET
FOUR-MILE CR.
SUNSET MILL & MINES
Colorado and North-Weste
SUGAR LOAF MOUNTAIN
WASHINGTON AVE.
SMOKY HILL
LIVINGSTON MINES
PRESTON TUNNEL AND WATER POWER
GREAT WESTERN EXP. COS TUNGSTEN MINES
FOURTH OF JULY MINE
UPPER RANCH
DENVER TUNNEL
NORTH BOULDER CR.
MIDDLE BOULDER CR.
AUGUSTA
INDIA
U.S. GOLD CORPORATION'S MINES
POORMAN CARIBOU
CARIBOU
BOULDER COUNTY MINES
CARDINAL
BOULDER COUNTY MILL
NATIONAL G. M.-L. COS MINES
NEDERLAND
REVENGE
ELDORA
BIRD'S NEST
MOGUL TUNNEL
BOULDER COUNTY
GILPIN COUNTY
Denver, North-Western & Pacific Ry. (Moffat Line)

1904 map, Ed Bathke Collection

1999 photo by Tom Noel

Tom Noel Collection

Denver Public Library, Western History Department

Denver Art Museum

Peter Pollock Collection

The Shining Mountains

Chapter *One*

Before the earth was inhabited it was covered with water. A pipe floated on top as a boat for the Great Spirit. In the boat with the Great Spirit were a duck, a beaver and a turtle. The Great Spirit knew that clay was at the bottom of the water so he asked the turtle to go down and bring Him some. But the turtle came back unable to reach the bottom. The beaver was also unsuccessful. The duck went next. He stayed longer and returned with some clay in his bill. The Great Spirit took the clay and threw it to the four different winds to form dry ground. Then He made the moon and after that men and women from whom The People descended. The sacred pipe was given to them and they were instructed as to its care. The pipe was made of wood so hard and so shining that many thought it stone.

—Arapaho Creation Myth

◆ (Opening photo with kids) No photograph survives of Niwot, leader of the Boulder band of Southern Arapaho. He struck one pioneer, Julia Lampert, as "the finest looking Indian I have ever seen. He was over six feet tall, of muscular build, and much more intelligent than the average Indian. [He] did not braid his hair; it hung loosely over his shoulders. When wearing his war bonnet and full warrior's regalia, he looked every inch a chief." The 1985 red stone sculpture of Chief Niwot by Thomas Meagher Miller is on Boulder Creek at the southeast corner of 9th and Canyon. Boulder children, unlike their great-great grandfathers, fancy the famed Arapaho chieftain.
1999 photo by Tom Noel

With his left hand, the newborn Arapaho reached for his mother. So she named him Niwot (Left Hand). He was given the usual indulgent Arapaho childhood and breastfed until the age of four. By then Niwot was eating jerky — dried buffalo meat that his mother mixed with dried chokecherries, strawberries, currants and cattail roots. He grew tall, with the light skin and large nose that distinguished the Arapaho from other Plains tribes.

The name Arapaho may come from the Pawnee word for "trader," because the Arapaho were great traders. Lakota Sioux referred to the Arapaho as "Blue Sky People." Some other tribes called them the "Tattooed People" because they scratched their breasts with a yucca leaf needle, then rubbed wood ashes into the wound to make an indelible chest tattoo. The Arapaho called themselves "Our People" or the "Bison Path People."

As a youngster, Niwot first saw the High Plains and Shining Mountains from a cradleboard on his mother's back. The Southern Arapaho kept moving with the seasons and with the buffalo.

In the spring the tribe left Boulder Creek for the prairies that stretched eastward as far as the eye could see. In those days Niwot could ride his pony all day and never get beyond the huge buffalo herds that darkened and shook the plains like thunderstorms. By July, the High Plains turned hot and dry and brown. The buffalo headed northward and into the cooler mountain valleys. The Arapaho followed, first north to Wyoming and then westward into the mountains. In North Park they found water, greener grass for their horses and game for their families. Following a circular route, the tribe then headed back toward Boulder Creek. Niwot's people climbed the Continental Divide and the Indian Peaks, where they camped and hunted at the top of the Shining Mountains.

Even as a youngster, Niwot fancied the glistening snowbanks on the breast of the Continental Divide, the perpetual ice fields such as Arapaho Glacier. When the first snows whitened the high country, when the creeks began to freeze, the Arapaho migrated down Boulder, St. Vrain and Left Hand canyons to their winter camps on Boulder Creek. At the base of the Shining Mountains, cottonwood groves protected them from the blizzards that blasted the mountains and the High Plains. Along the creek, their horses found grass that stayed green much of the winter. At this leeward base of the Rockies, they prayed for the winter chinook winds that warmed their lodges.

Sometimes Niwot wondered if the winds would blow down the tipi, but his mother, grandmother and aunts somehow made the tipis so strong that even 100-mile-an-hour blasts did not knock them over. Yet the Arapaho women could take down the same tipis in less than two hours when the tribe needed to move fast to escape the Utes or to catch the buffalo.

During deep winters, when snow stayed on the ground for weeks, the horses gnawed on the cottonwood twigs. In the worst of times, both horses and the

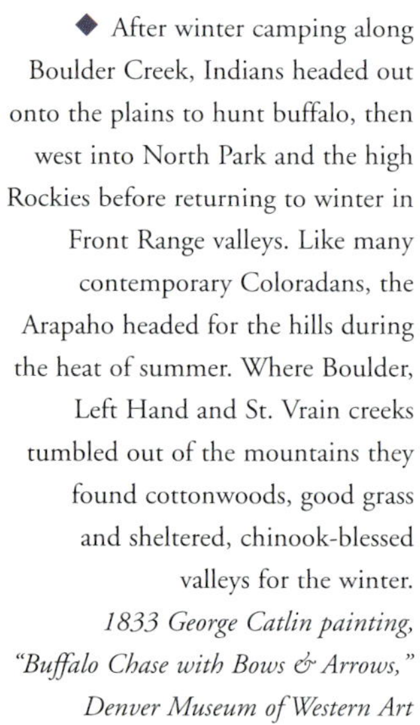

◆ After winter camping along Boulder Creek, Indians headed out onto the plains to hunt buffalo, then west into North Park and the high Rockies before returning to winter in Front Range valleys. Like many contemporary Coloradans, the Arapaho headed for the hills during the heat of summer. Where Boulder, Left Hand and St. Vrain creeks tumbled out of the mountains they found cottonwoods, good grass and sheltered, chinook-blessed valleys for the winter.
1833 George Catlin painting, "Buffalo Chase with Bows & Arrows," Denver Museum of Western Art

Arapaho women and children dried and cured buffalo meat for the winter ahead as depicted in this diorama at the Colorado History Museum in Denver.
Tom Noel Collection postcard

◆ This unidentified Arapaho woman has the light skin, prominent nose and round handsome face that distinguished her tribe. Of Arapaho women, Thomas Jefferson Farnham wrote enviously about Arapaho husbands in *Travels in the Great Western Prairies... and Rocky Mountains...* (1841): "His wife takes care of his horses, manufactures his saddles and bridles, and leash ropes and whips, his moccasins, leggings, and hunting-shirts, from leather and other materials prepared by her own hands; beats with a wooden adze his buffalo robes, till they are soft and pleasant for his couch; tans hides for his tent covering, and drags from the distant hills the clean white-pine poles to support it; cooks his daily food and places it before him. And should sickness overtake him, and death rap at the door of his lodge, his squaw watches kindly the last yearnings of the departing spirit." *Denver Public Library, Western History Department*

Arapaho ate the cottonwood roots and branches. Here among the trees, the tribe always had at least bark soup. Finally spring thaws would bring snowmelt gushing down Boulder Creek where cottonwoods, wary of late spring freezes, slowly and cautiously budded into their big hearted leaves. Grass grew green again. Game reappeared. A hungry but, warmer tribe found the strength to begin its annual journey.

This seasonal migration of Niwot's people followed a circular pattern that various prehistoric and historic tribes had used for more than 10,000 years. Clovis and Folsom peoples probably first developed this path used by later Native Americans along Front Range waterways. These creeks and the South Platte Valley form an erosional trough at the base of the mountains. In a dry land, the piedmont valley accumulated extra water, which kept it wet even in drought years. A combination of mountain timber and rock and plains vegetation also made the river and creek bottoms attractive to settlers. In these sheltered valleys, winter temperatures were generally warmer than in the mountains or on the High Plains.

On their circular, seasonal migration path, Niwot's predecessors staged annual hunts at traditional sites, where they constructed stone game runs. Stone walls, funnel-shaped and stretched for a hundred yards or more, have been found in the mountains of Boulder County. Some date as far back as 7,000 B.C. One game drive in Rocky Mountain National Park had three walls nearly 200 yards long. Near its granite walls, dozens of stone hunting points have been found, along with the butchered bones of mammals. Paleo-Indians left campsites excavated in recent decades by archaeologist James B. Benedict on Arapaho Pass, Blue Lake, Caribou Lake, Coney Creek and Fourth of July Valley in the Indian Peaks Wilderness. Benedict found Lyons Sandstone grinding slabs and handstones, as well as Kremmling chert chipped-stone tools.

Archaeologists have also found stone hunting blinds, such as those of Native American sheep hunters that give Sheep Mountain above Ward its name. Other stone circles have been identified as tipi rings or vision quest religious sites. Stone piles on elevated ridges and summits, including Longs Peak, served as eagle catching traps. Inside these bunkers of stone, Niwot's forerunners waited under evergreen branches, clutching a dead rabbit or other bait. When an eagle dove for the animal, they would grab some of its feathers. A few eagle bites and scratches were a small price to pay for such treasured plumage.

Arapaho Indians in 1914 accompanied Oliver Toll on a trip through Rocky Mountain National Park to provide information for Toll's booklet, *Arapaho Names and Trails — A Report of a 1914 Pack Trip*. The Arapaho showed Toll many ancient stone cairns used as trail markers. They also pointed out three stone piles that marked vision quest sites where individual Indians sought healing power and help from a guardian spirit by fasting in a sacred place such as on a mountaintop or in a cave.

The Arapaho, like Indians for thousands of years, moved down from the high country every autumn to winter in their piedmont camps until spring. When days grew longer and warmer, they explored nearby waterways such as Boulder, Left Hand and St. Vrain creeks and the South Platte River. By the 1830s, however, the Arapaho found disturbing changes taking place in the valley of the South Platte.

Palefaces, who had been seen sporadically coming from the south and the east for more than a century, became regular visitors. Ceran St. Vrain, a Frenchman working with the Bent Brothers, built Fort St. Vrain on a hill overlooking the confluence of St. Vrain Creek and the South Platte in 1837. Pierre Louis Vasquez, another trader, established Fort Vasquez nearby. Another adobe trading post arose at what has become the town of Fort Lupton at about the same time. These trading posts, all on the South Platte River in what is now Weld County, transformed Indian lives. The tribes became addicted to white trading goods. Niwot's band suffered much greater exposure to white diseases, from which they had no immunity. These diseases, such as cholera and small pox, killed far more Indians than did bullets.

The Arapaho and Cheyenne, as historian Elliott West argues in his book *The Contested Plains* (1997), had been drastically reduced in numbers and strength before the 1858-59 Gold Rush. White diseases and the exhaustion of cottonwoods and grasses in their winter camps began weakening the Arapaho in the early 1800s. Niwot's tribe, who numbered some 10,000 in 1800, had been reduced to less than a third of that before the 1858-59 Gold Rush began.

As one of the smallest and friendliest tribes of Plains Indians, the Arapaho became regular customers at the Platte River trading posts. They exchanged buffalo robes, beaver skins and deer hides for metal goods, knives and shining beads.

Niwot may have seen his mother trade her soft, beautiful animal robes for a metal pot. From the beginning, he was fascinated by the palefaces. He did not hide from them like other children. Instead he went to their trading posts to watch them and listen to them talk.

In 1833, Niwot's sister, MaHom, married trader John Poisal, a 24-year-old Kentuckian who worked at Bent's Fort, the great trading post on the Arkansas River in southeastern Colorado. Poisal took an interest in MaHom's bright-eyed little brother. He taught Niwot to speak English. The boy learned quickly. Soon he spoke better English than any Arapaho.

Those were still happy days for Niwot's people. They got along with the Cheyenne and the Sioux and the whites, with nearly everyone but the Utes. The Utes had occupied the Shining Mountains and the front range for hundreds, perhaps thousands, of years. They regarded the Arapaho as aggressive newcomers to be driven away: it had not been until around 1800 that the Arapaho moved from the Black Hills into today's Northeastern Colorado, including Boulder County.

The Arapaho scoffed at the Utes — a shorter, darker, squatter tribe. The Utes, as Niwot's father probably told him, were always trying to kidnap Arapaho women in order to breed with them and thus improve the looks of the Ute tribe. The Utes, as Niwot may have learned later, said the same of Arapaho men chasing Ute women.

Niwot took less interest in fighting the Utes — and other peoples — than in talking with them. He wanted to learn their language, to find out what they thought. White men were astonished by this outgoing Arapaho youth who spoke their language so well.

◆ Col. Ceran St. Vrain established an adobe trading post, the now-gone Fort St. Vrain, and gave his name to Boulder County's St. Vrain Creek.
Colorado Historical Society

◆ Fort Vasquez was established by Pierre Louis Vasquez, a Creole from St. Louis, near the confluence of the established St. Vrain Creek and the South Platte River. Many Arapaho and Cheyenne came to the fort to trade buffalo robes, beaver pelts and buckskins for the white man's trinkets and ironware. Reconstructed as a museum by the Colorado Historical Society, this adobe relic of the fur trade is a nifty trip into northeastern Colorado's past.
Colorado Historical Society

◆ Like the Arapaho and the buffalo, black-tailed prairie dogs have become an endangered species in Boulder County, threatened by human enemies, raptors and rattlesnakes. *Photos by J. W. Jackson, Denver Museum of Natural History*

The young Arapaho grew up with a special fondness for the creeks of Boulder County. Their fringes of greenery attracted mule deer, pronghorn antelope, buffalo, elk and bighorn sheep. Sometimes Niwot's mother pointed out mountain lions and brown bears. Once they even saw a snowshoe hare chased by a lynx.

Little Niwot watched the animals closely. He listened to their voices, tried to understand their language. He marveled at the prairie dogs. He visited their villages and lay on the ground watching and listening. He heard their strange barking, their cries, their complaints about being displaced by newcomers. Prairie dogs, Niwot may have mused, were like his people and the buffalo. When palefaced developers came, they would all be evicted, if not slaughtered. The Arapaho would be a devastated, desperate tribe by the time Niwot became their Boulder band chief in the 1850s. The white man's guns, and much more so his diseases, had reduced the tribe to a few thousand survivors. Their main chief, Little Raven, and subchiefs like Niwot, pursued peaceful relations with whites as the tribe's best hope.

With many males killed by disease or enemies, the Arapaho resorted to polygamy. Although Niwot apparently never took more than one wife, Little Raven had seven. Niwot's friendship with the whites was advanced by the 1849 marriage of his niece, Margaret Poisal, to Indian agent Thomas "Broken Hand" Fitzpatrick. Fitzpatrick, one of the most respected mountain men and Indian agents, tried to protect his wife's people. He negotiated the Peace Treaty of Fort Laramie in 1851. There, the Southern Arapaho and their allies, the Southern Cheyenne, were promised the land between the Platte and the Arkansas rivers at the eastern base of the Rockies. Niwot attended that treaty signing at Fort Laramie and heard Fitzpatrick and other white leaders promise the Boulder Creek country to his people forever.

Despite the treaty and the promises, whites moved into Arapaho territory whenever they pleased, shooting buffalo, deer, antelope and Indians as if they were nothing but practice targets. As whites killed their game, Fitzpatrick reported that the Indians were in a "starving state... Their women are pinched with want and their children constantly cry out with hunger." Some desperate Arapaho offered their women in prostitution for money or alcohol. So drunkenness and sexually transmitted diseases, as well as smallpox and cholera, further weakened the tribe.

Arapaho troubles became the overwhelming concern for Niwot after he was made a chief in the 1850s during a Sun Dance Ceremony. It may well have been the Arapaho head chief, Little Raven, who pronounced Niwot a chief with the ritualistic warning: "You will stand in a high place where everyone can see you.... Do not be discouraged when they blame you, or ashamed when they laugh at you. Walk straight ahead, and do your best for your people."

Cloudy days grew darker for the Arapaho with the 1854 death of their friend Thomas Fitzpatrick. Four years later, whites found gold in the South Platte and swarmed up the river and its major tributaries such as St. Vrain and Boulder creeks. The whites chopped down cottonwood trees to build cabins and furniture and fences. Trees that the Arapaho had shared for shade, shelter and firewood kept disappearing. William Bent, who followed Fitzpatrick as the Arapaho Indian agent, reported to the Superintendent of Indian Affairs that gold seekers were "making large and extensive settlements and laying off and building towns [in] the best part of the principal hunting grounds."

After Boulder City was founded on February 10, 1859, Niwot moved his band away from Boulder Creek to prevent clashes. He took them 15 miles north to the South Fork of the St. Vrain. Even there, trouble pursued the Arapaho. While Chief Niwot and his warriors were out hunting on April 14, 1860, Charles Gardner and other drunken whites attacked the Arapaho camp on the St. Vrain. They raped females of all ages, probably including Niwot's wife and 10-year-old daughter. Gardner was well known to the Arapaho. He had married one Arapaho and then eaten her during a winter blizzard, earning the nickname "Big Phil the Cannibal" for this huge man from Philadelphia, the City of Brotherly Love.

Even after the attack on the Arapaho women, Niwot refused to let his young men fight the whites. Niwot decided to follow the advice of his white friends and try to change things peacefully through elections. He showed up for a January 26, 1861, election in Denver, strode into the log voting hall and asked for a ballot. Startled Denverites refused. Niwot demanded an explanation and was told that the Indians could not vote because they did not pay taxes. Niwot had already figured he would be denied the vote, but thought his effort at participatory democracy might be an interesting lesson in civics.

Niwot also astonished whites by asking Editor William N. Byers of the *Rocky Mountain News* to retract untrue stories about Arapaho atrocities. The *News* on June 12, 1861, reported that Chief Niwot and his warriors attacked the Ohio House, a tavern in the foothills. Niwot's warriors supposedly demanded whiskey and clothing and then pillaged the place owned by A.B. Adams. Byers had second thoughts on June 19 after "a visit this morning from the Arapahoe chief, Left Hand, who called to contradict the report published by us." Byers investigated and concluded that "The Indians... killed no ox in that neighborhood, nor did they commit any other outrage." Adams had made up the story in order to claim damages.

On another occasion, Niwot jumped on stage at the Apollo Theater on Denver's Larimer Street after a play to give the wide-eyed audience a lecture on the peaceful intentions of his people. Despite all his dramatic efforts to pursue peace, Chief Niwot was caught up in a tragedy.

As whites illegally poured into the land promised to the Arapaho by the Treaty of Fort Laramie, Indian agents told Niwot and Little Raven that the Arapaho must negotiate another treaty. By the Fort Wise Treaty of 1861, the Southern Arapaho and Cheyenne surrendered the Colorado Front Range for a tiny reservation in the arid flats of southeastern Colorado. Many Indians later repudiated the treaty, which the U.S. Senate never ratified.

Although Niwot did not sign this treaty, he would be forced to abide by it. Niwot continued to camp with his people in the Boulder area through the winter of 1861-1862. The last Boulder Valley hunt of Niwot's band produced a meager winter meat supply of deer, elk, antelope and a few stray old buffalo. As Boulder City and other white towns prospered, both game and the Arapaho dwindled. Niwot's village became desperately poor, hungry and diseased. Starving warriors killed white men's cattle and stole to feed their families.

◆ The Colorado Gold Rush doomed the Southern Arapaho. The whites called them "the ugly ones," for faces scarred by the white man's smallpox. One tribesman, begging for assistance at Fort Laramie, told whites: "Our old people & little children are hungry for many days & some die. Our sufferings are increasing every winter. Our horses, too, are dying, because we ride them so far to get a little game for our lodges... We wish to live." The Arapaho complied with white orders to go to the Arapaho and Cheyenne Reservation in Oklahoma. They even posed, like this unidentified peacepipe smoker, for photographers despite their physical and spiritual scars.
Denver Public Library, Western History Department

◆ A giant over six feet tall and weighing more than 250 pounds, John M. Chivington came to Colorado as an itinerant Methodist minister, who preached in Boulder, Gold Hill and other mining towns. With the start of the Civil War, Reverend Chivington sought a "fighting" rather than a "praying" commission with the Colorado Volunteers.
Tom Noel Collection

◆ Some Boulder County residents refused to fight Niwot. Robert Hauck, a German immigrant, came to Boulder County from Wisconsin. He was aided by Chief Niwot, who helped him find a winter retreat near the confluence of Left Hand and Boulder creeks. In gratitude, Hauck refused to join the Colorado Volunteers who were hell bent to exterminate Niwot and his Arapaho band in 1864.
Longmont Museum

◆ These emaciated Arapaho boys, sons of Sharp Nose, are a reminder that the Arapaho and other tribes often were facing starvation when they fought with whites. When asked if Indian children should be spared in his attack on Sand Creek in 1864, Col. John M. Chivington replied, "Kill and scalp all Indians, little and big... nits make lice."
Denver Public Library, Western History Department

As violence increased in 1863, Niwot reluctantly moved his village out of the Boulder area. Even far out on the plains, however, he found peacekeeping a full-time job. In 1864, he bought a 17-year-old white girl, Laura Roper, from her Cheyenne captors, in order to return her to angry whites. Niwot turned her over to Major Edward Wynkoop, commander at Fort Lyon on the Arkansas River in southeastern Colorado. Wynkoop questioned the girl. She said the Cheyenne had threatened to cut her throat before Left Hand rescued her. He treated her well and promised her in English that he would return her because "she belonged with her people."

Margaret Coel of Boulder, author of *Chief Left Hand*, points out that "For an Indian to ride into a white camp with a white teenage girl on his pony and give himself over as a hostage, as Left Hand did, was an act of stunning courage." Major Wynkoop was impressed, but his superiors relieved him of his command at Fort Lyon for treating Indians too leniently. They decided that he had let Indian gestures of goodwill mislead him about their intentions. In Denver, Col. John M. Chivington complained that "Left Hand was in command" at Fort Lyon. Maj. Scott Anthony replaced Wynkoop on November 5, 1864. Like Wynkoop, Anthony continued to reassure the Arapaho and Cheyenne that they could safely camp near the fort on Sand Creek. Unlike Major Wynkoop, Major Anthony was not a man of his word.

Indians felt the treaty guaranteed their safety on Sand Creek. Their campsite was within the new reservation where they were promised that the federal government would feed them. Among several hundred Indians camped there were Niwot and his people. Instead of promised safety and food, the Indians received a surprise attack in the dark and freezing pre-dawn hours of November 29, 1864. Col. John M. Chivington and some 550 Colorado Volunteers swooped down on the sleeping village. White traders in the camp rushed out of Indian tipis and tried to stop the troops. Indians raised the white flag and the American flag as signs of peace but were answered with bullets and cannon balls. By day's end, 163 Cheyenne and Arapaho, mostly women, children and old men, had been slaughtered.

Among the Southern Arapaho camped at Sand Creek were Niwot and a dwindling band of about 50 to 60 Arapaho. Although seriously ill, Niwot ran toward the charging troops with his palms outstretched in a sign of peace. He was shot down despite his pleas in clear English. Niwot survived that day. He crawled away from the piles of dead, dying and mutilated Indians. Somehow he made it into an Indian camp on the Smoky Hill River. There

◆ The second Chief Left Hand posed in Washington, D.C., for this 1872 portrait by Alexander Gardner, eight years after the first Niwot (Left Hand) was fatally wounded at Sand Creek. His successor and namesake guided the Southern Arapaho during their early reservation years in Oklahoma. *Colorado Historical Society*

◆ The Arapaho were chased out of Colorado and put on reservations, but some have returned to Boulder and the greater Denver metro area. These four Arapaho women worked in Colorado as welfare workers during the 1930s. *Denver Art Museum*

◆ Chief Niwot's ghost lingers in this bust on the county courthouse lawn. Under the name Niwot or the English translation, Left Hand, he also lives on in many Boulder County place names, including a creek, a ridge, a mountain, a town and a brew pub. c.1998 *Photo by Tom Noel*

Niwot died. Details of his final days and his burial remain unclear.

At least his body did not suffer mutilation. Many soldiers at Sand Creek cut off Indian scalps, fingers, toes, ears, breasts and genitals from the dead or wounded. When asked about this afterwards, Colonel Chivington claimed that the mutilators "were simply obtaining trophies, to preserve as reminiscences, to bequeath to their children, of the glorious field of Sand Creek."

Capt. David H. Nichols, who led Boulder's Company D of the Colorado Volunteers at Sand Creek, came back to Boulder City, boasting that he had brought down the great Chief Niwot. Nichols and other Boulder troopers, including townfounders Thomas Aikins, A.A. Brookfield, Marinus Smith and Fred Squires were toasted and treated as heroes. The few Southern Arapaho who survived the 1860s Indian wars were forced out of Colorado by the Medicine Lodge Treaty of 1867, which sent them to a reservation in what would become northwestern Oklahoma.

On their Oklahoma Reservation, the Southern Arapaho found a new leader, a chief who took the name of the Arapaho he most admired — Niwot. So a second Niwot arose to help his people through the ordeals of reservation life.

The name of the original Niwot has survived. Left Hand Creek is where he was supposedly born. He once hunted on Niwot Mountain and along Niwot Ridge, and camped at what is now the town of Niwot. All are in Boulder County where he had championed harmony among oldtimers and newcomers to the Shining Mountains.

Boulder County children, like those everywhere in the United States, grew up playing cowboys and Indians. Boulder native Jack Smith, shown here at his landmarked family home at 308 Pearl Street in 1938, had doubts about who the good guys were. Even as the pensive nine year old shown here, the future famed archaeologist of Indian life suspected that "Maybe Niwot and his people were really the good guys."
Photo by George Edward Smith, courtesy of Susan Collins

Colorado Historical Society

Tom Noel Collection

Photo by Tom Noel

1970 photo by Hugh McGinty

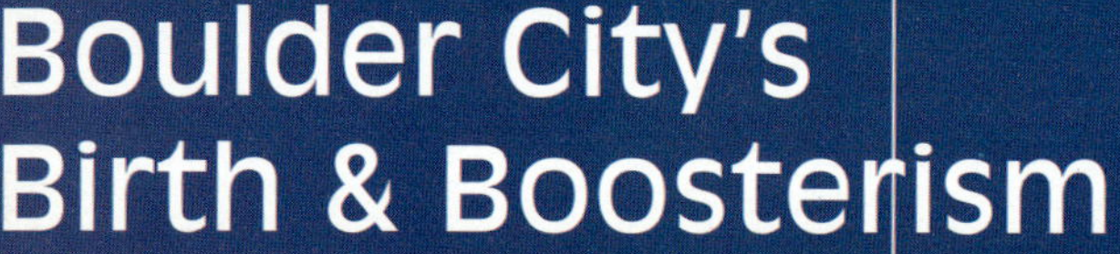

Boulder City's Birth & Boosterism

Chapter *Two*

"I mounted the walls of the old fort, and with the field-glass could see that the mountains looked right for gold, and the valleys looked rich for grazing. [I] could discern bands of Indian ponies and antelope feeding together [in] the most beautiful of all the valleys."

—Townfounder Thomas A. Aikins

This often-repeated account of Boulder's birth on October 17, 1858, came from an entrepreneur interested in selling real estate. Naturally he promoted Boulder as the most fertile, most golden, most beautiful Garden of Eden in all Colorado..

From the beginning, Boulder's history has been wrapped in golden myths and bold boosterism. To this day, Boulder puffs itself as a most scenic, liveable and progressive community. The myth persists, it should be added, because Boulder really is an extraordinarily fine place to live.

Townfounder Aikin's glowing words were recorded by Amos Bixby, Boulder's greatest early booster and the author of the "History of Boulder County." This 54-page account, the bible on which subsequent Boulder County history rests, is a chapter in *History of Clear Creek and Boulder Valleys, Colorado.* That 713-page volume was published in 1880 by the Chicago firm of Oliver L. Baskin, which

◆ (Above) Capt. Thomas A. Aikins, the founder of Boulder City, was a Maryland native who had farmed in Ohio, Illinois and Missouri before catching gold fever in 1858. He recruited the young mayor of Nebraska City, Alfred A. Brookfield, to join his crew of prospectors. Besides Brookfield, the Aikins party consisted of Aikins' son and nephew and about a dozen other gold seekers. Aikins' luxuriant beard, thick enough to hide mice, became a standard for subsequent Boulder longhairs. *Carnegie Branch Library for Local History, Boulder Historical Society Collection*

specialized in booster histories glorifying the pioneers. These were subscription books sold in advance to customers who could negotiate to include their biography and, for an additional consideration, a portrait. The hefty, gold-edged, ornately stamped Morocco-bound opus sold for $12 at a time when the average American made around $1,000 a year. That was a considerable sum in 1880, almost as expensive in relative dollars as the $450 it commands in today's antiquarian book market.

Boulder historian Thomas Meier first questioned Bixby's account in his well-documented 1993 booklet, *The Early Settlement of Boulder: Set in Type — Cast in Bronze — Fused in Porcelain "It Ain't Necessarily So."* Meier painstakingly tracked Boulder's creation myth through primary sources and also along the supposed route of the Aikins Party. He convincingly questions Aikins' supposed view, the October 17, 1858, founding date, and even the exact number of pioneer settlers.

As Meier asks, how could Aikins have seen grazing animals, much less distinguished Indian ponies from mule deer and antelope from Fort St. Vrain 25 miles away? One insurmountable obstacle is terrain that blocks the view of Boulder City. And how could a farmer who had just arrived from Missouri accurately pronounce an area rich in either soil or gold from such a distance? The Aikins' account, as Meier points out, was apocryphal. Bixby first published it in the *Boulder County News* October 17, 1873, as he reputedly heard it from Aikins. Bixby refined the 1873 quote for his 1880 book, deleting the last phrase in the quote heading this chapter. Aikins, who died in 1878, was not around to protest.

Boulder is now large, secure and prosperous enough to accept the truth about its origins. The fact — and the folklore — begin with the role of the native Arapaho Indians. Folklore has the Indians welcoming the palefaced land grabbers. The simple savages, as Aikins, Bixby and company tell the story, succumbed to the white man's bacon and cigars.

The truth is another story. As Boulder historian Margaret Coel points out in her 1981 book, *Chief Left Hand*, Niwot's band of Southern Arapaho was distressed to find the Aikins party camped on Boulder Creek in the fall of 1858. The Arapaho also saw thousands of other whites flooding into Colorado after the summer gold strikes on the South Platte around Cherry Creek. So many settlers were going west that some Arapaho suggested the tribe head east. Surely the white man's old country must be emptied by the huge emigration.

Whites were drawn by gold fever, which reached epidemic heights in 1858-59. Newspaper accounts titillated the nation with promises of instant wealth. The *Leavenworth Times* for August 21, 1858, reported "Diggers are obtaining from $50 to $60 a day, and pieces of gold have been found varying from $50 to $150

◆ Fortune seekers such as these portrayed in Frank Leslie's *Illustrated Newspaper* for August 20, 1859, were lured west by sensational headlines: "Gold! Gold!! Gold!!!" and popular songs: "Oh the Gold! The Gold — they say 'Tis brighter than the day, And now 'tis mine, I'm bound to shine… '" *Tom Noel Collection*

in value… Furthermore, it is stated to us on the most reliable authority that… pearls have been found, the largest of which are about the size of peas." Such exaggerations turned gold fever into a national disease.

Golden opportunities were especially seductive as hard times had fallen on the Missouri River Valley frontier. Many Americans who had tripped and stumbled along fortune's road now looked for a way to regain their stride.

Horace Greeley's *New York Tribune* reported on January 29, 1859, "an immense migration, especially from our western states, to the new Eldorado. The extensive failure of crops in 1858, the universal pressure of debt, the low prices realized or promised for the fruits of the husbandman's labor, the deadness of enterprise, the absence of thrift, render such immigration inevitable."

While Boulder city fathers promoted its golden origins, the town's first mayor, Al Brookfield, told another story in his private correspondence. "My impression of the mines is that they are a d—d humbug… I pronounce them a pack of lies, written by a set of petty one-horse town speculators calculated to ruin many a poor devil besides your humble servant."

Pursuing golden dreams rather than dirty reality, thousands poured into the new Eldorado. Most of the

◆ Alfred A. Brookfield wrote accounts from the Boulder diggings that reflect the transformation of frustrated prospectors into boosterish townbuilders. On March 5, 1859, Brookfield wrote from "Boulder City, Rocky Mountains, N.T. [Nebraska Territory]" to the *Nebraska City Times:* "I did not come out here for town speculation, but after we made what are considered by far the best discoveries of the 'precious metal,' we thought as the weather would not permit us to mine, we would lay out and commence building what may be an important town."
Tom Noel Collection

◆ (Opposite page, center top) Amos Bixby, born in Maine in 1822, typified versatile frontier boosters whose enthusiasms and loyalties were migratory. Bixby tried farming, lawyering and mining, before hitting his stride as a booster journalist. In 1873 he moved to Boulder to edit the *Boulder County News*, serve as postmaster and compile the first county history. Wherever Bixby landed, he quickly took to print to promote his new hometown. Soon after publishing his glowing 1880 account of Boulder County as America's new Garden of Eden, Bixby moved to California, where he died in 1894.
Tom Noel Collection

◆ Boulder City was initially called Red Rocks for the spectacular formation on the north bank of Boulder Creek. Today the Red Rocks are the centerpiece of Settlers Park.
Tom Noel Collection postcard

◆ Colorado's first public school was this clapboard building with a fireplace, shingle roof and Greek pediments over the front door and windows. Youngsters were often distracted by Arapaho Indians who patronized the water barrel under the eaves.
Tom Noel Collection

argonauts traveled the South Platte River road to Denver City, as had Aikins. Rather than follow the Platte to Cherry Creek, however, the Aikins party stopped at the ruins of old Fort St. Vrain, where Aikins made his alleged field-glass discovery of "the most beautiful of all valleys."

The Aikins party probably then followed St. Vrain Creek west to its junction with Boulder Creek, which they followed to the "Red Rocks," the jagged formation backdropping today's Settlers Park in Boulder. Aikins' party apparently included his son and a nephew, Alfred A. Brookfield, and between 10 and 19 others who had headed west from Nebraska City, Nebraska Territory. They pitched their tents beside the boulder-strewn creek where it emerged from the foothills. There, Niwot visited the newcomers and astonished them by speaking in English.

"Go away," Niwot told Aikins, "you come to kill our game, to burn our wood, and to destroy our grass." The whites supposedly placated Niwot with sugar and coffee, bacon and cigars. Just let us stay for the winter, they told the Arapaho chief, promising to push on when spring came.

Niwot consented. Bear Head and Many Whips turned against him, saying the tribe should slaughter or chase away the palefaces before they multiplied. Niwot, they argued, had been corrupted by his family's intermarriage with whites. They had taught Niwot to speak English and to accept the white man's ways. Other older chiefs supported Niwot, saying the white people's invasion was in the stars. A thousand stars had fallen on November 13, 1833, as the palefaced traders first began building forts on the South Platte. Donati's Comet was a heavenly sign, as Bear Head put it, that the stars have fallen "as thick as the tears of our women shall fall when you come to drive us away."

Spring came. The whites did not leave. Alphonse Wright found a promising gold claim on the south

Boulder was renamed for the rocky stream and piles of rock upon which it lies. Townfounders optimistically added the word "city" although Boulder consisted of a rural huddle of mud-floored log cabins. Certainly Boulder City sounded more promising than another proposed early name, Deadwood Diggings. Among many visitors unimpressed with Boulder was New York newspaperman Horace Greeley, who wrote in June 1859: "We camped for the night opposite Boulder City, a log hamlet of some thirty habitations covering the entrance to Boulder Diggings, twelve miles westward in the mountains. Here we found ... men, who, having taken a look at this gold region, had decided to push on for California."

1997 photo by Tom Noel

bank of Boulder Creek, where the city's first smelter, the Boyd Mill, would be built in 1874. Other settlers marveled at the huge herds of antelope, mule deer and mountain sheep. Even if prospecting did not pan out, there was game galore. And the snowmelt flooding Boulder Creek promised all the water anyone could want.

During the mild winter of 1858-59, Captain Aikins' son, James, and a few others prospected Boulder, Four Mile, St. Vrain and Sunshine creeks. Up Boulder Creek they took a fork, Four Mile Creek, to a place where they found color on January 16, 1859. They called the diggings Gold Run. This jackpot evolved into Boulder County's first great mineral bonanza —Gold Hill. There David Horsfal found the rich Horsfal Lode. It and lesser finds began yielding gold in paying amounts. By fall, Thomas J. Graham had lugged in a three-stamp mill. He used Left Hand Creek to power his 500-pound contraption to crush ore. By 1860, upper Boulder Creek and its tributaries had surrendered an estimated $100,000 in pay dirt.

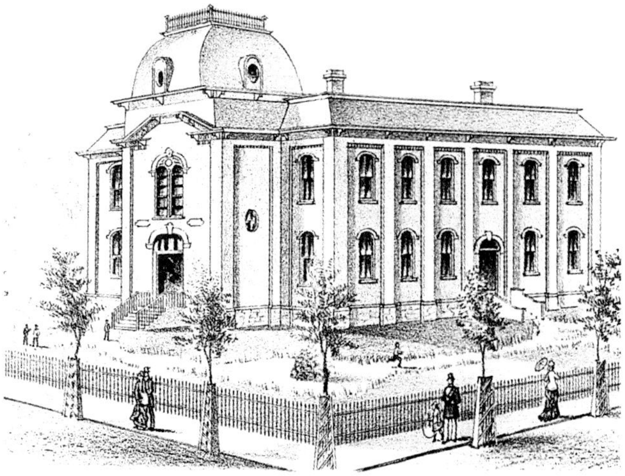

◆ (Right and opposite page, top) Central School, finished in 1873, exemplified the fine materials, design and consideration Boulder put into its schools. Demolition of Central, despite widespread community protest, inspired the 1971 formation of Historic Boulder Inc. to protect Boulder County's heritage. Although the school fell, HB has won many subsequent building battles. No building as significant as Central School has been lost since HB lost its initial preservation battle.
Historic Boulder, Inc.

Many more fortune seekers rushed in and found other riches of the earth — fine building rock — sandstone, granite and limestone. Others found coal in what became Marshall, Canfield, Louisville, Lafayette and Superior. Still others dug into the earth and found clay beds that made good red bricks. The Boulder Pressed Brick Company soon opened on the site where Casey Middle School now stands.

Such riches of the earth prompted Aikins and his party to renege on their promise to Niwot. "As the weather would not allow us to mine," Brookfield explained, "we would lay out and commence to build what may be an important town." They founded the Boulder City Town Company on February 10, 1859. The baby town held its first election, selecting Al Brookfield as town company president and Tom Aikins as vice president.

Aikins, Brookfield and company platted a two-mile-long town in the mouth of Boulder Canyon. They divided the town into lots measuring 50 by 140 feet instead of the 25 by 125 foot parcels used in Denver and most other cities. The Boulder City Town Company put 4,044 such lots up for sale at $1,000 each. The community's early interest in elbow room was also reflected in the generous assignment of land for public space, including 80-foot-wide roads and 20-foot-wide alleys. Not everyone agreed with Boulder's first growth-control decision. The same Amos Bixby who chronicled the townfounding fumed in the 1880 *Boulder Valley News*:

> Early in the affairs of the Town Company, two parties arose — one in favor of holding the lots high, in order to make a 'big thing' for themselves; the other in favor of giving away alternate lots to those who would build on them, or doing most anything to induce population and capital. Unfortunately, the high-priced party prevailed, but the lots were not taken at $1,000 each....

Consequently, Bixby lamented, Boulder failed "to have centered here the men of money and enterprise [who would] have made Boulder what Denver afterward became, the leading town of the Territory."

The Boulder City Town Company not only limited growth by offering only large, expensive lots but they also imposed strict building regulations foreign to most infant western settlements. Cabin walls had to be higher than eight and one-half feet, with chimneys inside the cabin. To avoid the raw, half-finished look of other frontier towns, Boulder required that cabin foundations be built in seven days and the whole cabin completed within 60 days.

Cabins were to be oriented north and south in orderly rows along the public streets.

Boulder aspired to be not only the best planned but also the best educated town in the state. The quest for schooling that would bring the state university to Boulder began early with the construction of Colorado's first public schoolhouse. Abner Roe Brown, a native of Connecticut who had taught school in New York and Iowa, recalled later his amazement "as I passed through the little nest of some 20 log cabins in Boulder, Colorado, on June 1, 1860 [at] the number of school age children playing in the streets." Brown, a carpenter as well as a teacher, helped build the frame school house with a shingle roof. Townsfolk donated glass from their picture frames for the windows.

To reward Brown, Boulder mothers held a "Gold Dust Dance," charging 25 cents per person. They raised $42 to pay Brown, purchased him a proper teacher's suit and persuaded him to forsake prospecting and stay on to teach in what was named Pioneer School. To the dismay of young students avoiding homework, their parents even took turns feeding and housing schoolmaster Brown. Whereas Denver and other towns merely rented shacks for teaching purposes, Boulder boasted the tidy edifice at 15th and Walnut streets, a shining example of civic virtue which the town painted lily white.

"Boulder is better supplied with public schools than any other town," crowed the *Boulder County Pioneer*, February 10, 1869. Editor Junius E. Wharton argued further that Boulder was "the gem of all the counties of Colorado" with "the finest agricultural land" and "an intelligent and dense population." In subsequent issues of the *Pioneer*, Wharton claimed Boulder had Colorado's largest vegetables and best people, while Denver excelled only in "political shysters."

Denver ignored such Boulder boosterism, leading Wharton to editorially fume that "Denver almost totally ignores the existence of Boulder County… the ignorant barbarians... in Denver ought to be ashamed of their deficiency in the knowledge of the geography of Colorado."

In 1872, overcrowded Pioneer School was replaced by the $15,000 Central School. Brown, who had graduated in 1871 to the county school superintendentship, championed public education for all. His efforts to get students to wear their trousers outside their boots, however, failed. Western boys, like their fathers in the mines, tucked their trousers inside their boots to the distress of cultivated easterners, such as Brown, who aimed education at dress and manners, as well as reading, writing and arithmetic.

Miss Mary L. Thomas became assistant principal at Central School in 1876 and helped establish seven separate grades. She turned one room of the school into a library and helped acquire an organ which transformed the school into a town concert hall. Born in Battle Creek, Michigan, in 1852, Thomas had graduated from the Indiana Female College in Indianapolis at age 15, then studied for six years at Michigan State Normal School. Upon receiving her diploma in 1873, the spunky schoolmarm headed west. She worked for two years in Central City before becoming assistant principal in Boulder. In 1877, she became principal of the Boulder Schools.

◆ Miss Mary L. Thomas joined the Central School faculty in 1876. She turned one room of the school into a library, helped establish seven separate grades, and acquired an organ which made the school a town concert hall. The next year the Boulder School Board made her the principal.
Tom Noel Collection

◆ Children at Pine Street School learned John Greenleaf Whittier's poems "Snow-Bound," "Barbara Frietchie" and "Columbia: Gem of the Ocean" by heart. They wrote to the great literary lion whose warm reply inspired children and teachers to rename their school for him in 1903. To celebrate Colorado's oldest school in continuous use, Historic Boulder Inc. spearheaded reconstruction of the belltower, shown here, for the school's 1982 centennial. *Historic Boulder, Inc.*

◆ Boulder easily attracted school teachers because they often relished the idea of summers off to explore the Rocky Mountains. These two adventuresome schoolmarms tackled Longs Peak in 1910. *Photo by Ed Tangen, Carnegie Branch Library for Local History, Boulder Historical Society Collection*

Miss Thomas, Mr. Brown and other Boulder citizens soon opened more schools. In 1882, Colorado's premier architect, Frank Edbrooke, was hired to design the Pine Street (now Whittier) School at 20th and Pine streets. On Fred Squires' pasture at the southwest corner of Mapleton Avenue and 20th Street, the Mapleton School was erected in 1889. Highland School followed in 1891, a Romanesque Revival-style gem by architects Ernest P. Varian and Frederick J. Sterner. Washington (1903), Lincoln (1903), University Hill (1905) and Boulder High (1937) are among other schools of architectural merit to survive.

Boulder's high aspirations attracted the attention of Denver's *Rocky Mountain News*, which reported in October 1859: "We are strongly reminded of a New England village... the morals seem to be above the ordinary rate." Tom Aikins' son, Lafayette, was appointed constable to chase out bums and riff-raft. Horsethief William Tull was hanged in 1867 from a creek side willow tree and found not guilty later. Luckier criminals were only banished forever from Boulder after being branded as morally unfit. Vigilant Boulderites shaved one side of the villain's head bald and then eliminated the whiskers on the other side of his face.

Efforts at better government led Boulder to incorporate as a city. In May, 1871, an angry letter to the editor of the *Boulder County News* urged the formation of a municipal government to keep the town from going to the dogs: "not another small town in the world can support as many useless, cussed dogs as Boulder. Oh, for a municipal government so that we can have a poisonous, killing, exterminating dog law." Incorporation came in 1871, and one of the first ordinances declared that "the constable will kill all dogs for which the owners have not obtained a license." He was paid $1 for each unlicensed canine killed and disposed of outside the city limits.

Human arrests netted the sheriff $2 a head. A growing number of prisoners led Boulder to rent a shack from Anthony Arnett in 1874 for use as the town jail. Constable Aikins was also charged with reprimanding anyone using "indecent and improper language within the town limits." Malefactors unable or unwilling to pay fines, according to another

◆ The Tommy Jones Stage Station, the oldest building in the Boulder Valley, is the only pioneer remnant of old Valmont. Built in 1860, it became the transportation hub and post office for the town laid out by Jones. After the Denver & Boulder Valley Railroad reached Valmont in 1873, the stagehouse on Indian Road and Boulder Creek became Emma Gould's Boarding House. Emma, a widow with nine children, ran the boarding house until 1910.
1970 photo by Hugh McGinty

1871 ordinance, "shall labor upon the streets of the town of Boulder."

Besides coping with its own troublemakers, Boulder also faced upstart competition from a rival town — Valmont — five miles down Boulder Creek. Tom Aikins, A. P. Allen, Al Brookfield and other pioneers settled there in 1859. After promoting Boulder City as a golden utopia for others, these city fathers returned to farming and business — their pre-gold rush occupations.

Valmont farmers flourished by feeding the county's miners and the struggling population of Boulder City. By the early 1860s, Boulder found itself eclipsed by this uppity rival. Valmont boasted a newspaper, a school, two drugstores, five general stores, three saloons and a cheese factory. Valmont Butte, the town's major landmark, yielded igneous basalt used for cobblestones in Denver as well as for other pretentious communities unsatisfied with dirt streets.

Valmont started the county's first newspaper, the *Valmont Bulletin*, on New Year's Day in 1866. The

◆ (Left)
Mangy dogs such as these led to the incorporation of the City of Boulder on November 4, 1871. Residents organized a government to pay a dogcatcher $1 for each unlicensed canine he exterminated.
Photo by Mary Sullivan

◆ While dogs suffered persecution, cats were highly prized in new Boulder County settlements. In his classic account of the mining frontier, *Roughing It*, Mark Twain eulogized one particularly prized feline, Tom Quartz, (below) who could sniff out gold ore.
Tom Noel Collection

◆ Cement-filled coffee cans serve as section markers in Valmont Cemetery, the final resting place of many Boulder pioneers, including town founder Thomas Aikins. When the Boulder Historical Society acquired the historic funeral grounds in 1964, the long feud between the rival towns was reignited. Angry Valmonters accused Boulder of stealing even their dead. *1998 photo by Tom Noel*

Bulletin made Valmont the center of attention as well as the center of population. Boulder boosters silenced their rival by stealing the *Bulletin's* hand press in the middle of one April night in 1867, after sedating Editor D. G. Scouten with alcohol and a $25 bribe. The press reopened upstream as the *Boulder Valley News*, later renamed the *Boulder County Pioneer*, and then the *Boulder County News*. As in most western towns, newspapers frequently came, went, changed names and consolidated. Boulder had no shortage of gazettes to celebrate its emergence as the county hub. By 1890, the *Valmont Bulletin, Rocky Mountain Eagle, Boulder Valley News, Boulder County Pioneer, Boulder Sentinel, Boulder County Bee, Boulder County Courier* and *Colorado Banner* had all come and gone.

Lucius C. Paddock came to Magnolia in Boulder County in 1878 as a miner and school teacher, but also worked as a correspondent for the *Boulder County News*. In 1891, Paddock and his father-in-law, Valentine Butsch, purchased the *Daily Camera*. "Our presses are run by the finest water power west of Niagara Falls," Paddock claimed. "It is derived from Boulder Creek, which makes it a powerful paper." The *Camera* was so named, recalls Lucius' grandson Laurence T. Paddock, because it used more pictures than any other newspaper. The name stuck and it's the only newspaper of that name in the United States.

"Bug Town," as Boulderites called Valmont, shriveled without its newspaper. The disheveled Valmont Cemetery became a haven for Boulder's rejects. The cemetery's founders prescribed "none shall be refused Buryal [sic] on account of poverty, race, color, religious belief, Moral Carictar [sic] while living, or any other pretence or cause… the Dead shall find in the bosom of the above described land a quiet resting place until the Resserection [sic], leaving all questions of Religion and fitness for the Judge of all Worlds."

Such tolerance did not characterize Boulder, where the town's moral guardians remained ever vigilant. In the 1880s, they grew outraged over the ultimate civic embarrassment. A red light district popped up near the railroad depot near 9th Street between Canyon Boulevard and Boulder Creek. The first locals to greet disembarking train passengers were often the "Brides of the Multitudes." Worst of all, the Pioneer Schoolhouse, the pride of Boulder, had become a whorehouse by 1886.

Editor Lucius G. Paddock of the *Boulder Daily Camera* raged "Never in the history of Boulder did vice present its hideous front with more brazen daring!" Paddock and others who may have prayed for God's vengeance on the "soiled doves" had their prayer answered by the 1894 flood. It swept away the red light district in a divine fit of urban renewal. Subsequently the city has built its library and municipal buildings on the site, leaving no trace — not even an historic marker — of the bad old days.

As Bixby noted in his 1880 history: "The temper of the Boulder people has always been in favor of the regular administration of law and justice." To that end, in 1875, the city hired night watchmen to enforce the midnight saloon closing law. Nocturnal shenanigans in the groggeries irked Boulder newspapers, preachers and righteous citizens. They were determined to make life miserable for the drinking class.

Perhaps to duck reproach, Boulder's tipplers were better behaved than most. A reporter for the *Boulder County News* marveled: "I have never seen a city of this size with so many saloons and so few drunks." Boulder taxed its taverns heavily — licenses cost $240 a year by 1883. By then, the 19 saloons listed in the 1883 Boulder City Directory had become a major source of municipal revenue. Editor Lucius Paddock got off his usual high horse to defend saloons as important to the city's budget: "A touch of the old Pilgrim spirit is a good thing in any community, that is to say, a little of it, just enough to give flavor like... a few drops of vanilla in a barrel of ice cream."

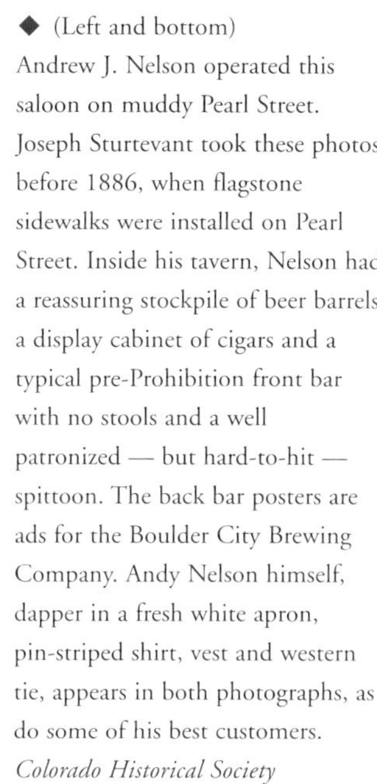

◆ (Left and bottom) Andrew J. Nelson operated this saloon on muddy Pearl Street. Joseph Sturtevant took these photos before 1886, when flagstone sidewalks were installed on Pearl Street. Inside his tavern, Nelson had a reassuring stockpile of beer barrels, a display cabinet of cigars and a typical pre-Prohibition front bar with no stools and a well patronized — but hard-to-hit — spittoon. The back bar posters are ads for the Boulder City Brewing Company. Andy Nelson himself, dapper in a fresh white apron, pin-striped shirt, vest and western tie, appears in both photographs, as do some of his best customers. *Colorado Historical Society*

Many local puritanical "pilgrims" disagreed that Boulder needed "vanilla." In 1869, the International Order of Good Templars formed Boulder's Golden Sheaf Lodge No. 19 to champion sobriety. In 1881, some 30 Boulder ladies organized the local chapter of the Woman's Christian Temperance Union (WCTU). A month later, the WCTU had grown to 139 ladies who began their meeting with the WCTU pledge to overthrow "king" alcohol. The WCTU and their allies raised liquor licenses in 1888 to $1,000 a year, forcing half of Boulder's taverns to shut their doors.

◆ A pair of wealthy Germans, Frank S. Weisenhorn and August Voegtle, opened the Boulder City Brewery in 1889 at 9th and Arapahoe. Catering to the cold water as well as the warm beer crowd, the Teutonic duo reorganized their company in 1898 as the Crystal Springs Brewery & Ice Company. Boulder's first brewery, W. G. Cook's, in a Pearl Street alley between 12th (Broadway) and 13th streets, had opened in 1870 and closed in 1872. Not until the 1990s renaissance of local brewing would Boulder see its third (Boulder Brewing Company), fourth (the Walnut Brewery) and fifth (Oasis Brewery) commercial beer makers.
Colorado Historical Society

chlorine, Better Boulderites spearheaded a 1907 countywide vote to ban alcohol. Reformers had convinced voters that this drastic measure would dry up not only drunkenness but also prostitution, vice, family violence and labor problems. Nativists argued further that Prohibition would discipline beer-chugging Germans, whiskey-guzzling Irish, and wine-drinking Italians. With the exception of 3.2 beer taverns, the great Boulder County drought began in 1909 and did not end until 1933.

The dry crusade picked up more steam in 1900 with the formation of the Better Boulder Party. Although somewhat distracted by their equally earnest campaign to keep the municipal water supply free of

Boulder City remained dry until 1967.

With staggering pedestrians and strutting prostitutes eliminated, the *Camera* turned its attention to speeding bicyclists "scorching down University Hill on

◆ Boulder's beautiful setting, captured in this *1876 Bird's Eye View*, led Dr. F. Ferrard to pen his "Tribute to Boulder:"

"The Alpine hamlet thy dim eyes have seen Lost in their beauty, as some vision, when We view the past through childhood's happy sheen; But loveliest vision of this magic spell, to where the Boulder from its mountain height Merges from rippling, darken'd, snowy dell, daily and sparkling, into golden light. And here the loveliest of thy hamlets stands, The spot of all thy mountain cities best.... "

Carnegie Branch Library for Local History, Boulder Historical Society Collection

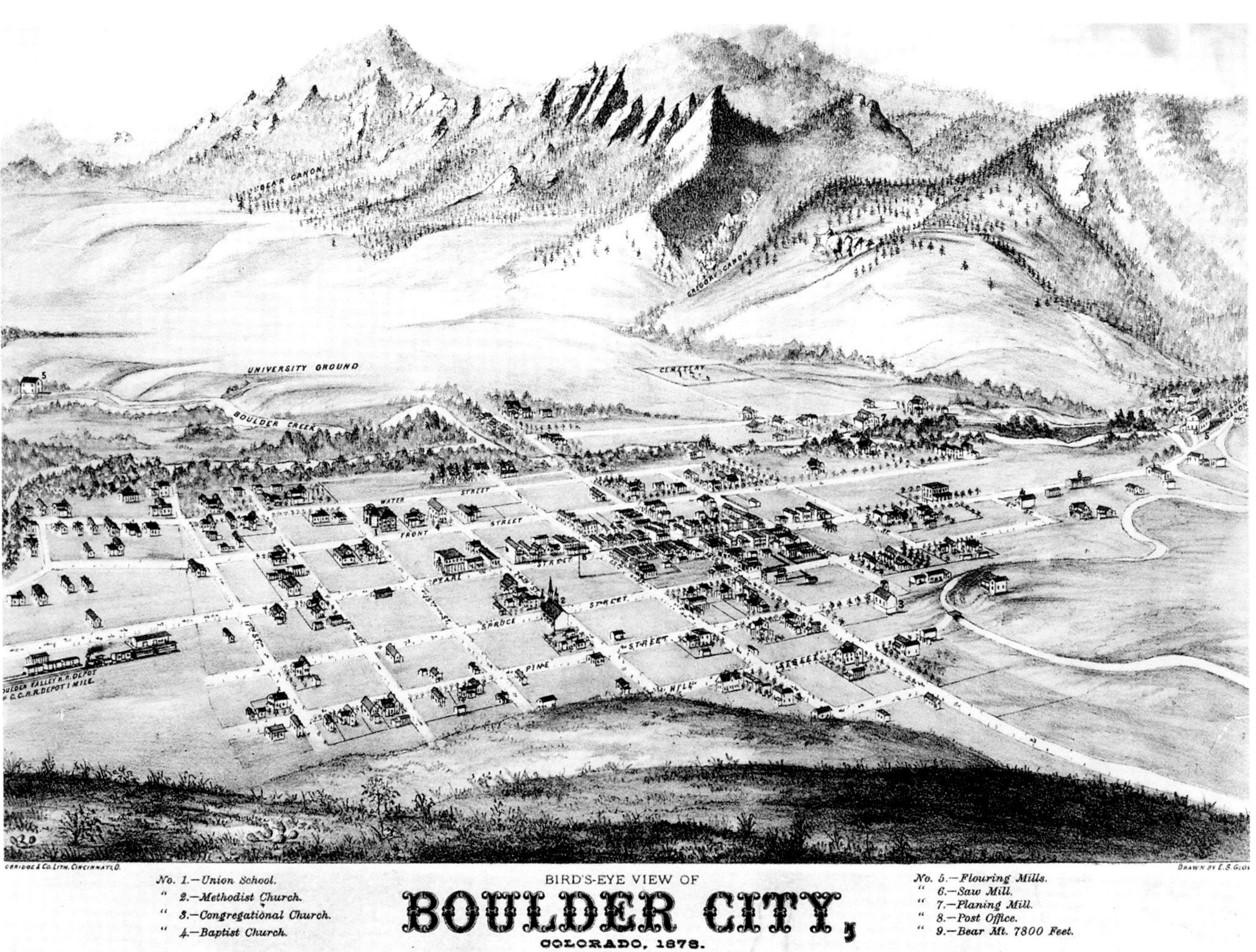

German-born people comprised Boulder County's largest foreign-born group until World War I. Deutschlanders gravitated to Teutonic taverns such as the German House on Pearl Street.
1880s photo by Joseph Sturtevant, Colorado Historical Society

◆ Boulder's 1883 County Courthouse celebrated the town's rush to respectability — and its mineral base. Booming Caribou silver mines paid for the $59,950 Second Empire-style edifice. On February 9, 1932, a fire started in the cupola and sent the 700-pound clock crashing through the structure, spreading flames in its descent. The county sheriff saved the prisoners in the basement jail and a fireproof safe protected county records.
c. 1910 postcard
Peter Pollock Collection

◆ Boulder County's 1932 courthouse is one of the few built in the Art Deco style.
1999 photo by Tom Noel

sidewalks." Speeding bicyclists soon had to compete with speeding motorists. After banker Andrew J. Macky bought one of the first automobiles in 1902, a $1,325 Mobile Steamer that whizzed through town at 40 m.p.h., the *Camera* began fretting about the "don't care attitude of automobile drivers." Speeding bicyclists and motorists proved to be persistent problems that trouble Boulderites to this day.

Like other rough-hewn frontier towns, Boulder City lusted after at least a veneer of civilization. Boulder's Curran Opera House opened in 1906 at 1132-34 Pearl Street, and the town turned to building a university and fine residences and churches as prized ornaments of culture during the rush to respectability that followed the gold and silver rushes. Having become a stable and permanent county seat, Boulder City became confident enough in 1878 to drop "city" from its name. Now that it really was a city, Boulder began to blossom as a homey yet cultivated pacesetter among Colorado communities.

The 1932 Boulder County Courthouse became the town's brightest Christmas ornament.

Peter Pollock Collection

Nurit Wolf

1969 photo by Tom Noel

Photo by James Baca

Colorado Historical Society

University of Colorado photo by J. Martin Natvig

Boulder Blossoms

Carnegie Branch Library for Local History, Boulder Historical Society Collection

Chapter *Three*

"Boulder is a hideous collection of frame houses on the burning plain, but it aspires to be a 'city' in virtue of being a 'distributing point' for the settlements up Boulder Canyon, and of the discovery of a coal seam."

—Isabella Bird, *A Lady's Life in the Rockies*, 1873

Thirty-five years after English travel writer Isabella Bird spent a November night in "hideous" Boulder, the esteemed landscape architect Frederick Law Olmsted, Jr. visited. He found that the crude frontier town had evolved into "a city of agreeable homes."

Guided not only by boosterism but also by environmental and ethical sensitivities, Boulder shunned industry and strove to become the "the Athens of Colorado," as Editor Lucius Paddock of the Boulder *Daily Camera* said. The new Athens, Paddock wrote in his June 11, 1896, edition, boasted "churches and excellent schools, cultural society, happy homes, and the University of Colorado." By emphasizing the quality of life, not the quantity of its population and products, Boulder became a model town.

After building Colorado's first public school, Boulder captured the state university as well. In the political scramble for territorial institutions, Boulder lost the Capitol to Denver and the penitentiary

◆ (Right and below right) Mining minds, Boulder emerged as an educational center that rode out the booms and busts that wiped out 50 other county towns. Old Main, shown here shortly after its 1877 opening, was restored a century later when the third floor became the University Heritage Center. *University of Colorado*

◆ A veteran of the California Gold Rush, Marinus Smith reached Boulder in 1859 and grew crops and fruit trees. With his agricultural skill and his Marinus Express Company, a horse-drawn stage and freight service operating between Boulder and Denver, Smith prospered and donated land for Boulder's Pioneer School, as well as the university. The 1894 flood wiped out many of his fields and left him stranded atop his house (near today's Boulder High School). This experience demented Smith, who was sent as "a raving maniac" to the State Insane Asylum in Pueblo. *Carnegie Branch Library for Local History, Boulder Historical Society Collection*

to Cañon City. That, anyway, is the myth, despite no known evidence that Boulder ever aspired to house either institution. Boulderites settled for the University of Colorado (CU). In those days, town boosters preferred prisons to universities: prisoners could be hired as cheap labor, but both faculty and students were widely regarded as poor and unproductive. The Colorado legislature treated the university as little more than a joke when the bill to create it was introduced in 1861. Lawmakers facetiously nominated presidents Abraham Lincoln and Jefferson Davis to its board of trustees. Although Territorial Governor William Gilpin signed the bill, no money was appropriated for 13 years. Furthermore, the legislature forbade the embryo university to mint its own money — one proposed solution. Boulder finally forced the issue in 1874 when David Nichols was speaker of the house and James P. Maxwell was president of the Senate.

Nichols and Maxwell, both Boulderites, negotiated a $15,000 appropriation on the condition that

Boulder provide matching funds. To secure the local match, Nichols supposedly made his famous "midnight ride" from Denver to Boulder. The following snowy January morning, he returned to the Capitol with a promise of $15,000. Marinus Smith pledged $1,000 and the smallest contributor, sheriff William Corson, tossed in $15. Anthony Arnett, Andrew J. Macky and others donated a site on a bluff overlooking Boulder Creek.

◆ (Left)
Mary Rippon Outdoor Theater, home of CU's summer Shakespeare Festival, commemorates CU's first woman professor.
1995 photo by Tom Noel

◆ (Above)
During Mary Rippon's 31-year career at CU, she became chair of the Department of Modern Language and Literature. President Sewall praised her as a model of "exalted womanhood," never knowing about her romance with a young student who fathered her secret love child. In many ways, "Miss" Rippon shattered the mold in which 19th-century men wrapped women. Her full story came to light in 1999 with the publication of Silvia Pettem's book, *Separate Lives: The Story of Mary Rippon. Photo courtesy of Silvia Pettem*

Boulderites rejoiced at the July, 1875, groundbreaking for "Old Main." Shortly after its mansard tower was completed and topped with slate, however, high winds blew it down. Architect Erastus H. Dimick designed a sturdier brick structure with a lighter roof that opened on September 5, 1877. "Old Main," the university's only edifice for several years, attracted 44 students with its promise of free tuition. Dr. Joseph A. Sewall of Illinois Normal University was hired as CU's first president. President Sewall enlisted John Dow, the principal of Boulder's high school, to help him teach classes. In 1878, Mary Rippon became the third faculty member and began a distinguished career teaching French and German.

The legislature continued to snub the university, but CU survived with local donations. Local high school students went to the struggling "university" to pad enrollments. President Sewall, his wife, son and three daughters, were given the first floor of Old Main as their living quarters. Grateful, the Sewalls moved in despite the noisy students boarding on the third floor. President Sewall resigned in frustration in 1886, complaining "Ten years of my life were mostly filled with sadness, disappointment and sorrow... I tried to be hopeful, but it was bitter work."

During the presidencies of Horace M. Hale (1887-1892) and James H. Baker (1892-1914), CU evolved from a glorified high school into a university of 1,200 students and 200 faculty with a $300,000 budget. By 1914, CU had a medical school (1883), a football team (1890), a law school (1892), an engineering school (1893), a college of education (1908), a business school (1908), a graduate school (1909) and a Denver Extension Division (1912). The Hale Science Building, completed in 1894, honored president Hale, who adorned the campus with trees and Varsity Lake.

President Baker threatened to close the school in 1899 after five years without any state funding. When

◆ From the first floor of Old Main, CU President Joseph Sewall graduated to this president's house in 1884. Designed by Denver architect Ernest Philip Varian, it has been restored as the Koenig Alumni Center. Old Main is in the background and a predecessor of CU's buffalo mascot, Ralphie, in the foreground.
Colorado Historical Society

◆ Andrew J. Macky arrived from Wisconsin in 1859 with three ox teams of provisions. He built one of Boulder's first fine frame houses at 14th and Pearl. Macky's home doubled as the first county courthouse and a community meeting place for political, religious and social events until he built Union Hall to get all those groups out of his house. Macky became president of Boulder's First National Bank and left a chunk of his considerable fortune to the University of Colorado.
Tom Noel Collection

◆ (Top) Charles Klauder's 1919 model of his masterplan for the Boulder Campus has been followed fairly well, earning the CU campus praise as America's best designed state university. Some local critics, however, called the buildings too rural, too primitive and too Italian, inspiring Governor Oliver H. Shoup to suggest: "I suppose you could stucco them."
Photo by Ed Tangen, Amon Carter Museum

the legislature crowned the $2.8 million State Capitol in Denver with a gold dome, Baker protested that the dome alone cost more than the university.

Boulder residents continued to sustain the university. Andrew Macky, president of the First National Bank, left $300,000 upon his death in 1907 to build Macky Auditorium. After it was finally finished in 1922, the entire student body met there every Thursday morning for prayer and pep talks.

They prayed and rooted for CU's football team — which desperately needed help. The slow-starting "Boulders" lost their first game in 1890 to the Denver Athletic Club, 20 to 0. This defeat was sweeter than the next. In the first official football game ever played in Boulder, CU lost to the Colorado School of Mines, 103 to 0. CU President Horace M. Hale, an elderly bearded man, became terribly distressed. According to a player, "President Hale threw off his coat, jumped over the ropes and started to clear up the adversaries single-handed, and he weighed only 100 pounds." Renaming the team the "Buffalos" did not help. CU did not capture national respect until 1937, when they were led by future Supreme Court Justice Byron "Whizzer" White to an unbeaten season.

◆ Workmen prepare to install the red terra cotta tile roof on Hellems Hall, March 24, 1921.
Photo by Ed Tangen, Amon Carter Museum

CU gained architectural as well as academic respectability during the 1919-1939 presidency of George Norlin, who joined the faculty as a professor of Greek in 1899. As president, he hired Philadelphia architect Charles Z. Klauder to masterplan the campus. Klauder and his partner, Frank Miles Day, had used the Collegiate Gothic style at Cornell, Princeton and Wellesley, but Boulder's "robust environment" changed Klauder's mind. It reminded him of his 1890s trip to Tuscany with its rough-faced stone buildings capped with red tile roofs and dove cot chimneys. Klauder used a variety of local sandstones under orange roof tiles with a sprinkling of brown, buff, purple, blue and red tiles. These design elements give the campus a rustic, casual air. Yet most of the buildings are aggressively symmetrical, with refined Florentine details such as the lions, cartouches and other neoclassical details carved into the limestone trim. The campus is perhaps Colorado's best example of a consistent, well-planned architecture and has earned CU national recognition as America's best designed state university.

Macky Auditorium's exotic architecture may be traced to President James H. Baker's orders to architects Aaron M. Gove and Thomas F. Walsh. He gave them, as he wrote in his autobiography, pictures of the Palazzo Vecchio in Florence, King's Chapel at Cambridge, the Magdalen Tower at Oxford, an edifice at Princeton University and a New York City Church and asked them "to harmonize the elements, if possible, and make 'something different.'"
University of Colorado photo by J. Martin Natvig

Besides fine schools and the state university, Boulder also aspired to erect noble churches. Congregationalists erected the first church in 1870, a square-towered structure on Pine Street replaced by today's Carnegie Branch Library for Local History. The flock moved across the street in 1908 into the English Gothic-style First Congregational Church built of Mt. Sanitas sandstone and designed by prominent Colorado Springs architects Thomas MacLaren and Thompson D. Hetherington.

Methodists formed the first congregation in Boulder and met in the Pioneer School, the courthouse, and the Congregational Church before erecting their own house of worship in 1872. The original red brick church was replaced in 1891 by the First United Methodist Church at 14th and Spruce, a Romanesque Revival gem in rough red sandstone. The original design of Harlan Thomas is complemented by a dramatically modern 1960 addition by Boulder architect Hobart Wagoner, who matched the original gables with six repeating gables of concrete and glass block.

Presbyterians organized in 1872. After meeting in the pioneer Court House, in A.J. Macky's Union Hall and in the Episcopal Chapel, the congregation in 1877 moved into its own red brick Gothic church on 16th Street. They raised funds with necktie socials — gentlemen bought a necktie matching the outfit of their favorite church lady. If either party was dissatisfied with the partnership, they could buy a divorce for 25 cents.

◆ Buff, pink and red Lyons Formation sandstone from local quarries, red tile roofs and distinctive dove cote chimneys unite otherwise diverse buildings on the University of Colorado's Boulder campus. (above) *photo by Tom Noel* (right) *photo by J. Martin Natvig*

◆ (Left photos)
Boulder's Congregational Church traces its origins to a July 17, 1864, meeting in a cottonwood grove along Boulder Creek in Valmont. This 1870 photograph of Boulder's first church building shows the Congregational Church on the site of today's Carnegie Library. The funeral service is for pioneer Jonathan Tourtellot who used water from Farmer's Ditch (center of photo,) to grow crops and landscape his house in what is now downtown Boulder. In 1908 the Congregationalists moved into the sandstone English Gothic edifice at the southwest corner of Broadway and Pine Street.
Carnegie Branch Library for Local History, Boulder Historical Society Collection & 1910 postcard from Peter Pollock Collection

Episcopalians erected a frame chapel at 15th and Walnut streets, then a red brick Gothic church at 14th and Pine. E. H. Dimick, architect of CU's Old Main, designed the First Baptist Church on the east side of 16th Street, between Pine and Spruce. The Episcopalians later moved to their current church at 1235 Pine.

Boulder became the first Colorado town with two Catholic parishes. Bishop Joseph P. Machebeuf established Sacred Heart of Mary Parish in 1867. The Bishop, a shrewd French-born missionary, paid $500 for 160 acres in South Boulder as a home for Sacred Heart of Mary Parish. The Benedictine Order took over the Parish in 1886 and established a monastery and farm. In 1930, the Benedictine nuns of St. Walburga, fleeing Hitler's Nazi Germany, opened their convent on the site and took over operation of the farm. As South Boulder became prime real estate and the sister's quiet, contemplative way of life grew threatened in the 1990s, they sold the 150-acre site and moved to Virginia Dale in rural Larimer County. While Sacred Heart of Mary and the Walburga Monastery served South Boulder and outlying rural areas, downtown Catholics in 1875 founded a second parish, Sacred Heart of Jesus, which thrives to this day at 14th and Mapleton.

◆ Boulder's First United Methodist Church showcases locally quarried red sandstone in a good example of the Romanesque Revival style.
1988 photo by Tom Noel

◆ (Far left)
Reflecting high hopes for the dead, tombstone angels point heavenward. With burials dating back to 1873, The Sacred Heart of Mary Catholic Church cemetery on South Boulder Road is a history lesson taught by pioneer immigrants.
1969 photo by Tom Noel

◆ (Right photos) The St. Walburga Benedictines established their South Boulder Road convent on St. Joseph's Day in 1935. In these photos, Mother Superior Mary Thomas read her prayers while Sister Angela prepared breakfast in May of 1985. In 1998 the nuns left this enclave for a quieter rural retreat in Virginia Dale near the Wyoming border.
Photos by James Baca

in 1871. An evangelical missionary, she walked the streets handing out religious tracts, even invading Pearl Street saloons to offer salvation to sodden souls. She helped establish the Seventh Day Adventist Church in 1879. Her health conscious sect acquired 90 acres at the western end of Mapleton Avenue and in 1896 opened a large sanitarium there for tuberculars. Patients basked in the cool Colorado sunshine on expansive front porches. They lived on vegetarian diets similar to those of the Battle Creek, Michigan, Sanitarium where Dr. John Harvey Kellogg invented cornflakes. Vegetarians found their dietary sentiments reinforced by the stuffed animal exhibits of Amy Dartt's daughter, Martha Dartt Maxwell. After the discovery of penicillin and other tuberculosis-curing drugs, the Colorado Sanitarium became Boulder Memorial Hospital.

Boulderites erected splendid residences. Frederick A. Squires built a fine stone house in 1865 at 1019

Catholics built Boulder's first private school, Mount St. Gertrude Academy, on Boulder's southwestern outskirts. After buying the site from Anthony Arnett, Sisters Mary Theodore, Thecla, Faustina and Luminia in 1892 opened their red brick academy on the block bounded by Aurora and Cascade avenues and Lincoln Place and 10th Street. At first, these Sisters of Charity of the Blessed Virgin welcomed boys and girls, Catholics and non-Catholics. As classrooms became overcrowded, they began accepting girls only in grades one through 12. In 1919, the sisters added two more stories to the main building, two large wings, a music conservatory bungalow and a chapel. Mount St. Gertrude remained Boulder's leading private school until its 1969 closing. Thirty years later, the grand old landmark reopened as The Academy, a mix of detached and communal senior housing.

"Grandma" Amy Dartt, a pioneer Seventh Day Adventist, came to Boulder

◆ Mount St. Gertrude's Academy, an 1892 design by Denver architect Alexander Cazin at 9th and Aurora Avenue, is red brick with red sandstone trim with Romanesque Revival stylings. Following a devastating 1980s fire, it was reconstructed and expanded for a 1998 renaissance as a housing complex, The Academy.
Noré Winter & Company

◆ (Far right) Martha Maxwell began collecting and mounting creatures for her Rocky Mountain Museum on Pearl Street, where this photo was taken around 1875. A year later her taxidermy collection, ranging from hummingbirds to a grizzly bear, starred in Colorado's display at the 1876 Centennial Exhibition in Philadelphia.
Colorado Historical Society

Offering tuberculars "air that only the angels have breathed before," Seventh Day Adventists opened the Colorado Sanitarium in 1895. This foothills haven at the west end of Mapleton Avenue boasted Colorado's salubrious climate cure, a "home-like atmosphere" and a holistic approach "treating the whole person rather than just the physical ailment." The five-story, 100-room, $70,000 sanitarium promoted itself as "a haven for the sick and robust, where all the comforts of a modern world are enjoyed." Tuberculosis bacilli, patients were assured, "will be arrested by an altitude greater than 5,000 feet with a dry atmosphere."
Photo by Harry Hale Buchwalter, Colorado Historical Society

◆ (Top photos) J.D. Long opened a flower and vegetable seed business in 1905 at 3240 Broadway along the 1862 Farmer's Ditch. Long published his first catalog in 1908 and began to specialize in Iris. J.D.'s son, Everett, expanded Long's Gardens into a nationally prominent business that ships some 600 different bearded iris rhizomes all over the world. Locals can still dig their own for $3 per plant at the historic Long House and Gardens on North Broadway at Iris Avenue.
Photos by Tom Noel

Spruce Street. He moved in with his wife Miranda, and her identical twin, Maria, who married Fred's business partner Jonathan Tourtellot. The two families operated a mercantile, the *Boulder County News* and raised cows on their Mapleton Hill Farm. They all lived together in the Squires-Tourtellot House, now restored as the oldest residence in Boulder.

Another notable architectural survivor is the Second Empire-style residence of Willamette Arnett at 646 Pearl Street. Will was the son of Anthony Arnett, a Frenchman who opened the Boulder House in 1864 and replaced it a decade later with the Arnett Hotel. Enriched by his hotel-keeping and investments in mining and real estate, Anthony donated part of the site for the state university. In his frame house at the corner of Pearl and Broadway, Arnett and his wife raised nine children. As that corner became the busiest and most dangerous in town, they moved to 741 Pearl. Their son Will had architect George King design a domicile of Boulder brick with stone trim. It is distinguished by a three-story mansard tower, steep pitched gables, scrolled bargeboards,

◆ Willamette "Will" Arnett built this gingerbread house in 1877 at 646 Pearl Street for $4,000. Still guarded by the original wrought iron fence and cottonwoods, it is an exquisite example of the Second Empire style. Will, the son of a prominent Boulder City pioneer family, ventured north to Alaska for the Klondike gold rush, where he lost his life in 1900.
1998 photo by Tom Noel

ornate roof cresting and a matching wrought iron fence. This quaint, unusually ornate house at 646 Pearl Street would become a preservationist's dream.

Boulder's wonderful climate and small town charms seduced summer visitors. New York City stockbroker and chainstore owner J.H. Harbeck, for instance, bought several lots at 1206 Euclid Avenue near Mount St. Gertrude. Harbeck used quarry-faced stone for the house, porch columns, carriage house and a fine porch wall. A hospitable Dutch front door, Tiffany-style stained glass windows, Italian tile fireplaces and built-in woodwork cupboards and bookshelves are among the exquisite details making Harbeck House a museum-quality example of Boulder's "Home Sweet Home" ethic.

Kate Harbeck buried her pet dogs beneath marble slabs in the backyard and, upon her death in 1930, bequeathed $50,000 to start Boulder's Humane Society. The house's next owner, Milton Bergheim, proprietor of a Pearl Street haberdashery, lived there from 1939 to 1969. After he died, the City of Boulder bought the house, ultimately for use as the headquarters and museum of the Boulder Historical Society.

Although Boulder puffed itself as a veritable Garden of Eden, farmers found that most crops withered and died without irrigation. To water his orchards at 17th and Arapahoe, Marinus Smith dug the Smith and Goss Ditch in 1859 along Arapahoe to Boulder Creek. The Anderson Ditch dug in 1860 irrigated land in and around Columbia Cemetery and later helped to water the University of Colorado campus. The Farmers Ditch dug in 1862 carried water in a 10-mile-long canal with more than 100 miles of lateral ditches. It took a northeastern route through the current Mapleton Hill and Newlands neighborhoods. Anderson and Farmers ditches survive as do the open irrigation ditches that still water the historic quadrangle of the CU campus.

Water ditches turned the Boulder Valley into fields of grain which fed Boulder's mills, bakeries and breweries. The Douty (later Yount) Flour Mill at the mouth of Boulder Canyon and the Sternberg brothers "Lily White" mill, first located on the south side of Boulder Creek near 24th Street, appeared in the 1870s and thrived for decades.

Besides serving outlying county farmers and ranchers, Boulder continued to be the county ore processing center. Gold Hill and other gold towns patronized Boulder County smelters such as James H. Boyd's smelting works at the mouth of Boulder Canyon. By 1876, Boyd processed some 15 tons of ore per day.

Boulder blossomed, thanks to mining, agriculture and a maturing university. From a tiny town of 343 in 1870, it grew into a city of 6,150 by 1900. Railroads were the key to the town's growth as the county's commercial and population center. The Denver & Boulder Valley Railroad, a subsidiary of the Denver Pacific, steamed into Boulder from the South Platte Valley in 1873 via Brighton, Erie, Canfield and Valmont. A second line, The Colorado Central from Golden and Denver, reached Boulder and Longmont

◆ Animal-lover Kate Harbeck buried her pet dogs in the backyard at Harbeck House. Upon her death in 1930, she bequeathed $50,000 to start the Boulder Humane Society. Milton Bergheim, owner of a Pearl Street haberdashery, lived here from 1939 to 1969. The house later became the headquarters and museum of the Boulder Historical Society. That society formed in 1944 thanks to Alva Adams "Gov" Paddock, publisher and editor of the *Daily Camera*, who had farsighted vision not only for Boulder's future, but for preserving its past.
Drawing courtesy of Thomas Meier

◆ The railroad tracks are now Canyon Boulevard and the Boyd Smelter (at left) has been replaced by the Boulder Municipal Complex and a park along Boulder Creek. Boulder native Jack Smith, who lives nearby in his family home at 308 Pearl Street, recalls: "After the Boyd closed in 1918 we used their two smelter ponds as swimming holes — they even had sandy beaches." Smith, a noted archaeologist, spearheaded the 1998 campaign to designate the Boyd site as Boulder's first archaeological landmark.
Carnegie Branch Library for Local History, Boulder Historical Society Collection

in 1873. These pioneer railroads were later swallowed by the Union Pacific and Burlington Northern, which serve the county to this day.

Boulder's narrow-gauge railroad started out in 1882 as the Greeley, Salt Lake & Pacific. Reorganized in 1897 as the Colorado & Northwestern, it chugged from Boulder four miles up Boulder Canyon to Orodell. From this tiny mining camp, the line steamed up Four Mile Creek to Crisman, Salina, Wall Street and Sunset. In 1898, the C&NW built north from Sunset over to Left Hand Creek and up to Ward via Mount Alto Park, Gold Hill Station and Bloomerville. In 1904, the C&NW constructed another branch from Sunset through Nederland, and Cardinal to Eldora. Renamed the Denver, Boulder & Western (DB&W) in 1909, it served mining towns and also attracted fishermen, campers and sightseers. This slow, tipsy line earned a local reputation as the "Do Better Walking." As mining dwindled, promoters dubbed the DB&W the Switzerland Trail to help capture rubberneckers. The railroad's evolution from mining gold and silver to mining tourists reflected a county-wide economic shift that would characterize Boulder County's 20th-century history.

More than a dozen different railroads served Boulder County at one time or another. Most were short and short-lived, quickly absorbed by larger roads if they proved to be profitable. Even hard core rail buffs are hard pressed to remember tiny railroads such as the Denver, Marshall & Boulder and Golden, Boulder & Caribou.

Much better remembered is the Denver & Interurban Railroad (D&I). This electric, pollution-free, 60 m.p.h. train started running in 1908 between Boulder, Broomfield, Denver, Eldorado Springs, Lafayette, Louisville, Marshall and Superior. Before its 1926 abandonment, the D&I transported students, working people and tourists. In exchange for a Pearl Street right-of-way, the D&I helped pay for paving that street. Much of the D&I right of way is visible to motorists stuck in automobile traffic jams along U.S. 36. Motorists and 21st-century transportation planners alike dream of reincarnating this interurban electric marvel.

Boulder City fathers knew that water was another key to the town's prosperity. In 1874, they passed an $18,000 bond issue to build a reservoir at the mouth of Boulder Canyon. After mining waste water polluted

◆ (Right and opposite page, top) Boulder had seven railroad depots over the years. The surviving Union Pacific station, built in 1890, was moved in 1973 to 30th and Pearl Streets to save it from demolition. Rail enthusiasts and preservationists hope to move it once again — to Canyon Boulevard or to Central Park — where a narrow gauge locomotive, passenger coach and caboose commemorate the once mighty railroad network that made Boulder the hub of the county. *C. 1899 post card courtesy of Peter Pollock; 1999 photo by Tom Noel*

that reservoir, townsfolk approved a $150,000 bond issue in 1890 to build a larger reservoir at the mouth of Sunshine Canyon. In 1906, the city bought a third reservoir, Silver Lake. Boulder bought the Arapaho Glacier in 1929 from the federal government for $4,618 to refresh the municipal water supply and make Boulder the only city in the world to own its own glacier.

To celebrate its new ice water, Boulder inscribed its public drinking fountains "Pure Cold Water from the Boulder-Owned Arapaho Glacier." The Chamber of Commerce organized hikes to "the big snowfield" so tourists and locals could slide down the glacier on hot summer days. Like many other Boulder promotions, this one became controversial according to Boulder *Daily Camera* history columnist Silvia Pettem. Local environmentalists shot down a scheme to build a toll road to the glacier to "keep the area free from spoilation by the greed of commercial interests or irresponsible transient tourists."

Boulder's People

Since 1858, Boulder County's population has been dominated by native-born whites. Among immigrants, the largest foreign-born contingents have come from Germany, England, Ireland, Scotland, Canada, Sweden and France. The Indians, of course, were run out of the county in the 1860s. Niwot's people were not even invited back for Boulder's 50th anniversary gala in 1909. Instead, the city brought in the old enemies of the Arapaho, the Utes. Chief Buckskin Charley and his delegation from the Southern Ute Reservation joined in the parade, attended a CU football game and feasted at the semi-centennial banquet where Mrs. A. A. "Auntie Emma" Brookfield reigned as queen.

Townfounder A.A. Brookfield had brought his wife out to the male mining camp in 1860. Emma added considerable interest to pioneer dances and helped establish the Valmont Presbyterian Church in

◆ (Above and below) Eben Fine, a longtime Boulder druggist, became an avid photographer of the area's scenic attractions. He also championed construction of Boulder's first auto park in what is now Eben Fine Park (above). *Carnegie Branch Library for Local History, Boulder Historical Society Collection*

1863. Such churches were a haven for the pioneer ladies, who struggled to refine the raunchy mining and farming communities of young Boulder County. Unfortunately some Protestant churches also proved to be a breeding ground for one of the biggest blights on Boulder's past — the Knights of the Ku Klux Klan.

The Klan haunted Boulder and the rest of Colorado during the 1920s. Klansmen occupied the Colorado's governor's office, a U.S. Senate seat and other positions of power. Boulder's Kolorado Klavern #3 enlisted membership estimated at 500 to 1,000, and claimed 2,000 Boulder County members. One member at Boulder's Paris Dry Cleaning Parlor advertised: "Klothes Karefully Kleaned." Kluxers who did their own laundry were often betrayed by their clothes lines. An ungodly number of sheets and pillowcases were hung out to dry on Mondays after weekend rallies on Flagstaff Mountain where the Klan installed a giant 50-foot high cross in 1924.

Kluxers went after Black Boulderites but had a hard time finding any. Blacks have always comprised a tiny percentage of Boulder's population with an all-time high of 1.7 percent in 1910. Boulder's African-American community, unlike those in other Colorado cities and towns, dwindled instead of grew. Even fewer lived outside of the Boulder city limits — in 1910 only 20 blacks lived elsewhere in the county.

Boulder County's first black resident, miner Lorenzo Bowman, lived in Gold Hill from 1859 to 1862, when he moved to Gilpin County's gold fields. The early black immigrants to Boulder were primarily from the South and the border states of Kentucky and Missouri. They purchased homes all over town until greater discrimination in the Klan-infested 1920s confined the majority of black residents to Goss Street and Water Street (now Canyon Boulevard) — the town's flood prone, railroad infested bottomlands.

The social life of Boulder's black residents centered around two churches. The African Methodist Episcopal (A.M.E.) Church on the northwest corner of 18th and Pearl streets was acquired by three former slaves, Oscar White, Henry Stevens and Lewis Sheets, who mortgaged their homes to make the purchase. Reverend James Clay, the first minister, later left for a more lucrative white-washing business. The Second Baptist Church, formed in 1908, survives as an integrated congregation on East Baseline Road.

Oliver Toussaint Jackson, the famed founder of the Dearfield Colony for blacks in southeastern Weld County, was Boulder's best known black citizen. Born in Oxford, Ohio, he was a caterer in Denver and Idaho Springs before coming to Boulder, where he lived from 1892 to 1907. He managed the Chautauqua Dining Hall, then operated "Jackson's Resort" outside the city limits on 55th Street and Arapahoe Avenue.

◆ Rev. James Clay, captured here in a 1890s photo by Joe Sturtevant, at his 802 Marine Street home, arrived in Boulder in 1884 as the first minister of the African Methodist Episcopal Church. Early black residents mortgaged their homes to help build the church. After two years, Clay left the ministry for more lucrative work — painting and carpet cleaning. *Carnegie Library for Local History, Boulder Historical Society Collection*

Like Blacks, Jews were a tiny minority. Boulder County's Jewish population — about 75 in 1925 — did not even have a synagogue where Kluxers could plant one of their fiery crosses. Although Boulder Hebrews organized short-lived congregations in 1898 and 1919, Congregation Har HaShem ("Mountain of the Lord") did not establish an enduring synagogue until 1967. Boulder's growing Jewish population has since built a second synagogue, Bonai Shalom, at 1527 Cherryvale Road.

As Jews and Blacks were hard to find in Boulder County, the KKK focused on Catholics — who were numerous and visible. Klansman, according to the *Denver Catholic Register*, January 25, 1923, harassed Catholics by impersonating law officers and conducting "fake searches for liquor" and other "unlawful acts of intimidation and violence." Boulder's William Francis published the state KKK newspaper, the *Rocky Mountain American*, which rhapsodized on April 24, 1925:

"I would rather be a Klansman in robe of snowy white, Than to be a Catholic priest in a robe as black as night. For a Klansman is AMERICAN and AMERICA is his home, But a priest owes his allegiance to a Dago Pope in Rome."

"Dago" is a derogatory version of the name Diego. It also was what Italian laborers supposedly said at the end of the day when collecting their wages. Kluxers used the term to denigrate both Italian and Hispanic peoples, two disparate groups they stereotyped as dark, dangerous, swarthy, Catholic foreigners. Both groups did the hardest, most dangerous work in the county — coal mining — but the Klan stereotyped them as lazy, unproductive parasites.

"The Klan," proclaimed the *Rocky Mountain American* on January 31, 1925, fought "the immorality that permeated the government, the churches, the social and domestic life in the post-war saturnalia." Such pontification attracted Boulder County's Protestant puritans, who saw the Kluxing of Kolorado as a way to curb the orgy of bootlegging, cigarette smoking, risque dancing and "free love" that spiced the 1920s.

Editor Paddock of the *Daily Camera* courageously took on the spooks, whom he ridiculed as the "Komic Kapers Klub." University of Colorado President George Norlin also stood up to the Klan. He ignored Governor Clarence F. Morley's order to fire all Jewish and Catholic faculty. When U.S. Senator Rice Means, another Klansman, asked to participate in the CU-Utah football game, Norlin replied, "Mr. Means can kick-off anywhere he wants, except in Boulder." By 1925, the Boulder Klavern had folded. The statewide nightmare ended by 1927, although some spooky spasms continue to this day.

◆ (Opposite page, inside bottom) At this 1922 rally, Boulder Klavern # 3 initiated 200 new Klansmen. Initiates paid $16.50 each for the Klan manual and a fresh white sheet and hood. The Boulder Klan targeted Catholic immigrants, particularly the Irish and Italians. Boulder's Klan newspaper, *Rocky Mountain American*, sneered on April 24, 1925: "the list of names of those arrested in the booze and vice clean-up… looks like a page torn out of a city directory for the Holy City of Rome, with a sprinkling of Cork." *Denver Public Library, Western History Department*

◆ Besides managing Chautauqua's Dining Hall, O.T. Jackson opened his own resort in 1897 at the northeast corner of Arapahoe Avenue and 55th Street. His dinner club, which catered to whites, closed in 1907 when the county went dry. Some of the willows in this c. 1900 photo shade the Boulder Dinner Theater now occupying the site. *Carnegie Library for Local History, Boulder Historical Society Collection*

◆ Oliver T. Jackson, his wife Sadie and daughter pose with their carriage at their 2228 Pine Street home. Sadie also owned the two adjacent cottages. O.T., after managing the Chautauqua Dining Hall, founded the Dearfield Colony in Weld County, Colorado's only all- black agricultural community in 1911. *Carnegie Library for Local History, Boulder Historical Society Collection*

Urban Growth

Boulder Creek gave the town a bath with the flood of May 31, 1894. Unfortunately, the deluge left even more trash that it swept away. The City Council spent $10,000 to repair and replace bridges and build up the banks of Boulder Creek. Concerns persisted about garbage and other junk — such as "old boots, trunk covers, bones, green watermelons, decayed fruit, etc. scattered in all directions." Not until 1909 did the City Council adopt the Boulder City Improvement Association annual "clean-up day" — an ongoing tradition.

From Boulder's beginnings, citizens wanting a small, quiet, white-collar residential community clashed with those who wanted more growth. "Prospective industrialists were brought to the city, only to find meager encouragement," the *Daily Camera's* Paddock complained. "Boulder must have factories, and the only way to get them is to seize them when in sight. Sugar catches more flies than vinegar, and bilious traitors to their own city and to their own families should be weeded out." However, the opposition generally prevailed, stomping out such evils as a 1897 proposal for another stamp mill.

The Better Boulder Party, heartened by its success in passing local prohibition in 1907, took on reform of local government. They restructured city government in 1917 at a charter convention, where they enacted the city manager form of municipal government. Frederick Law Olmsted, Jr., had recommended this for Boulder as had other champions of more "scientific" government. From a field of more than 100 candidates, Boulder picked E. O. Heinrich of Pasadena as its first city manager. He resigned after a year in office, stating, "One's country may inspire one to die for it, but a municipality is scarcely worth the supreme sacrifice."

Heinrich grew frustrated with bitterly divisive issues, which even back then, included the "big question… to smoke or not to smoke?" Boulder women argued that they could straighten out local government and in 1918 elected the first female, Ida Campbell, to City Council, adding yet more ideas to an already contentious forum.

Boulder's Human Nature

"If God hadn't wanted to create argument, he never would have made Boulder," proclaimed the *Daily Camera* amid a bitter 1969 land use controversy. Citizens joke that there are at least 10 opinions on the nine-member Boulder City Council. Town meetings initially focused on lot size, railroads, the university, water supply, schools and other important community issues. During the 20th century, city government debated structural reform and adopted the controversial city manager form of government and the peculiar O'Hare election system whereby voters listed not only their first, but second and third choices. During the 1920s, Boulder addressed growth control by creating a planning commission and zoning.

As O. H. Wangelin, editor of the *Boulder County Herald* noted in the 1890s, "human nature… there is considerable of it in Boulder." Boulder writer Phyllis Smith added in her book, *A Look at Boulder From Settlement to City:* "Boulder's citizens have displayed a feistiness to fight over almost anything — liquor, the method of saluting the flag, paving of the town's streets, celebration of Christmas in the schools."

Even angels spark controversy in Boulder. During the 1990s, heated disputes centered on angel tree ornaments put on a tree in public open space. The quality of life in Boulder and the surrounding county has attracted people with diverse views on how to make Boulder Colorado's pacesetting community.

◆ Ira M. DeLong arrived in Boulder in 1888 to teach math at the University of Colorado. DeLong, who soon headed the department, also immersed himself in civic affairs. He helped to organize and served on Boulder's first planning commission in 1918, and chaired the 1917 charter convention which brought in the city manager form of city government which survives to this day. The professor poses with his wife Elizabeth and daughters Edith and Ruth during a 1901 outing to Ward.
Carnegie Library for Local History, Boulder Historical Society Collection

Carnegie Branch Library for Local History, Boulder Historical Society Collection

Photo by Tom Noel

Library of Congress

Photo by Louis C. McClure, Western History Department, Denver Public Library

Photo by Ron Ruhoff

Mountain Towns

Chapter Four

Despite claims of Boulder City boosters, lower Boulder Creek yielded very little gold. Miners were fooled by golden traces found in 1858 that had washed down from the mountain mother lodes. Deposited eons ago when volcanic activity brought molten material to the earth's crust, the gold spewed into fissures of ancient rock that became mountains. As glaciers and streams eroded the mountains, surface (placer) gold was washed downstream.

Seasoned miners followed Boulder Creek up into the hills to prospect its tributaries. They found gold at Allenspark, Eldora, Gold Hill, Jamestown, Sunshine, Ward and elsewhere. Silver surfaced at Caribou and tungsten in Nederland. Seventeen other small mining camps once showed enough promise to attract post offices — Balarat, Cardinal, Copper Rock, Crisman, Frances, Hessie, Magnolia, Orodelfan, Puzzler, Rockville, Rowena, Salina, Springvale, Sugar Loaf, Sunset, Tungsten and Wall Street.

These mountain mining communities became the life blood of Boulder County. Eight different ore processing plants arose in Boulder City to compete with an even larger battery of smelters at Black Hawk in Gilpin County. Gold and silver created Boulder County, and other riches of the earth sustained it. The county ranks among Colorado's top producers of coal, copper, crude oil, fluorspar,

◆ Orodell, as miners called Orodelfan, lay at the junction of Boulder Creek and Four Mile Creek. In this 1890s view, note the Switzerland Trail railroad track leaving Boulder Canyon to head up Four Mile Creek to the mining towns of Wall Street, Sunshine and Gold Hill. In 1993 Orodelfan became Boulder County's first designated landmark. *Carnegie Branch Library for Local History, Boulder Historical Society Collection*

lead, nickel and silver. Boulder tops all counties in the United States for production of tungsten.

After mineral booms busted, hard rock mining towns turned to mining tourists. Some mountain towns, such as Eldorado Springs and Peaceful Valley, sprang up to accommodate visitors. Only in Caribou, Boulder County's first million-dollar mining camp, has hard rock mining continued into the 21st century. Gold Hill, the first mining camp, remains the best preserved relic of Boulder County's golden age.

Gold Hill

When Boulder City did not pan out, smarter argonauts headed for the hills. They reckoned that the yellow sparkles found in the flatlands had washed down from mountain mother lodes. One of Captain Aikins sons, who had been with the party that founded Boulder City, finally struck a mother lode January 16, 1859. It lay on Gold Run Creek, a tributary of Four Mile Creek. Gold Run camp became Gold Hill town, where David Horsfal, Matthew McCaslin and others struck the big bonanza — the Horsfal Lode.

Gold Hillers created Colorado's first mining district in the spring of 1859. California gold rush veterans such as Anthony Arnett and Matthew McCaslin fathered "Mountain District No. 1" to impose some law and order and to regulate mining claims. They created a 25-cent filing fee and insisted that claims "must be marked with a stake at each corner [to] identify the persons claiming and the date." The Gold Hill Mining District allowed each miner one mountain claim and one gulch claim with water rights. Favoring working miners over non-resident speculators, the "Gold Hill Laws of 1859" required miners to work their claim at least one day in 10 or surrender it.

A stampede of argonauts swelled Gold Hill's population to 1,500 in the summer of 1860, according to the *Rocky Mountain News*. However, the 1860 U.S. Census accounted for only 487 official residents. Gold Hill produced more than $100,000 by 1861 to become one of the brightest spots in the newly created Colorado Territory.

As the heavy metal flowed out of Gold Hill, the town sought a mill to process its pickings. When word spread that the Culver Brothers were lugging a stamp mill to Black Hawk, Gold Hillers intercepted them and redirected the mill to their community. It arrived

◆ (Below far right) Gold Hill, Colorado's oldest continuously occupied mining town, arose with a January 1859 gold strike on Gold Run Creek, six miles west of Boulder. In this 1895 view, the community's celebrated hotel, variously known as Miners Inn, Wentworth House and Bluebird Lodge, is the two-story wooden structure behind the Gold Hill Billiard Hall & Sample Room. *Robert & Evelyn Brown Collection*

◆ Gold Hill Miners display the community spirit which still prevails in this informal, unincorporated town.
Robert L. & Evelyn Brown Collection

in time for the town's Fourth of July festivities, celebrated with a parade, speeches and pies made with fruit supposedly crushed in the new stamp mill.

Gold Hill originally sprang up on Horsfal Hill, east of the current town. This ridge attracted bitter winds and the Utes, who treated the newcomers less kindly than the peaceful Arapaho had. The Utes stole horses and whatever else they could find, killing one pioneer, "Old Man Barker," when he protested. His loss was balanced by the birth of Boulder County's first white baby — a girl — to Matthew and Miranda McCaslin.

The McCaslins and other residents were almost cooked by a May 1860 wildfire that consumed Gold Hill's ramshackle tents and log buildings. Some saved themselves by scrambling into mines and prospect holes. After the fire burned itself out, settlers rebuilt downhill on the current site. Despite the new location, Gold Hill fizzled. Not until the early 1870s did discovery of gold tellurides revive the town. Mines such as the Cash, Cold Spring, Red Cloud, Slide, Snowbound and St. Joe showered the town with gold.

All three approaches to Gold Hill — Sunshine Canyon from the east, Lickskillet Gulch from the north and Four Mile Canyon from the south — were too steep for railroad construction. The railroad never came any closer than Gold Hill Station two miles west of town.

Gold Hill, however, had plenty of burros. Several herds of 25 to 50 each ran wild in the town. George Cowell, a Gold Hill old-timer, told Gold Hill historian Lynne Walter: "People would put their egg shells and coffee grounds and potato peelings out in the street. About 6 o'clock at night the burros would come down out of the timber and eat up all this garbage, even the paper off the cans. Then they'd go down to the well in front of the saloon and drink from the watering trough. If you wanted a burro you never bought one. You picked out one that you liked and put your brand on him."

◆ "Gold Hill, by golly she was a rip snorter," recalled old-timer Martin Parsons. "She had quite a number of saloon bums. I can see their faces, but I'll be danged if I can recall their names." With its plank floor, rough stone fireplace and back bar nude, the Gold Hill Inn resurrects the friendly informality of fabled saloons of yesteryear. *1995 photo by Tom Noel*

◆ Samuel P. Conger (below) struck bonanzas twice, finding silver in Caribou in the 1860s and tungsten in Nederland in 1900. Conger lived long enough to be a guest of honor at Caribou's 1919 Silver Jubilee parade, saluted by 84 floats and four bands. He died in Denver at age 93. Four years earlier he told historian Forbes Parkhill in 1921: "I've prospected almost every foot of the mountains in northern Colorado." *Denver Public Library, Western History Department*

Gold Hill gained a first-rate hotel in 1872, when Charles Wentworth built the Miners Hotel. Sometimes called Wentworth House, this three-story, hewn log edifice attracted both tourists and miners, especially after it was immortalized by Eugene Field's poem "Casey's Table d'Hôte:

The bar wuz long 'nd rangy, with mirrer on the shelf, 'Nd a pistol, so that Casey...could help himself; Down underneath there wuz a row of bottled beer 'nd wine, 'Nd a kag of Burbun whiskey of the run of '59; Upon the walls wuz pictures of hosses 'nd of girls, — Not much on dress, perhaps, but strong on curls!

The hotel and its fabled saloon became more refined in 1921, when a group of Chicago ladies, the Blue Birds, bought it as a summer retreat. The groups' founder, Chicago philanthropist Jean Sherwood, sought a summer vacation retreat for working women suffering from "modern nervousness." Her bevy of businesswomen, school teachers and other professional ladies renamed Casey's Table d'Hote the Blue Bird Lodge. They removed its siding to expose the original hewn log construction. In 1926 they built the log dining hall next door. Besides putting the sparkle back into the eyes of Gold Hill's aging miners, these chicks revitalized the town, which had dwindled to 51 residents by 1920.

The Blue Birds flew back to Chicago in the 1950s and Barbara and Frank Finn bought the hotel and dining hall in 1962. They reopened it as the Gold Hill Inn, resetting

Casey's Table d'Hôte and restocking the bar which they adorned with a painted lady "not much on dress but strong on curls." The Finns rejuvenated the adjacent Wentworth/Bluebird Hotel as part of this blast from the past now operated by their sons Brian and Chris.

Caribou

Caribou lies 18 miles north of Central City and 22 miles west of Boulder City. At 10,000 feet, it became infamous as one of the coldest, snowiest and windiest of all Colorado mining communities.

A legend, apparently invented by John W. Buchanan in his 1957 booklet on Caribou, has an Arapaho princess falling in love with prospector Sam Conger.

◆ The Gold Hill Inn revives a frontier legacy with its log walls, stone fireplace and robust ambiance. *Drawing courtesy of Barbara, Frank and Brian Finn*

Her father forbade the affair, but she supposedly consoled Sam by showing him where he could find his fortune in silver.

Conger, who was born in Marietta, Ohio, in 1833, had struck out as a young man for the California gold fields, where he picked up more experience than gold. In 1859 he joined the Colorado rush. During the 1860s, while hunting elk on the future site of Caribou, he noticed blossom rock like the silver ore from Nevada's fabulous Comstock Lode.

Both the Comstock and the 1864 discovery of silver in Clear Creek County's Georgetown had paid off, making silver an attractive prospect. In August 1869, Conger and partners George Lytle and William Martin began big time silver extraction. Lytle named the place Caribou for the Cariboo Mining District of British Columbia where he had mined earlier. Before autumn blizzards set in, the Conger party had extracted a silver payoff. When Conger, Lytle and Martin returned to Caribou in the spring of 1870, they had plenty of uninvited company. A town sprang up and by December 1, 1870, the *Rocky Mountain News* reported:

"Its hotels are the Cariboo House, kept by Mrs. Wilson [who] sets a good table, but lacks accommodations. Mrs. Lyons... is keeping a hotel, having some beds and rooms. Mrs. Gilligan and Mr. Berger have boarding houses. Messers Tony & Fritz have a bakery and brewery, and Press W. Pierce, a fine, well filled butcher-shop, with an ample supply of vegetables, sufficient to last till next June. Leo Donnelly has a store with cellar attached, and a well selected, though small, stock of groceries, provisions, miner's goods, camping utensils, hardware. Sears, Werley & Co. have the largest building in the place, a fine, two story, well-finished frame house. The lower story is devoted to billiards and a saloon, while the upper story furnishes about a dozen rooms suitable for offices and sleeping rooms...

"There are at present neither doctors, lawyers, preachers nor school, though the presence of a score of youngsters indicates great need of the latter. Down the valleys skirting it are smaller settlements, where people live as easily as people are wont to do in such frontier primitive conditions."

◆ Most Caribou buildings had to be braced against the wind, but not the town's only one three-story structure, the Sherman House. This sturdy hotel and an instant town sprang up soon after *Caribou Post* editor Amos Bixby reported in 1870, "In a few weeks after the snow had disappeared there were from 300 to 400 hardy prospectors on the ground... as jolly and happy a set as we ever met. The scene after night-fall of the denizens of a populous mining camp gathered around the huge log fires was one to be remembered... in a little while all were stretched on their couches of fragrant pine enjoying the sweet sleep of healthful labor, and, perchance, dreaming of silver bricks, or the girls they left behind." *Ed Bathke Collection*

◆ Abel D. Breed, the first man to make a million in Colorado pay dirt, excelled at marketing as well as mining and milling (left). Breed (below) poses with the coffee service made of silver from his Caribou Mill. *Western History Department, Denver Public Library & Tom Noel Collection*

Caribou became official in 1871 when the federal government authorized a post office. The baby silver city glittered brightest of all the Boulder County camps in the 1870s, attracting eastern investors such as Abel Breed of Cincinnati. Breed's background as a highly successful patent medicine and casket salesman prepared him for the dicey business of mining. He bought Caribou mines and built his own Breed Smelter. As a publicity stunt, Breed paved the steps to Central City's Teller House with silver bricks from his Caribou Mine. When President Grant visited Central City in 1873, he stepped from the presidential stage onto Breed's shiny

◆ The Caribou School House, built in 1874, relied on log braces to resist the town's notorious winds. The single room school enrolled 77 students by 1879, making it one of the largest ungraded schools in the county. *Western History Department, Denver Public Library*

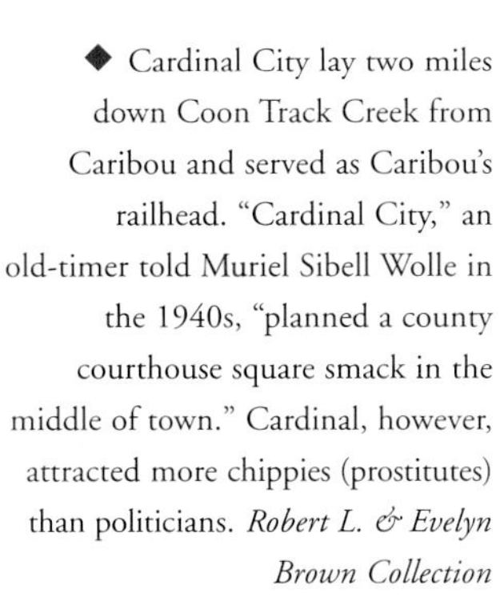

◆ Cardinal City lay two miles down Coon Track Creek from Caribou and served as Caribou's railhead. "Cardinal City," an old-timer told Muriel Sibell Wolle in the 1940s, "planned a county courthouse square smack in the middle of town." Cardinal, however, attracted more chippies (prostitutes) than politicians. *Robert L. & Evelyn Brown Collection*

product. With this nationally reported silver carpet, Breed's fame — and stock — soared. When potential investors called upon Breed, he offered them refreshment from a coffee service made of Caribou silver.

Breed, who had bought the Caribou Mine from Sam Conger in 1870 for $50,000, sold it to a Dutch company three years later for $3 million — the largest amount paid up to that time for a Colorado mining operation. When Cornish miners and mill workers struck against Dutch management, they called in Chinese laborers who became a target in the labor dispute.

The Dutch abandoned the mine in 1876. Denver entrepreneurs Jerome Chaffee and David Moffat subsequently picked up the $3 million operation at a sheriff's sale for $70,000. The two high rollers restructured Breed's empire as the Caribou Consolidated Mining Company and unloaded it on New York capitalist Robert G. Dun, who later became half of the famous Wall Street house of Dun & Bradstreet. Dun may have sunk as much as $1 million into his Caribou Mine, according to mining historian Duane A. Smith, in *Silver Saga: The Story of Caribou, Colorado* (Boulder: Pruett Publishing, 1974). The financier wrote of his Caribou misadventures in 1877: "That d — d old mine has harassed me almost to death aside from embarrassing pecuniarily. I only wish I were out of the operation and had back one quarter of what I have in it." Dun retreated to Wall Street, which he found far safer and more lucrative.

Without Breed around to puff the town, Caribou collapsed. After its mid-1870s boom, it shriveled and began to blow away, even though buildings were braced on the east side against 100-mile-an- hour gusts roaring down from the Great Divide. Caribou residents joked that summer lasted two days and winter three years. In winter residents used second-story windows to climb over snow drifts that buried one-story buildings.

Despite the inhospitable climate, Caribou strove for respectability. The Sherman House, a three-story edifice erected in 1875, became the town's social center, offering lyceum lectures and Caribou Silver Coronet Band performances. Townsfolk opened a school and a Methodist Church and, in 1881, persuaded the city fathers to close the notorious Shoo Fly Saloon and run its prostitutes out of town. These enterprising ladies set up shop two miles down Middle Boulder Creek at Cardinal, where red lights and scarlet women were welcome. Caribou's church, school and moral ways

◆ (Left and below)
The Potosi Mine Boarding House was intact in 1920, when Henry H. Lake drove up to Caribou to take this photo (bottom). Sixty years later, wind-blown, blizzard-blasted Caribou harbors little but the Potosi's stone ruins (left).
Denver Public Library, Western History Department & 1999 photo by John O'Dell

could not save it from the Silver Crash of 1893. Major fires in 1879, 1899 and 1905 and a 1903 earthquake finished the town. After peaking with an 1880 population of 549, Caribou declined to 44 by 1900 and became a ghost town in the 1920s. Survivors moved nine miles down Coon Track Creek into Nederland. Nowadays only summer tourists prowl the dead silver camp, scrutinizing the stone ruins of the Potosi Boarding House and the tombstone-less cemetery where residents slumber, free at last from the chilly winds.

Nederland

Although Caribou disappeared, its founder — Sam Conger — did not. He poked around Boulder County mining towns for decades, making his second and greatest discovery in 1900 — Tungsten, or "Black Iron" at Nederland. Previously cursed as "that damn black stuff," tungsten found 20th-century use for hardening steel and as the filaments of incandescent light bulbs. A tungsten mining and milling bonanza woke up the sleepy town on Middle Boulder Creek.

Initially known as Dayton, then Brownsville or Brown's Crossing for pioneer innkeeper Nathan Brown, it was christened Middle Boulder when the post office opened in 1871. When the Nederland Mining Company purchased the town and its mill from Abel Breed in 1873, they incorporated and renamed the town Nederland.

◆ In 1880s Nederland, the 1872 Hetzer House is in the foreground and Breed's Smelter in the left background. *Alisa Lewis Collection*

Nederland served Caribou as a mill town and also became a tourist haven. The *Caribou Post* in 1871 noted that the new wagon road from Boulder to Nederland and Caribou "affords opportunity for tourists to see Boulder Canyon, now the great attraction." Tally-hos — open wagons carrying 10 to 12 tourists — competed with ore haulers on the steep, serpentine Boulder Canyon Road. Boulder entrepreneurs spent an estimated $75,000 on the Boulder & Caribou Wagon Road, hoping to steer business — and rich ores — away from Black Hawk's smelters and Central City's many goods and services. Although notorious for its lack of turnouts, hairpin turns and more than 30 crossings over Boulder Creek, this toll road became jammed with ore and tourist wagons. Sightseers who survived the hair-raising ride found solace in Nederland's Brown's Mountain House, New Nederland House and Hetzer House, all up and running by 1877.

During the early 1900s, tungsten mining triggered Nederland's greatest boom. Breed's old Nederland silver mill was re-tooled as the Wolf Tongue Mill, named for a combination of two names for the same ore, "wolframite" and "tungsten." Several other tungsten mills hummed night and day during World War I, when the demand skyrocketed for this mineral to harden steel armaments. With the end of the war in 1918, the tungsten market collapsed. Nederland's wartime population of more than 1,000 fell to 291 by 1920. Conger's tungsten company did not close permanently until 1944. By then, tourism had become Nederland's economic mainstay.

Construction of Barker Dam in 1909 created Barker Lake to the delight of fishermen, boaters and sightseers. The Nederland Fish and Game Club stocked the lake with 50,000 trout and the nearby woods with elk relocated from Wyoming. Mary Roose's Antlers Hotel, which overlooked the lake from a craggy ridge, gave the town first-class tourist accommodations.

To construct the dam, its backers persuaded the Denver, Boulder and Northwestern Railroad to build a spur line from Sulfide Flats, near Eldora, to the construction site below Nederland. This rail line, best remembered as the Switzerland Trail, brought in tourists by the train load.

◆ (Far right) In this 1909 Ed Tangen shot of Main Street, Nederlanders are dressed up for July 4th festivities. *Carnegie Branch Library for Local History, Boulder Historical Society Collection*

◆ (Below) Colorado's premier mining historian Duane A. Smith published his master's thesis on Caribou. *1979 photo by Tom Noel*

When mining fizzled, Nederland courted tourists by promoting itself as a summer resort in "cloudland." These motorists probably reached cloudland via the scenic Boulder Canyon Road.
Ed Bathke Collection

◆ (Right photos) Barker Dam was constructed on Mrs. Hannah Barker's hay ranch in 1909 by the Eastern Colorado Power Company, a predecessor of the Public Service Company. It stores water for a power plant further down Boulder Canyon. *Peter Pollock Collection*

◆ (Below) Since 1874 Nederland has ridden the ups and downs of gold, silver and tungsten mining. The mountain town is now attracting flatlanders who have swelled its population to an all-time peak of almost 1,600, according to town clerk Pam Buckout in this miniature Town Hall. *1995 photo by Tom Noel*

◆ (Far right top) Historic Boulder, Inc. stalwarts Rebecca Waugh and Chellee Courtney led this fast-paced 1997 HBI excursion to Nederland for an inspection of the historic Pioneer Inn, one of Boulder County's most venerable liquid landmarks. *Photo by Tom Noel*

◆ (Far right bottom) In 1974 Nederland celebrated its centennial by organizing the Nederland Historical Society, which opened the Gillaspie House in 1975 as a museum. Built in 1906, this cottage housed Dr. Carbon Gillaspie, who ran the drugstore and once served as mayor. Gillaspie made his rounds by bicycle, even riding his bike down to Boulder, then putting it on the Switzerland Trail railroad for the ride back up to Nederland. The museum is officially open from Memorial Day to Labor Day, but the curator says "I'll open up if it isn't too snowy even in winter upon request, especially for school children." *1999 photo by Tom Noel*

Sightseers flocked to Nederland, which puffed itself as "cloudland," not only by rail but in a fleet of Stanley Steamer Mountain Wagons. The Hickox-Fields Livery Stable in Boulder bought two of these steam-powered vehicles and began regular summer excursions up Boulder Canyon. Other Boulder companies followed, giving the "Switzerland Trail" railroad more competition — competition that would ultimately derail the line. After a 1919 flood again washed out much of the trackage, the Switzerland Trail never rebuilt. To smooth the way for automobile tourists, Boulder Canyon Road was

◆ John Kemp built this cabin in 1894 for his family, including sons Donald and Robert in the horse-drawn wagon (below). When mining did not pan out, the Kemps logged Woodland Flats west of Eldora. Mr. & Mrs. Kemp and sons are atop the logs (left).
Denver Public Library, Western History Department

widened and straightened by laborers from the Colorado State Penitentiary.

Unlike most mountain mining towns that boomed in the 1800s and busted in the 1900s, Nederland remained a miniature community until its tungsten mining era began in 1900. Since then, its population of 182 has increased to more than 1,600.

During the 1960s, Nederland became a magnet for young, long-haired, blue-jeaned hippies resembling the miners who had rushed in a century earlier. Several decades of conflict between these "back to nature" newcomers and suspicious old-timers culminated in the bizarre murder of a young hippie by a county deputy sheriff. The generational riff has healed somewhat, however, as aging longhairs, with their locks shortened by balding if not by barbers, have become the old-timers. They have made Nederland an offbeat community wary of the growing threat of montane suburbanization.

Eldora

Six miles up Middle Boulder Creek from Nederland, the gold camp of Eldora was born with John Kemp's 1892 discovery of the Happy Valley Placer. Happy Valley was renamed Eldorado, but mail sent there often went to Eldorado, California, leading the post office to shorten the name to Eldora in 1897.

Typical of many mining camps, Eldora started out with spectacular growth and then sputtered. From a 1900 population peak of 395, the town shriveled into a near ghost town by the 1940s, and lost its post office in 1967. Although year-around residents became sparse, tourists fancied Eldora for its scenery and cool summers.

◆ John A. "Jack" Gilfillan, a mining engineer from St. Louis, settled in 1889 on the future site of Eldora. Jack, shown here with his best friend, found gold and built the Mogul Tunnel, anticipating a big time bonanza that never materialized.
Denver Public Library, Western History Collection

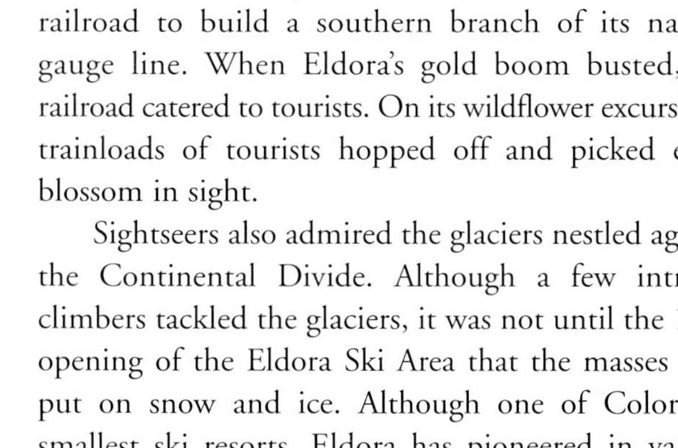

Eldora's mining boom led the Switzerland Trail railroad to build a southern branch of its narrow gauge line. When Eldora's gold boom busted, the railroad catered to tourists. On its wildflower excursions, trainloads of tourists hopped off and picked every blossom in sight.

Sightseers also admired the glaciers nestled against the Continental Divide. Although a few intrepid climbers tackled the glaciers, it was not until the 1962 opening of the Eldora Ski Area that the masses were put on snow and ice. Although one of Colorado's smallest ski resorts, Eldora has pioneered in various ways, including lighting the slopes for night-time skiing and offering regular bus service to the slopes.

Allenspark

Allenspark lies at the foot of Longs Peak on the eastern edge of Rocky Mountain National Park. It is named for Alonzo N. Allen, who homesteaded here in 1864. Allen, who also founded Burlington (Longmont), typified the prairie-mountain-prairie seasonal migration of whites, like the Arapaho before them.

◆ (Far right photos) Carl Talmadge & John Lilly's Stage Line ran from this Boulder depot on 15th Street between Pearl and Spruce, to the stage house in Eldora. The partners ran their daily Boulder- Nederland-Eldora service with the slogan, "Safest Teams for the Mountains."
Tom Noel Collection

◆ Despite great hoopla about a new California, a new Eldorado, Eldora proved to be slim pickings. The gold town flourished briefly from 1897 to 1898, then fizzled into a sparsely-settled summer tourist possibility.
1899 photo by Joseph B. Sturtevant, Ed Bathke Collection

◆ (Left photos)
Allenspark, a mountain community of 800 hardy souls, cherishes its past. Townsfolk have preserved the chimney of founder Alonzo Allen's log cabin and transformed St. James on the Mount Episcopal Church into their community house of worship.
Photos by Tom Noel

Allen and other miners dimpled the surrounding hills with prospect holes, triggering a brief flurry of gold mining. Although Allenspark received a post office in 1896, it has never incorporated. The town built a ski jump in the 1930s, but remained primarily a summer tourist destination. Each summer some 800 permanent residents host guests fleeing the flatland heat.

Among Allenspark's rustic marvels is St. James-on-the-Mount, which opened as an Episcopal church. Episcopalians had held preliminary meetings in the town's Dance-A-Lot Hall, which locals dubbed the St. Vitus Episcopal Church. To avoid all the jokes, the tiny congregation built this slab log chapel in 1925. Fifty years later it became the community church.

◆ "Upon this rock I shall build my church," Jesus said, providing inspiration for Monsignor Joseph J. Bosetti to build St. Catherine Chapel at Camp St. Malo Chapel. The Oscar Malo family donated $15,000 to build the chapel named in honor of Mrs. Malo's mother, Catherine Smith Mullen.
Photo by Ron Ruhoff

◆ Calvin Ward struck gold in 1860 and gave his name to the camp that developed around his discovery. The Columbia Hotel, seen here in 1899 was restored a century later. *Carnegie Branch Library for Local History, Boulder Historical Society Collection*

Bunce School, in a wooded setting with the Continental Divide as a backdrop, is named for its builder, a former mayor of Lexington, Kentucky. Its logs are square-notched at the corners and rest on stone rubble piers. One of two remaining log schools in Boulder County, Bunce School closed in 1940 but is still used as a community center.

Five miles north of Allenspark, Monsignor Joseph J. Bosetti, an avid skier and outdoorsman raised in the Italian Alps, opened Camp St. Malo in 1916. For the site, he selected 160 acres on the eastern edge of Rocky Mountain National Park. The crown jewel of the camp is St. Catherine's Chapel at the entrance, a 1934 masterwork by Colorado architect Jacques Benedict. Bosetti, the rector of Immaculate Conception Cathedral in Denver, persuaded the Oscar Malo family to build this $15,000 stone chapel named in honor of Mrs. Malo's mother, Catherine Smith Mullen. This roadside chapel built of massive boulders sits on a rocky crag which is incorporated into the structure.

Allenspark reveres its landmarks. Behind the town's strong sense of place is a remarkable group of women — the Hilltop Guild. Since the 1920s this club of 110 ladies has met weekly in their rustic lodge to discuss and undertake town improvements. They restored the one-room Bunce School and maintain the stone fireplace that is the sole remnant of pioneer Alonzo Allen's Cabin.

Ward

Prospector Calvin Ward struck gold at his "Miser's Dream" mine in 1860 in upper Left Hand Canyon. His neighbor Cyrus Deardorff discovered the Columbia Mine — a $3 million jackpot. In 1861 Ward and Deardorff founded the town named for Calvin. By the 1880s, half a dozen stamp mills thumping day and night kept Ward humming. The golden news led Boulder merchants William Davidson and Samuel Breath to form the Ni Wot Mining Company. They eventually bought out Ward and Deardorff and helped construct a wagon road to the 9,258-foot-high town, closely nestled to the snowy bosom of the Great Divide.

An estimated 600 people rushed to Ward in the mid 1860s, but the inevitable bust set in by 1870. Davidson sold out and went back to farm three miles east of

◆ In this March 30, 1899, Ward streetscape, Hazel Schmoll is the little girl bundled up in the middle of Rundell Avenue. She lived to be 99 and, besides serving as the state botanist, operated a dude ranch, the Range View Ranch, north of Ward. *Carnegie Branch Library for Local History, Boulder Historical Society Collection*

Boulder County's famous "Switzerland Trail" railroad began in 1881 as the Greeley, Salt Lake & Pacific. That narrow gauge underwent three subsequent corporate reincarnations. It was largely built between 1891 and 1894 by the Union Pacific, Denver & Gulf. The UPD&G abandoned the line in 1894, shortly after taking this bath in Four Mile Creek. The Colorado & Northwestern reorganized and expanded the line in 1898 and initiated "The Switzerland Trail of America" slogan. After floods and financial crisis derailed the C&NW, the line last operated as the Denver, Boulder & Western between 1909 and 1919.

Ed Bathke Collection

◆ Ward lay west of the current Peak to Peak Highway, according to folklore, until a fierce windstorm blew the ramshackle town downhill into its current gulch site. Ward enters the 21st century with much historic fabric intact, including the Congregational Church shown here.
1998 photo by Tom Noel

Valmont. About 300 persistent miners stuck it out in Ward despite the wicked winters. The town incorporated in 1896, anticipating growth with the impending arrival of "The Switzerland Trail" railroad. That narrow gauge line from Boulder finally chugged into Ward two years later. Governor Alva Adams alighted from the inaugural train to expound on "the whiplash route from the verdant valley of Boulder to the Cloud Kissed Camp of Ward," which dressed up in American flags and red white and blue bunting to greet visitors.

On the way up to this northern terminus of the Switzerland Trail, tourists marveled at Gold Hill Station, Brainard, Bloomerville and Mount Alto Park. Tourists came from all over the country to chill out in Boulder County's high country with its glaciers, alpine meadows, breath-taking scenery, and cool mountain air "that only the angels have breathed before."

A 1900 fire destroyed much of old Ward, sparing only the Congregational Church, schoolhouse and outlying dude ranches. Ward never really recovered. The population sank from an 1890 peak of 424 to only 10 in 1950. During the 1960s Ward began growing again as a haven for counter-cultural folk pursuing alternative lifestyles. As a symbolic denunciation of the work-obsessed, commuter world they left behind, some of these drop outs have decorated Ward with an exquisite collection of abandoned old cars and trucks, even a battered Citroen with Paris license plates.

Some of the newcomers moved into remnants of the Big Five Mines that pockmark the surrounding hills, although new growth pine, spruce, fir and aspen have erased most of the scars. The town is sleepy even in summer, with activity centered on the Ward Store, across Main Street from the dance hall, a crumbling stone ruins.

Behind the store sits the two-story frame Columbia Hotel with its asymmetrical roof. The Congregational Church, a white frame landmark built in 1894, has been rechristened the Ward Community Church.

Ward Store is not a modern supermarket. Built just after the 1900 fire, the clapboard, false-fronted building is jammed with health foods and other bare necessities of offbeat living in a town of eccentrics who fancy high, rarefied air. Storekeeper Jill Sturdevant tends her own children there and tended the town as its mayor during the 1990s. Near the counter she keeps Day-Glo Reflecto-Puppy bandannas to keep dogs — or small children — from being run over at night.

Big bins of raw foodstuffs range from cous-cous to Bear Mush Pearled Barley. "Kiss-my-Face Honey Moisturizer" is next to a barrel full of tie-dyed clothing. The store also has a Siberia-sized stockpile of anti-freeze and firewood.

"Ward is booming," Mayor Sturdevant boasted with a maternal pride in 1998. "Five babies were born here in 1997!" This explained the barrel outside labeled, "Diaper Service only." It stood next to a bare breasted wooden woman, a fertility totem pole.

With small town trust, Mayor Sturdevant lends the key to the town library to anyone who asks. Located in a rear annex to the 1898 Ward School, it is barely big enough for full-sized patrons and a librarian. A neat hand-printed sign urges patrons to "Please re-shelve books." The sign works. The library is the tidiest place in this disheveled town.

A tree trunk with log steps and tree branch railing leads to a balcony. The children's section is the five-foot-high alcove under the balcony. Most of the fiction corner is taken up by a cat-clawed old easy chair. *Webster's Second International Unabridged Dictionary* — the biggest ever compiled for the English language with over 600,000 entries — has its own hand-carved stand.

The front half of the old school contains the post office and free showers, a luxury in winter at 9,528 feet. One place with running fluids that never freezes over is Ward's Old Mill Site Inn, with its name spelled out in the log balustrade of the front porch along the Peak to Peak Highway. Opened as the Aspen Grove

◆ (Left and below)
Jamestown originated in the 1860s on James Creek as a mining camp. Locals sometimes call it Jimtown. Amos Bixby, in his 1880 history of Boulder County wrote that Jamestown's "scenic attractions are so striking that the first beholders called the place Elysian Park." Whatever you call it, the town remains an unspoiled community centered on the Mercantile — a general store, saloon and cafe with an upstairs meeting and music hall.
1998 photos by Tom Noel

◆ (Far left and left photo)
Wall Street was named by east coast investors who in 1902 built this immense Wall Street Gold Extraction Company Mill. Ruins of the mill still stand. The Wall Street Assay Office survives as the home of historian, Delores S. Bailey.
c. 1900 photo by Louis C. McClure, Denver Public Library, Western History Department,
1998 photos by Marti Anderson

Ivy Baldwin made the last of 86 tightrope walks across Eldorado Canyon in 1948 on his 82nd birthday. Baldwin, who ran off with a circus troupe at age 13, came to Colorado to perform at Elitch Gardens. He retired to an Eldorado Springs cottage to pursue his goal of 100 Eldorado tightrope performances.
Library of Congress

Inn in 1935, the inn has a cozy interior with bent wood furniture and a stone fireplace made from ore specimens of surrounding mines. Log posts holding up the bar are a mother lode of graffiti that includes a beautifully carved snow plow, the signature of plow operator Ed Martinek.

◆ "White gold" lured tourists to frolic in Boulder County's high country. This 1921 University of Colorado expedition to South Arapahoe Peak must have astonished old prospectors still scrounging around for gold.
Ed Tangen photo, Carnegie Branch Library for Local History, Boulder Historical Society Collection

Eldorado Springs

One of Boulder County's resorts served as an ancient sacred site for Native Americans who came to soak in its waters. This mecca lies where South Boulder Creek emerges from the mountains between 1,500-feet-high canyon walls. As tipis and tents gave way to log cabins and ranches, Frank D. Fowler and several partners formed the Moffat Lakes Resort Company in 1904. They established the resort town of Eldorado Springs, which gained a post office in 1906. As the centerpiece of the resort, the company constructed a 120-by 50-foot pool.

The standard gauge Eldorado Springs Railway arrived from Marshall, the coal camp three miles down South Boulder Creek. In 1908 the Denver & Interurban Line from Boulder reached Eldorado Springs. With a dozen runs a day during the summer tourist season, the D & I made Eldorado Springs a big splash.

Besides the pool filled by 76-degree artesian springs, Eldorado Springs boasted indoor and outdoor dance pavilions, a roller skating rink, picnic and camping grounds, gardens and shops.

◆ Jubilant South Boulder Creek carries trout through Eldorado Canyon to tease fishermen, old and young.
1998 photo by Tom Noel

◆ Toe-testing confirms that Eldorado Spring's warm springs pool has been heated deep within the earth to 76 degrees. Since 1906, this thermal wonder, enhanced with a bathhouse, sun deck and old fashioned water slide, has attracted water and sun bathers. *1998 photo by Tom Noel*

Accommodations ranged from private cabins and tents to the Eldorado, Grand View and Crags hotels. The Crags was reached by a funicular railway in operation from 1902 until 1912. A "crazy stairway" of 1,350 wooden steps climbed to the top of Chimney Rock (now Bastille Point) with picnic pavilions en route.

Glenn Miller's Orchestra played Eldorado Springs, whose notable visitors included Buffalo Bill Cody, Jack Dempsey, Jimmy Durante, Douglas Fairbanks, Gene Fowler, Mary Pickford and 1916 honeymooners Dwight and Mamie Eisenhower.

Eldorado's star, Ivy Baldwin, performed as "the greatest tight rope walker in the world." Every year he walked a one-inch thick wire between the pinnacles at the entrance to South Boulder Canyon. No safety nets impeded the view of the nervous crowd 580 feet below. During his walk across the 672-foot-long steel cable, Baldwin stopped to stand on his hands.

Regular Interurban train service was discontinued in 1926, leaving Eldorado Springs accessible only to the then minority of Coloradans who owned automobiles. A 1938 flood and a fire the following year destroyed many of the resort's amenities. The Baldwin and Eisenhower cottages remain, along with ruins of past resorts and even a few steel strands of Baldwin's tight rope.

Michael Hercules, a handsome, red-haired, showman, leased the pool from the Fowler family during the 1960s and renovated it, adding a snack bar, old fashioned metal water slide and sun decks.

◆(Right and opposite page) Tom Hendricks of Caribou, Dee Bailey of Wall Street and other champions of Boulder County's hard rock mining past raised money in 1997 to erect this statue in front of the courthouse. *Photo by Delores S. Bailey*

Visitors began returning to Eldorado, to be greeted at the pool entry by a stanza of Edgar Allen Poe's poem, "Eldorado" in black Gothic script:

Over the mountains of the moon,
Down the valley of the shadow,
Ride, boldly ride, the shadow replied
If you seek for Eldorado.

In 1975 Jack Fowler sold 200 acres of the resort to the state of Colorado for Eldorado Canyon State Park, which opened in 1978. Spectacular hikes, climbs and views reward visitors, as does the commercial hot springs pool and picnic grounds. Eldorado Canyon is one of Colorado's premier rock climbing meccas, with about 400 different ascents ranging from a beginner's walk to some of the most difficult rock climbs in the world. Watching human spiders climb the canyon walls remains a major attraction, although no one has yet matched Ivy Baldwin's aerial acrobatics.

Back to Mining

In the spring of 1971, a Colorado Springs native named Tom Hendricks walked into the clearing where the town of Caribou once stood. He saw in mountain-rimmed Caribou Park the same silvery possibilities that Sam Conger had seen a century earlier.

Hendricks, a geology student at the University of Colorado, decided that day to drop out and move into an abandoned miner's cabin at the Cross Mine. He started poking around in the mine, which had been opened in 1876 and abandoned in 1939. Hendricks knew that such mines had led many others to lose everything, including their lives. But like Conger, he took the plunge, sure he could beat the odds and strike it rich. Hendricks paid the owners $15,000 a year plus a 15 percent royalty on any gold he might find. In 1974 he bought the mine after laboriously deepening the shafts and constructing a drainage system.

With promotional genius reminiscent of Abel D. Breed, Hendricks enlisted corporate and individual investors. In 1980 he purchased Sam Conger's original Caribou Silver Mine. By the end of the year, he employed 47 people and extracted 80 tons of ore a day. Concentrates shipped to the Cominco Smelter in Trail, British Columbia, and the ASARCO Smelter in East Helena, Montana, yielded lead, zinc, copper, silver and gold in paying amounts. Hendricks actually began paying dividends.

Shrugging off almost three decades of hard, cold, lonely work, Hendricks reflected in 1998: "I guess I'm caught up in the romance and the history of Boulder County's mineral past, in the daily excitement of knowing that I may stumble across a rich vein."

Increasingly, Hendricks treats schoolchildren and sightseers to tours of his underground kingdom. Modern tourists marvel at the mine and at the stamina of men such as Tom Hendricks and realize that Colorado still has men to match her mountains.

Longmont Museum

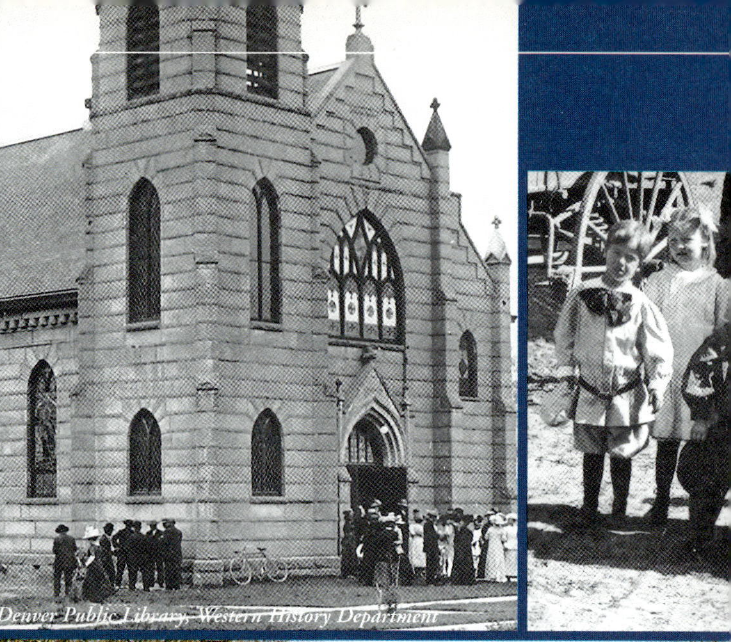
Denver Public Library, Western History Department

1999 photo by Tom Noel

1998 photo by Tom Noel

Longmont Museum

Denver Public Library, Western History Department

Longmont

Chapter *Five*

"There is no man integral within himself. We are all parts of one grand community, and it behooves every man to know what his neighbor is about."

—1871 Chicago-Colorado Colony Constitution and By Laws

With high communal hopes, the Chicago-Colorado Colony planted an agricultural community near the confluence of St. Vrain and Left Hand creeks. They named the place Longmont for Longs Peak — the 14,255-foot landmark on the western horizon.

The baby town, destined to become Boulder County's second largest city, was conceived in Chicago on November 22, 1870 by the Chicago-Colorado Colony Company. These Chicago idealists elected a Unitarian minister, Rev. Robert Collyer, as their president, Sidney H. Gay of the *Chicago Tribune* as vice president and Col. N. C. Pratt as secretary. William Bross, an ex-lieutenant governor of Illinois, also joined, adding luster to a company which attracted 300 stockholders by 1871.

The colony sent a representative, Seth Terry, to inspect sites within the land grant of the Denver Pacific Railway. Terry was escorted from Chicago to the promised land by William N. Byers, Colorado Territory's greatest booster. Byers, the founding editor of Denver's *Rocky Mountain News*, also moonlighted as the land

◆ Longs Peak, which commands the western horizon, inspired the Chicago-Colorado Company to name their colony Longmont. *1997 photo by Jim Havey*

◆ Seth and Jane Terry, two Connecticut Yankees, parented the baby town of Longmont. The Terrys, seen here in their 1895 25th wedding anniversary photo, helped populate the prairie hamlet by raising 11 children, some of whose descendants still reside in the town. *Longmont Museum*

agent for the National Land Company, the real estate arm of the Denver Pacific.

Byers kept his client in good humor. In his diary, Terry reported on January 20, 1871: "A magnificent day! Go to the Platte Canyon [with] Mr. Byers... One of the pleasantest days of my life."

The Chicagoans bought a 23,000-acre site for $5 an acre. They purchased another 30,000 acres from the federal government and some 7,000 additional acres from other parties. Seth Terry surveyed a square mile tract at the center of the colony as a town, which he christened "Longmont" on March 9, 1871. He platted the town, as the *News* noted, using antelope pronghorns as stakes.

Byers' *News* office also published the *1871 Chicago-Colorado Colony Constitution and By Laws* which declared that "Members of the Colony must be of strictly temperate habits and good moral character... Each member shall pay an initiation fee of five dollars and $150 for all rights and privileges of membership." Members were entitled to purchase two town lots, one for a residence and one for business, and were given access to outlying farmsteads. They created a model town with communal irrigation ditches, a street grid of tidy houses, schools, churches, a bath-house and one of Colorado Territory's first libraries.

◆ Water, as the 1871 *Chicago-Colorado Colony Company Constitution* put it, was "the magic touch" that would turn the Great American Desert into the Garden of Eden. This headgate siphoned St. Vrain Creek onto farmers' fields. By building its own water supply, Longmont is still in the enviable position of being a water seller instead of a buyer. *1998 photo by Tom Noel*

Settlers found nearby both the coal seams and good building stone that the town prospectus promised. Elm saplings were shipped from Chicago and planted along the dusty lanes of the baby town. Children watered the elms from street side laterals of the English, # 2, Left Hand Valley and other ditches.

Unlike most Colorado towns reluctant to dedicate park land that could not be either taxed or sold for municipal income, Longmont's founders actually built all three parks on the 1871 plan. Lake Park, named for Lake Michigan, was supposed to feature a large lake but only achieved that ambition in very wet years. The "lake" was filled in and converted to a horse racing track in what is now renamed Roosevelt Park. This park hosted the Boulder County Fair from 1891 to 1978. Collyer Park also materialized, as did Thompson Park. The largest parcel of the 1871 plat was set aside for "county buildings" in hopes of capturing the county seat from Boulder City.

Whereas Boulder City was founded by gold seekers, Longmont consisted of sober, hard-working farmers. "Agriculture," as the 1871 *Chicago-Colorado Colony Constitution* proclaimed, "is the basis of wealth, of power, of morality. It is the conservative element of all national and political and social growth; it steadies, preserves, purifies and elevates." Proving their virtue, Longmonters burned down the first saloon constructed in their temperance colony. Boulder might wink at saloons and brothels, but not Longmont.

Longmont tipplers, however, formed their own town of North Longmont in 1904. Besides saloons, North Longmont contained a jail, where intoxicated guests paid for their room with fines that financed the town.

This arrangement continued until 1913 when Longmont annexed its boisterous northern neighbor.

Spurred by aggressive promotion in both the *Chicago Tribune* and Denver's *Rocky Mountain News*, some 390 pilgrims flocked to Longmont during its first year. In 1871 the *Longmont Sentinel* was founded to further promote the new temperance colony as a Garden of Eden.

Although Longmont failed to capture the county seat from Boulder, it did erect Colorado's first public library. Mrs. Elizabeth (Rowell) Thompson, the wife of Boston millionaire Thomas Thompson, never moved to Longmont, but bought stock in the company to support its Christian and temperance principles. On one of her town lots, she built a 26- by 30-foot library, which opened on June 12, 1871, just three months after the first settlers arrived. Longmont's first Strawberry Festival celebrated the library's opening. However, because newly planted strawberries had not ripened, canned fruit was used. Some of this probably wound up on the 300 books, engravings and prints that Mrs. Thompson also donated.

Because Thompson Library initially served as a public hall, it was called Library Hall. Librarian William H. Terry, Seth Terry's 14-year-old son, rang the town bell atop the library at 7 a.m., 1 p.m., 6 p.m. and midnight. When school was in session, Billy rang an 8:45 a.m. bell to summon his classmates to join him at the library-schoolhouse.

◆ Isabella Bird, a British world traveler, rode into Longmont on September 25, 1873, and reported: "We came first upon dust-coloured frame houses set down at intervals on the dusty buff plain, each with its dusty wheat or barley field adjacent, the crop not the product of the rains of heaven but of the muddy overflow of Irrigating Ditch No 2. Then comes a road made up of many converging wagon tracks, which stiffen into a wide straggling main street."
Tom Noel Collection

◆ Saplings and frame storefronts in this 1872 photo (left) evolved by 1900 (below) into mature trees and brick commercial buildings. Longmonters determined ditch-digging and tree planting ultimately created an oasis town.
Longmont Museum

◆ Longmont's Library, the oldest in Colorado, is a cherished landmark at 335 Pratt Street. After service as a library, school and community hall, the 1871 edifice became a private residence, its use to this day. *1999 photos by Tom Noel*

Thompson Library likewise housed pioneer religious services until congregations could build their own churches. The Methodists built first in 1871, while Episcopalians erected St. Stephen's at 470 Main Street in 1881.

Longmont's Carnegie Library in 1912 replaced the Thompson Library, which had been converted to a private residence. The Carnegie Library was almost demolished in 1992 as preservationist Harriette Grigsby recalls, "They snuck in at night and demolished our 1975 library, but some of us saved the old Carnegie Library next door. We gathered 3,674 signatures in just 20 days to convince the city to save that treasure."

Old Burlington

Longmont blossomed and absorbed the older adjacent village of Burlington, which had been named by settlers from the city of that name in Iowa. Burlington originated in 1860 when Alonzo N. Allen and his stepson William Dickens built a hewn log cabin on the south bank of St. Vrain Creek. Allen, who came to Colorado as a gold seeker in 1859, enlarged his cabin in 1862 to accommodate the stage stop and a post office. This stage stop was enlarged again to become the Allen Hotel where Seth Terry and his committee stayed

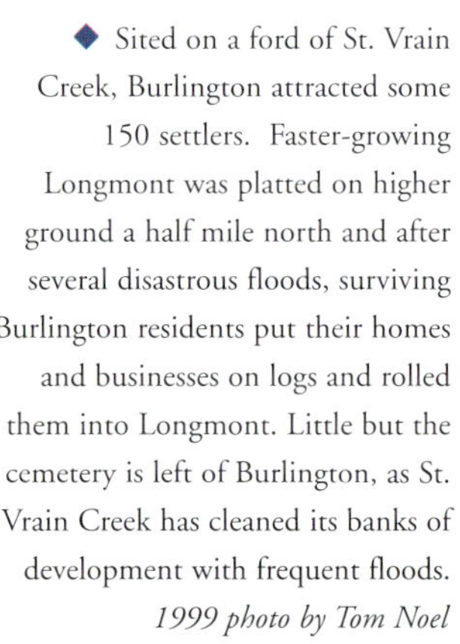

◆ Sited on a ford of St. Vrain Creek, Burlington attracted some 150 settlers. Faster-growing Longmont was platted on higher ground a half mile north and after several disastrous floods, surviving Burlington residents put their homes and businesses on logs and rolled them into Longmont. Little but the cemetery is left of Burlington, as St. Vrain Creek has cleaned its banks of development with frequent floods. *1999 photo by Tom Noel*

during their search for the Chicago-Colorado Colony townsite. Sited on a strategic ford of St. Vrain Creek, Burlington attracted some 150 settlers and its own newspaper, *The Burlington Free Press.*

The Allens, who had nine children, spearheaded efforts to start a Burlington school, which opened in 1864. One of their children, Alonzo H. Allen, recalled later:

The old Burlington School in 1864-65 was a shanty 18 by 24 feet, boarded up and down, and battened; rough floor with wide cracks; a center aisle with rough benches on each side; no desks. The boys sat on one side, the girls on the other... Our first teacher, Mrs. Mary Kinney, and about 30 kids waded through mud to get to school.

Floods ravaged the town, drowning dream after dream. Burlington's greatest aspiration was to become the home of the University of Colorado. Boulder not only captured the university but the other most coveted prize — the county seat. Floods erased most of Burlington, whose residents put their homes on logs and had horses and oxen lug them uphill to higher ground in Longmont.

Of old Burlington, subsequently annexed to Longmont, only a few souvenirs remain, such as William H. Dickens' farmhouse at the northeast corner of Main Street and St. Vrain Creek. Dickens, the son of Mary Allen by her first husband, became one of the town's largest landowners. His name lives on in the Dickens Opera House at the northeast corner of 3rd and Main. His mysterious 1915 murder while reading in his house was never solved, although one of his sons was a prime suspect.

Water & Steam

While Burlington drowned in too much water, Longmont's fortunes rose on its successful effort to build a bountiful municipal water system. Jessie Hall, who spent her entire life of some 90 years in Longmont, recalled the dry old days:

We had very little water. What we did have was brought from the St. Vrain River by Mr. R. F. Boze in a tank-wagon. At our back door were two tar barrels that he filled once a week for 25 cents per barrel. The barrels were covered with gunny sacks to keep out the dust and the bugs. An ice house was built at Fifth and Main where ice from Terry Lake and the St. Vrain was packed in straw and sold by the pound.

The collectivist Chicago-Colorado Colony dissolved in 1873 and the town of Longmont officially incorporated. Although the colony disbanded, the town it founded continued to grow. By 1880 Longmont boasted 773 residents. The population doubled by 1890, thanks to the community's diversified agriculture and good railroad connections.

The iron horse, as city fathers put it, was "the magic wand [which] would kindle a beauty unknown, lying hidden in the veiled bosom." To open the dry prairie bosom, the Colorado Central snorted into

◆ The City Bakery, shown here on Main Street around 1900, has been replaced by the Longmont National Bank. *Longmont Museum*

◆ In this January 2, 1903, glimpse of 3rd and Main streets, note the Dickens Opera House, right, built in 1882 by William H. Dickens, a pioneer resident of old Burlington. The Imperial Hotel, left, was constructed in 1881 by George Zweck, a Prussian immigrant, as the Zweck Hotel. Zweck struck it rich with his Prussian Mine on Left Hand Creek, where he supposedly extracted some $400,000 in gold. His 60-room hotel boasted solid oak furniture, Brussels carpeting and a restaurant with Haviland china, hand-blown crystal and fine silverware. After Charles F. Allen bought the hotel from Zweck in 1894, he changed the hotel's name from Zweck to Imperial.
Longmont Museum

town in 1873. By connecting Longmont with the rest of the world, the railroad enabled the town to grow as an agricultural hub. Renamed the Union Pacific in 1880, the line serves Longmont to this day.

Longmont also boasted a hometown railroad. The Great Western Railway was established in Longmont in 1902 to bring sugar beets into Great Western's Longmont mill. Ultimately the Great Western "sugar tramp" operated 75 miles of track, connecting beet dumps to Great Western mills at Eaton, Greeley, Johnstown and Windsor, as well as Longmont. The last standard gauge line in Colorado to regularly use steam locomotives, its puffing engines, clanging bells, and long, lingering steam whistles could be heard around town until the 1960s.

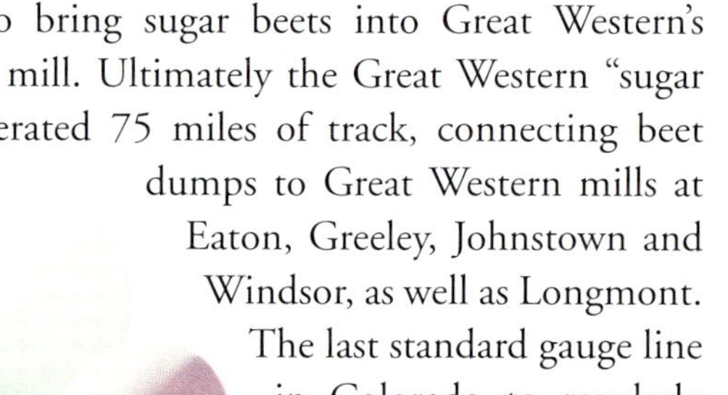

Minneapolis of the Rockies

Wheat put Longmont on the map, according to Enoch J. Coffman, who homesteaded on the site of Longmont in the 1860s. "I was taking a wagon load of wheat to Denver," he reminisced years later, "when I met the Chicago-Colorado committee looking for a site. We stopped to pass the time of day. Then they asked what I had in my sacks.

"'Wheat.'

"'Mind if I see it?' I opened several sacks and the men examined it closely. It was clean, plump and heavy... my load of wheat displayed at that chance meeting was one of the deciding factors in the location of Longmont."

The colony appointed Coffman superintendent of agricultural operations to oversee 1,000 acres planted in wheat and other crops. Coffman encouraged James W. Denio to construct the old Longmont Mill in 1873. Although it burned down in 1934, millstones weighing over 2,000 pounds survive. These heavyweights were turned by water power to produce fine

◆ (Bottom images) The old Longmont Mill site at 237 Pratt Street was converted to Old Mill Park in 1970 by the St. Vrain Historical Society. With a remnant of the Denio Mill Ditch, the 1860 Affolter hewn log cabin, and the 1860 stone milk house of Robert Hauck, this mini-park is a picturesque celebration of Longmont's earthy origins.
1998 photos by Tom Noel

◆ (Far left)
Longmont's largest 19th-century flour plant, the Farmers' Mill, opened in 1886 near today's Golden West Mill.
Denver Public Library, Western History Department

◆ R. Franklin Boze used his tally-ho coach as the St. Joseph School bus. He rewarded well-behaved passengers with chewing gum, which sometimes ended up on the underside of school desks. *Denver Public Library, Western History Department*

flour that made Longmont legendary. One stone now occupies a pedestal by the library, while another lies in Old Mill Park, a salute to Longmont's grainy past.

Coffman also served on the school board and in 1882 was elected to the Colorado Legislature on the Populist Ticket. Although Longmont abandoned its communal origins, Coffman remained a collectivist, helping to organize the Grange (Patrons of Husbandry) Mill in 1878. Another famed mill, the Longmont Farmers' Alliance operation on Main Street between 1st and 2nd avenues, is gone, replaced by a parking lot. It opened in the 1880s as the Longmont Farmers' Mill and lasted until the 1930s.

Appropriately, Longmont's dominant downtown landmark is the huge Golden West Milling and Elevator Company at the northwest corner of 1st and Terry. Opened in 1910 as a feed mill, it was converted in the 1920s to a flour mill, the Long's Peak Milling Company. In the 1930s it was renamed for its best known brand of flour, "Golden West." Golden West sold flour in 100 pound canvas bags, as well as smaller 20, 10 and 5 pound paper bags, all colorfully labeled.

Coffman, the pioneer wheat booster, took a lively interest in the Longmont Farmers' Milling and Elevator Company, a cooperative established in 1886. With this collective effort, Longmont area farmers grew, cleaned, milled, stored and sold grain on their own, rather than selling raw grain to milling tycoons such as Denver's John Kernan Mullen.

Mullen, an Irish immigrant, came close to monopolizing the Colorado grain market with his Colorado Milling and Elevator Company, which ultimately acquired three Longmont mills. For years Mullen schemed to capture the Longmont Farmers' Milling and Elevator Company, according to historian William J. Convery in *Pride of the Rockies: John Kernan Mullen*. Mullen called the Longmont mill "the best in northern Colorado" and "very hard competition."

Longmont Farmers' in 1906 erected a large concrete elevator in Denver along the South Platte River and railroad tracks at 20th and Little Raven streets. They

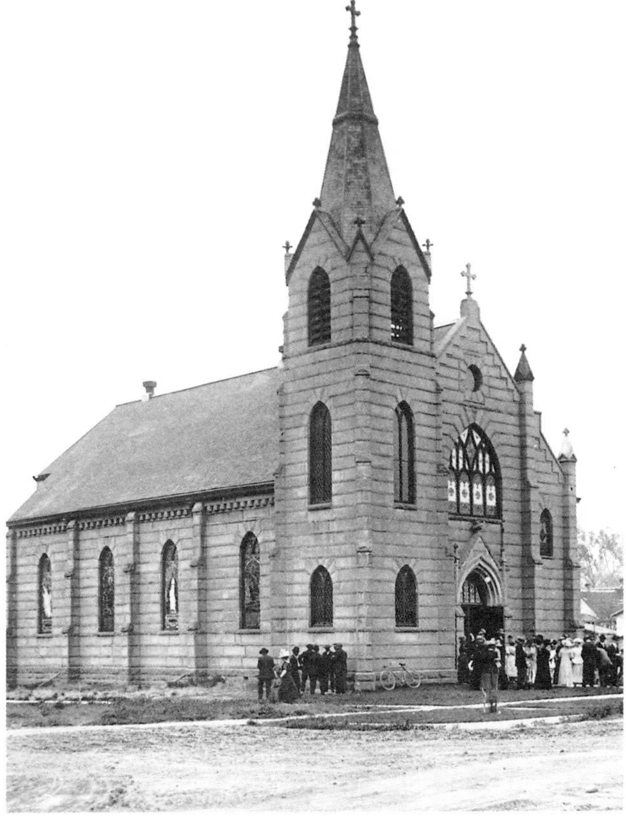

◆ St. John the Baptist Catholic Church, shown here at its July 22, 1905, dedication at 4th and Collyer, became the hub of a parish complex, with a rectory, convent, grade school and high school. The school opened accidentally in 1906. Mother Thecala and Sister Celestine, two sisters of St. Francis from Milwaukee, intended to start a school in Loveland. As their train neared Longmont, they mistook the conductor's cry and got off. Townsfolk persuaded them to stay and open an academy which attracted both Catholic and non-Catholic students.
Denver Public Library, Western History Department

painted their three Denver mill bins with a huge ad for "Pride of the Rockies," outraging Mullen who dominated the Mile High City market with his Hungarian Flour brand. Mullen, an Irish Catholic, became an easy target for the Ku Klux Klan, which had a powerful Longmont Klavern. In 1925 the Klan took over Longmont's city hall and announced plans to hire unemployed Klansmen to construct Chimney Rock Dam on St. Vrain Creek. Popular dissatisfaction with this controversial measure led to the Klan's ouster in 1927. The next city council used the left-over cement to pave Main Street.

◆ The Pride of the Rockies Flour Mill was not only an industrial but a baseball powerhouse, whose winning 1910 team is shown here with coach and mill management. *Longmont Museum*

With six mills humming during the flush times, Longmont could call itself the Minneapolis of the West. Twenty-four hours a day Longmont plants milled wheat, oats, barley and malt for flour and feed. The wheat industry thrived, peaking during World War I, when U.S. farmers found new markets in war-ravaged Europe. After the war, however, prices fell from a 1919 peak of $4 per bushel to $1.90 in the 1920s. Wheat sank to an all-time low in the mid-1930s of 80 cents a bushel. Not until 1924 did the Longmont Milling and Elevator Company sell out to Mullen's CM&E, which retained the popular Longmont brand name "Pride of the Rockies."

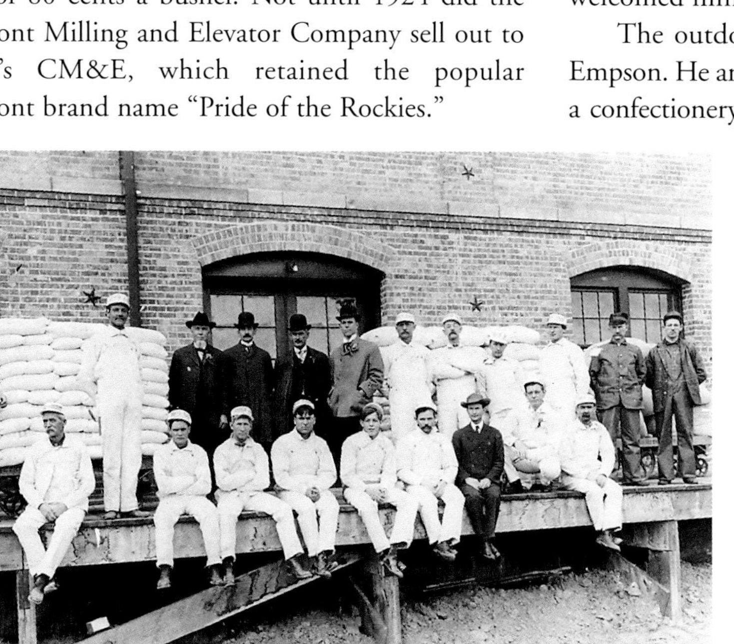

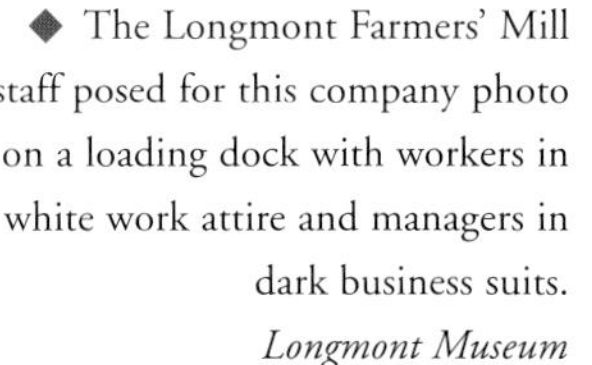

◆ The Longmont Farmers' Mill staff posed for this company photo on a loading dock with workers in white work attire and managers in dark business suits. *Longmont Museum*

J. Empson and Daughter

John H. Empson became one of Longmont's best known human landmarks thanks in no small part to his daughter Lida. Born in Cincinnati, Empson opened a confectionery there. When he developed tuberculosis, his seven-year-old daughter Lida persuaded him to go west to Colorado. Empson agreed: his wife had died shortly after Lida's birth and he hoped to live long enough to raise his daughter. Empson went to Estes Park, where the noted naturalist Enos Mills welcomed him to his Long's Peak Inn.

The outdoor life and Rocky Mountain air cured Empson. He and his daughter moved to Denver to open a confectionery. When the candy business soured, they headed for Longmont to open a cannery in 1886 under the name "J. Empson and Daughter Canning Company."

Lida and John thrived on canning fruit and vegetables. Not content to just outsell rivals, the Empsons pioneered innovations. Instead of traditional copper cooking kettles, they developed silver kettles for making jams and jellies. Colorado, "The Silver State," welcomed the new use for its main mineral resource. Empson's original kettle, made with 4,000 melted down silver dollars, is in Denver's Colorado History Museum.

During the 1890s, when many less solid agricultural enterprises withered with drought and the depression, J. Empson and Daughter expanded. They acquired or built canneries in Berthoud, Greeley and Ft. Lupton. They hired Luther Burbank, the California plant wizard, to develop a smaller, sweeter pea. Colorado's cool, snowy springs were ideal for growing snow sugar peas, which ripen and are harvested in spring. By 1905 the Empsons ran the world's largest pea cannery, with some 400 workers.

Empson also specialized in asparagus, green beans, red beets and, of course, Longmont's legendary pumpkins. These giant orange squash inspired Longmont to launch its annual harvest festival — Pumpkin Pie Day in 1899. Besides free pie, visitors feasted on coffee in souvenir tin mugs and ham sandwiches. The festival featured a parade, horse racing, tightrope walkers crossing Main Street and a "most beautiful baby" contest in Thompson Park.

The Empsons sponsored Pumpkin Pie Day floats and helped provide "pie in the sky" postcards, poetry, political addresses and samples served "by the prettiest girls in Longmont, which means the prettiest girls in Colorado." These local beauties passed out Empson canned pumpkin pie filling which became another of the firm's best sellers.

In 1920 Empson sold his Longmont plant to a group of local investors headed by local farmer Charles Lewis Hover. Hover and his associates ran the company until it merged with the Kuner Pickle Company in 1927. After selling out Empson and Lida, who had served as company vice president since she was 16, took a trip around the world together.

John H. Empson died in 1926. Lida, who lived in Longmont until her death in 1956, donated funding, art, and books to the Longmont Public Library. In gratitude, the library has made J. Empson and Daughter a centerpiece of its artful welcome arch in front of the 1993 library.

The Empson Cannery, at 15 3rd Avenue, has been restored and given substantial additions that mimic the original architecture. It now serves as the Cannery Apartments, one of Colorado's first and best recyclings of an abandoned agricultural plant.

◆ John and Lida Empson made J. Empson and Daughter a successful cannery, selling asparagus, green beans, beets, peas and pumpkins throughout the Rockies. As benefactors of the Longmont Public Library, the Empsons are commemorated in this artistic library welcome arch, completed in 1993 by sculptor George M. Greenameyer.
1998 photo by Tom Noel

◆ Longmont staged its first Pumpkin Pie Day in 1899 with a parade and display of all the things that could be made with pumpkins. The Sunshine Girls assembled a pumpkin coach and enlisted Cinderella to join the celebration. In 1971 the St. Vrain Historical Society revived the festival as a community fall antique show.
St. Vrain Historical Society

◆ The Empsons built this sunny Craftsman-style house in 1907 at 1228 3rd Avenue in Longmont's West Side Historic District.
1999 photo by Tom Noel

◆ Great Western Sugar Beet Company recruited some of the world's most able and industrious farmers — the Japanese — to transform the Longmont area into a sugar bowl. Here Mrs. Y. (Mui) Nishida prepares cold frames for early spring planting. *Longmont Museum*

Agricultural Industries

By 1900 Longmont boasted a population of 2,201. During the 20th century, this prairie hamlet grew into a hub city for agriculture. The Great Western Sugar Beet Company (GW) in 1904 acquired the Longmont Sugar Company refinery built in 1903 on the outskirts of Longmont. GW blanketed the countryside with signs: "Wanted: 500 Farmers to Raise Sugar Beets."

Among many respondents to GW's plea for workers were Japanese immigrants. Japanese families proved to be the perfect work force — productive, respectful and quick to learn. The only problem was that they saved their money, bought land and ultimately acquired their own businesses and farms. The Tanaka Family became one of Colorado's largest vegetable growers. The Nishidas became prominent truck farmers. The Kanemoto family, who arrived in 1910 with the immigration of Goroku Kanemoto from Hiroshima, donated a park and "The Tower of Compassion" to Longmont. The Japanese also recycled buildings for their own purposes. For instance, they bought the abandoned Burlington School and converted it to a Buddhist Temple.

With Japanese, Germans-from-Russia and Hispanic labor, the Great Western Sugar plant stayed open until the 1980s. Although the plant is now closed, it left a diverse population who grew, cultivated, harvested and processed the large beets. They continue to be productive groups in Longmont to this day.

High Tech Industry

Longmont has mushroomed from a town of 11,489 in 1960 to a city of some 63,000. Establishment of the huge Hewlett Packard plant in 1960 triggered a high tech industry boom reminiscent of the original agricultural boom.

In 1962 Longmont became the home of the Federal Aviation Agency's Denver Air Traffic Control Center. The $12 million, 10-acre center was built as part of the FAA's campaign to decentralize strategic sites that might be targeted by enemy missiles. Controllers there supervise the Rocky Mountain region, helping to guide some 2,000 planes a day in and out of airports with the help of radar.

◆ The Great Western Sugar Beet Company acquired this Longmont refinery in 1904, the year after it was built by Longmont investors. GW soon became the town's single largest employer, and persuaded many farmers to switch from wheat to the big, sweet beets. *St. Vrain Historical Society*

The Great Western Sugar Beet Company built this hotel in 1919 at the southeast corner of 3rd and Kimbark to house 100 men in 50 dorms. During World War II it housed 180 German and Italian prisoners of war who worked the sugar beet fields. The hotel is now transitional housing, the Inn Between.
Longmont Museum

Agriculture remains part of Longmont's economy although many fields have disappeared in a sea of new residential subdivisions, strip malls and office parks.
1994 photo by Jim Havey

◆ A weigh station survives by the now-abandoned Great Western Sugar Beet mill and elevators, which have dominated Longmont's skyline since 1903.
1999 photo by Tom Noel

The rapid population growth and the shift in economic base that began in the 1960s brought incredible change to our town. We felt it was vital for Longmonters — both long-time residents and newcomers — to understand and appreciate our roots. This historical perspective will reinforce modern Longmont's sense of community. Preserving our historic landmarks is a major focus for us, a way to assure a future for our proud and colorful past.

The huge 1965 IBM plant along the Boulder-Longmont diagonal, Longmont's Mini-Scribe computer company and other high tech firms triggered growth that is ongoing. During the 1990s Longmont emerged as the disc-drive capital of the world with firms such as Maxtor and Seagate building Longmont area plants.

Longmont, with its small town charms, also boomed as a bedroom community for Boulder, Denver and other employment centers. To welcome newcomers, Mrs. Millie Seawalk established the Hi Club in the 1960s. Besides her cheery newsletters, Millie greeted new arrivals with gifts and information about Longmont's community resources, including its fine library and excellent municipal museum. Millie strove to have coffee with every "Mrs. Newcomer," theorizing that "she who sups with me cannot be my enemy. I want her to like me, for if she does, she is well on her way to liking her new town."

One of the things newcomers like most about Longmont is its strong sense of place. To preserve that historical perspective, the St. Vrain Historical Society and other groups have worked to ensure that Longmont's rich heritage is celebrated to promote a greater sense of community. Dale Bernard, executive director of the St. Vrain Historical Society since 1985, explained:

With almost 100 locally designated landmarks, Longmont has emerged as a state-wide pacesetter in historic preservation. Successes range from the Cannery Apartments to recycling of the Presbyterian College for affordable housing. The elegant 1930s Longmont Post Office has been reborn as a child care center.

The Fox Theater, a classic 1930s Main Street movie house, has been recycled as a performing arts center. Dick Klein bought the struggling theater in the 1950s. He ran films for mostly empty houses. Longmont preservationist Harriette Grigsby remembers calling Klein up and asking what time the movie started.

"Madame," he told her, "what time would you like it to start?" Such poor attendance led Klein to sell the movie house to the Longmont Theater Company, which since the 1950s had been staging performances

◆ Central School occupies the block between 4th and 5th avenues and Bross and Gay streets, a site initially reserved for a university. The original wing, built in 1878 at a cost of $2,725, still stands with 1881 and 1908 additions to this still active school.
1999 photo by Tom Noel

◆ Vertical lines and the geometical ornament of the Art Deco style distinguish the Fox Theater on Main Street, which has been reborn as a performing arts center.
1999 photo by Tom Noel

as the Potpourri Players. With a new art deco sign and marquis, the rejuvenated theater is now a handsome Main Street attraction.

Besides many in-town preservation projects, Longmont purchased the Sandstone Ranch in 1998 to convert it to open space. The old city dump at the confluence of Boulder and St. Vrain creeks is being rehabilitated as part of a hike-bike trail and park system.

Longmont also boasts one of Colorado's finest municipal museums. Begun in 1940 as a private organization, the baby museum started out in the carriage house of the city-owned Callahan House at 312 Terry Street. As the carriage house soon became cramped, the growing collection was moved to the basement of the Memorial Building in Roosevelt Park in 1954.

In 1970 the museum became an official municipal department and moved into a former city garage at 375 Kimbark Street. With the aid of many volunteers, the museum prides itself upon cataloging, cleaning and preserving every artifact that comes in — within a month! To help house its 26,000-item collection, the museum has restored the old Longmont Power Plant as storage.

"Our museum," reported Director Kent Brown in 1999, "collects and exhibits not only history, but art and science. We also welcome a lot of traveling exhibits — so that Longmonters always have a new reason to visit us, especially after we move into the Golden West Flour Mill. This will be especially true in the millennium when we move into much larger quarters."

Longmont's efforts to preserve the best of its past amid a flood of new development has been epitomized by the struggle to save the town's grand old estate, Hoverhome at 1309 Hover Road. Thanks to the St. Vrain Historical Society and a history-conscious city, the home and part of the surrounding gardens and farm survive amid a sea of new houses. This Jacobethan

◆ "The St. Vrain has swallowed the Chicago River," proclaimed the *Longmont Call* on December 25, 1908. Longmont's 17-man high school squad of "Beet Diggers" had just pounded Chicago's Englewood High 30-0 to capture the National Football Championship, a coup celebrated in this *Call* cartoon.
Longmont Museum

◆ Longmont's Golden West Mill at 123 Terry Street, which closed in 1979, awaits creative reuse. One possibility — lofts — have drawn inspiration from the successful conversion of the Longmont Farmers' Mill in Denver, which preservationist-developer Dana Crawford reopened in 1999 as the Flour Mill Lofts. *1998 photo by Tom Noel*

Revival mansion, one of the finest historic homes in Boulder County, was built by Charles Lewis Hover. Hover and his brother William operated a large and profitable wholesale drug company in Denver.

Charles retired early to look for a pleasant small town where he could become a gentleman farmer. That search led him and his wife Katherine to Longmont. To design their dream home, they selected Robert Roeschlaub, Colorado's first licensed architect. Roeschlaub had designed the now landmarked and restored Hover Company offices at 14th and Lawrence in Denver. Roeschlaub and his nephew, Frank, produced an exquisite country estate with fine Craftsman style detailing.

Upon its opening in 1914, this country villa on 161-acre grounds was the marvel of the county. Built of rusticated red brick with creamy terra cotta trim, it sports steep rustic gables, a port cochere, garage and English border gardens. The interior shimmers with built-in golden oak shelves, pantries and woodwork;

◆ (Right and opposite page bottom) Dale Bernard, executive director of the St. Vrain Historical Society, helped save Hoverhome, one of Longmont's finest country estates. Constructed in 1913-1914, this red brick Jacobethan mansion is a rambling, multi-gabled country estate now available for special events. *1914 & 1926 photos from Colorado Historical Society; 1999 photo by Tom Noel*

burlap wall covering, art nouveau stained glass windows and lighting, and the latest in appliances. Katherine Hover's trademark yellow Harrison roses blossom in the stained glass, in the carved wood and, of course, throughout the grounds.

The Hover's adopted daughter, Beatrice, lived in the house until 1982. Reluctant to leave the grounds, she moved to Hover Manor, the first phase of a retirement community that her mother had always dreamed would be built on Hover Farm. There she spent her final years helping to preserve both the old family home and build new facilities, such as the Beatrice Hover Personal Care Unit for seniors. She conveyed the home to the Hover Community, Inc. for preservation as a cultural center for the retirement community and the town. In 1997 the St. Vrain Historical Society bought Hoverhome to preserve it for community use and as a reminder of Longmont's agricultural roots, as Beatrice had always wished.

◆ Pioneer turkey farms have evolved into big business. Longmont Foods, founded in 1951, has become Colorado's largest turkey dealer. Besides Thanksgiving dinners, the company processes turkey for hot dogs, ground meat, luncheon meats and sausage. Many health-conscious Coloradans have substituted turkey products for beef. In 1987 Omaha's huge Con-Agra Conglomerate bought out the company, but still sells its products world-wide under the Longmont Foods name.
1939 photo by Arthur Rothstein, Library of Congress

1999 photo by Tom Noel

1998 photo by Tom No

Louisville Historical Museum

Louisville Historical Museum

Louisville Historical Museum & contemporary photos by Tom Noel

1999 photo by Tom Noel

Louisville, Lafayette & the Coal Towns

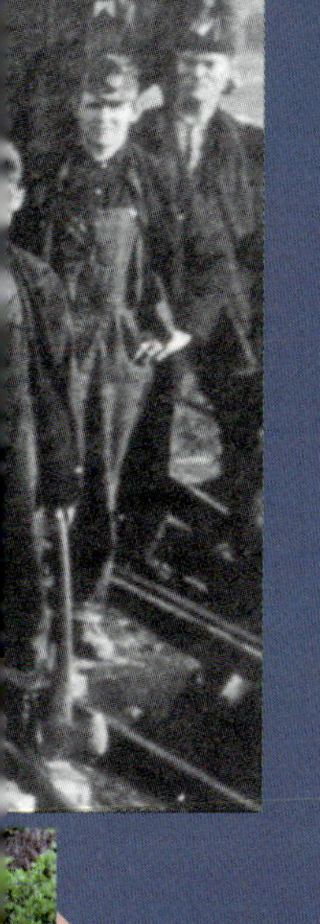

Chapter *Six*

Boulder County's once dominant coal industry is now almost as hard to find as the memorial to one of its fallen heroes — Joe Jaramillo. He disappeared in Boulder County's worst mining accident. On January 20, 1936, at 6 a.m., the Monarch Mine (a few miles southwest of Louisville) exploded in a storm of coal dust.

Joe Jaramillo had returned to the mine to check on the comrades he left behind. Rescue crews dragged seven other bodies out of the mine, but could not find Jaramillo. If the accident had come 20 minutes later, after the morning shift started, the tunnels would have been full of men and fatalities probably would have been much higher.

Only a few old-timers, like Louis Varra, remember Joe Jaramillo. "I went to work one morning and the mine exploded," Varra recalled in Maria Rogers' book, *In Other Words* (Golden: Fulcrum, 1995). "There were eight that got killed down there. Joe Jaramillo, the mule driver. He's still down there, buried alive. He was bringing the mules out that morning when they had the explosion." Varra claims that mine owners treated the mules better than the miners. Mules knew when it was quitting time. And when it was lunch time. If they usually pulled only one ore car and somebody put on two, they'd go on strike.

◆ Black-rimmed prairie dog holes alerted miners to Boulder County's rich coal veins lying just under the surface. The furry pioneers first excavated the soft coal, although they and their homes became blacker and grittier. The same fate awaited miners who followed them into the earth. *Photo by J.W. Jackson, Denver Museum of Natural History*

The Rocky Mountain Fuel Company, which operated the Monarch Mine, erected a memorial to Joe Jaramillo beside the Denver-Boulder Turnpike (U.S. Highway 36). Joe's marker, however, was moved in 1998 to make room for Broomfield's new FlatIron Crossing regional shopping mall. Mall developers promise to install a shrine to Joe in Boulder County's newest shopping paradise, a far different world from the dusty coal mines Joe knew. All those mines are gone now, buried under residential subdivisions and shopping malls.

The Monarch Mine explosion was the deadliest of many fatal accidents in Colorado's Northern Coal Fields. This "black gold" replaced gold, silver and tungsten to become Boulder County's mainstay by the 1920s. Seven county communities owe their existence to the hard work of miners such as Joe Jaramillo. Coal miners remain the county's unsung heros: in life they were often snubbed by uppity Boulder and Longmont merchants and white-collar folk. In death they often received little more respect than has Joe Jaramillo. Descendants of the miners remain prominent in these former coal towns, where they have fought to preserve and celebrate their mining heritage.

◆ Joe Jaramillo's monument is one of the few remnants of Boulder County's coal mining era. Most of the mining buildings, tipples and the miners themselves are gone. This memorial to one of eight miners killed in the 1936 Monarch Mine explosion was moved in 1998 to accommodate developers of the FlatIron Crossing regional shopping mall. In 1998 Joe was re-obliterated by construction of what boosters say will be Colorado's largest shopping center, the FlatIron Crossing regional shopping mall, which promised to find a new home for Joe's marker. *1999 photo by Tom Noel*

Long before these towns emerged, Native Americans first used Boulder County coal as fuel, although they did not mine it. Anglo-Americans, as Marshall historian Joanna Sampson wrote, went to a great deal more trouble: "A miner lies on his side to undercut the coal seam with his pick, often working in water. He would then drill holes into the face of the coal with a hand auger and into these holes he tamped cartridges filled with black powder to blast the coal down. Undercutting the face was necessary because a solid face of coal weakened the mine roof and produced smaller, less valuable lumps."

Miners dug underground chambers and braced them with timbers, which often rotted because of the moisture. Twin entries were built every 25 to 35 feet, creating a maze of tunnels. Coal and waste rock were excavated using mules, creatures that spent their lives underground and caught only brief glimpses of daylight.

Generally speaking, the deeper the tunnel, the better quality the coal. Tunnels still underlie Marshall, Louisville, Lafayette and Superior. Mining companies made little effort to clean out or secure the tunnels. Subsequently they collapsed, creating subsidence problems, especially in Louisville. Underground fires, as well as subsidence, are persistent problems as coal dust induces spontaneous combustion and fires which smolder to this day.

Mining proved to be dangerous work, cursed by accidents and fatalities. When Boulder's Green Mountain Cemetery opened in 1904, the first grave was filled by Archie Chalmers, a Scottish immigrant killed by a runaway mine car. Mine strikes also led to fatalities. Five miners shot by the Colorado National Guard for a pro-union demonstration during the 1927 Columbine Mine Strike were dumped into unmarked graves in the Lafayette Cemetery.

Unlike gold and silver miners, coal miners rarely dreamed of getting rich. They struggled to eke out a living in miserable circumstances, often owing their soul to the company store. Exacerbating the already unsteady finances of workers, many mines closed during the summer when demand for heating coal was low, and workers were laid off. All five former coal towns have shaken off the coal dust and are now primarily white collar residential communities. Computers now generate far more county jobs than coal.

The many dangers did not stop coal mining from becoming Boulder County's most lucrative industry in the early 1900s. The "black gold" boom began in the 1870s, when railroad development made coal mining profitable and spurred the prosperity of commercial hubs such as Boulder and Longmont. "To coal and the Boulder Valley Railroad, the town of Boulder owes no inconsiderable part of its prosperity," proclaimed the *Boulder News-Courier* on January 8, 1875. Indeed, the towns of Marshall, Canfield, Louisville, Lafayette and Superior owed also their existence to coal.

Marshall

Joseph W. Marshall purchased a surface coal mine five miles south of Boulder City in 1864. He opened this coal bank to customers who came to load and haul away their own coal. On his land, where coal had first been found in 1859, Marshall also mined iron deposits. To make iron from his coal and iron, Marshall built a blast furnace, which he called Belmont. There he produced the iron for the first cannon cast in Colorado Territory.

Marshall did not wait for railroads to come to his coal town, but ordered his own steam engine from England and built a line into Golden. Extending his empire into Denver, he formed a partnership with Augustine Langford, who operated a pioneer iron

◆ The Monarch Mine, where some of their fathers died, took miners' children to school in this black metal contraption, a distant ancestor of the bright yellow school buses serving Louisville's new Monarch High School. The school's name commemorates the mine that used to be the fate of many Louisville children. *Louisville Historical Museum*

◆ Marshall, founded in 1859 on Coal Creek by Joseph W. Marshall, emerged as Boulder County's first coal mining town. The rail connection shown here made Marshall's "black gold" payoff. *Carnegie Branch Library for Local History, Boulder Historical Society Collection*

◆ (Right and opposite page photos) The tiny town of Canfield near the Weld County Line was once a coal and farming hub. The four-story Wise Elevator, shown here in its 1886 heyday, has become a ruin (opposite page, bottom photo) along Jasper Road. Canfield also thrived as a mining town with large and lucrative mines such as the Boulder Valley, whose crew posed for this 1920s portrait. *Historic photos from Sarah Wise; 1998 mill photo by Tom Noel*

foundry on Larimer Street. Langford's key role was commemorated by the adjacent town of Langford, which merged with Marshall in 1892.

Boulder County's pioneer coal town experienced one of the first major coal mining strikes in 1880. Langford, as general manager of the mining company, ordered the strikers out of the company-owned town. "Miners may quit if they don't like the wages," Langford declared, "but when they undertake to say that no one else shall work, they go a step too far." Setting a precedent for future labor conflicts, Langford quickly replaced striking miners with scabs.

With not only the Marshall but the Black Diamond and Gorham mines as major producers, Marshall became a town of around 500 by the 1880s. During the flush times, Marshall contained several hundred homes, a post office, rail depot, school and a half dozen saloons. One youngster, town historian Joanna Sampson, found that Marshall's watering holes were far more entertaining than the school: "There were lots of bars. On weekends the kids used to roam up and down the valley watching the fights. You'd hear 'fight, fight at Binello's [Saloon]' and the kids would all run up there to watch." Marshall never had a church, but did not lack spirits. Even after Prohibition came in 1916, several whiskey stills turned out a particularly potent local beverage known as "White Mule."

This foothills community reached a peak census year population of 813 in 1910 and then began dwindling. Marshall's coal mines survived the labor wars and even the economic downturn spurred by the 1929 stock market crash. The end did not come until the 1946 bankruptcy of Marshall's last mining company, the Rocky Mountain Fuel Company. The town's population migrated to livelier communities. The current hamlet is haunted by persistent underground coal fires which sometimes reach the surface. In 1974, for example, flames shot up three to four feet above ground at the Peerless Mine.

Today Marshall has disappeared from most maps, but a few pioneer buildings survive, most notably the three-room schoolhouse in a meadow north of town. This frame landmark has been restored as a private residence near the intersection of Colorado 170 and Cherryvale Road. Marshall Mesa has been acquired as Boulder City Open Space where observant hikers will find traces of this once rambunctious town.

Canfield

Prime farm land and asthma brought the Oliver E. Wise family from Wisconsin by covered wagon in 1868. Their eastern Boulder County homestead became hot property after they noticed prairie dogs excavating black dirt — a sure sign of coal. Isaac Canfield and his brothers discovered a six-foot-thick coal bed and joined with the Wises in 1878 to establish Canfield. Wise served as Canfield's postmaster. His son, William O., also held that job as well as editing the *Erie-Canfield Independent*, and later served as a state representative.

Coal, not crops, put Canfield on the map. By 1880 it boasted 53 residents and 20 buildings huddled around Isaac Canfield's Rob Roy Mine and the Wise

family's Star Mine. Besides the coal mine, the Wises operated a large hay and corn fodder mill, a giant grain storage elevator, a blacksmith shop and the Canfield General Store. Thanks to a balanced combination of coal and agriculture, Canfield grew into a town of approximately 500 that remained unusually stable for the boom and bust state of Colorado.

In recent decades, however, much of Canfield has been annexed by fast-growing Erie, a larger coal mining town two miles east in Weld County. By the 1990s, Erie had become a bedroom community for Boulder County. Erie also began commercial development along Interstate-25. In 1999 Erie began paving its streets and announced plans to become a city of some 50,000 in the new millennium.

Canfield, meanwhile, has become a ghost town. One of the few remaining residents is Sarah Wise, the great-granddaughter of Oliver, who returned to the old family farm after a teaching career. Dr. Wise tends the family farm and looks after a few decaying landmarks. "I don't know why I work so hard to keep up this place and to preserve what's left of Canfield," she said in 1998 with a sigh. "I guess because no one else will do it. And there are so many newcomers — and their kids — who don't know anything about our past. See those big old cottonwoods along the road? Believe it or not I planted those back in the 1920s when I was a little girl. Most of the other old timers are gone. So are the railroad depot, the mines, even the Canfield baseball diamond. So I'm donating the 1872 Wise Family Homestead as a museum which I'll help preserve and maintain for the next millennium. Canfield should not be forgotten."

◆ Dr. Sarah Wise, a professor of education, retired to Canfield to run the family farm at 11497 Jasper Road. Sarah, shown here with her trusty tractor, reports that she and many other women have run farms by themselves.
1998 photo by Tom Noel

◆ The Wise Homestead in eastern Boulder County is a relic of the once humming coal mining and agricultural town of Canfield. Sarah Wise, who lives in the house built by her great grandfather, has become the town's champion for historical preservation. She is preserving the Wise homestead, including its mill and blacksmith shop, because "so many newcomers — and their kids — don't know anything about Canfield's past." She is donating the white clapboard family homestead house for use as a museum in this hamlet built by her ancestors.
1998 photo by Tom Noel

Louisville

Like Marshall, Louisville was born as a coal mining town. After railroads made coal mining profitable, prominent Golden capitalist Charles Clark Welch hired a Polish prospector, Louis Nawatny, to search for coal in eastern Boulder County. In August, 1877, Louis found coal 200 feet below David Kerr's farm — which Welch quickly bought. Nawatny, who proved to be an entrepreneur as well as a prospector, purchased land nearby. On October 24, 1878, he platted a town and named it for himself. Then Louis became a real estate agent, greeting newcomers and selling them lots in his newly formed Louisville.

The *Boulder News and Courier*, on September 26, 1879, described Louisville as having "about 200 inhabitants [with] churches and a school." By 1890, the population reached 966 and included ethnic enclaves such as "Kimbertown" for the Cornwellians, "Frenchtown" and "Little Italy." These new immigrants, as well as their English and Irish predecessors, rarely got together except during brawls on saloon-lined Front Street. Ethnic hostilities were exacerbated by the mine owners' practice of bringing in new, different worker groups less likely to form union bonds with veteran miners. English-speaking, western Europeans tended to get the best jobs in an ethnic hierarchy based on language, ethnicity and skin color. Whenever one group became disgruntled and union prone, however, an antithetical group was recruited. To replace WASP workers, for instance, Italian laborers were often initially recruited as strike-breakers — until they too began to seek union solidarity.

Saloons proliferated as fast as immigrant newcomers. Some 13 saloons ruled Front Street by 1900. The Old Louisville Inn at Front and Spruce streets displays one of the oldest and most splendiferous back bars in Colorado, a mahogany altar resplendent with its mirror and fancy bottles. After Louisville's saloons finally closed in the early morning, tipplers could sleep it off at the Commercial Hotel, which opened at 328 Pine Street in May, 1881. Its back rooms rented for 50 cents, while fancier front rooms rented for $1 per night.

◆ In this earliest known portrait of Louisville, Spruce Street in 1881 boasted the two general stores. Note the schoolhouse bell tower in the distance.
Louisville Historical Museum

◆ (Far left)
Louis and Kathinka Nawatny, both Polish immigrants, founded the town named for him. She served as the first postmistress.
Louisville Historical Museum

◆ (Left and below)
The Louisville Beer Hall (bottom left), shown here in 1909 at 720 Front Street, competed with a dozen other taverns that made Louisville Boulder County's wettest community. The Old Louisville Inn (left and below) at 740 Front Street contains a magnificent neoclassical backbar. This altar of king alcohol stands 12 feet tall and 25 feet long in shimmering cherry, mahogany and glass.
Louisville Historical Museum & contemporary photos by Tom Noel

Louisville immigrants boasted of their bars and their brawls. The story of the 63 round "prize fight" of February 1882 still circulates in surviving saloons such as the Pine Street Junction and Old Louisville Inn. Irish miner Charley McGaugh had it in for Canadian George Elliott. The mines had closed that winter and miners had little to do other than egg on the two enemies. One day, Elliott struck back while cornered, knocking McGaugh down. Claiming he was the better man, McGaugh demanded more. To the dismay of his Irish friends, McGaugh went down 63 times before they finally carried him away. Elliott suffered only a few scratches.

Celeste Romano is wearing a tie and vest in the rear center of this beer-clutching fraternity. His legendary and long-lived Louisville beer and pool hall at 809 Main Street still hides behind a frame false front on a tiny hipped roof house. Celeste turned his shanty into a long, skinny saloon. The American flag draped over the back bar asserts the Americanism of these Italian immigrants.
Louisville Historical Museum

Perhaps both men went to confession after this hard lesson. They would not have had trouble finding a church, because Louisville, unlike Marshall, boasted several. Catholics built Saint Louis as Louisville's first church in 1884. Father Cyril Rettger helped his parishioners unionize and was repaid with a bullet. The near miss left a bullet hole in the stained glass window nearest the altar.

The Methodists purchased two lots for $2 from C. C. Welch to build their fine church at Jefferson Avenue and Spruce Street. This 1892 edifice had a rose window that was covered because of the sun's glare in the minister's eyes. During the 1920s the minister also may have protected his eyes with a Ku Klux Klan hood. Kluxers visited his church on Sundays, tossing dollar bills to adults and candy to children. At St. Louis Church, the Klan made a different kind of donation — their fiery crosses.

◆ Louisville's many groggeries inspired dry reformers to open this temperance hall where women and children, as well as men, were welcome. This 1904 photograph was taken three years before Boulder County banned the sale of alcohol. During the dry spell, many saloons became "soft drink" parlors but usually had some bootleg spirits on hand for trusted regulars.
Louisville Historical Museum

Louisville's first school, according to town historian Carolyn Conarroe, consisted of classes in Wesley Jacobs' stone milkhouse. Two years before Nawatny's 1877 coal discovery, the milkhouse was replaced by the first school in the Coal Creek Valley. Although the first

◆ Churches consoled immigrants hungry for old country ways. Father Benedict Ingenito, O.S.B., kept a stern eye on this First Communion class, posing in front of the $40,000 brick church he built in 1942 to replace the 1884 original. In 1905 the parish opened the "St. Louis School and Business College." Despite the proud name, the "college" could afford only one textbook, the *Baltimore Catechism,* which the Benedictine nuns also used as a reader and a speller.
Louisville Historical Museum

◆ Louisville immigrants proved their Americanism by fighting in World War I and by organizing this November 13, 1918, Armistice Day Parade float to proclaim "Kaiser Bill Gone to Hell But Not Forgotten."
Louisville Historical Museum

◆ While other residents had their own homes, many Louisville miners lived in company housing such as these provided by the Hecla Mining Company. The Hecla became the focal point of the 1910-1914 strike pitting the United Mine Workers of America against the Northern Coal and Coke Company. Striking miners and their families were hastily evicted from these homes and replaced by scabs.
Louisville Historical Museum

teacher, Miss McCarty, resigned after teaching half a day, her successors taught all grades in the one-room schoolhouse by the railroad tracks at Short and Front streets. Louisville built a roomier school at Spruce and Main streets and a third one at Spruce and Jefferson. Memory Park, dedicated in 1974, marks the site of the third schoolhouse, which was demolished in 1962 and replaced by several fine new edifices. Louisville's immigrant miners repeatedly contributed to building new schools so their children might graduate into better jobs than the dank, dangerous, subterranean world.

Some miners put their meager savings in the Louisville bank, which closed in 1915, when a receiver foreclosed on the bank. The miners lost all their savings. Prompt action by local citizens created Louisville's First State Bank one month later, before unwanted "Boulder bankers can step in." Louisvillians had little liking for Boulder, whose merchants sometimes refused to wait on coal miners.

Louisville's newspapers proved more stable than its banks. Although the first gazette, *The Louisville Miner*, failed within a year of its 1887 birth, *The Louisville Times* has been published since 1913.

Louisville's coal mining heritage still haunts the town. Tunnels of the Acme Mine, which extracted two million tons of coal from beneath the community, have caused serious subsidence problems. The town sued the Louisville Mining Company in 1895, 1912 and 1914 for causing streets to sink, but received little, if any, compensation. In 1923 Josephine Roche's Rocky Mountain Fuel Company negotiated a land trade to settle Louisville's subsidence claim. Subterranean mines have also been a blessing since that agricultural land that was too dangerous to develop has been left as open space.

To preserve the town's rich — if sooty — history, the Louisville Historical Commission formally incorporated in 1983, drawing on enthusiastic volunteers who had staged Louisville's centennial celebration in 1978. The commission restored the 1903 Tego Drug Store and converted it to the Louisville Historical Society Museum at 1001 Main Street. The pharmacy/museum sports a gloriously restored "Coca-Cola" sign on the south side. Next door to the north, a small

◆ Louisville miners pose with their carbide head lamps, lunch pails and the mine mule. The lunch pail typically contained hot soup or coffee which kept the meat pie warm in the upper compartment.
Louisville Historical Museum

◆ Mules had been replaced by trucks in this 1940s view of the large Hi-Way Mine on U.S. 287 southeast of Louisville. It was among the largest of 33 Louisville-Lafayette area mines operating between 1877, when the Welch Mine opened, and 1954, when the Hi-Way Mine closed.
Louisville Historical Museum

◆ To honor coal miners, Louisvillians erected this statue in front of City Hall during Colorado's 1976 Centennial-Bicentennial celebration.
Photo by Tom Noel

miner's cottage has been furnished with artifacts reflecting a typical mining family household. The city and the historical commission also collaborated to install the bronze statue of a miner, with his lunch pail and shovel, in front of City Hall. Beginning with the 1970 opening of the huge Storage Technology Company, Louisville has flourished as a white collar city of more than 20,000. Thanks to the work of the Louisville Historical Commission, newcomers and oldtimers, including many high tech workers, enjoy landmarks, museum and public monuments celebrating Louisville's sooty underground roots.

Lafayette

In Lafayette, farming preceded coal mining as the first industry. George Pierce and Stephen Goodall received land patents near the present community of Lafayette in 1864. William St. John's 1868 patent became the site of the town, soon acquired by Boulder County pioneer Lafayette Miller and his wife, Mary. Lafayette Miller, named for the French Marquis de Lafayette, who fought with the American revolutionists, became the namesake of a town where French and other immigrants were welcome.

After Lafayette's death in 1878, his widow, Mary, hired John Simpson of Louisville to look for coal on her 1,280-acre holdings. In 1888, he developed the Simpson coal mine, the first of many in the Lafayette area. To supply the emerging coal hub, Mary platted a town, naming it for her late husband.

"My grandparents [were] Lafayette Miller and Mary

◆ The Lafayette Public Library wears a large mural celebrating the town's history. Townfounder Mary Miller and her husband Lafayette pose with a mine tipple, miners and a mine dog. *1998 photo by Tom Noel*

Miller," Ralph Miller recalls in Maria Roger's book, *In Other Words* (Fulcrum, 1995). "My grandfather filed a homestead which runs from Baseline Road to the Louisville Road... Then there wasn't a tree in this part of the county... They lived right up there by the mine... There were a lot of tent houses in Lafayette. The tents were wood about three feet up with a canvas top and a dirt floor. Grandma said it was very uncomfortable... living in a rag house."

Mary Miller, a religious woman and staunch prohibitionist, ran on the statewide prohibition ticket for state treasure. Townsfolk dubbed her "Queen Mary" for her pretentious ways — she even had indoor plumbing. "Queen Mary" strove to make Lafayette a model town. She placed covenants on all town lots precluding the sale of liquor, a dry condition that continued until 1980. She also aided Congregationalists in building Lafayette's first church at 300 East Simpson Street in 1892. The church doubled as the town's hospital during the 1918 influenza epidemic and as the town library for much of the 20th century. Mary also encouraged the Methodists, whose first meetings were 1894 revivals conducted by husband and wife preachers Kent and Alma White. Alma White later moved to Denver to found the large and popular evangelical Pillar of Fire Church. The Baptists organized in 1907, holding services in a railroad car chapel before constructing the church at 200 West Cleveland Street in 1912.

Hoping for a model, saloon-less town of churches, schools, libraries and fine homes, Mary Miller platted large house lots 50 by 140 feet in 300-square-foot blocks with 60-foot streets and 20-foot alleys. Her ideas were implemented by her son, Thomas, the town's first mayor, who oversaw incorporation in 1889 of a town of about 400 people.

Mary nurtured her town through its formative years, establishing a two-room school in 1889. She also ran the Lafayette Bank, at 400 East Simpson Street, supposedly as the only female bank president in the world. Mary, who died in 1921, lived most of her years in the still-standing house at 409 East Cleveland

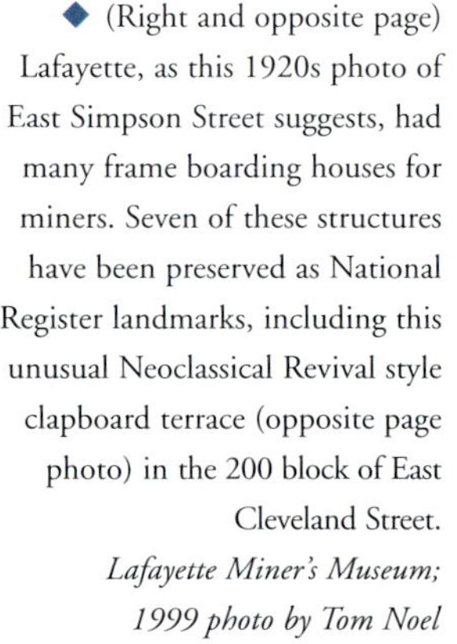

◆ (Right and opposite page) Lafayette, as this 1920s photo of East Simpson Street suggests, had many frame boarding houses for miners. Seven of these structures have been preserved as National Register landmarks, including this unusual Neoclassical Revival style clapboard terrace (opposite page photo) in the 200 block of East Cleveland Street. *Lafayette Miner's Museum; 1999 photo by Tom Noel*

◆ (Far right)
Lafayette Knights of Pythias Hall, like its brother lodges all across America, staged skits explaining the Greek tale of Damon and Pythias. Pythias, condemned to death for plotting against the king, begged to leave to arrange his affairs. His friend, Damon, pledged to give his own life if Pythias did not return. This scene shows Pythias returning just in time to take his own place at the execution. King Dionysus was so impressed by their loyal friendship that he released both lads.
Lafayette Miner's Museum

◆ (Top left)
Lafayette's Brass Band led town celebrations including the most important one for coal miners — the Labor Day Parade.
Lafayette Miner's Museum

◆ (Bottom right)
Adeline Beckett Davis, who took this photo in 1916, recalled that Lafayette "was small enough that all the residents could hear the bell on top of City Hall. During summer months the bell was rung to tell residents when they could turn on water for irrigation, and rung again when the water had to be turned off."
Lafayette Miner's Museum

◆ (Bottom left)
Neither sleet nor storm nor snow kept Sam Carlisle from picking up mail at the railroad depot six days a week and carrying it to the Lafayette Post Office.
Lafayette Miner's Museum

Street. Her son, Thomas, lived nearby at 501 until his accidental decapitation in the Strathmore Mine.

Lafayette lacks the intact historic main street that has become the pride of Boulder, Longmont, Louisville and Niwot. A fire on January 24, 1900, destroyed most of the bustling business district on East Simpson, the original main street. Buildings such as the two-story Rocky Mountain Fuel Company store (now Boulder County Social Services) were rebuilt. After the Post Office moved to Public Road (U. S. 287) in 1970, that street became Lafayette's new "Main" Street. The new business district lacks the colorful signs of old main street. Dentist J. B. Hurt, "The Painless Dentist," Chevrolet dealer C. L. "They All Come to Grief" Grief, and Erna Dollar's "Earn a Dollar" Red and White Store gained tiny Lafayette recognition in Ripley's "Believe It or Not."

Like Louisville, Lafayette was infested with the Ku Klux Klan in the early 1920s. Both towns included many Catholic immigrants, whom the Klan harassed. After *Lafayette Leader* publisher Emil Sands editorialized against the Klan, they kidnapped him. He was "indoctrinated" on a hill near the Blue Ribbon Mine east of town, an experience that terrified but did not silence him. The Klan also pursued bootleggers, including Deputy Sheriff Raymond Bailey. He was arrested during Prohibition in 1925 for operating an illegal 250-gallon still near Lafayette and possessing over 4,000 gallons of mash. Sheriff Blum stated, "This raid undoubtedly will eliminate one of the largest channels of liquor distribution in the district." No charges were brought against Bailey, who switched from mash to mining. Along with Joe Jaramillo, he lost his life in the Monarch Mine explosion in 1936.

After the 1950s demise of mining, Lafayette became a sleepy town unawakened until Boulder County's explosive growth in the 1970s. The 1980 town of 5,593 has mushroomed into a city of some 20,000.

To provide historical perspective and a sense of place for thousands of new residents, the Lafayette Historical Society formed in 1975. The William Lewis frame miners cottage from the Gladstone Mine was moved to 108 East Simpson Street and restored as Lafayette Miner's Museum in 1976. Lewis' widow, Hannah, had occupied the six-room frame cottage until her death in 1975. The Lafayette Historical Society converted it into a splendid local mining museum. The museum has a good collection of mining artifacts and also offers books and literature, including a lavishly illustrated 382-page history of Lafayette.

Superior

An 1864 flood along Coal Creek exposed a coal bank, giving birth to a coal camp located 10 miles southeast of Boulder. William C. Hake turned the coal seam on his farm into the Industrial Mining Company. Hake platted the town in 1895, naming it for his former residence in Wisconsin. Even before Superior earned a post office in 1896, it became a stop on the Denver, Marshall & Boulder Railroad and The Denver & Interurban. Superior organized one of Boulder County's first school districts in 1863. These districts were often the first effort at organizing a community, by taxing a population for a community goal. School District boundaries often became town boundaries.

Hake became the mayor of Superior and his large frame house and even larger miners' boarding house

◆ (Left and below)
Jim and Beth Hutchison have spearheaded the operation of the Lafayette Miner's Museum. James is a Lafayette native and a CU-trained engineer who worked 30 years for the Colorado Department of Transportation. He then operated the Lafayette Conoco Station. "I've appreciated education and museums ever since the day I got frustrated with school and told my parents I was quitting. The next morning my father woke me at 4:30 a.m. and handed me a shovel and a lunch bucket. He took me to work with him in the Monarch Mine. That was the hardest day of my life. Next day I went back to school — and I stayed in school as long as I could. Here, in our museum, we show kids that a miner's life was no picnic."
1999 photos by Tom Noel

◆ (Far left)
Jessie Irwin and Arlene Schofield loved their jobs as the pioneer operators for the Lafayette Telephone Exchange. This strategic listening post allowed them to be the first to hear local news and gossip.
Lafayette Miner's Museum

◆ (Photos this page and opposite page bottom) Superior was christened by town-founders from Superior, Wisconsin. Although surrounded by huge coal mines .such as the Industrial, shown here in its flush times before closing in 1945, downtown Superior amounted to little more than this mercantile company. With the 1990s development of the Rock Creek residential subdivisions, this once inferior burg has become Colorado's fastest-growing community. *Louisville Historical Museum*

old-timers. Richmond would provide the town all the water it needed. All Superior had to do was to annex a little land over the hill and let Richmond put up some new homes to raise the town's tax base.

Thus began the enormous Rock Creek housing subdivision of some 5,000 houses. This sea of new development has transformed sleepy Superior into the fastest-growing community in Colorado.

Daniel Kupfner, a sixth generation Superiorite, shook his head in disbelief during a 1999 interview. "Rock Creek developers promised us free water if we'd annex the old ranch and let 'em develop it. They said they'd keep the old town the way it was and development would be hidden over the hill. But look at all these homes, and the traffic and dust and noise. We've even had to appoint a town marshall — a post that had been empty since my granddad and dad were marshals in the old days."

dominated the little town. After the Industrial Mine closed, the town did not merit its own phone book listing but was treated as part of Louisville. Superior faced chronic water shortages as its well water became undrinkable and even its ditch water scarce. The town government began buying bottled water which it distributed out of the town hall.

At that point developers with Richmond Homes approached the town with a bargain — a devil's bargain in the opinion of some

STRIKES!

Boulder County's coal mining towns all became scenes of clashes between miners striking for better wages and conditions and recalcitrant mine owners.

The first strike, which broke out in the Canfield-Erie coal fields in 1871, introduced the first strike-breakers to Boulder County.

Strikes began to turn bitter in 1903, when Louisville miners struck for an eight-hour day and a 15 percent wage increase. The United Mine Workers of America sent in Mother Jones, then in her 70s, to rally the strikers. With help from this guardian angel of the working class, Louisville strikers won concessions and even improved mine safety.

Unionists next undertook a four-year strike which began in 1910 and put 2,700 miners out of work. Mine owners fought the strike, just as they did at the Ludlow Massacre of April, 1914, in the Southern Colorado Coal Fields. Hatred loomed between strike-breakers, management and scabs. Like the UMWA, Boulder County Sheriff M. P. Capp found, "The mine operators are the most intemperate men I have ever dealt with." To end fighting between striking miners, scabs and mine guards, Governor Elias M. Ammons sent in the state militia. Gunfire drove townspeople to their cellars, including the William Lewis family, whose home became the Lafayette Miner's Museum.

Unlike the anti-union state militia, the more neutral federal troops were well-received. A band played, the town staged a parade and a soldier and a local girl were married to public acclaim. The strike ended with a 20 percent wage increase and increased safety in working conditions. Management, however, refused to recognize unions until compelled to do so by New Deal legislation of the 1930s.

◆ The United Mine Workers of America organized this local in Louisville to crusade for better pay ($3 a day), shorter hours (40 hours a week), safer working conditions and management's acceptance of unions.
Colorado Historical Society

◆ Major strikes shook Boulder County, in 1898, 1903, 1910-14 and 1927. In most disputes, mine owners persuaded the Colorado governor to send in state and federal troops to defend their mine property and their scabs. In this April 1913, view in Louisville, the Army is moving in to suppress strikers.
Louisville Historical Museum

Although the 1910-1914 strike was the longest, the 1927 strike proved to be the bloodiest in Colorado's Northern Coalfield. During the 1927 strike at the Columbine Mine near Canfield, company guards fired upon strikers, killing six and wounding about 20 more. The shooting began after a mine guard grabbed an American flag from a miner's son. Five slain miners were buried in unmarked graves in the Lafayette Cemetery. The U. S. Cavalry galloped in to end the violence. The strike had a rare happy ending complete with a

◆ Josephine Roche, at the age of 12, asked her father if she could go to work with him — his Rocky Mountain Fuel Company owned many Boulder County coal mines. "No," he told her, "it's too dangerous." She replied, "Then how is it safe for the miners?" Her father had no answer. Josephine ultimately inherited her father's company and investigated coal mining conditions. She improved mine safety and, in 1928, raised Columbine Mine wages to $7 per day — the highest paid to Colorado miners.
Colorado Historical Society

fairy godmother: social worker Josephine Roche inherited the Rocky Mountain Fuel Company, which operated the Columbine Mine, from her father. She raised wages, to the dismay of other mining companies. When they retaliated by lowering prices, Roche's employees loaned her some of their wages to keep the company afloat. Grateful working people helped Josephine Roche become Colorado's first female gubernatorial candidate in 1934. After she lost the Democratic Party nomination to Ed Johnson, Josephine went to Washington as President Franklin D. Roosevelt's U.S. assistant secretary of the treasury.

Although labor-management wars damaged the coal business, the final blow came with the 1930s introduction of natural gas, which replaced coal for heating. Coal mining gradually ceased, although the last Boulder County mines did not close until the 1970s. By then these mining towns were reborn as thriving residential communities.

OIL

During the early 1900s another resource — oil — became a new bonanza. Oil, like coal, evolved out of decayed vegetation from the tropical Mesozoic era. During the Cretaceous Period 135 million years ago, the region filled with seaweed and marine life as inland seas appeared and covered the land. Even after the great inland seas receded, a still-marshy Boulder County hosted lush vegetation and prehistoric creatures. As the climate grew drier and colder, vegetation dried up and was buried by sediment from the erosion of the ancestral Rocky Mountains.

Underground, the vegetative matter turned to oil and natural gas. In places, erosion exposed coal seams and oil seeps. Dr. Ferdinand V. Hayden, during his geological exploration of Colorado in the 1870s, announced that Boulder County lay "over a veritable sea of oil."

In 1892 the "Old Whiterock" oil well was drilled at the top of what is now Gunbarrel Hill. In 1901 the Boulder Oil Company began sinking wells around the county. Oil, however, was more a curiosity than a marketable product. Some used the greasy, black stuff in their lamps, as a cure for dandruff and to lubricate their wagons. Quack doctors recommended it as a cure-all.

With the automobile age, oil found a new market. By 1905 the Boulder Oil and Refining Company was digging and refining crude oil into gasoline. By 1910 Boulder County production averaged roughly 30,000 barrels of crude oil a year. More than 120 different oil companies sunk wells in the county by 1920. After drilling many wet and dry holes, geologists mapped Boulder oil field six miles long and two miles wide, stretching northeast from Boulder along the diagonal road to Longmont.

Although half of some 200 county wells were dry, others were gushers. Most of the wells produced crude oil and some offered an associated product, natural gas. By the 1920s, when Henry Ford and others were mass producing cars for sale to the middle class, America — and Boulder County — experienced its first great oil boom.

Like booms in gold and silver, tungsten and coal, the oil and natural gas bonanza ultimately fizzled. During the 1930s Depression, car ownership and the market for Boulder County's dwindling oil supply faded rapidly. Notwithstanding booster claims that Boulder County was a bottomless mineral chest, one boom after another busted. Boulder County began to look for other riches of the earth and found it in agricultural endeavors.

To boost morale and to lead the town's Labor Day Parade, the Lafayette Local of the United Mine Workers of America formed this brass band.

Lafayette Miner's Museum

1971 photo by Tom Noel

1999 photo by Tom Noel

Boulder Depot Museum

Longmont Museum

Ed Tangen Photo, Carnegie Branch Library for Local History, Boulder Historical Society Collection

1991 photo by Tom Noel

Sodbusters

Chapter *Seven*

"Chief Niwot scolded Jerome Gould as he plowed his field near Left Hand Creek: 'Wrong side up.' "

—Anne Dyni, *Pioneer Voices of the Boulder Valley*

Anne Dyni learned this story from Jerome Gould's granddaughter, Ruth Dodd McDonald: "Niwot didn't want grandfather to plow that nice native land. He wanted to save it for the wild game to feed on."

Niwot lost the plowing battle and the land he and his people loved. Gould and his wife, Amy, who had traded a team of oxen for 120 acres along Left Hand Creek near the town of Niwot, stayed and continued to plow.

Boulder County's first "crop" did not require a plow. Native prairie grasses were harvested by prairie dogs and deer, antelope and buffalo. Later arrivals used the grasses for their livestock. Farmers, however, soon began busting the tough prairie sod, hoping to plant crops for hungry miners. Some disgruntled gold-seekers actually became the area's first agriculturalists. Matthew McCaslin, for example, left Gold Hill in 1862 with his wife and baby daughter, both named Miranda. The McCaslins resettled on a farm near Hygiene along St. Vrain Creek. He began supplying miners with farm fresh milk and butter.

◆ Making hay is easy in Boulder County's cool, sunny climate. Skilled farmers like Longmont's David Boswick, shown here with six tons (168 bales), raised as many as three crops a year.
Longmont Museum

McCaslin ultimately acquired more than 1,000 acres for his ranch, where the 1862 stone milkhouse and 1871 farmhouse stand to this day. When the McCaslins retired to Longmont in 1902, their son Matt and his wife, Molly, took over the farm, now a county landmark. Matthew, his son Matt and his grandson Ted all became Boulder County Commissioners. McCaslin Boulevard in Louisville is named for Ted, a commissioner from 1944 to 1967.

Another agricultural pioneer, William Davidson, started a flatland farm before heading to the mountains to gamble on gold. Davidson arrived in Boulder County in 1859 and took up farming on Boulder Creek three miles east of Valmont before prospecting Ward's gold mines. After Ward's flush times came and went, he established the farming community of Davidson at the intersection of 95th Street and Baseline Road.

◆ Boulder County's intrepid farmers cultivated both mountains and plains. The Boynton-Coffin farm in Allenspark specialized in high country crops such as carrots, hay, lettuce, peas and potatoes. By 1900 Boulder County had 967 farms producing nearly $1 million annually.
Longmont Museum

The Wellman brothers — Henry, Luther and Sylvanus — arrived from Illinois on August 1, 1859. They took up a whole section around today's Foothills Parkway-Arapahoe Road intersection. The brothers planted turnips only to have them devoured by grasshoppers. After eating every plant in sight, the hoppers hopped into farmhouses. Inside, they ate curtains, clothing and anything else they fancied. In 1860 the dreaded hoppers spared the Wellmans, who raised the county's first wheat crop. Four years later, however, grasshoppers devoured 80 acres of Wellman wheat. Grasshoppers also stripped the fields of Anthony Arnett, who established the county's first ranch in 1860 with 100 cattle on his Mapleton Hill farm.

◆ Despite full irrigation ditches, good soil and bountiful sunshine, Boulder County farmers struggled. One of their biggest problems was grasshoppers. The Rocky Mountain locust (Melanoplus spretus) descended by the billions on Colorado in sporadic plagues that began in the 1860s. They devastated crops and swarmed onto railroad tracks, stalling trains. Boldly invading even Boulder City, they found this cast iron storefront less tasty than Boulder County's greenery. *Pikes Peak Library District, Local History Collection*

J. A. King of Valmont invented a vacuum cleaner to suck up the pests. J. Hitzel of Longmont patented a horse-drawn fire wagon to cook the creatures, while Jacob S. Flory of Hygiene patented a locust-catching and crushing machine. Despite an arsenal of weapons, Boulder County farmers still dread the grasshopper's hum.

Fruit farmers found the land around Boulder to be productive. Marinus Smith, who arrived in 1859, acquired 220 acres along Boulder Creek. Besides apples and cherries, he raised rhubarb, which earned him the nickname of "Pie Plant" Smith. Englishman John Brierley, who came to Colorado in 1859, planted orchards at the mouth of Boulder Canyon near his home at 201 Pearl Street. Smith and Brierley soon found competition from Joseph Wolff, whose north Boulder orchard surrounded his stately home at 1235 Elder Avenue. Bypassers marveled at the circular "grapery" on which he grew Concord grapes.

Brothers Frederick and Jacob Affolter built their 1860 cabin on Left Hand Creek west of Haystack Mountain. In 1862 these Swiss emigrants drove a herd of milk cows from Missouri to Colorado, where they opened Boulder's pioneer cheese factory. Their place became the scene of community celebrations such as weddings, dances, funerals and other public gatherings — including the 1864 return of the 100-day volunteers from Sand Creek. In 1971 the Affolter cabin was acquired by the St. Vrain Historical Society, which moved it to Longmont's Old Mill Park. Craftsmen reconstructed the cabin using the original stone foundation and re-joining the logs with wooden pins.

Many pioneer farms and ranches have disappeared, devoured by new residential subdivisions and strip malls. A notable exception is Lafayette's Ewing Centennial Farm at 1915 N. 95th Street. John Ewing, a Civil War veteran who survived Confederate prisons, bought his 40-acre prairie spread in 1885. Flora, Ewing's daughter, remembered riding on her father's plow to help him bust the tough prairie sod so they could plant wheat. His wife, Amanda, made butter so good that local grocers hid it under their counters for their best customers. She also made apple butter after Ewing planted Lafayette's first apple orchard. Ewing's venerable farmhouse is now a State Register landmark and honored as a Centennial Farm

◆ Bushy-browed William Davidson arrived in Boulder in 1859, hoping to make his fortune in mining. He soon left the diggings to become one of the county's largest agricultural landowners. Davidson's farm, three miles east of Valmont on Davidson Mesa, still harbors his 1870 barn. *Carnegie Branch Library for Local History, Boulder Historical Society Collection*

◆ Civil War veteran John Ewing, who brought his family from Kansas in 1880, purchased a 40-acre spread from William Davidson. Ewing erected this farmhouse in 1886 on 95th Street, just north of Arapahoe Road in Lafayette. Here, Ewing and his wife, Amanda, raised six children.
1999 photo by Tom Noel

by the Colorado Historical Society. Restored, it is now a solitary relic of times past amid a sea of new subdivisions.

German immigrants Adolph and Anna Waneka settled in 1860 on the south bank of Coal Creek on the west edge of Lafayette. Adolph lived in a cave while building a two-story house with stone he found along the creek. The Wanekas began cattle ranching and also served meals to hungry travelers. They prospered, becoming a large clan of landowners still prominent in the Lafayette and Longmont area.

The Wanekas and other farm families banded together to create rural school districts — often the first effort to define a rural community. Citizens in the defined area were asked to contribute money, or at least labor, to build a school. In 1861 Colorado's first territorial legislature established a common school system law. It required each county to establish school districts for a community with 10 or more children. Amos Widner, Boulder County's first superintendent, was followed by Valmont Presbyterian minister Charles Campbell. Ultimately, Boulder County established 66 school districts. Large, extended farm families sometimes dominated classrooms. The Beasley School, for example, located four miles south of Longmont, captured the attention of *Ripley's Believe It or Not* when all 29 of its students were related.

Early schools had simple architecture distinguished by a front gable and a belltower atop. Most schools were frame buildings painted white. The double front doors usually faced south or east away from Boulder County's winds. Although larger eastern schools often had separate doors for boys and girls, egalitarian western schools usually shared all facilities except the outhouses.

The Grange

The Patrons of Husbandry, popularly known as the Grange, also enriched the sense of community among isolated farm folk. Organized in 1867, this national organization strived to unite agrarians who felt increasingly exploited. Farmers received less and less of the price people paid for food, while grain merchants, railroad magnates, bankers and a seemingly endless line of middle men siphoned off the profits. Whenever farmers traveled into cities, they saw tremendous wealth that rarely flowed out to the hinterlands. The grange movement's primary goal was to serve the farmer a bigger piece of the American pie.

Besides acting as political centers, grange halls became social hubs. Lonely farm women especially enjoyed this chance for sociability. At first, grangers met in churches, schools and other halls, such as Valmont's Good Templar Lodge. Not until 1873 did Valmonters build the county's first grange hall, soon followed by 23 others.

◆ Since its 1900 construction for $384, the Boulder Valley Grange Hall has guarded the northeast corner of 95th Street and Isabelle Road in eastern Boulder County. Anne Dyni restored the hall and successfully nominated it for the National Register of Historic Places. In 1988 she sold it to the Pleasantview Grange, whose old hall at 47th Street and Jay Road was demolished for the Foothills Parkway.
1999 photo by Tom Noel

Boulder County's granger movement originated with an 1869 "farmers convention" at the first Boulder County Fair, where grangers congregated and enlisted new members. The *Boulder County News*, on June 12, 1869, reported that "about 100 of the county's heaviest farmers, fruit-growers, and stockmen" organized the Boulder County Agricultural Society. This non-profit organization elected Judge Granville Berkeley as president and purchased 40 acres between 28th and 30th streets south of Valmont Road for a fairground. Farmers feasted in the dining tent operated by Valmont Presbyterian Church women. Then they heard Judge Berkeley proclaim that the "one great mistake of the first settlers of the territory was that every effort, energy, and encouragement was given to the development of the mines, while agriculture seems to be lost sight of. Neither can prosper without the other." Farmers welcomed miners to the county fair, where "mineralogy" was one of the five classes of exhibits. Despite daily horse races to attract patrons, Boulder County's first fair closed $2,500 in the hole. The fairgrounds were sold in a sheriff's sale.

In 1871, the same year that the Chicago-Colorado Colony settled in Longmont, Longmonters formed the Northern Colorado Agricultural Society. The Society purchased the 80-acre Lake (later Roosevelt) Park as its fair site. That event soon outdrew Boulder's Fair and the county fair was moved to Longmont, where it remains. This fair draws some 75,000 each August and in 1978 was moved to a larger site at the northeast corner of Hover and Nelson roads. Here Coloradans can see, feel, sniff and taste the products of Boulder County's agricultural communities.

Valmont

Tommy Jones named his 1860 stage stop by combining the words "valley" and "mountain." Former miners such as Boulder City founders Tom Aikins and Al Brookfield were among many disappointed gold-seekers drifting downstream to the community that sprouted around Jones' stagehouse. After hosting the first county elections in 1860, Valmont aspired to eclipse Boulder as the county's political seat. In 1867 Boulder officially became the county seat, and Valmont dropped its big city aspirations, never even bothering to incorporate.

Judge Alonzo P. Allen platted Valmont in 1865, the year the town gained its own post office. The settlement harbored a handful of businesses, including Tommy Jones' "Valmont House" and had bedrock support from the Boulder Valley Presbyterian Church, which had organized on September 6, 1863, in Emma

◆ The Altona Grange first met in the Bader School at 41st Street and Nelson Road in 1891. Five years later, grangers built this $350 hall on land donated by Alonzo Allen at the southeast corner of 39th Street and Nelson Road. The Altona Grange had an orchestra, chorus, horseshoe pitching, softball, square dancing and oyster suppers.
1999 Photo by Tom Noel

◆ The Boulder County Agricultural Society built this round, conical-roofed exhibit hall for the Boulder County Fair in 1870. Measuring 30 feet in diameter and 12 feet in height, it housed agricultural and mineral exhibits. It was demolished when the fair moved to Longmont.
Carnegie Branch Library for Local History, Boulder Historical Society Collection

◆ Much of Valmont has faded into oblivion today, leaving only a few faded photographs, such as this 1914 view showing buildings clustered on Main Street (Valmont Road). Three saloons situated there led Boulderites to call Valmont's Main Street "Devil's Row." Fighting the devil, Valmont Presbyterians built their first church in 1866, then replaced it with the 1899 clapboard church at 3262 61st Street. Located in the center right, with Boulder Creek in the background, this church was Valmont's finest structure. It burned down in 1979 and was replaced by the current Valmont Community United Presbyterian Church.
Norris Hermsmeyer

◆ Valmont erected Boulder County's first brick schoolhouse in 1869, a one-room structure with an anteroom and a belfry. Earlier, classes had been held on the hard benches of Valmont's 1866 Presbyterian Church. The third school, this 1911 cement-block edifice on 61st Street, awaits adaptive reuse.
1999 Photo by Tom Noel

◆ (Right top) This silo and milk house are remnants of the south Valmont farm of Irish immigrant Edward Donnelly, who also ran Valmont's general store.
1999 Photo by Tom Noel

Brookfield's parlor. The congregation's first minister, Reverend Charles Campbell, arrived in 1865 and oversaw the construction of the county's first church in 1866. The Methodists opened their church three years later.

To save farmers a trip to Boulder, Peter Housel and John DeBacker opened a Valmont flour mill in 1865. Besides the county's first newspaper, Valmonters also claim the county's, and perhaps the state's, first brick schoolhouse. The 1869 one-room structure was built just south of the still-standing 1911 school which replaced it.

The 1870s saw Valmont develop as a commercial and social center. In 1873 two railroads — the Colorado Central and the Denver and Boulder Valley — reached the prospering community. That same year a second flour mill, the White Rock, opened on Boulder Creek at 75th Street. Valmont Butte, the town's distinguishing landmark, was quarried to produce cobblestones for Denver and other markets. Young Valmonters picnicked and boated on Weisenhorn Lake on the south side of the butte. Keeping pace with Boulder's cultural claims, Valmonters organized a Literary Society in 1874. In 1877 one of Valmont's pioneer industries, Hayden's Cheese Factory, opened west of the Presbyterian Church, churning out 16,582 pounds of cheese in its inaugural year.

Fire ended Valmont's flush times. The White Rock Flour Mill burned in 1878 and the cheese factory melted in a blaze four years later. An 1884 spark ignited the ice house next to Edward Donnelly's store. To preserve what is left of the historic town, descendants of pioneer settlers formed "Rural Historic Valmont" in the 1990s. The old stagecoach stop, the pioneer cemetery, the 1911 school and the old Wells/Chambers residence at 3902 N. 63rd Street are relics of a largely vanished Valmont. Remaining residents savor a rural lifestyle amid rapid growth in surrounding towns.

◆ This 1870s building at 6095 Valmont Road was one of Valmont's two blacksmith shops. After horseless carriages replaced horses, blacksmith Frank Polzin became a car salesman. During the 1970s the old smithy became Valmont Auto Wrecking.
1980 Photo by Carole Gunter

Jacob S. Flory established Hygiene's grandest structure, this 1882 Hygiene House sanitarium on 75th Street north of the current elementary school. Despite Flory's claims that Hygiene's mineral water and sunshine would rescue even the sickest tubercular from the edge of the grave, the sanitarium failed, becoming a home for alcoholics, a music school, an orphanage and a hotel before its 1926 demolition.
Longmont Museum

Hygiene

Hygiene started with the "Hygiene House," a sanitarium for tuberculosis patients established in 1882 by the Church of the Brethren. Popularly known as the Dunkards for their baptismal practice of immersing a person three times, this German Baptist sect also built a church, school, farmhouses and irrigation ditches off St. Vrain Creek.

Not only in their creek dunkings, but also in their village life the Dunkards were led by a remarkable pioneer. Reverend Jacob S. Flory had piercing eyes, a six-inch goatee and golden oratory. He directed construction of the Hygiene House and also of Hygiene's 1880 Dunkard Church, which survives at 7811 Hygiene Road. Inside handsome sandstone walls, the church's plain plaster walls and pine flooring reflect the sect's austerity. Now a National Register landmark, the church is the oldest surviving Colorado Church of the Brethren. Hygiene also boasts an impressive red brick 1905 Methodist Church at 7542 Hygiene Road.

Caring for both physical and spiritual needs, Reverend Flory drove invalids to the supposedly curative waters of a sulfur spring on the south side of Rabbit Mountain. There he constructed a pergola over the spring so patients could sip in the shade. For sicker, immobile patients, the good reverend hauled water by wagon to the sanitarium, whose crowning glory was a third-story solarium with a blue glass cupola. Flory promoted Hygiene as a health spa and agricultural colony in his newspaper, the *Home Mirror*. Despite the *Mirror's* claims, the Hygiene House was never a healthy business and was soon recycled for other uses.

◆ Cottonwoods, the only sizeable native prairie trees, offered shade, firewood and shelter. The St.Vrain Valley grove in Hygiene hosts the nation's largest cottonwood, measuring a giant 105 feet tall and 36 feet in circumference. *1971 photo by Tom Noel*

Flory became Hygiene's first postmaster in 1883. When not sorting and delivering mail, the enterprising minister introduced alfalfa to the area for its bee-enticing blossoms. By 1900 Hygiene's honey production reached 14,000 pounds a year. To protect Hygiene's fields from grasshopper plagues, Reverend Flory did more than pray. He invented and patented a locust-catching and crushing machine.

Thanks to Reverend Flory's far-ranging talents and dynamic leadership, Hygiene eclipsed its neighbor to the south, Pella or Fort Pella. Named after Pella, Iowa, this 1860s settlement was also known as the "Upper Crossing" on St. Vrain Creek. By the 1870s Pella had a blacksmith shop, general store, post office, grist mill and school. The hamlet declined when the railroad bypassed it for nearby Hygiene. In 1886 Pella lost its post office — and its identity.

Hygiene, however, is still dominated by prosperous farmers and ranchers on the western fringe of fast-growing Longmont. Hygiene boasts America's largest cottonwood, a giant in Crane Hollow that is 105 feet high, with a circumference of 36 feet and a crown spread of 93 feet, according to the American Forestry Association's *National Register of Big Trees.* Thanks to sturdy trees and sturdy agrarians, Hygiene has changed little since the *1904 Boulder County Directory* described it as "well supplied with two stores, creamery, and cheese factory, a neat church owned by the United Brethern, a well equipped school, post and express offices and feed mill. The village of Hygiene must be seen ere it can be fully appreciated. Population about 300."

◆ The Hygiene Cheese Factory was built by the George Zweck family. George Sr., a German immigrant, traveled to Colorado by an ox-team in 1860. Charmed by the St. Vrain Valley, he imported dairy cattle to produce his memorable cheese. The blizzard of 1881 nearly wiped out his cattle and bankrupted him. Fellow Dunkards stabled his surviving milk cows at their farms to hide them from creditors. *Longmont Museum*

Joaquim and Jocy Ann Armas converted the Hygiene School to the Old Prague Inn in 1977. Their tavern is adorned with paintings of Old Prague and a portrait of the famous Czech author and president, Vaclav Havel. The Czech bartender amuses guests by floating coins on a foamy head of Prague's Urquell pilsner.

Niwot

Born in 1873 as the Colorado Central Railroad section house halfway between Boulder and Longmont, the site was first called Modoc. When platted in 1875, the settlement was renamed for the left-handed Arapaho chief fatally wounded at Sand Creek. The Union Pacific Railroad, which bought the Colorado Central in 1880, lured farmers to Niwot by promising to build cattle guards at railroad crossings. When the railroad reneged on its promise, farmer William Caywood ran a fence across the tracks and pulled out a section of rail with a team of oxen. Although the railroad's attorneys charged Caywood with obstructing the U. S. mail, a jury of locals acquitted him.

Niwot's diagonal street grid paralleled the railroad tracks that preceded today's Diagonal Highway. Porter

◆ Niwot's 1873 depot was one of the first structures in the town platted two years later by Porter Hinman and Ambrose Murray. Both passengers and livestock were boarded in this now-gone board-and-batten depot on the Union Pacific line. *Carnegie Branch Library for Local History, Boulder Historical Society Collection*

◆ Chilly winter weather did not keep girls off the dirt court at Niwot School in 1915. *Ed Tangen Photo, Carnegie Branch Library for Local History, Boulder Historical Society Collection*

Hinman and Ambrose Murray, who surveyed the town in 1875, named the streets on either side of the tracks for themselves. Hinman's side became the original town hub after the Niwot Depot located there. The railroad steamed into town twice a day, connecting Niwot with markets in Boulder, Longmont and Denver. Fertile fields and plentiful underground water produced abundant crops, dairy products and livestock.

◆ In a rare respite from hard work, this Mexican migrant family posed in a sugar beet field on the outskirts of Niwot in 1908. Migrant laborers still do much of Boulder County's hardest work. *Ed Tangen Photo, Carnegie Branch Library for Local History, Boulder Historical Society Collection*

Townsfolk planted trees, shrubs and flowers, creating a tiny urban oasis.

The main street commercial district east of the railroad tracks had mercantile, drug and grocery stores, as well as a blacksmith shop, hotel, creamery, newspaper, post office and bank. The latter was robbed in December, 1916, by unlucky burglars whose railroad handcar escape was foiled by deep snowdrifts.

Niwot's most colorful merchant, United Brethren minister William Taylor, operated the "Niwot Bee" grocery. Reverend Taylor held services on the second floor where he gave memorable sermons on farming and merchandizing as well as religion. Announcements of his sermons in the *Niwot Tribune* promised to save souls, while his ads promised to save folk's money on meats, groceries and his soda fountain concoctions, not to mention free candy for the children. In 1986 his false-fronted frame church/store was reborn as "Rev. Taylor's Country Restaurant."

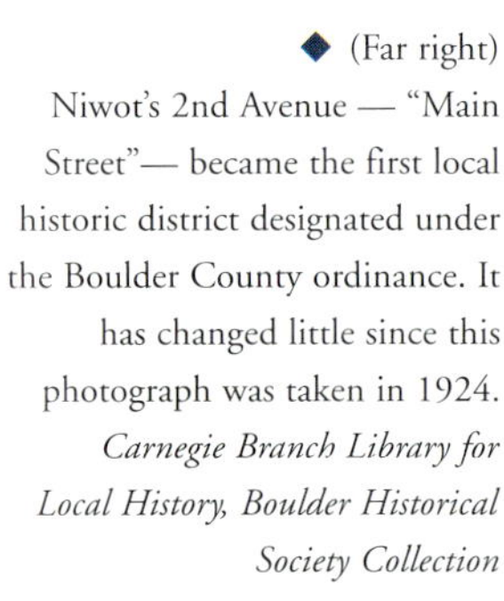

◆ (Far right) Niwot's 2nd Avenue — "Main Street"— became the first local historic district designated under the Boulder County ordinance. It has changed little since this photograph was taken in 1924. *Carnegie Branch Library for Local History, Boulder Historical Society Collection*

Although Reverend Taylor's place survives, 1959 construction crews for the Diagonal Highway knocked down the west half of town, including the historic depot. Also sacrificed for the four-lane, median-divided highway was Niwot's 1910 two-story brick schoolhouse, demolished in 1972 for the southbound lanes.

The surviving eastern half of Old Niwot has been rejuvenated as a an antique shop mecca. Quaint, well-preserved 2nd Avenue earned 1993 designation by Boulder County commissioners as a historic district.

◆ (Left and below right) Ryssby Church and Cemetery crown the hill south of Nelson Road on 63rd Avenue. Stonemason Charles Olson and blacksmith Andrew Lindberg built this Gothic gem in 1882 with fieldstone from August Olander's farm. Candlelight "Julotta" services and "Midsummer Day" services around the June 21st Solstice are still celebrated in Swedish, as are weddings. Churchyard tombstones reveal that many of the 14 founding families hailed from Ryssby in Sweden's Smaland province.
1991 photo by Tom Noel

Ryssby

Ryssby, located on North 63rd Street south of Nelson Road, commemorates Boulder County's Swedish settlers. As churchyard tombstones testify, many hailed from Ryssby in Sweden's Smaland province. Some 14 Swedish families built a fine stone church in 1881 as a house of worship and the social center for the small community, which also had a school and blacksmith shop. The Swedes brought the floor plan and design from the old country, and used a nearby quarry for the sandstone walls. On the inside, craftsmen applied beaded tongue-and-groove siding to the vaulted ceiling. A pot-bellied stove still provides the only heat in the church. In 1914 the dwindling congregation merged with Longmont Lutherans, who keep up the rustic, history-rich Ryssby Church for use on special occasions.

◆ (Left) Niwot's 1874 Cemetery, lying a mile northwest of town near 75th Street, has 287 residents and is still growing. Granite and marble tombstones, far more substantial than their pioneer dugouts and sod house and shanties, commemorate Boulder County's trailblazers.
1999 photos by Tom Noel

Broomfield

Broomfield traces its origins to Henry and Sarah Church, who began ranching in 1864 at what is now 104th Avenue and Old Wadsworth Boulevard. The Churches also opened a stage stop on their spread and welcomed travelers. Their congeniality — and home-grown and home-cooked meals — attracted other settlers. Church's, as the community was first called, attracted Adolph Zang, a Denver beer baron. In 1879 Zang bought 4,000 acres and started raising French Percheron horses, fruit trees and berries on his Elmwood Stock Farm.

Church's became a town after the 1881 arrival of the Union Pacific Railroad. Around the depot, a community sprang up and took its name from surrounding fields of broom corn. In 1884 the first postmistress, Druella Coulson, persuaded postal officials in Washington to use the name Broomfield, although some called the settlement Church's after the pioneer family or Zang's Spur after Adolph Zang's huge spread.

The town remained a rural hub with its elevators and railroad depot for 70 years, not passing the 100 resident mark until 1950. The biggest business, Zang's Farm, sprawled over both Boulder and Jefferson counties, including the current sites of the Jefferson County Airport and Great Western Reservoir. Zang, whose farmhouse still stands at 680 Poppy Way, made Broomfield famous for auctions of "Colorado's Oldest and Largest Breeders of Purebred Percherons."

◆ (Right and below) This 1909 Broomfield Depot included comfortable living quarters for the agent and his family — a parlor, a kitchen and two bedrooms. The depot originally stood along the railroad tracks just north of 120th Avenue. In 1976 Broomfield's Jaycees moved it to Zang's Spur Park, where it has been the city's history museum since 1983. In addition to the depot, the park contains a honey house, pumphouse and an outhouse from the farm of early Broomfield historian Miles Crawford.
1946 Photo by Charles S. Ryland; 1989 photo by Tom Noel

Around Zang's trackside grain elevator, small businesses sprouted. Mary Merkle Wright, who came to Broomfield with her husband Robert in 1888, operated a Broomfield cheese factory from 1890 to 1910. Despite the aroma, this edifice, the town's largest building, hosted church services, dances and meetings.

Children walked to the 1880 rural schoolhouse, which predated Broomfield's founding. This one-room, white frame building stood at Main Street and 10th Avenue, just east of Lakeview Cemetery. It was replaced in 1921 by a fine brick structure, which was later augmented by four houses on 1st Avenue used as "Cottage Schools" for grades kindergarten through six.

Although Boulder County Broomfielders could attend school without crossing a county line, they had to leave the county to find a church. The Methodists built the first church in the Broomfield area in 1888. That old church at 120th and Allison, now a taxidermy studio complete with a rooftop giraffe, hosted community as well as church gatherings.

Dr. R. D. Elmore, Broomfield's first physician, started making horse and buggy house calls in 1899. In 1916 he bought a Model T, which he never considered as reliable as old Dobbin. "Never will forget the night the new Lizzie got stuck in a snow drift," Doc Elmore reminisced. "I drained the radiator and spent the next two days in a farmhouse during the storm and finally walked home. The car stayed in the drift for a week."

By the 1930s Broomfield boasted two giant grain elevators, a feed mill, general store, blacksmith, pool hall, hotel, lumber yard, barber shop and the Crescent Grange Hall. This hall served as a community center after its construction in 1916 on land donated by the Zang family.

As early as 1923, the Zang Investment Company began selling off parcels for residential lots, but the 1952 Denver-Boulder Turnpike quickly ended Broomfield's pastoral era. In 1955 the Turnpike Land Company bought a large chunk of the Zang spread and built Broomfield Heights, complete with a shopping center. Houses and stores, new schools and churches sprang up almost overnight. In 1963 Broomfield built a library, named for Denverite Mamie Doud Eisenhower, who personally dedicated it. Broomfield Heights incorporated in 1961 as the City of Broomfield with a population of 4,700, a figure that doubled by 1980.

Broomfield's explosive growth delighted Aksel Nielsen, president of the Title Guaranty Company and a Denver real estate tycoon. The Danish-born developer helped put together the Turnpike Land Company and recalled in 1983: "Broomfield was our most spectacular deal. K.C. Ensor, Carl Norgren, Bud Knight, Balmore Swan, John Sullivan and I bought the old Zang Ranch and turned it into the city of Broomfield."

During the 1980s and 1990s, the once tiny hamlet in the southeast corner of Boulder County sprawled into neighboring Weld, Adams and Jefferson counties. This governmental overlap led to creation of a separate new county, which Coloradans approved in a 1998 statewide

◆ Old Broomfield's grainy past is commemorated by two elevators along the Union Pacific tracks, a square 1923 Coors grain elevator and the rounded towers built in 1916 by Adolph Zang.
1999 photo by Tom Noel

◆ (Below left)
The 1916 Crescent Grange Hall at 7901 West 120th Avenue is a souvenir of Broomfield's agricultural roots. As one of the town's first civic groups, the Crescent Grangers pushed for free rural mail delivery.
1999 photo by Tom Noel

◆ Mary Merkle Wright and her husband Robert arrived in Broomfield in 1888. Mary, Broomfield's first businessperson, operated her cheese factory from 1890 to 1910 and became Colorado's first female Dairy and Cheese Commissioner.
Broomfield Depot Museum

◆ Besides fielding a baseball team, the Broomfield Lumber Company at 7905 West 120th Avenue served both town residents and outlying farmers. They grew broom corn as livestock feed and to make brushes and brooms.
Boulder Depot Museum

election. By 2001, when Broomfield formally becomes Colorado's 64th county, its population may exceed 40,000.

Residential subdivisions and shopping malls have consumed much of the land where broom corn, sugar beets, wheat and other crops once flourished. Ranches, replaced by subdivisions of ranch houses between the 1950s and the 1970s, are now often being subdivided for two- and three-story mansionettes with three- and four-car garages. Home on the range is no longer a place where deer, antelope and prairie dogs play. Wildlife, like livestock and crops, have been sacrificed as Broomfield exploded with growth, including high-rise hotels and office buildings along U.S. 36 that are taller than any in Longmont or Boulder.

◆ (Far right) The Denver Boulder Turnpike, first envisioned by CU civil engineering Professor Roderick Downing in 1912, opened in 1952. Motorists paid 25 cents between Boulder and Denver, 15 cents from Denver to Broomfield, and 10 cents from Broomfield to Boulder. Many more motorists than expected enabled the Colorado Department of Highways to remove the toll booth in 1967, 13 years ahead of schedule.
Tom Noel Collection

◆ Now a city park, Broomfield's 1890 Lakeview Cemetery on 10th Avenue west of Main Street was deeded to the city in 1973. In the oldest of 120 graves lies an 1889 newborn.
1999 photo by Tom Noel

◆ Broomfield initially had the only U.S. 36 exit between Denver and Boulder — the clover leaf shown in this 1957 aerial photo. After the Denver-Boulder Turnpike opened in 1952, Broomfield blossomed.
Tom Noel Collection

◆ (Far left)
Turnpike Land Company Vice President Pete De Longchamps helps Marianne MacDonald, Miss Broomfield Heights of 1958, break ground for that new subdivision on August 4, 1958. Broomfield Depot Museum Director Peggy Atkinson bought her three-bedroom Broomfield Heights home that year for $14,000.
Broomfield Depot Museum

◆ This towering sign was Broomfield's most prominent landmark from 1958 until its 1994 removal to make room for a Target store. The 18- by 22-foot neon monument originally boasted yellow letters on a blue background. Broomfield preservationists wanted it restored, but city officials balked at the $20,000 cost.
Broomfield Depot Museum

Photo by Ron Ruhoff

Photo by Tom Noel

Peter Pollock collection

Carnegie Branch Library for Local History, Boulder Historical Society Daily Camera Collection

Peter Pollock postcard

1969 photo by Ron Ruhoff

Planning Ahead at Boulder City and CU

Chapter *Eight*

"Tumbleweed straggles on the railroad track where children balance safely on the rail; the interstate blots out the cattle track, a sulphur flag waves from the giant stack. The houses crawling up the mountain lack deep roots — may they not slide into the vale. And, can you tell the schoolhouse from the jail? You never really were a peaceful town — snatched from the Indians for greed of gold, hard against unions with a burning cross, hooded and sheeted against black and brown. Your errors are impossible to gloss, nor will your beauty abdicate its hold."

—Florence Becker Lennon,
Boulder Poet and Environmentalist, 1983

Boulder's determination to manage growth has made it a national prototype. This abiding concern about improving the quality of civic life began with town founders. Back in 1859 they decided to plat a town with unusually large lots and generous public amenities. By 1900 the city had acquired more than 1,800 acres of park land and adopted visionary plans for acquiring much more during the 20th century. Consequently, Boulder enters the 21st century endowed with a superb greenbelt, exhilarating mountain parks and a first-rate city park system.

◆ (Right and below) Chautauqua opened in 1898 with tent housing. In Cottage No. 6, three Texas teachers practiced their song and dance. *Carnegie Branch Library for Local History, Boulder Historical Society Collection*

magnificent natural setting inspired residents to establish America's pioneer open space program in 1967. Critics blasted this controversial scheme as new-fangled nonsense, forgetting that Boulderites had overwhelmingly supported mountain parks acquisitions and development of recreational and cultural activities as early as the 1890s.

To protect its park-like setting, Boulder's City Council unanimously passed a resolution in 1907 to limit the city's physical size. Not until 1941 did the city annex additional land with the proviso that developers help pay for the infrastructure, including "water, light, sewer systems, streets, etc." Respect for Boulder's

Chautauqua

The pretty, tree-shaded town captured attention as far away as Austin, Texas, where the University of Texas decided to cool off with a summer school in Colorado. The Texas-Colorado Chautauqua Association was formed in 1897 to establish a Boulder Chautauqua. The Seneca Indian word "chautauqua" ("moccasins tied together") came from the peculiar shape of Lake Chautauqua in western New York,

◆ In this1899 photo, Chautauquans pose on Old Chautauqua Rock, the most photogenic boulder in Boulder. *c. 1900 postcard Peter Pollock*

where the first program opened in 1874. Rural adults hungry for education and culture flocked to the movement, which quickly expanded nationwide, offering educational and inspirational lectures and programs. By 1898 more than 150 Chautauquas dotted the country. President Theodore Roosevelt called Chautauquas "the most American thing in America."

Boulder was not the only Colorado city to woo the Texans. Denver also wanted the prize and Colorado Springs offered $100,000 as a lure. Lucius Paddock, editor of the Boulder *Daily Camera*, argued that "the prize is too big to be allowed to slip away." At a public meeting in 1898, Boulder citizens urged city fathers to secure the Chautauqua. Boulderites, editor Paddock proclaimed, must put "shoulders to the wheel and pull altogether [so] Boulder will land upon the summit of prosperity's wave."

By a 35 to 1 margin, voters approved a bond issue to establish Chautauqua on the 75-acre Bachelder Ranch south of Baseline Road. An additional 96

◆ Joseph Bevier "Rocky Mountain Joe" Sturtevant (1851-1910) came to Boulder in 1884 as a sign painter, but quickly took up photography. Named the Official Chautauqua Photographer in 1898, he built this studio on the site of the current Community House. Sturtevant, on the left in buckskins, offered guided mountain excursions to the Texas school marms, who were charmed by his tall tales. *Carnegie Branch Library for Local History, Boulder Historical Society Collection*

◆ (Far Left) Gloriously restored in the 1980s, Chautauqua Dining Hall now offers lunch and dinner year round. *1994 photo by Tom Noel*

◆ Boulderites celebrated Chautauqua's 100th birthday on July 4, 1998. After the traditional *Daily Camera*-sponsored concert on the green, celebrants marched single file into the auditorium waving American flags to "Stars and Stripes Forever." Following this speech by Chautauqua Executive Director Leslie Durgin, the Chautauqua Board of Directors hosted an old-fashioned ice cream social.
Colorado Chautauqua Association

◆ On summer evenings, classical music of the Colorado Music Festival fills the antique auditorium.
1998 photo by Tom Noel

acres — Boulder's first mountain park — were later purchased on the west side of Chautauqua.

To capture the long-skirted Texas school marms, Boulder donated land, constructed permanent buildings and laid a streetcar line out to Chautauqua. In exchange, the Texans promised summers of entertainment and education to Boulder's citizens and tourists.

The Chautauqua Auditorium and Dining Hall were built in 45 days, opening on July 4, 1898. Four thousand celebrants heard seven hours of speeches from 17 speakers, including Colorado Governor Alva Adams and Boulder Mayor Crockett Ricketts. Subsequent programs featured William Jennings Bryan, Rev. Billy Sunday and Sen. Robert LaFollette as well as John Philip Sousa's band. Silent movies were introduced in 1898. To this day, programs also include lectures on current issues, as well as the Colorado Music Festival, which has made Chautauqua its home since 1978.

The National Trust for Historic Preservation in 1990 honored the Colorado Chautauqua Association and the City of Boulder for revitalizing not only the structures but the edifying public programs. The Dining Hall, noted for fine views and fine food, has been open year round since 1998.

Boulder's Mountain Park System

Delighted with the Chautauqua teachers and tourists — and their dollars — Boulderites continued to purchase land for parks, civic improvements and public uses such as Chautauqua's smorgasbord of cultural and recreational programs. In the early 1900s, Boulderites enjoyed one acre of park land for every two citizens, a proportion still maintained by purchasing additional open space. In 1942 Parks Commissioner Louise Cheney estimated that only two other cities in the United States — Denver and Phoenix — owned more park land per capita.

Park fever grew after the 1898 Chautauqua purchases and re-organization of the Colorado and

◆ Chautauqua Meadow attracts skiers as well as hikers galore. In 1948 the Boulder City Council granted entrepreneur Harris "Tommy" Thompson the right to operate a ski tow. After clearing rocks with a bulldozer, Thompson opened the Mesa Ski Slope. It operated for only a few seasons, and the city rejected subsequent proposals for an amusement park-resort in the meadow.
Carnegie Branch Library for Local History, Boulder Historical Society's Daily Camera Collection

Coloradans, this brochure crowed, "need not go to Switzerland, to Italy or to France for sublime mountain scenery, with such a wonderful array of nature's wonderful beauties as you have displayed within easy distance." Col. William Jones spearheaded the campaign to develop Boulder County tourism by recycling the old mining line, the Colorado & Northwestern Railway, as the Switzerland Trail to mine tourists.
Ed Bathke & Tom Noel Collections

◆ Boulder owns more than 7,500 acres of mountain park land, ranging from Boulder Falls in Boulder Canyon to Fourth of July Campground in the Indian Peaks Wilderness, from Coot Lake on 63rd Street to 8,549-foot-high South Boulder Peak. *City of Boulder Parks and Recreation Department*

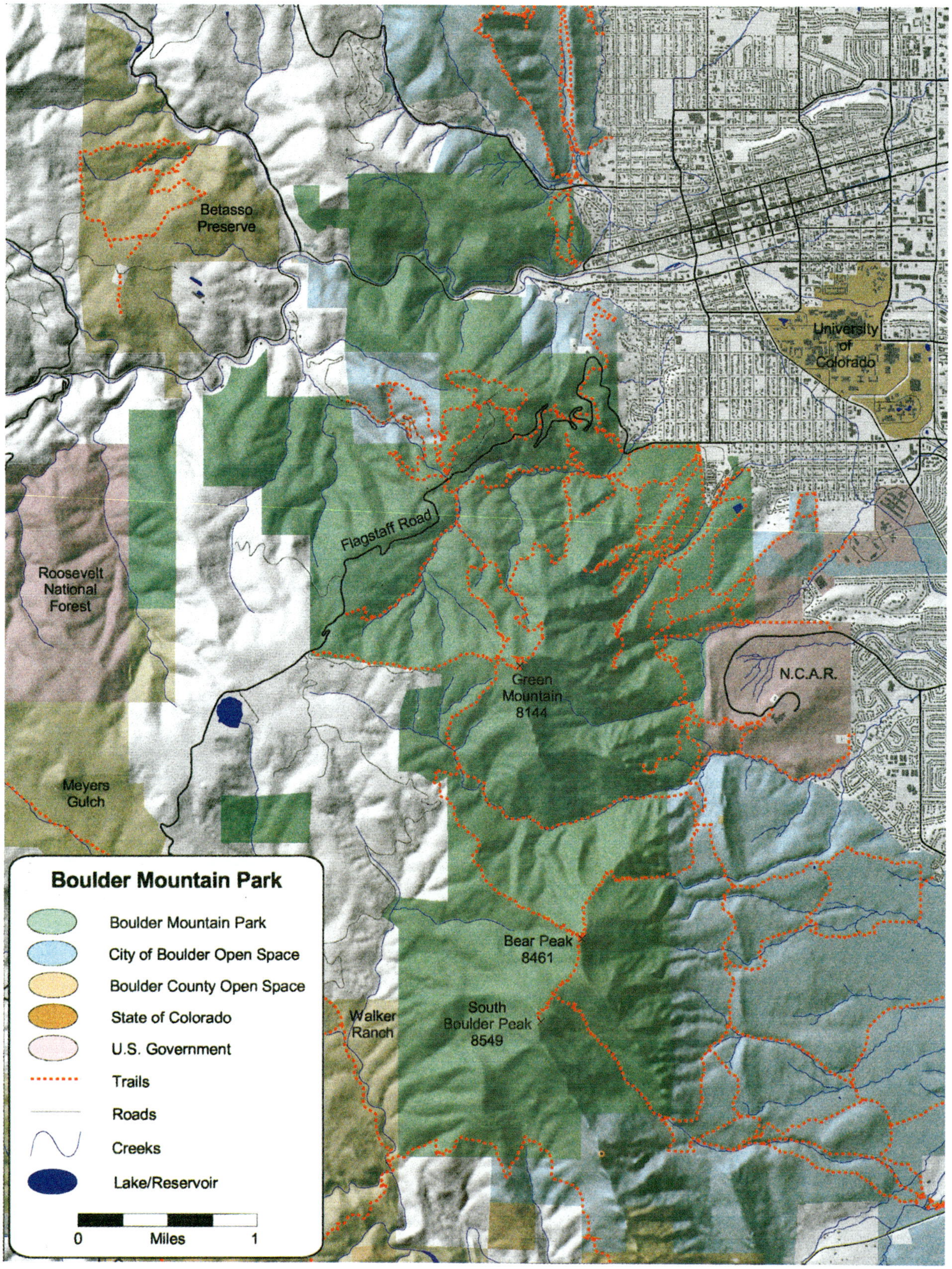

Betasso Preserve

University of Colorado

Flagstaff Road

Roosevelt National Forest

N.C.A.R.

Green Mountain 8144

Meyers Gulch

Bear Peak 8461

Walker Ranch

South Boulder Peak 8549

Boulder Mountain Park

Boulder Mountain Park
City of Boulder Open Space
Boulder County Open Space
State of Colorado
U.S. Government
Trails
Roads
Creeks
Lake/Reservoir

0 Miles 1

◆ Ernest "Dad" Greenman (1877-1960) championed Boulder's mountain parks. Whenever he could get away from his University Hill drug store, Greenman headed for the hills to work on trails, post fire danger and "no wildflower picking" signs or to plant apple trees along the Gregory Canyon trail. This 1922 shot captured one of his 101 climbs of the Third Flatiron. *Mary Ann Stevens Collection.*

Boulder Falls and its environs were donated to Boulder City as a park in 1914 by banker Charles Buckingham.
1969 photo by Ron Ruhoff

◆ Critics blasting modern-day Boulder environmentalists as tree huggers forget that earlier generations also loved trees. For decades tourists made pilgrimages to the Perfect Tree in Boulder Canyon, until it died naturally in 1898.
Peter Pollock postcard

◆ After an 1878 horseback ride through Boulder Canyon, Helen Hunt Jackson compared it in *Bits of Travel at Home* to "a joyous outburst of the soul of Beethoven or Mozart." Of her 16-mile ride from "Nederland Meadows" to "Bowlder City," she wrote "Bowlder people [are] lucky not in that gold and silver are brought down to their streets every day, but that they can walk of an afternoon up into Bowlder Canyon."
Western History Department, Denver Public Library

◆ Glaciers cling to the Continental Divide in the Arapaho (Indian) Peaks. The largest, Arapaho Glacier, is about a half mile long and wide, and about 200-feet thick. Early photos show a somewhat larger glacier although, despite global warming, Arapaho renews itself every winter.
1960 photo by Ron Ruhoff

Northwestern as a tourist railroad, the Switzerland Trail. Boulder persuaded the United States Congress to give the town an additional 1,800 acres of mountain backdrop in 1899. In 1912 Boulder purchased 1,200 acres from the federal government for $1.25 per acre, creating a mountain parks system which extended from Sunshine Canyon to South Boulder Peak. By the early 1930s Boulder owned 62 park acres within the city and 6,300 acres in the mountains.

Boulder's mountain lands included Arapaho Glacier, after the city bought it from the federal government for $4,618 in 1929. Rubberneckers soon began exploring this eternal patch of snow and ice snuggled up against the Continental Divide. Boulder parks booster Eben Fine used lantern slide shows and publications to organize hikes and horseback treks to the glacier. He fascinated audiences with stories such as this in his autobiography, *Remembered Yesterdays* (Boulder: Johnson Pub. Co., 1957):

Digging my heels in deeply at every step, I zigzagged my way to lessen the steepness of the grade. Suddenly I felt my left foothold breaking, and, realizing I was going to fall, I whirled around facing down hill. Grabbing my camera under my arm, I sat down in the mushy snow and ice and slid several hundred feet in less time than it takes to tell the story. I fully expected to land in that crevasse, but fortunately, managed to keep my feet in front of me, plowing up a furrow. As the grade slackened off a bit, I succeeded in stopping some distance above the crevasse, else I would likely be in "cold storage" today instead of here to tell the story.

While Fine championed Arapaho Glacier as the county's finest alpine slide, Boulder City engineer Fred Fair publicized two other glaciers, which he named Isabelle and Fair after his wife and himself. Fair urged the city to build a road up to the glaciers and negotiated with daredevil aviator Charles "Slim" Lindbergh, Jr., for a promotional glacier landing. Neither of these schemes got off the ground, thanks in part to warnings about over commercializing Boulder's natural beauties from the nation's foremost landscape architect.

Frederick Law Olmsted, Jr. Comes To Town

The Boulder City Improvement Association organized in 1903 to pursue the "improvement of Boulder in health, growth, cleanliness, prosperity and attractiveness." As a first step, the Association sought to create a park around Chautauqua and to acquire and develop other park lands. With the help of local landscape architect W. W. Parce, they created the Chautauqua "green." The Association lobbied for the creation of a Parks Board in Boulder in 1907 and persuaded the City Council to reject new annexations unless 10 percent of the land was set aside for parks.

◆ The Boulderado Hotel originated with a 1906 community subscription drive after no private parties answered appeals to build a first class hotel in the city. "Without a decent hotel," the *Daily Camera* argued, "you can never expect that Boulder will be a city of 20,000."
Peter Pollock postcard

To masterplan city parks, the Association retained America's premier landscape architect, Frederick Law Olmsted, Jr., of Brookline, Massachusetts. Although reluctant to come to a small town of only 10,000, Olmsted agreed for a fee of $700 plus traveling expenses. Arriving in Boulder during a May, 1908, snowstorm, Olmsted lectured at the University of Colorado, bicycled around town, climbed Mount Sanitas, hiked along Boulder Creek and rode horseback up Flagstaff Mountain and into Boulder Canyon. He produced a booklet, "The Improvement of Boulder, Colorado: Report to the City Improvement Association," a 1910 master plan that has guided Boulder ever since.

Olmsted praised the "pleasant pretty little town with a character all its own" as "a place where things seem ripe to happen." He saw Boulder as "a city of agreeable homes" and discouraged heavy manufacturing. Olmsted proposed converting a few wide streets into grand boulevards, including a foothills parkway along 5th Street. With accurate foresight, he identified 28th Street, then a dirt lane, as a major future artery. This prediction came true with the 1963 opening of Crossroads Mall. University Avenue developed as a result of Olmsted's idea of making it "a grand promenade worthy of a state university." He also urged Boulderites to outlaw billboards and bury power lines.

Olmsted's recommendations ranged from Herculean to easily implemented, such as avoiding soft cottonwoods and silver maples in favor of honey locust, red and white oak, ash and linden trees. He suggested that no development be allowed south of Baseline Road. Olmsted urged Boulder to convert 20 percent more land to parks so that every citizen would be within a quarter mile of a park.

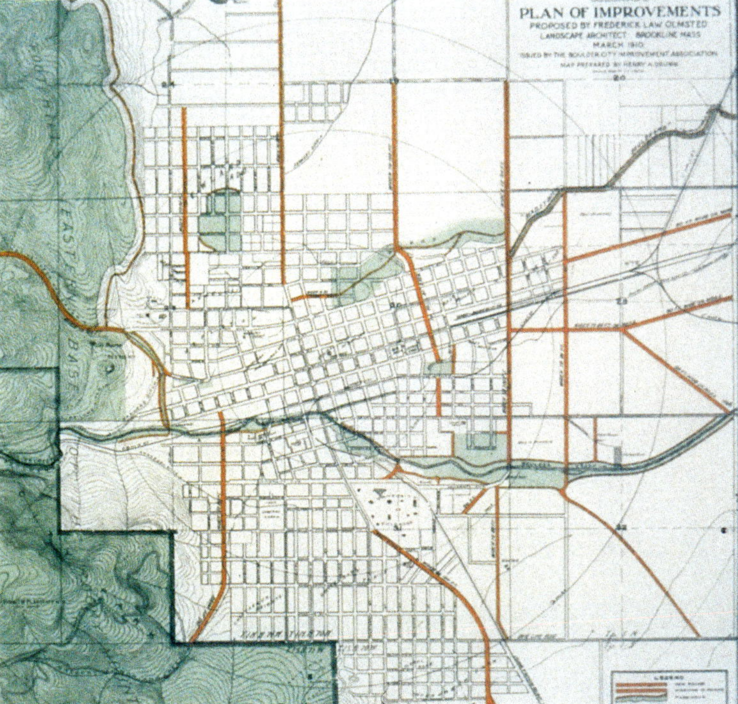

◆ Frederick Law Olmsted, Jr.'s 1908 visit to Boulder resulted in a 1910 masterplan for parkways and neighborhood parks, including a city park on North Broadway named for the famed Massachusetts landscape architect.
Peter Pollock collection

◆ Boulder courted tourists with this 1926 billboard installed by the American Legion at the junction of U.S. 287 and Arapahoe Road. *Photo by Ed Tangen, Carnegie Branch Library for Local History, Boulder Historical Society Collection*

Olmsted's most ambitious plans were for Boulder Creek, then an eyesore lined with mills, factories and a shantytown. Olmsted advocated a "clean park path running beside the murmuring water" with trees to screen the "rather unattractive clan of occupants." He pointed out that Boulder Creek's flooding could be reduced by creekside green space. When Olmsted returned 13 years later, he found the creek still unimproved. So he prepared a plan called "Improvement of Boulder Creek," urging the city to buy bottom land for a streamside park and a new city hall.

Many of Olmsted's green dreams came true. Boulder aggressively bought creekfront property and in the 1980s installed its prize-winning Boulder Creek Path. Several of Olmsted's park prescriptions were filled, including Canyon and North Boulder parks. Boulder also followed his stream-side recommendation for city hall in 1951. The reclaimed creek became the site of Boulder's current Municipal Building. Boulder, with encouragement from Olmsted, returned to its creek-side roots, to the waterway which gave the city its name.

◆ (Right and opposite page top) Boulder's shantytown, which locals called The Jungle, lay between Boulder Creek and the railroad tracks (now Canyon Boulevard) from Broadway to 9th Street. During the 1920s the homeless were moved to build Olmsted's creekfront park. The old trail is now a paved recreational path. *Carnegie Branch Library for Local History, Boulder Historical Society Collection; 1997 photo by Tom Noel*

Zoning & Saco DeBoer

Boulder's 1917 charter created a Planning and Parks Commission to produce "a comprehensive plan for the physical improvement of development in the city." In 1921 Olmsted urged Boulder to adopt a zoning ordinance. After the legality of zoning was upheld in 1926 by the United States Supreme Court in the landmark case of *Village of Euclid v. Ambler Realty Company*, City Manager Scott Mitchell and the City Council agreed to hear a zoning proposal from Denver planner Saco R. DeBoer. This Dutch immigrant had become the region's most prominent proponent of parks, planning and zoning. DeBoer, who worked on zoning plans for Denver and Grand Junction, charged $2,000 for his plan. He recommended 17 small neighborhood shopping centers, 13 of which the City Council approved. His 1928 zoning plan created Boulder's first height restrictions, limiting downtown buildings to 75 feet and neighborhood shopping districts to 35 feet. Not all citizens were enamored with the new-fangled concept of zoning. One vocal opponent complained to the City Council in 1927 that Boulder was already over-regulated "and now someone proposes to tell us what kind of houses we can live in."

◆ Shantytown has given way to a hike-bike path (above) and Boulder's Municipal Building, designed by local architect James Hunter. Shown here at its 1952 dedication, this International-style city hall originally faced Broadway, but was re-oriented to face Canyon Boulevard during a renovation. *Carnegie Branch Library for Local History, Boulder*

Between 1890 and 1920 Boulder grew from 3,330 to 11,223. During the next 20 years, the population increased by only 2,000. Boulder suffered less than most cities from the Depression because of the stabilizing effect of the university, whose enrollments and employees seemed relatively unaffected by Colorado's boom and bust cycles.

DeBoer cautioned Boulder that its growth as a residential center could "do more harm than good and might destroy what the city is proud of." In 1938 he recommended further planning outside the city to protect the greenbelt of mountain parks and agricultural land. Such extra-territorial schemes became another hallmark of Boulder's planning.

Besides open space, DeBoer focused on transportation. He recommended a direct highway between Boulder and Denver — the turnpike approach, which had been advocated by University of Colorado civil

◆ (Right and below) Boulder's Pearl Street has long bustled as the commercial center of Boulder County. Since its 1977 conversion to a pedestrian mall, people watchers as well as shoppers flock there to encounter local celebrities such as historian Silvia Pettem, shown below with Historic Boulder, Inc.'s Kathryn Barth. They are discussing the 1999 landmarking of downtown Boulder. *1946 Peter Pollock postcard; 1998 photo by Tom Noel*

engineering professor Roderick L. Downing since 1912. Also foreseeing the Diagonal Highway, DeBoer suggested a direct route to Longmont as the crow flies.

When DeBoer updated Boulder's zoning code in the 1948, he recommended gradually annexing land around the city to gain control of surrounding development and to increase the city's tax base. He argued, "It is better to extend the city limits now while there is little building activity than to wait until large areas are built up and many problems incurred in connection with annexation."

The Danish Plan

DeBoer's advice was heeded. During the years following World War II, Boulder experienced an unrestricted growth surge until the 1976 passage of the controversial growth-limiting Danish Plan, named for Councilman Paul Danish. A CU history student who edited the *Colorado Daily* during the 1960s, he gained notoriety as a ringleader of Boulder's "green necks," who pursued radical environmental goals. His Danish Plan restricted residential building permits to an increase of two percent per year. After serving on the Boulder City Council from 1976 to 1982, Danish became a Boulder County Commissioner.

As a CU graduate, Danish knew well the university's ambitious growth pattern. Thanks to the G. I. Bill and the huge influx of people after World War II, the university population more than doubled between 1940 and 1950 — from 3,846 to 8,866. It has since tripled. Appalled at such huge increases, Danish rallied those wary of the Chamber of Commerce crowd addicted to growth. The growing, land-hungry university would be caught up in the controversy.

Not only the university, but many business people wanted a bigger Boulder. Boosters cheered the Chamber of Commerce's 1949 donation of a site to the subscription division of *Esquire* magazine (now Neodata). A similar 1950 subscription drive led to the city's purchase and donation of 217 acres of land south

◆ Cattle grazed at Enchanted Mesa before the construction of the National Bureau of Standards helped launch Boulder's post-World War II growth boom. *Carnegie Branch Library for Local History, Boulder Historical Society's Daily Camera Collection*

of town for the National Bureau of Standards (now the National Institute for Standards and Technology). After the bureau built below the mesa, a developer proposed a large luxury hotel there as well. Alarmed opponents hosted a 1962 Fourth of July fund-raising picnic on the mesa to advertise the threat. This began a successful crusade to persuade Boulder voters to approve a $105,000 bond issue to purchase 155 acres to stop the development. This scheme preserved the mesa for hikers, dogwalkers, sledders and those who just wanted to sit on outcropping rocks and enjoy a sweeping view of the foothills.

This success on Enchanted Mesa followed some setbacks such as the 1955 Beech Aircraft plant, which scarred otherwise rural foothills north of Boulder. That same year the Boulder Industrial Park opened east of the city. The first tenant, Ball Brothers Research Corporation, launched a still booming high-tech industry. Ball Brothers, the progeny of a Muncie, Indiana jar maker, became Boulder's largest employer, with 3,000 on the payroll. Further development came with the state's 1960 donation of a 530-acre Table Mesa site for the National Center for Atmospheric Research (NCAR).

Outside the city, the Atomic Energy Commission's 1951 research plant at Rocky Flats also accelerated growth. Initially, Boulder officials dismissed concerns about this huge facility for making plutonium triggers for nuclear weapons. Boulder Mayor J. Perry Bartlett

◆ The National Bureau of Standards, dedicated by President Dwight D. Eisenhower in 1954, was built on 217 acres of land donated by Boulder citizens. As this 1955 photo shows, the first houses soon popped up east of Broadway while Green Mountain Cemetery residents slumber across the street in their tree-shaded enclave.
Carnegie Branch Library for Local History, Boulder Historical Society's Daily Camera Collection

◆ Boulder officials smiled at Rocky Flats' 1951 groundbreaking, calling it economic progress and motivation to pave the road between Boulder and Golden. The plant, which manufactured plutonium triggers for nuclear bombs, became a hot spot by 1983, when these pacifist protesters tried to encircle Rocky Flats plant. Allen Ginsberg, the great American poet, entertained demonstrators with his "Plutonium Ode," noting that the deadly stuff was named for Pluto, Greek god of death and the underworld. Such protests led the plant to close in 1989 and begin a multi-billion dollar clean up of its toxic wastes.
Carnegie Branch Library for Local History, Boulder

proclaimed, "I feel no alarm over any potential hazard from the location of the plant near Boulder." As a result of these new job-generating industries, South Boulder expanded with new housing in Highland Park and Martin Acres.

Boulder was also affected by rapid growth in the entire Denver metropolitan area after World War II. The Denver-Boulder Turnpike made Boulder a convenient bedroom community for commuters. The Chamber of Commerce promoted the road, which shortened the trip to Denver from one hour to 30 minutes. The turnpike's completion in 1952 accelerated Boulder's growth greatly. The little college town of 1940 tripled to 37,718 people by 1960 and almost doubled its population again between 1960 and 1970.

Growth led to more ambitious planning. A Boulder Valley-focused Planning Commission consisting of representatives from the city, Boulder County and the school district was formed in 1950, with Trafton Bean as coordinator. A year later Boulder voters approved a charter change separating the Planning Board from the Parks Board. The Boulder City Council adopted a "Guide for Growth" map in 1958. It prescribed increased density in the city's core, new industrial zones and neighborhood shopping centers. Developers wanting their land annexed to Boulder in order to gain city services, were required to donate parks.

◆ Trafton H. Bean became Boulder's first planning director in 1952. As the joint regional planner for the city, county and school district, he launched Boulder County's first attempt at intergovernmental cooperation and master planning. Bean's many innovations included requiring developers to dedicate park land in residential subdivisions — a Colorado first. *Brent Bean Collection*

PLAN-Boulder

Just as the old Boulder City Improvement Association emerged in the 1900s, a new civic group appeared in 1959 to advocate planned growth. It started with a citizens' initiative to stop development in Boulder's scenic foothills by refusing to provide city water services above a 5,750-foot "blue line." CU Professors Robert McKelvey and Albert Bartlett hiked the threatened area and spearheaded this scheme. To implement the "blue line," the two professors and their compatriots formed PLAN-Boulder (People's League for Action Now) to promote "a more imaginative and enlightened pattern of community development."

PLAN-Boulder put the "Blue Line" on the ballot and Boulder voters passed it 2,735 to 852. PLAN-Boulder next successfully pushed through a 1962 ballot measure to purchase Boulder's Enchanted Mesa, thus saving it from hotel development.

PLAN-Boulder's greatest achievement was the 1967 creation of the first open space tax in the United States. The group's chair and attorney, Ruth Wright, later became a state legislator. She spearheaded PLAN-Boulder's agenda along with City Manager Francis J. "Ted" Tedesco, and others. Their proposed sales tax increase to purchase open space won with a 57 percent majority. An Open Space Board of Trustees was created six years later to identify, purchase and maintain open space lands. Encouraged by the open space success, PLAN-Boulder in 1971 placed a 55-foot building height limit on the ballot. This campaign, inspired by plans for a high-rise hotel, also gained voter approval.

◆ This poster urges voters to support Boulder's 1967 open space ballot measure. It worked. Boulder became the first U.S. city to use a sales tax to purchase open space. *1967 photo by Harold Malde, poster courtesy of PLAN-Boulder County*

Comprehensive Boulder Valley Planning

The mountain parks, Blue Line and open space were only the beginning of Boulder's efforts to control development outside its city limits. The city began to push growth control countywide. Although the techniques changed, the vision remained constant — a compact city surrounded by open space.

A 1964 Boulder City Planning Department report, "Boulder's Fringe Area Objectives," stated that growth could occur in three ways: through high-rise development, through sprawl or through the use of semi-autonomous sub-communities, each with their own retail areas and schools. The sub-community approach was recommended. Gunbarrel became the guinea pig when IBM built its huge plant in that northeast Boulder neighborhood in 1965.

The first Boulder Valley Comprehensive Plan of 1970 was jointly signed by four bodies — the Boulder City Council, the Board of County Commissioners and the city and county planning commissions. A more detailed 1978 document required all four governmental bodies to approve any changes.

A citizen-initiated "Zero Population Growth" ballot measure to limit Boulder's population to 100,000 failed in 1971. Five years later, voters approved the 2 percent residential growth limitation of the Danish Plan for an experimental five-year period. Subsequent ordinances continued to limit the number of residential building permits. Because of the negative effect on business planning, a controversial attempt to also limit commercial and industrial building permits was abandoned in 1997. Current planning challenges include affordable housing options for Boulder's middle-class, which is being priced out of the home ownership and rental market by soaring land values.

Historic Boulder, Inc., like the Boulder City Improvement Association and PLAN-Boulder, began as a grass-roots effort. HB formed in the early 1970s to fight the demolition of significant historic buildings. Whether the cause is historic preservation, increased green space parks or growth management, an active citizenry has made Boulder a pacesetter. As Boulder Planning Director Peter Pollock observed, "Only citizen advocacy can give courage to politicians to initiate community deliberation over a long-range plan and then implement that vision."

◆ Allen J. Lefferdink built downtown Boulder's only highrise, the nine-story Colorado Building with a rooftop heliport. During its 1950s-1960s heyday, Lefferdink Enterprises, Inc. included Allen Enterprises, Inc., Allen Investment Company, Allied Colorado Enterprises, Boulder Cemetery Association, Boulder Industrial Bank, Commonwealth Industrial Bank, Colorado Stock Transfer Corporation, Magic Mountain, Inc., Midway Oil Company, Mountain Savings & Loan Association and Tower Merchandise Mart, Inc. Lefferdink also bought what was then Lakewood's largest shopping center, Villa Italia, and Denver's grand old downtown landmark, the Daniels & Fisher Tower. Lefferdink's career, like that of mining magnates, followed a boom-bust trajectory that left his empire in bankrupt shambles. *Woody Eaton Collection*

CU: The Flush Times

While Boulder City curtailed growth, the University of Colorado planned to grow into a major research university. This dream started with the first president, science professor Joseph Sewall, but did not materialize until after World War II. Even before the war, CU established its High Altitude Observatory near Climax in 1940. The war slowed university growth, but CU captured some wartime programs to pick up the slack. Although far from an ocean, CU set up a Naval Reserve Scientific Training Unit in 1941 and converted dormitories into naval barracks.

CU lost students to the war effort but boomed when peace came in 1945. To meet the demands of post-war enrollment increases, university personnel went door-to-door seeking extra sleeping rooms for students. When there were not enough Boulder beds to meet the demand, the university built "Vetsville." This village of trailers and Quonset huts at Folsom and Arapahoe still left hundreds on the waiting list.

Besides wrestling with growth, CU faced a communist witch hunt in the 1950s. Despite the human rights legacy of President George Norlin who had defended Catholic and Jewish faculty against the KKK in the 1920s, Philosophy Instructor Morris Judd lost his job in 1952. After he refused to answer questions about past membership in the Communist Party, he was dismissed as a "pedestrian" academic.

◆ The National Center for Atmosphere Research on Boulder's Table Mesa was the dream of Dr. Walter Orr Roberts of Boulder. Roberts commissioned I.M. Pei, the world's best known living architect, to design NCAR. Pei drew inspiration from Indian pueblos of the American Southwest and used local soil and rock for the masonry aggregate, giving NCAR its rosy skin. *1993 photo by Tom Noel*

◆ CU's 1965 Engineering Center combines red tile shed roofs and sandstone trim, a concession to the traditional campus architecture of Charles Klauder, with the dramatic verticality and raw concrete of the Mine Shaft Modern Style. *1998 photo by Tom Noel*

President Norlin, after a long and distinguished tenure, was succeeded in 1939 by CU's sixth president, Robert L. Stearns (1939-1953). During the early 1950s, McCarthy-era persecutors of communists focused on Philosophy Professor David Hawkins, a one-time member of the Communist Party who had refused to incriminate friends and relatives before the House Un-American Activities Committee. The Colorado legislature accused Stearns of coddling commies.

"Stearns," asked one legislator, "is it true that you're teaching communism at CU?"

"Yes. We are teaching communism in Boulder. And we are also teaching syphilis at the medical school in Denver. But we advocate neither."

Stearns weathered the storm, despite pressure to curb free thought and free speech on campus. During one protest he was struck on the head by a rock, but he, his wife and four daughters continued to live in the heart of the campus in the president's house.

◆ Boulder's tallest structures are at Williams Village, shown here under construction in 1966. Boulder architect Hobart D. Wagoner designed the152-foot-tall towers on land donated by the Williams family at 30th Street and Baseline Road. *Carnegie Branch Library for Local History, Boulder Historical Society's Daily Camera Collection*

◆ (Far right) One of America's favorite mid-20th-century poets, Robert Frost, died in 1963 but lives in this 1997 bronze by George Lundeen in front of CU's Old Main. Frost visited Boulder during the 1920s and 1930s to see his daughter, Marjorie, a patient at the Colorado Sanitarium. CU recruited the New England bard to lead its Writers Conference, put him up at the Hotel Boulderado and, in 1939, awarded him an honorary degree. *1999 photo by Tom Noel*

CU President Quigg Newton (1956-1963) found the post even more turbulent than the job he had just left as mayor of Denver. Newton, the last president to live on campus, recalled in 1999: "I was hung in effigy outside my door for firing a winning football coach and accused of protecting communists on the faculty. We fired Everett 'Sonny' Grandeluis in 1962 because he had violated NCAA rules, even though we had beaten the University of Oklahoma, captured the Big Eight title and taken the Buffs to the Orange Bowl."

◆ Red tile roofs and light-colored masonry structures characterize the University of Colorado at Boulder. The unique "Tuscan style," transplanted from the foothills of northern Italy to Colorado's foothills, distinguishes one of America's most attractive and well-planned campuses.
1998 photo by William L. Breeder

While humbling the mighty, Newton defended the persecuted. He protected professors such as Hawkins against critics clamoring for their dismissal. Newton steadfastly pursued academic excellence. CU captured nationally acclaimed Harvard scientist Walter Orr Roberts and the National Center for Atmospheric Research (NCAR) as well as the National Bureau of Standards and the Joint Institute for Laboratory Astrophysics (JILA). Compatible industries such as Ball Brothers Research Corporation, Beech Aircraft and IBM were courted for public-private partnerships.

CU's scientific investment paid off. CU astronauts include Malcolm Scott Carpenter of Boulder and Vance Brand of Longmont. In 1989 university chemist Thomas Cech became the first Coloradan to receive a Nobel Prize.

CU's development required new buildings that, for the most part, remained true to Charles Klauder's architectural master plan for the campus. Most notable is the 1953 University Memorial Center, built with donations to honor CU's World War II dead. To ensure that future design decisions would follow these examples, CU established a Design Review Board in 1964. University architect William Deno has overseen designs that reflect Klauder's spirit while providing flexibility for more contemporary buildings as CU grew to more than 25,000 students by the year 2000.

CU, as president John Buechner noted on the eve on the millennium, cherishes its reputation as one of America's most beautiful and well-planned campuses. President Buechner, a former Boulder mayor, added that CU drew inspiration from its setting in one of America's most beautiful and well-planned cities.

◆ University expansion and parking threaten the Craftsman-style bungalows in the Grandview Terrace neighborhood on the northwest border of campus. In 1999 Colorado Preservation, Inc. placed the terrace on Colorado's Most Endangered Places list.
1999 photo by Tom Noel

1973 photo from Daily Camera

Historic Boulder, Inc. Collection

1999 photo by Tom Noel

1999 photo by Tom Noel

Longmont Museum

Preserving Boulder County

Chapter *Nine*

"Thank God for Boulder County's Open Space and Historic Preservation programs. They've helped us protect Lyons with open spaces like Hall and Heil ranches. That's a 10,000-acre buffer on the southwest side of town to stop all these homes creeping up into the mountains."

—LaVern Johnson of Lyons, 1999

"I'm not against growth," LaVern Johnson explained. "I'm against fast growth. I always go to every town board meeting to keep an eye on things. Some newcomers, especially developers, think nothing happened until they came here.

"Lyons is a paradise, but we've had to fight to keep it that way. Back in 1982, they wanted to build Coffintop Reservoir with a 400-foot-high dam that would have flooded St. Vrain Canyon. Fortunately we buried that plan. I hope to die here and be buried with the rest of my family under our local headstones. Lyons is paradise, with less wind, snow, cold and people than Boulder. But Lyons must fight to keep its open space, scenery and historic sandstone buildings."

1998 photo by Tom Noel

Boulder County owes much to dedicated citizens such as LaVern McConnell Johnson. Her great grandfather, John Reese, arrived in 1862 to join Edward S. Lyon in forming the town where LaVern was born in 1927. Ed Lyon and his wife Adeline came west from

◆ LaVern Johnson, the guardian angel of Lyons, has championed parks, preservation and cautious growth. She helped erect this memorial in Sandstone Park to her husband, who was also named LaVerne but with an "e." He helped her make Lyons a model for both preservationists and conservationists "My philosophy," she reports, "is that if you want something done, do it yourself. Take whoever will come along with you and hope the rest will leave you alone. If they're not helping, they don't get to criticize."
1999 photo by Tom Noel

◆ (Far right) The Hugh Murphy Quarry crew posed for this company photo sometime between 1881, when the quarry opened, and 1915, when it closed. Later renamed the John Brodie, this red sandstone quarry stood on the north side of Lyons. Of a dozen quarries, only the Ohline Quarry on Blue Mountain never closed. The Sprague and Buster quarries have reopened to provide Lyons sandstone for restorations and new construction.
Lyons Redstone Museum

◆ Lyons has preserved both its natural and built environments. Both are dominated by the local "red" sandstone, which actually varies from red to orange to pink to grey.
1999 photo by Tom Noel

Connecticut for his health. His cousin Nathan, a Civil War hero, had given his name to Fort Lyon in southeastern Colorado.

Ed Lyon went first to Black Hawk, then Boulder. Still restless, he took weekend horseback rides looking for a better place to settle. Where South and North St. Vrain creeks join, he found a valley that offered spectacular scenery, good water and beautiful red sandstone. His Lyons Townsite & Quarry Company, established in 1880, received a post office two years later.

The town was rich in sandstone and lime which is used to make mortar and plaster. Townsfolk took the stone and lime in wagons down the St. Vrain Creek Road to Longmont until the Union Pacific built a spur line to Lyons in 1884. From the little Lyons depot, sandstone was shipped all over the United States. Lyons residents also used the soft pink stone for their homes and for many local buildings, including the 1881 schoolhouse, the 1882 hotel, the 1885 railroad depot and the 1894 Congregational Church. By 1890 eight quarries were in operation.

Lyons incorporated in 1891, anticipating a future as rosy as its stone. Despite being showcased on the CU campus, sandstone went out of style during the early 20th century. Cement, cast stone, terra cotta and brick all proved to be cheaper, more weather-resistant and more popular. When most of the quarries closed, Lyons residents turned to apple and cherry orchards, ranching, growing meadow hay, lumbering and working in mines at Jamestown and Nederland.

While the quarry business ebbed, a flood of tourists to Rocky Mountain National Park sustained Lyons. The town erected a Welcome Arch across U.S. 36 in 1932. At the wooden gateway, tourists faced two equally scenic alternatives — the north or south St. Vrain Canyon routes to the high Rockies.

Lyons resisted the blatant commercialization that blighted Estes Park. It remains a small, prim town of less than 1,700 souls, wary of growth. The town still glories most in its sandstone. Townsfolk have restored many landmarks and earned a National Register District designation for a well-preserved collection of 15 rustic sandstone landmarks, ranging from a dynamite shed to the McAllister Saloon. A prime agitator behind all this was LaVern Johnson.

"We formed the Lyons Historical Society in 1973," LaVern explained in 1999, "to save the old depot, which the Union Pacific wanted to tear down. We restored it as the public library. Since then we've also recycled the old sandstone electric plant next to the library as our town hall, converted the 1881 school to the Lyons Redstone Museum and restored the 1934 WPA river rock picnic shelter in Meadow Park. We've also passed a 1 percent sales and use tax to buy and improve parkland. We tax developers 75 cents per square foot to fund recreation. We've used that money for Sandstone Park (1985), Meadow Park (1987), Bohn Park (1993), and South St. Vrain Trail (1996), Olson Park (2000) and the old Griff Evans homestead, ice house and stage stop, where we hold our Blue Grass Festival."

◆ In this 1908 Ed Tangen photo of Lyons, the rail cars are loaded with local sandstone. The sandstone school on the hill is now the Lyons Redstone Museum.
Carnegie Branch Library for Local History, Boulder Historical Society Collection

◆ Lyons erected this Welcome Arch to greet tourists but took it down in 1940 because motorists kept running into it.
Lyons Redstone Museum

◆ Sandstone Park opened in 1985 on the site of the old sandstone sales lot. Lyons sandstone walkways feature carvings of local wild animals such as this mountain lion.
1999 photo by Tom Noel

Conservation & Preservation

Preservation, which Lyons has handled particularly well, has appealed to a county experiencing rapid growth. Boulder County's preservation movement, like many others across America, sprang out of the 1960 conservation movement. The environmental activists of PLAN-Boulder launched the city's innovative open space program in 1967. Besides protecting the natural environment, some conservationists also began to focus on saving historic-built environments and cultural landscapes.

Since the 1970s Boulder County has encouraged preservation at the local level. Three preservation firsts came in the 1970s. Historic Boulder, Inc. (HB), a private non-profit organization formed in 1972, became the county's first preservation advocacy group. The Longmont City Council enacted the county's first municipal preservation ordinance in 1971. The 1979 Louisville City Council empowered the Louisville Historical Commission to survey buildings for National Register eligibility.

In 1992 Boulder became the first county in Colorado to enact historic preservation legislation. Subsequently, even tiny mountain towns such as Nederland, Gold Hill and Ward have created their own preservation programs. In 1996 Canfield passed a local preservation ordinance. Lafayette in 1999 likewise passed legislation authorizing municipal designation of local landmarks.

Boulder County and its local communities have tried different preservation tactics. Each community has approached the issues differently, sometimes with innovative programs that have captured national and state awards. Appropriately, preservation efforts began in the county's first mining town.

Gold Hill

Gold Hill, Boulder County's first important mining camp, struck it rich again with the first historic preservation zoning in unincorporated Boulder County. Residents in 1968 successfully lobbied the Board of County Commissioners to establish a historical zoning district. The Gold Hill Organization to Safeguard the Town (GHOST) also proposed preserving 3,000 acres of their mountain environs, but the county commissioners limited historical zoning to the townsite itself. In 1972 Gold Hill wrestled from the county the right to review all building permits for new construction in the town.

Gold Hill's charm is epitomized by its general store which is an antidote for Colorado's ubiquitous strip

◆ Gold Hillers fought to keep their quaint three-room school open, becoming one of the few towns in America to successfully resist consolidation into a larger, more distant modern school.
1996 photo by Ron Ruhoff

◆ The Gold Hill Store is the town's year-around hub, offering groceries, newspapers, coffee, monster chocolate chip cookies, the work of local artists, a public library in the attic and a loafers' bench in the front.
1995 photo by Tom Noel

malls and shopping centers. Hugh Moore, a fourth-generation Coloradan, owns and operates the Gold Hill Store as a year-round town center. Inside this 1880s frame antique, the pot bellied stove has footrails to warm your toes. As this is the only store in town, Hugh sells nearly everything from hardware to software, from deli lunches to chocolate chip cookies. He donates the store attic for the town's 3,000-volume public library. To promote the lost art of loafing around the general store, he put benches in front and chairs and tables in the backyard.

Not only this vintage general store but Gold Hill's 1874 two-room schoolhouse are still in use — Gold Hillers successfully fought efforts to bus its children to a consolidated, modern school. Another landmark, St. James Catholic Church, is a round log edifice built in 1938 by Tim Walter. The town restored St. James in 1999 as the municipal museum and archives.

Pursuing an antiquated lifestyle in a new age, Gold Hillers refuse to pave even Main Street. They resist the "progress" that has transformed other mountain towns into residential subdivisions, preferring bumpy dirt roads to the city slickers. General storekeeper Hugh Moore reflects: "We love this place because it hasn't changed much in 100 years, even though we're now only 10 miles from a metropolis of two million people. Our dirt roads have become our moat." With the help of a National Register Historic District Designation and a local preservation committee, Gold Hill shines as one of America's best preserved mining camps.

Historic Boulder, Inc.

Both public and private agencies have championed preservation. Historic Boulder, Inc., a private group, was organized to deal with rapid growth and demolition of cherished older structures in the county seat. Boulderites strove to protect the town's main street with the creation of the Pearl Street pedestrian mall in the 1970s. The mall district focused on preserving historic architecture, public spaces and mountain views. Interest in saving Boulder's downtown gained support after construction of the nine-story Colorado Building at 14th and Walnut streets, inspiring a 1971 citizens' initiative establishing a 55-foot height limit downtown. Boulder's 1986 Urban Design Plan called for construction on a pedestrian scale, compatibility with existing buildings and respect for solar access and mountain views.

◆ A time warp at the end of a rugged dirt road, Gold Hill tiptoed into the 20th century warily. With the help of a National Register Historic District Designation and a local preservation committee, Gold Hill enters the 21st century as one of America's best preserved mining camps. *1995 photo by Tom Noel*

◆ (Left photos and following page) Boulder's 1890 Union Pacific Depot was home for the Switzerland Trail, shown (next page) in its virgin run. To preserve the depot, the Boulder Jaycees bought it in 1973 and moved it from 14th and Canyon Boulevard to the Pow Wow grounds at 30th and Pearl streets.
Carnegie Branch Library for Local History, Boulder Historical Society's Daily Camera Collection,
1890s postcard Peter Pollock Collection, Colorado Historical Society

Colorado Historical Society

While the mall enhanced and enriched downtown's ambiance, the rest of Boulder's built environment was still endangered during the 1960s and 1970s boom. Joyce Davies, a founder of Historic Boulder, Inc. and its first president, recalls that "many small older buildings were being demolished. Money started flowing in and the developers said the bigger the better."

◆ (Right and below) Highland School narrowly escaped the clutches of a developer bent on replacing it with a high-rise apartment. Historic Boulder, Inc.rescued this handsome, historic school on Boulder Creek near 9th Street and Arapahoe Avenue, now elegantly restored as office space.
1995 Photo by Tom Noel; Rob Pudim Cartoon from Historic Boulder, Inc. Collection

Davies and like-minded citizens formed Historic Boulder, Inc. in 1971 to stop proposed demolitions of the 1873 Central School at 15th and Walnut streets, the 1890 Union Pacific Depot at 14th Street and Canyon Boulevard, and the 1891 Highland School at 9th Street and Arapahoe Avenue. HB incorporated in February, 1972, two years after the birth of its prototype, Historic Denver, Inc. Mayor Robert Knecht, Planning Director Bill Lamont, *Daily Camera* editor Laurence Paddock and other civic leaders nourished the baby organization.

Historic Boulder, Inc. activist Margaret Hansen and others were outraged by statements such as that of the developer planning to level the Highland School. He promised to use stones from the wreckage to build a wall around the high rise that would replace it and told protesters, "What more can you ask?"

HB asked for more. It saved Highland School by raising money and obtaining loan guarantees to purchase the school in 1972. Historic Boulder, Inc. then lobbied the City Council to enact Boulder's Historic Preservation Code. Council responded in 1974 by creating the Landmarks Preservation Advisory Board. The Board has since designated more than 120 individual landmarks and some 900 other buildings within six local historic districts. To foster greater awareness of newer, architecturllly important buildings, the Board has also designated more than 64 Structures of Merit. Among these are I. M. Pei's National Center for Atmospheric Research (NCAR) and the highly original residential designs of Boulder architect Charles Haertling.

In 1994, at the urging of the Boulder Landmarks Board, the City Council passed a demolition ordinance requiring Landmarks Board review before demolition permits can be granted for any building over 50 years old. If such a building does not meet the requirements for an individual landmark, alternatives for its continued use are explored with the building's owner.

◆ The extraordinary designs of architect Charles Haertling (1928-1984) are found throughout Boulder. Here, Haertling inspects one of his expressionist masterpieces, the "Aspen Leaf" House in Pine Brook Hills. Many of Haertling's designs have been designated as Structures of Merit by the Boulder Landmarks Board, on which he served as well as being a city councilman.
Joel Haertling

◆ (Far right) The Whiteley-Hellems House was saved by Historic Boulder's revolving preservation fund. Richard Whiteley, a lawyer and state legislator, built the Queen Anne-style residence of Lyons sandstone in 1891. His sister, Hortense, married Dean F.B.R. Hellems of the University of Colorado and lived here after Richard died. Following Hortense's death, Hellems married her sister Zena and continued to live here.
Historic Boulder, Inc. Collection

◆ In 1979 Historic Boulder, Inc. members signed a one-year lease with an option to purchase the Art Deco-style Boulder Theater. This 1936 structure was designed by architect Robert Otto Roller to compliment the new Deco courthouse across 14th Street. HB used its revolving fund to save this colorful, fanciful theater.
1999 photo by Tom Noel

After getting the school landmarked, HB sold Highland School to a preservation-minded developer, using the proceeds to create a preservation revolving fund. That fund enabled Historic Boulder, Inc. to lease the endangered Boulder Theater in 1979. HB members sold popcorn, showed second-run movies and obtained landmark status for the theater. HB arranged a facade easement to give future owners a tax break.

Before the theater was secure, Historic Boulder, Inc. helped save the Whitely-Hellems House at 1709 Pine Street from the wrecking ball, giving that Queen Anne a second chance as condos. HB next bought the circa-1905 Edwardian cottage at 2104 Bluff Street in 1983. The house was redone by on-site restoration classes. This novel experiment impressed the National Trust for Historic Preservation, which gave HB its 1986 National Preservation Honor Award for the house's restoration.

"Preservation in Action," HB's slogan, took a new twist with the Technical Assistance Program (TAP). HB initiated TAP to help smaller Boulder County communities

◆ This Edwardian cottage at 2104 Bluff is Historic Boulder, Inc.'s national award-winning ROAR (Renovate Our Architectural Resources) House.
HB sold it in 1984, making a profit to pump into a revolving fund for other preservation projects.
Historic Boulder, Inc. Collection

HB's TAP PROJECTS:

- A preservation plan for Gold Hill's 1941 St. James Chapel and community design guidelines
- The Louisville Downtown Preservation Master Plan
- An archival project for the Lafayette Miner's Museum and Lafayette Public Library
- A preservation plan for Superior's 1890s Grasso Park collection of historic structures
- Restoration of Allenspark's 1888 Bunce School
- Restoration of Ward's 1898 Town Hall
- A preservation plan for Canfield's 1872 Wise Farmhouse
- Preservation plans for Nederland's 1937 Old Stone Garage and 1905 Gillaspie House
- Partnership with the Boulder County Parks and Open Space Department to landmark properties located on county open space.

and rural areas preserve their assets. TAP is the brainchild of Historic Boulder, Inc. Board members Betty Chronic and Margaret Hansen and former Executive Director Sandy Priester. To direct the program, HB hired a professional preservationist, Rebecca Waugh. Rebecca explained, "Our program, started in 1996, has helped outlying communities identify, preserve and celebrate their landmarks. Through this partnership approach, HB ensures that control of a project remains where it belongs — in the hands of the community." Colorado Preservation, Inc. (CPI), a statewide organization, honored this innovative program with its Dana Crawford Award in 1998.

HB opened its first office in the Highland School in 1978, then moved on to other quarters which it saved and restored. The early 1870s Woodward-Baird House at 1733 Canyon Boulevard housed HB from 1978 to 1993. This fine example of a small worker's cottage was affectionately called "The Little Grey House." Since 1993 HB has resided in the elaborately detailed 1877 Arnett-Fullen House at 646 Pearl Street. HB continues aggressive advocacy for threatened historic structures. In 1999, for instance, HB took on the University of

◆ Nederland's Stone Garage was designated a county landmark in 1997. Nederland cleaned up decades of motor oil, gas and diesel spills to convert this to the Nederland Mining Museum.
1999 photo by Tom Noel

◆ Historic Boulder, Inc. in 1978 renovated the Culver-Bixby-Woodward-Baird House, an 1870s National Register-listed workers cottage at 1733 Canyon Boulevard. Depicted here as a square of HB's world-traveling Boulder-landmarks quilt, it was owned for two years in the 1880s by newspaper editor and Boulder promoter Amos Bixby. *Historic Boulder, Inc. Collection*

Colorado, which planned to demolish the National Register-eligible Grandview Terrace neighborhood for parking space. This picturesque collection of bungalows and Craftsman-style homes, located on the north edge of campus overlooking Boulder Creek, once housed CU professors and small campus offices.

Longmont's Landmark Designation Commission

Longmont passed a preservation ordinance in its centennial year of 1971. Harriette Grigsby and other members of the St. Vrain Historical Society spearheaded this virginal piece of preservation. They feared that urban renewal efforts such as those that leveled much of downtown Denver might also devastate Longmont. To save Longmont's downtown from the wrecking ball, Harriette and her husband Robert contacted other cities around the country for advice, then drafted a historic preservation ordinance. County Commissioner Jack Murphy championed the ordinance before the City Council. "Jack assured me that he would do the talking, since I wasn't used to public speaking," Harriette Grigsby recalls. "Golden oratory flowed. His eloquent presentation compared Longmont's preservation battle with the 1814 Battle of New Orleans."

Longmont's City Council, persuaded by Murphy's eloquence and Grigsby's persistence, created a nine-member Landmark Designation Commission. Commissioners first focused on the 1892 Callahan House at 312 Terry Street. In 1938 the Callahan family had donated it to the

◆ The Nomad Playhouse, a 1951 Quonset hut, was designed as a theater by prominent Boulder architect James Hunter. This low budget theater was built on donated land at 14th and Quince in north Boulder. *Photo by William Cramer*

◆ (Far right) Genteel older homes find new uses as bed and breakfast inns. Boulder carpenter Jason L. Dwight built this cottage at 1305 Pine Street, which Col. John H. Nicholson enlarged in the Colonial Revival style. *1994 photo by Tom Noel*

city as a civic and social center for the women of Longmont. This use continues although well-behaved men are now also permitted inside. The Commission's second landmark was the St. Stephens' Episcopal Church at 470 Main Street. Instead of the proposed demolition, this 1881 Gothic gem is now reincarnated as an art gallery. Old Mill Park at 237 Pratt Street showcases structures moved to this site to avoid demolition, most notably the 1860 Affolter Cabin, the 1860 Hauck Milk House and the 1890 Billings Cabin.

◆ (Left photos)
Thomas M. Callahan lived in this 1892 home at 312 Terry Street with its elegant gardens and Grecian statuary. Callahan's Golden Rule Store on Main Street did so well selling dry goods that he opened a chain of similar stores in other towns. One of his employees, J.C. Penney, later bought out the Kemmerer, Wyoming, Golden Rule to establish his own chain of J.C. Penney's stores. The carriage house is the home of the St. Vrain Historical Society.
1998 photo by Tom Noel

In 1994 Longmont enacted a 90-day delay for demolition permits for landmark-eligible buildings more than 50 years old. Such delays give owners and preservationists time to consider alternatives to the

◆ Tom Callahan brought the first automobile to Longmont, a 1902 Locomobile steamer with a fringed canopy on top. Keeping up with her husband, Alice Callahan bought this electric car.
Longmont Museum

◆ (Right and below) St. Stephen's Episcopal Church, a lovely Gothic chapel, still stands at the southwest corner of 5th and Main streets, thanks to its 1974 designation as Longmont's second local landmark. *1998 photos by Tom Noel*

proposed demolition. In fast-growing Longmont, the Landmark Designation Preservation Commission also won the legal right to comment on historic and cultural resources in areas considered for annexation.

Longmont now boasts more than 85 local landmarks as well as a proposed Main Street district. Besides local landmarks, Longmont has three National Register Historic Districts —the East and the West Side Residential Districts and the Hoverhome Farmstead District.

Colorado's First County Landmark Ordinance

In 1990 Colorado passed a law permitting each of its 63 counties to enact historic preservation ordinances. The new legislation, which had been pushed by HB and Colorado Preservation, Inc., gave citizens a local tool to preserve landmarks outside of town and city limits. Boulder County preservationists and planners lost no time in taking advantage of the new legislation.

To prevent bickering, Republican Betty Chronic and Democrat Margaret Hansen developed a bipartisan team to work with the county commissioners and citizens concerned about property rights and the level of design review. Chronic, an advisor to the National Trust for Historic Preservation and National Register Review Board member, recalls, "It took more tact and working together than any previous historic preservation endeavor."

In 1992 the county commissioners added preservation amendments to the Boulder County Land Use Code. These new provisions created a Historic Preservation Advisory Board (HPAB) empowered to designate historic

◆ Reflecting small town America, Longmont's landmark-studded Main Street retains many of the one- and two-story commercial emporiums seen in this 1920s street scene. *Tom Noel Collection postcard*

◆ (Far left)
Anne Dyni poses in front of Niwot's former blacksmith shop, which she has converted into a store. Old Town Niwot, a charming block of Second Avenue, is Boulder County's first local historic district.
1998 photo by Tom Noel

◆ In the mountain town of Ward, the Columbia Hotel became a Boulder County Landmark in 1995. Built in 1900, it has three front doors and two second-story back doors on the uphill side. Restored in 1999, it once again welcomes guests.
1999 photo by Tom Noel

landmarks. This Board also reviews building and demolition permit applications for structures 50 years of age and older. If the structure is judged eligible for landmarking, a 120-day stay can be implemented to discuss alternatives to demolition or detrimental alterations.

Boulder County's HPAB designated the first county landmark on July 1, 1993 — the Orodell Townsite at the confluence of Boulder and Four-Mile creeks. Little remains of the town whose name is Latin for "gold vale." Besides a smelter, Orodell boasted a mill, stage stop, boarding house and general store. A devastating 1891 fire, 1894 flood and the ravages of time have obliterated most of this once rip-roaring gold camp.

Since Orodell's listing, more than 30 other county landmarks have been designated, including the Old Town Niwot District. The HPAB worked with towns such as Lafayette, Nederland and Ward to give their locally selected landmarks county designation.

The Lafayette Historic Preservation Board

Dana Coffield and her husband, Douglas Conarroe, admired the Queen Anne-style farmhouse on Baseline Road west of Lafayette. After the farm was annexed to the city in 1994 and faced demolition for a subdivision, they bought the house and moved it to 513 Elm Street. They donated the façade easement to Historic Boulder, Inc. for a tax break that enabled them to afford restoration. Subsequently, they persuaded Lafayette to establish a Historic Preservation Board in 1996 to make it easier to save other noteworthy structures. At first, buildings were designated under Boulder County's ordinance. Not until 1999 did the Lafayette City Council empower the Historic Preservation Board to locally designate landmarks. Lafayette's first landmark, the 1893 "Trader Jacks" building at 501 East Simpson Street, is the sole survivor of downtown's 1900 fire.

Led by local historian Steven Mehls, Lafayette's Historic Preservation Board initiated educational programs, such as the videotaping of long-time residents' recollections. In 1998 the Lafayette City Council set the pace for statewide arboreal preservation by creating Colorado's first "Tree Board." This citizen group identifies historic trees and works with owners to designate them as city landmarks. Although no other Colorado communities landmark trees, Lafayette's peers in arboreal appreciation include Los Angeles and New York City.

◆ The 1880s Anna Waneka Greenlee Thomas House was slated to be demolished for a subdivision development. Anna, the daughter of pioneer Adolph Waneka, raised 11 children in this Queen Anne-style home. It was moved to town in 1995 by Dana Coffield and Douglas Conarroe to spare it from demolition.
1999 photo by Tom Noel

◆ Lafayette's Miner's Museum has a treasure trove of memorabilia. This prized photograph captured the Lafayette Volunteer Fire Crew, which won the 1924 State Championship in hose racing.
Lafayette Miner's Museum

The Louisville Historical Commission

Louisville is blessed with many pioneer families and multi-generational businesses. To celebrate these roots, *Louisville Times* owners Percy and Carolyn Conarroe, Mayor John Waschak, City Manager Leon Wurl and the Louisville City Council created the Louisville Historical Commission in 1979. The Commission's first task was to survey the town for buildings eligible for the National Register of Historic Places. They successfully landmarked 13 structures, ranging from the 1908 Denver Grain Elevator to Steinbaugh Hardware at 801 Main Street. Among the landmarks is the 1908 Ginacci House at 1116 LaFarge Street, a coal miner's cottage with a spaghetti-making machine. The Ginaccis used this apparatus to supplement family income during the summer months when coal mining dwindled. One other landmark, the 1903 Tego Drug Store at 1001 Main Street has been restored to house the Louisville Historical Commission's museum.

The Downtown Business Association of Louisville, Historic Boulder, Inc. and preservation consultants Winter & Company of Boulder developed a 1998 Louisville preservation master plan. This plan includes design guidelines to deal with new three-story buildings disrupting Louisville's historic city scape. By the year 2000 Louisville preservationists hope to have in place an ordinance which permits local landmark designations.

City of Boulder Open Space

Motorists driving into Boulder on U.S. 36 are greeted by cattle grazing on historic open space ranches along the freeway. This pastoral relief from metropolitan sprawl is no accident. The City of Boulder has acquired more than 60,000 acres of open space since 1967, including farms and ranches which account for 60 percent of its holdings. Eighty-five percent of these have been bought outright, 10 percent protected through conservation easements, and 5 percent safeguarded through the purchase of development rights. Lessees of Boulder open space lands are typically life-long Boulder County residents with a family history of farming and ranching.

Ann FitzSimmons of the city's Open Space Department explains, "Grazing is the largest component of the agricultural program used to balance natural resource conservation and agricultural production."

◆ (Far right) This proto-typical false fronted clapboard store is happily recycled as the Louisville Historical Museum.
1995 photo by Tom Noel

◆ Steinbaugh's Hardware Store, which opened on Louisville's Front Street in 1892, operated there until 1997, when big chain hardware stores put it out of business. Renovated in 1999 by architect Eric Hartronft, it has been reincarnated as a mixed-use structure.
1995 photo by Tom Noel

Albert Viele and his family homesteaded in 1882 at South Boulder and Cherryvale roads. By 1900 the Viele's Meadow Brook Farm delivered 250 pounds of butter weekly to Boulder. Lynn Van Vleet purchased the property in 1942 to breed Arabian horses. The Van Vleets sold their magnificent acreage to the city's open space department in 1978. Now a city landmark, the picturesque working farm treats U.S. 36 motorists to a pastoral approach to Boulder instead of the usual strip malls and billboards.

1999 photo by Tom Noel

◆ (Far right) Atop Sheep Mountain, the Arapaho, and probably earlier Indian tribes as well, used these stone pits as blinds for hunting Big Horn sheep. Such archaeological landmarks await the attention of preservationists. *1999 photo by Tom Noel*

◆ Open Space embraces and protects cultural resources such as the Dunn Homestead, which preserves an 1860s stone farmhouse. *City of Boulder Open Space photo*

◆ In the tiny mining town of Eldora, one of the few lively businesses is the Gold Miner Hotel. This 1897 log resort, reborn as a Bed and Breakfast Inn in 1984, is one of more than 70 Boulder County listings on the National Register of Historic Places. *1930s watercolor by Muriel Sibell Wolle*

Open Space also protects and uses historic water ditches for agricultural purposes as well as to support wetlands and wildlife habitat.

The Boulder Valley contains both natural and cultural resources needing protection. Typical of the rural cultural landscapes is the Dunn House on City of Boulder open space at the south end of the Mesa Trail. After homesteading here in the 1860s, John DeBacker found tipi rings and arrowheads in the surrounding fields still used to grow hay. DeBacker's daughter, Emma, who was born in the house in 1877, lived there with her husband, John Dunn, until his death in 1953. With family support, the city has preserved it as an open space farm.

◆ (Left and below right)
The Walker Ranch hosts living history performances sponsored by the Boulder County Parks and Open Space Department. These shows introduce Boulderites and visitors to James Walker, whose 160-acre ranch remains a relic of Boulder County's puppy days.
Boulder County Parks and Open Space Department

Other sites range from aboriginal prehistoric remains such as stone hunting blinds to historic homesteads, from defunct coal mines and oil wells to railroad and stagecoach lines, from irrigation ditches to outhouses, from specimen trees to the Arapaho sheep hunting pits on Sheep Mountain. Because all but a small portion of Boulder open space lies outside the city limits, the city works with the county's historic preservation program to landmark sites.

Boulder County Open Space

Boulder County's open space program preceded its historic preservation ordinance. The county first bought open space in 1973, although a sales tax to fund such purchases was not approved by the voters until 1993 after two unsuccessful efforts. Preservation of agricultural land is the primary goal in a county where, between 1959 and 1992, farm and ranch acreage declined by 45 percent, from 287,000 to 157,000 acres.

◆ (Far left)
Tom Hendricks, Boulder County's best-known miner, has preserved much mining heritage at his Cross Mine above Caribou, including the original miners cabin shown here.
1999 photo by John O'Dell

◆ Rebecca Waugh, Historic Boulder, Inc.'s preservation specialist, inspects the sandstone foundation of the Geer Homestead barn. *1999 photo by Tom Noel*

◆ In Allenspark, the Bunce School's first teacher, Vella Booth, poses with her pupils. Kenny Tallman, who helped to restore the school, recalls, "I was in the last class to graduate back in 1940. Because of the long, deep winters, we had to carry coal and firewood to school with us." *Carnegie Branch Library for Local History, Boulder*

Of the county's 60,000 acres of open space, 22,000 continue as agricultural lands. Lease revenue from agricultural open space land often exceeds the property tax collected when the farm or ranch was taxable private property. About half of Boulder County's agricultural open space is protected through conservation easements, which keep farmers and ranchers on the land. The county's population explosion led the county commissioners to take these aggressive measures to preserve agricultural land. "When the open space program began, Boulder County had fewer than 130,000 residents," according to the county commissioners. "Since then, the county's population has more than doubled, and open space is more important than ever."

The commissioners' efforts are facilitated by many long-time county residents who want their farms and ranches preserved. The negotiation skills of the late open space director Carolyn Holmberg helped such families as the Trevartons maintain their historic ranch near Meeker Park. Octogenarian Lillian Trevarton and her children were more interested in preserving the ranch than subdividing it for homes. Trevarton explained, "I didn't want this area to ever be developed. It will always be a working ranch… that's just too beautiful to be destroyed by development."

◆ Rock Creek Farm serves as a bucolic buffer between fast-growing Broomfield and Lafayette. Recently renamed in honor of the late county Open Space Director Carolyn Holmberg, the farm features a 1912 Craftsman-style farmhouse and the Rock Creek Archaeological Site. *1999 photo by Tom Noel*

The Big Elk Ranch near Meeker Park showcases this 80-year-old "Barn Again!" restoration of the National Trust for Historic Preservation. Lillian Trevarton, whose family has owned the ranch since 1928, sold the development rights to Boulder County for $1,000 per acre to keep it as a working ranch.
Boulder County Parks and Open Space Department photo by Richard W. Koopmann

1971 photo by Tom Noel

1999 photo by Tom Noe

St. Vrain Historical Society

1998 photo by Tom Noel

Boulder City Open Space

Into the 21st Century

Chapter *Ten*

Boulder County's most daring and controversial open space buy came in 1999 when the City of Boulder paid $8.75 million for two parcels in Jefferson County along Colorado 93. The Jewell Mountain and Van Fleet ranches added 1,500 acres to Boulder's open space buffer. The purchase stunned some Boulderites, and many living in Jefferson County and Arvada. The latter two governments had planned to develop the site as part of a 28-square-mile Jefferson Center — a huge commercial project larger than the entire city of Boulder. Jefferson County Commissioners blasted their cagey northern neighbor for being "out of bounds." Boulder's foray into development-happy Jefferson County demonstrated the growing importance of open space purchases in growth management.

This was not Boulder's first pre-emptive strike to strategically purchase undeveloped land. In 1997 the city bought 250 acres from IBM to reduce growth along the Boulder-Longmont Diagonal Highway. The county has encircled fast-growing Longmont on three sides with open space, causing Longmont officials to complain that they can only grow eastward into Weld County. In aggressively pursuing growth management, Boulder City and Boulder County are insulating the planned C-470 beltway with open space. Even at the risk of outraging neighboring governments, Boulder continues to insist on elbow room.

◆ This pioneer farm of Lafayette's Waneka clan, once surrounded by grain fields, is now overshadowed by a "Mall Wart," as local preservationists have dubbed Wal-Mart. This unprotected Lafayette landmark, like many Boulder County farms, is endangered as land values soar. *1999 photo by Tom Noel*

Wary of the million new residents expected to settle along Colorado's Front Range between 2000 and 2020, Boulder is concentrating on quality rather than quantity of life. Sister cities and towns, overwhelmed by new development, are also beginning to wonder if bigger is better.

Boulder's growth management is not problem-free. It has shifted residential growth to smaller nearby communities — especially Lafayette, Longmont, Louisville and Superior. These communities are suddenly experiencing their own growing pains: traffic congestion, lack of affordable housing and a shortage of open space. Boulder County mountain dwellers who once lived in isolated peace are likewise being inundated with newcomers building huge homes on multi-acre parcels and then demanding paved roads and urban services. These and other issues led the Boulder Valley League of Women Voters to issue a 1998 report entitled "Will 'Success' Spoil Boulder County?" Stressing a county-wide approach, the League concluded, "Strong political leadership will be needed to carry out comprehensive plan goals for housing diversity and affordability, transportation, land use and open space and agricultural preservation."

"WESTCOR, HO !"

◆ Rob Pudim's 1972 cartoon proved prophetic. Westcor is the developer of Broomfield's new FlatIron Crossing, scheduled to open in 2000 with aspirations of replacing Douglas County's Park Meadows as the largest regional mall in the Rockies. *Carnegie Branch Library for Local History, Boulder*

During the 1990s, Boulder County's population climbed a steep 33 percent — from 225,000 to more than 300,000. Vehicle registration sped during the 1990s from 173,000 to almost 250,000 and employment rose from 128,000 to 164,000 workers. The average selling price of a single-family home doubled from $124,000 to over $250,000, pricing many low and middle income families out of the market.

At the end of the 20th century, Boulder leads all Front Range counties with its 4.5 percent job growth rate. As housing grows more expensive than in surrounding counties, more new jobs than residents are expected. This imbalance pushes county housing prices even higher.

To cope with change, several communities toughened their growth management standards in the 1990s. Boulder lowered its 2 percent growth limit to one percent in 1995 and included an affordable housing component. The city's 1997 rezoning strove for slower employment growth.

Other communities wrestle with growth management as well. In 1993 Louisville set an annual cap on building permits and capped its population at 21,000. In 1995 Lafayette citizens followed suit with a ballot measure limiting yearly permits to 3 percent of the existing housing stock. Even blossoming Broomfield has curbed residential building permits to 300 per year, a compromise designed to counter a more restrictive citizens' initiative.

Acquiring open space has not been as popular as growth control tactics. Even though open space tax measures passed in Louisville in 1993 and Broomfield in 1994, similar proposals failed in Longmont in 1995 and in Lafayette three years later. Louisville's open

◆ (Both photos)
Nyland CoHousing Community became Colorado's first major co-housing project when it opened in 1993 on the west edge of Lafayette. Denver architects Barker, Rinker, Secat and Partners designed it with parking limited to the periphery and replaced streets with sidewalks.
1999 photos by Tom Noel

space now exceeds 1,700 acres, with additional joint purchases planned with the county. Broomfield plans to expand its 450 acres to augment Boulder County's open space along its northern border.

Use of green space has skyrocketed, generating conflicts between recreation and ecosystem preservation. In 1998, for example, Boulder's Dry Creek open space trail, which is popular with dog walkers, was re-routed to avoid a prairie dog colony. One irate dog owner protested to the Boulder City Council that prairie dogs enjoy being chased by dogs. Officials are realizing that open space can't be all things to all people.

Since 1970 Boulder County has lost more than 100,000 acres of agricultural land to new construction. County officials view rural preservation as a way to manage growth and preserve the quality of life. A transferable development rights program now permits more clustered housing in exchange for setting aside open space. Agreements between the county and its cities also preserve agricultural land, as do conservation easements that leave land for crops and livestock.

With traffic on U. S. 36 expected to double between 2000 and 2010, regional planning advocates have focused on that thickening jam. Proposals range from adding HOV lanes to reviving the Denver and Interurban electric railway that whisked traffic between Denver and Boulder from 1908 and 1926.

Too much traffic and too little housing have inspired some creative projects. Nylands in Lafayette was the county's first co-housing development, with such innovations as group housing, group parking and group recreational facilities. Nomads, Boulder City's first co-housing, opened at 15th Street and Quince Avenue in 1997. Iris Hollow is Boulder City's first "New Urbanism" experiment with pedestrian friendly planning. Longmont's Prospect neighborhood adopted the same concept with similar amenities.

◆ (Both photos)
Nomads, Boulder's first co-housing project, is a curved roof design by Richard Epstein, mixing low and middle income units next to the Nomad Theater, whose rounded hut top inspired this novel plan.
Richard Epstein

◆ Boulder's Iris Hollow is a "New Urbanist" complex that mimics some of the architectural elements in a pre-existing single-family neighborhood. Boulder is banking on such projects to mitigate its affordable housing crunch.
Coburn Development, Inc.

◆ Longmont's New Urbanist "Prospect" community at Pike and Main streets borrows architectural styles and pedestrian-friendly streetscapes from "the good old days." Developer John "Kiki" Wallace kept a 100-year-old family farmhouse and barns as the center-piece of this 80-acre development. Front porches and alley garages downplay autos while promoting walker-friendly sociability.
1999 photo by Tom Noel

Such developments suggest that compact, mixed-use housing with higher densities along transit corridors can accommodate growth while preserving landscape.

Historic preservationists cheered such approaches to the urban sprawl that is their top 21st-century issue. National Trust for Historic Preservation President Richard Moe wrote *Changing Places* (1997), urging Americans to return to their urban cores. In 1999 Preservation Action, the national lobbying group, stated, "We must secure a national commitment to preserving and restoring our nation's existing houses, work-places and transportation networks." Meanwhile, Boulder County's inhabitants are wrestling with growth and other issues by using distinctive approaches in each community.

The City of Boulder

Some growth control activists trace their activism to Vietnam War-era protests that first challenged the status quo. The University of Colorado 1997 riots protesting alleged police harassment brought back memories of the early 1970s hippie invasion and anti-Vietnam War protests. CU's Regent Hall was occupied by anti-Vietnam war protesters in April, 1970. One year later, in May, 1971, three days of anti-war protest led to looting and destruction of property.

A liberal philosophy emphasizing universal human rights has led the City of Boulder to adopt its own foreign policy. It has banned nuclear weapons within the city limits and removed city funds from enterprises in countries that ignore human rights. The city has urged alleviation of global warming and the greenhouse effect. It seconded United Nations' sanctions against Iraq in 1990. It condemned the 1998 Multilateral Agreement on Investment that excused international corporations from honoring local environmental regulations.

Human rights have made progress since the ouster of City Councilman Tim Fuller and the near-recall of Mayor Penfield Tate in 1974. They had supported a gay rights amendment to the city charter, which opponents claimed would turn

◆ (Right and opposite page) Boulder's lively interest in foreign affairs was rewarded in 1987 with a $1 million teahouse from Boulder's sister city of Dushanbe, Tajikistan. It opened in 1998 next to Central Park in a handcrafted building that became an instant landmark.
1998 photos by Tom Noel

◆ In 1974 Boulder City Councilman Tim Fuller was ousted for endorsing gay rights and Mayor Penfield Tate narrowly avoided recall. Irate Boulder voters overturned their liberal gay rights ordinance by a two-to-one margin. In 1987 voters reversed themselves by 300 votes to approve a gay rights ordinance. This 1974 City Council portrait shows, left to right, top row first: Karen Paget, Robert Trenka, Ruth Correll, Walter Slack, Frank Buchanan, Ken Wright, Penfield Tate, Janet Roberts and Tim Fuller.
Boulder City Council

Boulder into a "sexual deviate mecca that will become as vile and corrupt as Sodom and Gomorrah." Boulder voters defeated gay rights in 1974, but changed their minds 13 years later. In 1987 they approved legal protection for persons discriminated against because of their sexual orientation. When these rights were threatened by Colorado's 1992 Amendment 2, Boulder, along with Denver and Aspen, led the legal battle to declare it unconstitutional. A United States Supreme Court victory was celebrated in 1996, with Boulderite Jean Dubofsky, a former Colorado Supreme Court Justice, as the advocate.

In 1979 the city established the Boulder Arts Commission to increase public awareness and funding for the arts. By 1993 The Boulder Cultural Plan undertook community programs such as the Boulder Museum of Contemporary Art, the first such museum in Colorado. Located in the City Storage and Transfer warehouse, a designated city landmark, this museum stages live performances as well as exhibits.

The sciences are also pampered in Boulder. In 1998 the National Oceanic and Atmospheric Administration (NOAA) dedicated the 372,000-square-foot David Skaggs Research Center. This followed a decade of protest spurred by concerns about open space, height and Native American archaeological sites the complex might displace.

Broomfield County

While "The People's Republic of Boulder" has pontificated on foreign policy and human rights as well as growth and sprawl, Broomfield has been much more laid back. For eight decades following its 1880s founding, this rural community was best known for fields of broom corn. Lounging on a ridge between

◆ Congressman David Skaggs led the battle to locate the National Oceanic and Atmospheric Administration's research center in Boulder, persisting in a long political struggle to get the government to comply with Boulder's strict land use regulations. Opened in 1998, it is set back from Broadway with the first floor below grade to soften the visual effect. Its name honors the U.S. representative who made it possible.
NOAA

◆ (Far left)
Boulder's Public Library, a glass and Lyons sandstone edifice spanning Boulder Creek, has a coffee bar and aquariums offering a closer look at the aquatic life in the creek below.
1997 photo by Tom Noel

◆ Boulder's hometown hero — astronaut Scott Carpenter — is honored by a city park, where would-be astronauts enjoy this spaceship.
1998 photo by Tom Noel

◆ (Far left bottom)
Whittier, Boulder's oldest school, has been landmarked and restored as the showpiece of Pine Street.
1999 photo by Tom Noel

Rock Creek on the north and Big Dry Creek on the south, the town avoided the rapid growth of the Boulder and St. Vrain creek valleys. Rapid growth after the 1952 opening of the Denver-Boulder Turnpike led Broomfield to incorporate as a city in 1961.

Now that flush times have come, the city is addressing quality of life concerns. Broomfield is planning a recreational greenway along the Community Ditch which bisects the city as well as pedestrian-friendly green space in and around the 1994 Municipal Center. On November 3, 1998, Colorado voters approved Broomfield's request to become its own county on November 15, 2001. Broomfield asked for county status because it had spread in recent decades into four counties and six school districts.

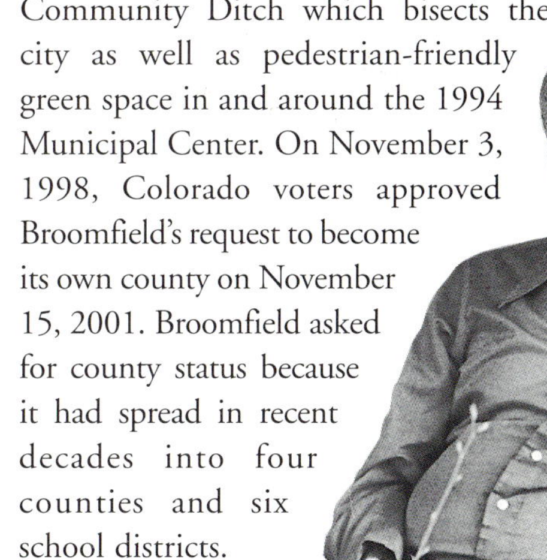

◆ (Below)
Boulder County historians Forest Crossen and Silvia Pettem share shaggy dog stories on the front porch of his old cottage at 2002 Spruce Street.
1987 photo by Tom Noel

Boulder nightlife centers on the Pearl Street Mall with its many opportunities for liquid refreshment in vintage buildings.
1999 photo by Tom Noel

(Above and following page top photos)
Boulder County residents can recharge their psychic batteries in the Indian Peaks Wilderness Area on the western edge of the county. This Alpine paradise offers trails, lakes, glaciers and wildlife, such as this marmot sunbathing on the rim of Lake Isabelle.
1998 photos by Tom Noel

Broomfield's new residents will not lack employment opportunities. Over 50,000 new jobs are expected, primarily in the large Interlocken business park that opened in 1984 and the FlatIron Crossing regional shopping mall that will open in 2000. The first new county created since 1913 expects to surpass Boulder City as a commercial hub.

Longmont

Longmont boasts a better balance of jobs-to-residents than any other Boulder County city. Fifty-seven percent of its workers live in the city. Longmont's 1991 community-based strategic plan, "Envision 2020," strives to maintain this balance, which means less commuter traffic — and better odds that Longmonters can walk or bicycle to work.

Cultural diversity is also a goal of Envision 2020. Memories of 1980s racial violence after a Longmont

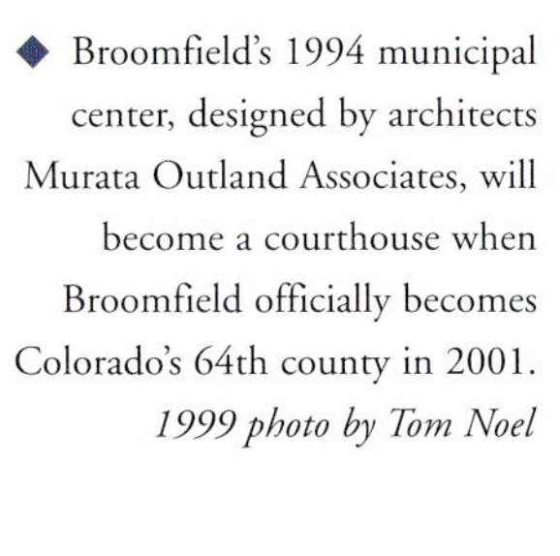

◆ Broomfield's 1994 municipal center, designed by architects Murata Outland Associates, will become a courthouse when Broomfield officially becomes Colorado's 64th county in 2001. *1999 photo by Tom Noel*

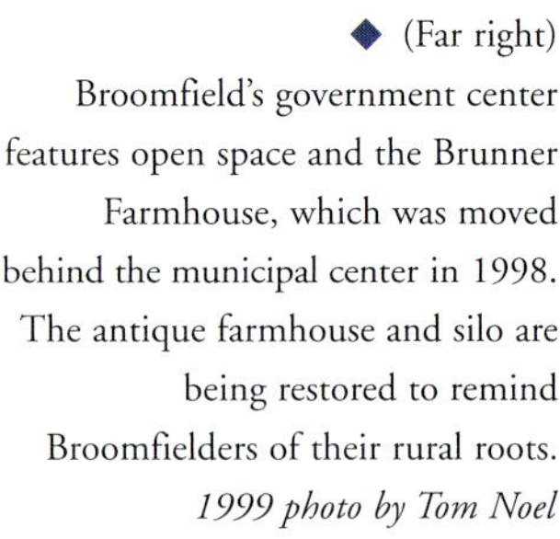

◆ (Far right) Broomfield's government center features open space and the Brunner Farmhouse, which was moved behind the municipal center in 1998. The antique farmhouse and silo are being restored to remind Broomfielders of their rural roots. *1999 photo by Tom Noel*

◆ (Left and far left)
Longmont's 1993 civic center and library, planned by RNL Design architects, has an entry arch to the library that playfully displays themes from Longmont's colorful history. Similar bowed entry signs characterize both Postmodern edifices in a graceful contemporary Civic Center.
1998 photos by Tom Noel

police officer shot and killed an Hispanic youth still haunt the city. Longmont's Hispanic population is 11 percent and growing since the city offers some of the most affordable housing in Boulder County. Tensions between recent Mexican arrivals and the established Hispanic population resulted in 1998s Community Gang Task Force, which is promoting partnerships, prevention and education.

◆ Longmont's 1907 firehouse, which replaced an earlier fire station on the site, was designed by Benjamin Viney, architect for both Longmont's and Boulder's Carnegie libraries. Since 1988 the Longmont Council for the Arts and the Arts Studio has been on call there.
St. Vrain Historical Society

◆ IBM's 1965 plant between Longmont and Boulder began Longmont's rise as a high tech center. Fine landscaping and a low building profile hide the enormous size of this campus which triggered Boulder County's explosive growth as Colorado's Silicon Valley. *1999 photo by Tom Noel*

Longmonters are also planning for recreation. Their St. Vrain Greenway incorporates the historic Burlington townsite, where the first "Longmonters" settled. The Greenway will follow St. Vrain Creek to its confluence with Boulder Creek, where the former town dump is scheduled to become a park. In 1998 the city made its most significant open space purchase: The 313-acre Sandstone Ranch on the eastern edge of the city in Weld County contains an 1880s house to be preserved for civic use. This new open space will be needed to serve Longmont's burgeoning population since its emergence as a high tech mecca.

◆ (Right and bottom photos) Giant earth movers have transformed fields and farms into 4,500 residences in Superior's Rock Creek subdivision. Natural prairie does, indeed, end at Rock Creek's "Prairies End," one of many new neighborhoods that made Superior Colorado's fastest-growing town at the turn of the 20th century. *1999 photos by Tom Noel*

Superior

Once-tiny Superior, a coal mining town for much of its history, became Colorado's fastest-growing city in the late 1990s. Before that, few could say where Superior was — and residents liked it that way. Water quality problems sparked the change. After sprawl-conscious Boulder refused to extend water utilities, Richmond Homes promised free water to the town's citizens in exchange for a flagpole annexation to the south for its Rock Creek residences. Thanks largely to these Rock Creek subdivisions, Superior's 1990 population of 250 is swelling to a projected 25,000 by 2020.

Rock Creek offers new homes at relatively affordable as well as astronomical prices, making the American dream of home ownership easier in expensive Boulder County. Long-time Superiorites, however, have reservations. Dan Kupfner, a sixth generation resident, states, "All this development is god-awful — they're going to push us old-timers out."

While some long-term residents are voluntarily leaving Superior, others have been forced out by town-initiated condemnations to provide land for tax-generating mega-stores along U. S. 36.

◆ Superior's Grasso Park on Coal Creek is the setting for a pioneer homestead, an outhouse, a root cellar and a barn. These antique reminders of Superior's small town past are showpieces of an open space refuge surrounded by the huge Rock Creek subdivision.
1999 photo by Tom Noel

Louisville and Lafayette

Zooming residential growth has led both Louisville and Lafayette to scramble for sales tax-generating strip malls, shopping centers and big box superstores to pay for rapidly expanding city services. After seeing dizzy growth on their fringes, both communities have tried to regain their balance by focusing on their historic downtowns. Without these historic cores, individual identities are swamped by a flood of generic residential and commercial development. To meet their mutual goals, cooperation between the two towns has improved since 1888, when Lafayette posted guards at its borders during a diphtheria epidemic to keep out germy Louisvillites. Louisville later retaliated with similar tactics when Lafayetters got the flu.

Since 1986 the Lafayette-Louisville Downtown Revitalization partnership has set up a revolving low-interest loan fund to renovate downtown buildings, such as the Old Louisville Inn and Lafayette's West Antiques on Public Road.

Downtown Louisville, forgotten for decades except as a mecca for Italian restaurant lovers, exploded with growth in recent decades. In 1998 the City Council enacted a moratorium on downtown construction to stop an epidemic of three-story buildings

◆ (Left and following page top photos) Downtown Louisville, with its coal miner statue, colorful signs and picturesque one- and two-story storefronts, is a delightful trip down memory lane.
1998 photo by Tom Noel

that overshadowed one-and two-story Main Street landmarks. Not all are happy with these restrictions on downtown: a few disgruntled developers claim that big box retailers on the city's fringe can get what they want while downtown development is stymied. Many old-timers and some newcomers, however, strive to save old downtown Louisville with its fabled spaghetti houses and vintage saloons.

In Lafayette, city officials are focusing on two historic downtown streets. Simpson Street, Lafayette's original commercial center, was eclipsed by Public Road after World War II. Residents hope to transform one mile of Public Road into an old-fashioned Main Street. Town boosters view Public Road as "A Mile Long Gold Mine" ready to be exploited. On Simpson Street, Lafayette's Historic Preservation Board is recreating old time ambiance by encouraging renovations and restorations. Lafayette's vision statement for downtown emphasizes small businesses to preserve the town's "panoramic view of the Rocky Mountains that inspires our view into the future."

Louisville and Lafayette now adjoin Superior and Broomfield in a conglutination that will be further cemented by the northwest quadrant of metro Denver's C-470 beltway. A race to put up highrises has begun with Broomfield's 1999 11-story Omni International Resort. Other such 21st-century giants are far larger than the old-time highrises — the coal tipples and grain elevators that have all but vanished from the landscape.

Nederland

Nederland's tumultuous 1990s battles over growth resulted in a turnover of 36 town board members in less than three years as well as seven town administrators in six years. Anti-growth forces have prevailed, requiring developers to face a town vote and to prove that the current size of the town "is wrong." The town's last annexation, in 1989, provided land for a new elementary school. Through such measures, tiny Nederland, which is surrounded by United States Forest Service land and Boulder County open space, has maintained its historic character, small town scale and woodsy setting.

◆ Among Lafayette's downtown landmarks is this 1925 Lafayette High School. The 1890 Lafayette School, which handled all 12 grades, had to be torn down after coal companies undermined it. *1998 photo by Tom Noel*

◆ The Omni International Resort opened in 1999 is a 132-foot-tall hotel that is taller than any of the coal tipples that once dominated the area's skyline.
Omni International Resort

Lyons

Lyons languished after its sandstone quarries closed in the early 1900s. Some newcomers to the scenic town, however, are now threatening to transform it. New mansionettes have given this one-time blue collar community Boulder County's highest housing prices, forcing out some old-timers. In response, Lyons began rationing water taps to 20 per year in 1996. This effort to maintain community character can be traced to a 1982 citizen protest over Coffintop Dam, which would have plugged up St. Vrain Canyon. Lyons' spunky, independent-minded residents have grown accustomed to fighting such "progress."

The town of 1,500 has developed an award-winning parks and open space program with the help of the community's 1985 tax on developments, which is used

◆ The Lyons Historical Society formed in 1973 to save the old Union Pacific depot, which has been recycled as a library.
1999 photo by Tom Noel

◆ These furry rodents, moralistic critics point out, are promiscuous and passionate, breeding often and indiscriminantly. Nevertheless, while people are proliferating, prairie dogs are declining in Boulder County, which in 1999 set aside 17,500 acres for the persecuted creatures. *Denver Museum of Natural History*

to procure park and open space lands. Lyons native LaVern Johnson, chair of the parks board, has written over $500,000 in successful grant requests for parks, open space and historic preservation. About the only proposal Johnson has not written is one for managing the town's prairie dogs. Her solution is, "Let the eagles eat 'em.'"

Where Did All The Prairie Dogs Go?

During the late 1990s both the Arapaho and the buffalo made a comeback in Colorado. Both populations have risen in recent decades, despite predictions that both would be exterminated.

Another pioneer species has not fared so well. Prairie dogs — once Boulder County's most numerous animal — are disappearing. As the county's human population has jumped to more than 300,000, new residential subdivisions are displacing prairie dog villages.

While human and animal rights have been extended to practically every other species, prairie dogs remain down in the dirt. In fact, the 1999 Colorado legislature made the furry little pups a primary target by declaring that they could not be spared by moving them to another county without the support of the commissioners in the relocation county. As neither developers nor county commissioners in possible relocation counties will abide the rodents, this law amounts to a death sentence. Not even the liberal-minded Boulder *Daily Camera,* Longmont *Daily Times-Call* or *The Denver Post* defended prairie dogs against such hate legislation. Governor William Owens quickly signed the prairie dog death bill into law with a joke about "burrowing into the prairie dog problem."

Once prairie dogs are gone, Boulder County will also lose badgers, bobcats, burrowing owls, coyotes, eagles, foxes and hawks that rely on this critical link in the food chain. The once ubiquitous black-tailed prairie dog is now threatened and the rarer white-tailed and Gunnison dogs are nearly extinct. The Great Plains once hosted an estimated 2 billion prairie dogs. Shooting, poisoning and loss of the grasslands they feed on has devastated prairie dogs by an estimated 90 percent.

Boulder County has long prided itself not only on picturesque scenery but also on tolerance for different kinds of people and animals. If the past is prologue, residents of Boulder County will have a wonderful fracas and then sit down to resolve problems in innovative ways. Moreover, compassionate and creative solutions pioneered in Boulder County will point the way for other communities also struggling with predicaments ranging from suburban sprawl to prairie dogs to historic preservation.

Part II

Partners in Boulder

Building a Greater Boulder
188

Business & Finance
204

Manufacturing & Distribution
216

Marketplace
224

Professional Services
258

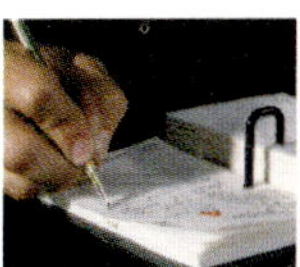

Quality of Life
272

Technology
292

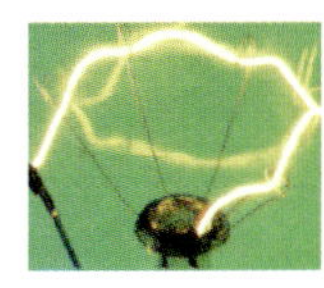

Chrisman Construction	190
Flatiron Companies	192
Prudential Wise-McIntire Realtors	194
The W.W. Reynolds Companies	196
Coburn Development, Inc.	198
Dean Callan & Company	199
Mock Realty and Mock Property Management Companies	200
RE/MAX of Boulder, Inc.	201
Wright Kingdom Realtors, Inc.	202

Real estate, development and construction industries shape tomorrow's skyline, providing working and living space for the people of Boulder.

Building a Greater Boulder

Chrisman Construction

In today's world, it is not often that two companies seal a $3.5 million business deal with a handshake. Nonetheless, this did not deter Jim Chrisman, owner of Chrisman Construction, from making such a deal to remodel the old Head Ski facility in Boulder. He takes pride in knowing that Complex Tooling and Molding hired him in part due to his policy of "rigorous honesty." This policy, along with an excellent group of quality employees, accounts for Chrisman Construction's remarkable success since its inception in 1985.

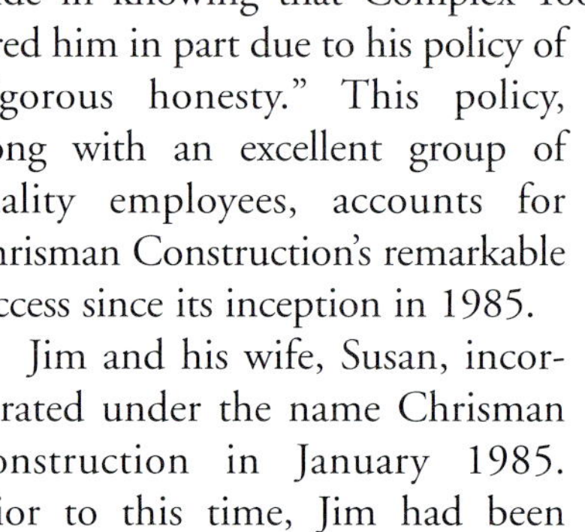

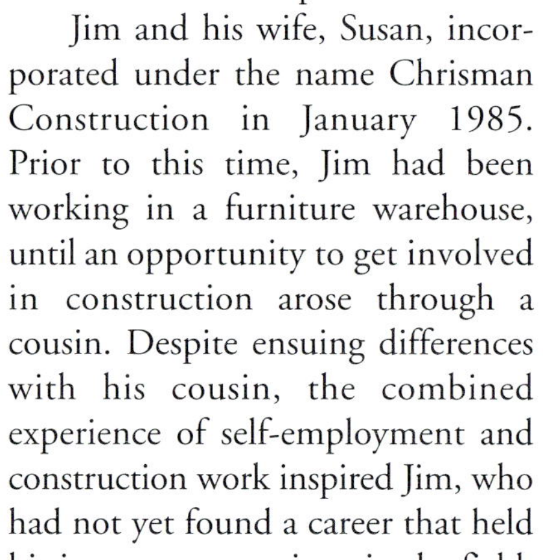

◆ An internal view of Complex Tooling and Molding

Jim and his wife, Susan, incorporated under the name Chrisman Construction in January 1985. Prior to this time, Jim had been working in a furniture warehouse, until an opportunity to get involved in construction arose through a cousin. Despite ensuing differences with his cousin, the combined experience of self-employment and construction work inspired Jim, who had not yet found a career that held his interest, to continue in the field.

Discovering satisfaction and motivation in construction, Jim recruited Susan to assist with the business and accounting end of the company. Her help proved instrumental as Chrisman Construction worked to establish itself in the Boulder community. Though Susan later relinquished her official position in the company to pursue her career as a commercial real estate broker, she has maintained an active role in Chrisman Construction, and is viewed as the CFO by Jim and the employees.

Jim and Susan's dedication to creating a company that would strive for continuous quality within budget standards drew not only clients, but also a group of talented employees. Chrisman Construction's employees take pride in their finished work, recognizing the value of each individual involved in the creation of the final product. Indeed, Jim attributes much of the company's phenomenal growth to the employees' commitment, which he believes stems in part from his policy to treat each employee the same way he would like to be treated.

Aside from terrific employees, a key factor in Chrisman Construction's success has been the contribution of Jim's father, Byron Chrisman, a well-known retired tax attorney in Boulder, who has become an avid real estate developer. Much of Chrisman Construction's work has come from the elder Chrisman, who has hired the company to construct buildings and do tenant finishes for entities with which he is involved. Other than his father, Jim believes that most of the company's business comes through word-of-mouth. His reputation as an honest, budget-attentive, quality-oriented business owner has grown over the years.

Since Chrisman Construction's first days, Jim has made a point to always conduct business with strict attention to honesty. His attainment of sobriety in 1990 only served to enhance his integrity. While undergoing this process, he recognized that absolute honesty and morality, not only in business, but in all aspects of his life, would provide the only acceptable path to which he could subscribe. Jim has found that both customers and employees respond positively to his genuine commitment to his work and the pride he takes in the finished projects.

Buildings constructed by the company have certainly made their mark in Boulder County. Chrisman Construction is responsible for hundreds of tenant-finish jobs, in which the shell of the building is complete, but the interior has yet to be divided and finished to tenants' specifications. The company has constructed numerous light industrial projects, and research and development facilities as well. In 1996, Chrisman Construction completed the building that currently houses its own offices, providing a much-needed space gain from the small sublet in which the company was previously headquartered.

While most of its business has been in Boulder County, the long waiting period for building permits in Boulder and the limited amount of building space have prompted Chrisman Construction to expand its horizons. One newer project involves the construction of a retail shopping mall in Steamboat Springs. This project has been a learning experience for the company, in that the weather and altitude, not to mention cost differences, contrast sharply with Boulder projects. Encouraged by this project and the company's success within Boulder County, Chrisman expresses with certainty that the company will continue to grow and that the scope of its projects will increase as its reputation develops.

The strength of the economy and the development of new technologies and better products have contributed and will continue to contribute to Chrisman Construction's success. Construction products are constantly changing and improving, and while some naysayers may comment that "they don't build things like they used to," Jim, for one, believes that his company builds things better than they used to, citing the fact that his employees are detail- and quality-oriented. Partnered with the fact that construction materials are much improved, he believes his company provides a winning combination.

Along with better building materials, new technology has only increased the efficiency of Chrisman Construction's building process. The company uses the Internet frequently, especially to facilitate the design process. Chrisman Construction helps the clients design their space on the computer. The file is then transmitted to engineers, who perform the necessary work to prepare the design for the blueprint company, which also receives the plans via the Internet. The blueprint company then produces the blueprints and delivers them. This process represents a remarkable increase in speed, cutting as much as two weeks out of the construction process. Thus, Internet use has assisted the company in its efforts to ensure the highest quality of service to its customers.

In addition to high-quality customer service, Chrisman Construction has made itself known in the community, largely through its commitment as a primary sponsor of the Eldora Mountain Ski Club. Jim serves on the board of this nonprofit ski-racing team for young athletes, of which both of his children are members. Susan is involved with the Boulder Valley Rotary Club, serving as its treasurer, as well has being a board member for AAHOP (Accessible and Affordable Housing Options, for the physically challenged). As Jim has multiple sclerosis, both he and Susan are also very active in raising money for the Multiple Sclerosis Society.

Chrisman Construction has proven itself to be a valuable addition to the Boulder community since its incorporation in 1985. As a detail-oriented, honest business known for its ability to finish projects on time and under budget, the company's reputation and work force have grown remarkably over the years. Grossing nearly $10 million in 1998, Jim continues to aim high with his long-term goal of building his business into a company with yearly revenues of $20 million. With an owner so committed to truth and quality, Chrisman Construction's continued growth is virtually assured.

◆ The Lakeshore Building in Boulder

Flatiron Companies

From building Foothills Parkway to local parking lots, from open space and park land to the gleaming buildings of Flatiron Park, Flatiron Companies has helped to create the Boulder of today.

As construction material suppliers, paving contractors, bridge builders and business park developers, the entities known as the Flatiron Companies have been headquartered in Boulder for five decades. Quality, innovation and competence have been the constant as the Companies have evolved.

The first Flatiron company was a small, ready-mix concrete company, founded in 1947 by James and Mildred Milne. They were joined in 1953 by Harold Short, whose vision and entrepreneurial spirit led to rapid expansion. Short's achievements and business acumen have earned him a place in Boulder County's Business Hall of Fame. He has been a director of the Chamber of Commerce of the United States, and chairman of the Mountain States Employers' Council among many other distinctions.

When Flatiron Companies celebrated its 25th anniversary in 1972, more than a dozen companies with over 500 skilled employees were then a part of Flatiron. Operating together, yet separately managed, the affiliated companies had plants and operations in Boulder, Longmont, Loveland, Fort Collins, Windsor and Greeley, and mobile operations throughout much of Colorado and adjacent areas.

◆ Reclamation area near the White Rocks

◆ Flatiron concrete truck

In 1971, Flatiron Park Company was formed to develop the 200-acre, master-planned business park, on the east side of Boulder, known as Flatiron Park.

By the late 1980s, the need for capital to keep the various companies growing resulted in the sale of the paving contracting companies and the construction material companies to a large publicly held company. Those parts of Flatiron became units of what is now known as Lafarge. Former Flatiron managers now hold many key positions with Lafarge.

Prior to the sale to Lafarge, Flatiron employed more than 800 men and women. Many significant projects were built by Flatiron, including the Hanging Lake bridges and other structures in Glenwood Canyon, Foothills Parkway, the re-paving of Trail Ridge Road, and roads and bridges throughout Colorado. Flatiron concrete, sand and gravel were used across northern Colorado, and in such notable Boulder buildings as the National Center for Atmospheric Research, the University of Colorado, Community Hospital and IBM. Flatiron's success has been primarily the result of all those who worked so proudly and with such motivation on this myriad of projects.

With a reputation for finding solutions to difficult problems, Flatiron is known as a leader and an innovator in mining and reclamation of mined lands. The company has been recognized three times by the Governers of

◆ Building in Flatiron Park

Colorado for reclamation excellence. The reclamation of the mined area south of Boulder Creek near the White Rocks garnered the National Conservation Award from the Wildlife Society, and an outstanding reclamation award from the National Sand and Gravel Association. Over the past 25 years, Flatiron has donated more than 600 acres of reclaimed land to the open space systems of Boulder and Fort Collins, and has donated land to Colorado State University, the University of Colorado and the state of Colorado.

With the sale to Lafarge, Flatiron energy and capital were used to significantly expand Flatiron Park and Flatiron Structures Company. By 1993 Flatiron Structures had again outgrown Flatiron Companies' ability to provide capital, and Structures was sold to Scott Lynn, its president, and his European financial backers.

Today, Flatiron Park Company develops, owns and manages buildings in Flatiron Park. With more than 2.5 million square feet of software, research, manufacturing and related office space, Flatiron Park is the largest business park in Boulder. Its unique site, surrounded by trails and open space, is now home to many of the most highly regarded companies in Boulder.

The development, leasing and management team at Flatiron Park, headed by co-owner Larry Frey and Vice President Dick Hedges, prides itself on providing creative solutions to the needs of the businesses they serve. Most owners build projects with the intention of selling them. Flatiron buildings are constructed with the goals of long-term ownership and effective management.

Scott Patten and Ed McDowell are the current managing partners of Flatiron Companies. They provide vision and management for the more than 1,000 acres of land in northern Colorado that are being mined and reclaimed for future productive use. Open space, residential areas, reservoirs, recreation uses and commercial buildings will occupy various portions of these lands.

The owners and managers expect to continue the example set by Chairman Emeritus, Harold Short, in giving back to the communities in which they operate, both through meaningful contributions and leadership roles in encouraging others to give to capital campaigns that have special significance. Over the years, Flatiron has made significant commitments to the YMCA, Junior Achievement, Valmont Community Church, chambers of commerce, University of Northern Colorado, Colorado State University, University of Colorado, Little League, Hospice, Colorado Open Lands and others.

Flatiron looks forward to the future and the many opportunities and challenges that will be forthcoming. Changing with Colorado, yet never forgetting the community from which it grew, Flatiron Companies has surely earned its place in the history of Boulder.

◆ The Hanging Lake bridges in Glenwood Canyon

Prudential Wise-McIntire

Realtors

In the world of business, there are those who believe in luck, while others believe in making their own luck. Such was the beginning of a remarkable partnership between two men who built a business that forever changed the face of the Boulder community.

Dennie P. Wise Jr. and Robert McIntire were fortunate to have met early in their real estate careers. Wise had been wounded in the Korean War and arrived home realizing he had no real training with which to make a living. Deciding upon real estate, Wise found tremendous pleasure in selling homes and properties his clients truly desired. Wise had owned his own business, Wise and Co., for three years before meeting Robert McIntire in 1967. McIntire had been in the industry for one year, and his company, Kent Realty, was located in an office building that Wise owned. The two men realized they shared common interests, values and goals, and together they founded Wise-McIntire. Through the years, they enjoyed both a prosperous partnership and a rewarding friendship.

◆ The Prudential Wise-McIntire building

From 1967 to 1990, the firm was involved in the development of many significant properties in the Boulder area. One of Wise and McIntire's favorite projects was the Valentine Building. Valentine Hardware had been around for many years before Wise and McIntire bought the building and began working on it. They had to sandblast the structure and endure the gossip throughout town about that "spectacle on Broadway and Pearl." They succeeded, however, in beautifully remodeling the building, while preserving its integrity and original style. Wise and McIntire felt immense satisfaction when their building was nominated for a Boulder historic award. This was one of the first steps in revitalizing downtown Boulder, including what is known as the Pearl Street Mall.

◆ The Randolph Center

Wise and McIntire bought the old Armory building on West Pearl Street, which had once housed a shooting range in the basement and later a basketball stadium for the University of Colorado, Boulder. During the war years, the main area was used as a dance floor while big bands like Glenn Miller played in the balcony. Wise, McIntire and Richard Paquette envisioned converting it into an office building, so they formed a partnership and purchased the property. Within days, they received a letter from the fire department demanding that the building be immediately demolished, due to an unsound floor and foundation. Instead of razing the building, they were able to salvage much from the original structure. Now a uniquely beautiful building graces Pearl Street and currently houses Urban Outfitters.

Another interesting project in the downtown area that Wise and McIntire developed was the office building/parking structure known as The Randolph Center. The original property on Broadway and Walnut contained a local icon called The Carnival Café, a popular hangout for many 60s-generation students. City Councilman Paul Danish and others with similar foresight into the growing needs of the community believed that building a parking structure downtown was a great step in reducing traffic pollution in Boulder. The structure was completed through cooperation between the city of Boulder and Broadway Walnut Company, which consisted of Wise, McIntire and Frank Day, owners of The Randolph Center. The completion was part of other trendsetting, downtown projects for Wise and McIntire, including The Edwards Center, the Boulder City Building, The Willard Building — which once housed the

◆ The Armory building

Aristocrat Steak House — and the old telephone building on Spruce Street.

Wise and McIntire's interests reached beyond downtown Boulder. They developed, with East Park Associates, what is known as East Park, which included Arnold Brothers Ford and the Regional Transportation District's (RTD) maintenance facility. East Park drew in high-tech industries such as Storage Technology and NBI and is currently the location for Exabyte. In addition to East Park, Wise and McIntire developed two other business parks, including Valmont Industrial Park and Longbow IV.

Through the years, Wise-McIntire's reputation for integrity, ethics in business, and service became widespread. As the business developed, two other integral players joined the team. Dennie P. "Chip" Wise III, Dennie's son; and Thomas W. Tyrrell, Dennie's son-in-law, both came on board as agents in 1978. Chip's degree in art gave him an aesthetic advantage in working with renovation and property development. He invested time and energy to become a certified property manager (CPM) by 1993, then earned the title of certified commercial investment member (CCIM) by 1997. Chip's expertise became instrumental in the continued development of commercial real estate, including sales, leasing and professional property management. The company consistently manages about 220,000 square feet of commercial property in Boulder.

Tom Tyrrell's influence on the business has also been extraordinary. With a degree in business and previous experience as sales manager for Meyers Jewelers, Tyrrell focused on the residential side of the business, while assisting Chip with commercial sales and leasing. Tyrrell's passion for residential sales facilitated the building of a stronger sales division than the company had ever known before, and he now has 30 agents working with him. From a minor emphasis in years past, Tyrrell and his team have brought residential sales to make up 70 percent of the company's revenue. His sales team serves all of Boulder, Louisville, Lafayette, Longmont and Broomfield.

Tyrrell and the younger Wise became owners of the company in 1989, and began playing integral roles as the elder Wise and McIntire prepared to retire the following year. Tyrrell and Wise became affiliated with Prudential that same year, forming Prudential Wise-McIntire Realtors. This affiliation has allowed for expanded and improved services to meet a wider variety of client needs. The company is continuing to build its residential staff and services while exploring commercial development. With the acquisition of the Prudential Wise-McIntire Building in Southcreek Office Park, and the recent development and construction of the Hanover Building at Hanover and South Broadway, the company continues in the tradition of the founders. Prudential Wise-McIntire Realtors has become one of the top firms in commercial and residential sales with the same emphasis on personal service offered from the beginning.

◆ The old telephone building on Spruce Street

Although many of the properties Wise and McIntire were involved with have been sold, and the partnership and business relationships that were instrumental in their success have ended, the historical significance of their effect on the Boulder community lives on. Despite the fact that it has been difficult to let go of the reigns, Wise and McIntire both agree that their successors have based their work on the same values as they did when they built the company years ago. Their commitment to business ethics and building relationships within the Boulder community ensures that Prudential Wise-McIntire will continue to shape the face of Boulder for years to come.

The W.W. Reynolds Companies

In 1980, the area east of downtown Boulder offered little more than community leftovers. What is now the continuous Pearl Street, Boulder's east to west main drag, stretching from its western inception in the foothills of the Flatirons to 55th Street, ended just beyond downtown. In fact, Pearl Street emptied into a seemingly unplanned wasteland as it approached Valmont Butte. Junked cars, construction debris and overgrown weedy lots proliferated in that area near Boulder Creek. The site was a disaster waiting to happen if urban sprawl took an indifferent course.

That did not happen. Fortunately, at that point, visionary William ("Bill") Reynolds, founder and president of The W.W. Reynolds Companies, imagined a research and development office park. The companies had already completed the Table Mesa Shopping Center, a retail mix with a grocery store anchor and a similar development, the Sunrise Center, at 30th and Arapahoe. Although office and industrial developments were a new twist and a gutsy risk for the companies, the project area wasn't a complete frontier. Reynolds owned another office building near the area where Pearl Street petered out. Recognizing that Boulder's retail market was approaching an overcrowded glut, with too many developers chasing too little money, Reynolds pushed his vision.

Persistence drove all of the companies' moves. Modeling their philosophy after Teddy Roosevelt, proclaiming that it was not the critic who counted, but the guy who was willing to try and fail, the Reynolds Companies pushed their vision to fruition.

◆ The W.W. Reynolds Companies' office building on Pearl East Circle

◆ A jogger passes the northwest corner of W.W. Reynolds.

Fortifying his dream with the strong business sense of partner Gerald ("Jerry") Lee, Reynolds convinced the banks to back his project. The resulting 540,000 square feet of light industrial and office space bespeaks the companies' goal of creating an aesthetically pleasing environment compatible with the physical and social aspects of the surrounding community and appealing to the needs of future tenants. Pearl Street East encompasses 35 acres along Boulder Creek and offers a web of pedestrian and bicycle paths that weave into Boulder's bike path system. Trees, shrubs, grass, and flowering plants sprawl over 12 acres, an extension of Boulder County's commitment to open space embracing contained development.

Most telling of the companies' community ethic is their unique sculpture garden joining the Boulder Bike Path and the Foothills Bike Path, a project lauded by both community and art experts. Conceived of as a memorial to Reynold's father, the garden plays with a watering hole metaphor, the place where diverse species meet. The design offers drinking fountains for people and a pond where dogs drink by day, and deer and other indigenous wildlife drink on the dark side of sunset and sunrise. Rocks taken from the area combine with xeriscape planting appropriate to Boulder's ecosystem to establish a naturalized setting. Kids climb on the rocks, rollerbladers and bikers drink from the fountain, and office workers eat lunch on benches. Like the W.W. Reynolds Companies, the garden transforms vision rooted in the Boulder landscape into a functional, attractive entity.

The companies began serendipitously in 1966, when Reynolds earned his real estate and broker's license in a state that was waiting to grow. An avid skier, he bought and sold mountain property in Aspen for several years before returning to Boulder to build the Table Mesa Shopping Center in South Boulder on a leftover parcel of land from the Martin Acres subdivision. The Sunrise Center followed.

Reynolds grew up in the Mapleton Historic District and attended Mapleton Elementary School, now over a century old. Although Boulder runs in his blood, so does a persistent desire to nudge new frontiers. The companies expanded their operations to Fort Collins with Prospect Park East, an office, research and development park similar to Pearl Street East. Not only does it feature the trademark pleasing architecture and inviting landscape complete with a lake, jogging trail, fitness stations and picnic areas, it also keeps clients' interests at the forefront. A policy of flexible space availability — "incubator" space — allows a young company to start small and then lease additional footage as it prospers.

An eye to the future needs of a business world entrenched in rapidly changing technology guides The W.W. Reynolds Companies' designs of their properties. Clean, simple spaces respond more easily to a dynamic and

◆ Decorative fountain at the northeast corner of the W.W. Reynolds building

◆ View to the southwest and Flatirons

changing world than striking images and experimental architecture that lapse into anachronism in an amazingly short time. All of Reynolds' other projects in Boulder and Fort Collins, including the LakeCentre, Airport Plaza One and Tierra Centre, offer the same simple well-lit spaces, window-clad for sunlight and well-sited views, and an understated professional atmosphere. Comfort and function, not opulence, guide the clients who choose Reynolds Companies' properties.

Expanding the parameters of academia, the Reynolds Companies helped initiate the University of Colorado's Real Estate Center, a rigorous graduate and undergraduate program offering an interdisciplinary curriculum. Students may select courses from the colleges of engineering, architecture and planning, law, geography and other departments to uncover viable approaches to real estate for the future within the context of established communities.

Reynolds brings his historic knowledge of the community to all his undertakings. Deeply respectful of the city's tight building restrictions to save its historic open spaces and architectural integrity, Reynolds lauds its founding fathers for their vision. That is what shaped the unique environment Boulder enjoys today. Protector of the past, prophet of the future, proponent of both historic and progressive Boulder, the W.W. Reynolds Companies' stated hope is to create what their community likes and values.

Coburn Development, Inc.

For over a decade, Coburn Development, a Boulder-based company, has specialized in historical renovation and urban infill projects, winning recognition and national acclaim for its architectural contributions to one of the most walkable cities in the West.

Founded in 1985 by William Coburn and his wife Ann, Coburn Development is a design/build firm with a mission — to preserve Boulder's old Victorian houses, to restore neighborhood environments and to foster affordable housing in a community where million-dollar homes are no longer rare.

A Boulder native, Bill Coburn has successfully concentrated the firm's redevelopment efforts in central Boulder. The company has long revitalized neglected alley and backstreet lots with new Victorian-style houses, featuring gables, hip roofs and covered porches which harmonize perfectly within classic 19th-century neighborhoods while retaining their own distinctive charm.

Many of Coburn's historical renovations have been awarded landmark status by the city of Boulder. Work on local treasures, such as the "Annie House" and "Carlston's Folly," has been recognized with Historic Boulder's Annual Award of Merit.

◆ Iris Hollow — Boulder's first New Urbanist neighborhood

Occasionally the company's preservation efforts involve moving architectural gems to save them from demolition. Walnut Hollow is one such project. On a 43,000-square-foot parcel, two historic structures were transplanted, two existing houses were renovated, and five new single-family homes were constructed. The resulting pocket neighborhood — built around a narrow, brick-inlaid lane with front porches and detached garages encouraging neighborhood interaction — was featured in *Metropolitan Home* and *Better Homes and Gardens, Home Plan Ideas.*

Another magazine favorite is the Painted Ladies project at 14th and Pine Streets, where a Queen Anne Victorian was landmarked and renovated into five units and a new, single-family Victorian house and a Victorian duplex were constructed on this downtown corner parcel, winning national acclaim.

◆ Painted Ladies

With Iris Hollow, Coburn Development has created Boulder's first New Urbanist neighborhood, emphasizing appropriately scaled streets and pedestrian zones in a mixed-use community. Primarily consisting of single-family homes, the development also features cottages and condominiums. Amenities such as a Montessori school, a guest house, business studios and green spaces for recreation make this a distinctive addition to Boulder's housing structure while contributing over 40 homes to the city of Boulder's plan for permanently affordable housing. Iris Hollow received the Governer's Smart Growth Award in 1997.

The same principles were applied when Coburn Development was hired to refurbish the old Boulder Steel site. Wanting to create a unique mixed-use neighborhood, with a loft-style residential character, the company came up with a design for Steel Yards which includes a park, Montessori school, light industrial and retail spaces, offices, residential lofts and rowhouses. The result promises a pedestrian-friendly live/work neighborhood with a sense of place and character all its own.

Offering complete planning, designing and building services for residential and commercial use and site development, Coburn Development brings quality to every project, integrating Boulder's historic past with exciting possibilities for its future.

Dean Callan & Company

When Dean Callan founded Dean Callan & Company, Inc. in 1963, Boulder was in the initial stages of commercial and industrial development. Since that time, the company has been one of the driving forces in Boulder County real estate, having been involved in a number of sizable transactions involving shopping centers, office and industrial buildings, and large land acquisitions. In many ways, these transactions helped shape Boulder's future.

Dean Callan & Company, Inc. has primarily been known as a leader in the brokerage business. However, the company has also been active in the development arena, having developed several office and industrial buildings including The Greens Industrial Park, The Flatiron Terrace and the 777 29th Street building. Dean Callan's knowledge and personal approach built a foundation of integrity that created early success and a reputation for honesty that brought clients back time after time. Today Dean Callan and Company is a full-service company specializing in development, brokerage, management and acquisitions.

Honesty, integrity and attention to the needs, desires and best interests of the client continue in the family tradition at Dean Callan & Company, where Scott, Becky and Bruce join their father (in-law) as principals in the successful operation of the business. Scott oversees the property management division, which manages nearly 1 million square feet of commercial space in Boulder County. With a degree in business and real estate from the University of Colorado and more than 20 years of real estate experience in Colorado and Arizona, he brings a significant amount of knowledge and resources to the company. Becky, a graduate of The University of Texas, manages the brokerage division where she has successfully handled the sales, leasing and marketing of several high-profile projects. These include representing the buyers for the largest single real estate transaction in the history of Boulder, as well as representing the owners for the leasing and marketing for two of downtown Boulder's largest class "A" office buildings. Bruce Gamble, Dean's son-in-law, is the director of acquisitions for the company. This division partners with private and institutional funds that actively pursue investment and development opportunities in the Front Range.

The Callan family's contributions to the community are not limited to quality real estate. Dean has served on many boards, including the boards of directors for Boulder Community Hospital, Colorado National Bank, Frasier Meadows Manor and the Senior Foundation. He is also a longtime member of the Buff Club and its president in 1974. Scott, Becky and Bruce are also longtime supporters of the University of Colorado, with Becky following in her father's footsteps, as the first female president of the Golden Buffalo Scholarship Fund in 1996-97 school year. In addition, both Bruce and Becky are actively involved in the YMCA and Boulder Junior Soccer as volunteer coaches.

◆ (L-R) Becky Gamble, Bruce Gamble, Scott Callan, Dean Callan

Dean Callan & Company's generosity is seen throughout the Boulder area. It financially supports many organizations within the community including the University of Colorado, Boulder Valley Schools, YMCA and Special Olympics.

As a longtime resident in the community, Dean Callan & Company brings a perspective that combines personal history with knowledge, and future vision to guide Boulder's real estate market well into the future.

Mock Realty and Mock Property Management Companies

The family team of Ed and his sons, Gail and Bruce Mock, personifies the innovative and dedicated business leadership that has helped shape the vitality of the Boulder community. They have created premier real estate brokerage and property management companies whose trademark is superb customer service. The Mock family also has a longstanding dedication to community service throughout Boulder County.

In the late 1950s, Ed and his wife, Bernice Mock, saw Boulder's potential as a community whose natural beauty was matched by the creativity and energy of its residents. The Mock family moved to Boulder in 1959 when Ed began his real estate career as sales manager with Wheeler Realty and Phillips Construction Companies, the developers of the Table Mesa Subdivision in Boulder.

Ed opened Mock Realty on December 1, 1965. The firm's first sale was of a home on 39th Street that brought a sales price of $17,600. In 1966 the company moved to its new office building on South Lashley Lane. That same year, Ed served as president of the Boulder Board of Realtors. Ken, the oldest of the Mock's three sons, joined the company in 1968 and started a property management department in 1969. Ken left the company in 1978 when he moved to Steamboat Springs.

Ed has developed over 25 projects through partnerships. The elegant Spanish Hills, a residential subdivision, was his first project. Subsequent projects included several condominium and apartment buildings and three office buildings. Ed's latest project is the Black Diamond Center, a commercial and retail development in Lafayette.

Gail Mock began his real estate career in 1973, joining Mock Realty as a salesman. He received his broker's license in 1976 and became sales manager in 1980. In 1991, Ed sold Mock Realty to Gail and Mock Property Management Company to his youngest son, Bruce, a real estate attorney and broker. The two companies moved in 1993 to their present location on South Broadway in Boulder.

Gail has expanded the Mock Realty team to include 25 realtors and four support staff who provide exceptional service to their clients. Gail served as president of the Boulder Area Board of Realtors in 1997-98 and focused on defining real estate services for the Boulder community for the 21st century.

Mock Property Management, under Bruce's leadership, has grown to include seven property managers/leasing agents and five support staff who offer unparalleled expertise in the Boulder area. The firm specializes in residential and commercial property management, leasing and commercial sales. A 1981 University of Colorado Law School graduate, Bruce practiced law with Dietze Davis and Porter in Boulder and later with Transamerica Title Insurance Company in Denver. His legal expertise has expanded and enhanced the range of services offered to clients of Mock Property Management.

◆ (L-R) Bruce, Gail and Ed Mock

The Mocks have always placed a high value on community service. Ed finds great personal satisfaction in helping others to achieve their best. He has mentored three sons and numerous employees and friends who have become successful business and civic leaders. Ed, Gail and Bruce serve as leaders of several charitable and civic causes that benefit the Boulder County community.

RE/MAX of Boulder, Inc.

Boulder, Colorado — one of the signature cities of the world! It is difficult to find someone who hasn't heard of Boulder. Many Boulder County residents are living proof of the truth of Niwot's curse. Chief Niwot is credited with saying, "Once you have lived in this area, you will never be happy anywhere else." Many of the students of the University of Colorado are living proof of the desire to stay in this area and do whatever they can to earn their fortunes. The area is now and always has been one of exceptional entrepreneurship.

In 1977 Tom Kalinski recognized this university town as an up-and-coming real estate market, desirable to those who wanted their own slice of the American dream in a beautiful setting. He established RE/MAX of Boulder, Inc., the first RE/MAX franchise in Boulder County, and only the fifth RE/MAX franchise in the United States. From its inception with just one other agent, this independently owned and operated office has become the highest-producing RE/MAX office in the Rocky Mountain region.

Boulder Revisited 1977

The community consisted of approximately 75,000 people. About 20,000 of those were University of Colorado students. In the fall of 1976, voters approved a two percent growth limitation on residential construction to be controlled by the number of building permits issued. Also in 1976, the voters approved the first of several taxes which would be used to purchase "open space" surrounding the city of Boulder, thereby dissolving the prediction that all the communities from Fort Collins to Pueblo would become one. The average sales price of a single family home in Boulder in 1977 was $59,630.

RE/MAX of Boulder Today

Much as when established attorneys, doctors or architects decide to form a partnership because they respect each other's professional conduct, RE/MAX of Boulder represents Realtors® mutually chosen for their proven dedication to high standards within the profession. Today the company includes more than 65 sales associates serving the real estate needs of Boulder County. All of these agents have a Broker's license, and 60 percent hold the Certified Residential Specialist designation, compared to just seven percent nationally. Cumulatively, RE/MAX of Boulder agents have over 1,000 years of experience. Their average of 17 years of experience is unsurpassed in the Boulder area. RE/MAX of Boulder's success at creating customer satisfaction is evident by the fact that over 70 percent of their business is from past clients or referrals from past clients.

For the RE/MAX of Boulder associates, it isn't just about selling homes. In nearly every facet of community involvement, including church, school, United Way, YMCA, YWCA, Buff Club, Historic Boulder, Special Olympics, Scouting, Boulder Hospice, Boulder Philharmonic, Habitat for Humanity, and more, you will find a RE/MAX of Boulder Realtor® involved.

RE/MAX of Boulder Realtors® have a dynamic and future-oriented philosophy using the most up-to-date technology. Their experience, knowledge, vitality and enthusiasm is sure to make the home-buying or home-selling experience a pleasant and positive one.

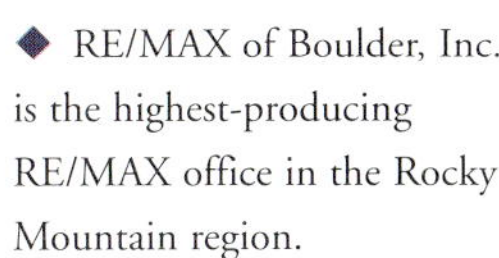

◆ RE/MAX of Boulder, Inc. is the highest-producing RE/MAX office in the Rocky Mountain region.

Wright Kingdom Realtors, Inc.

Wright Kingdom Realtors' prominence in the Boulder community stems from its firm commitment to upholding high standards in the local real estate industry. In 1976, Stuart Wright and Lew Kingdom decided to form Wright Kingdom due to a shared dedication to service and quality. Already experienced in the residential real estate business, the two men joined together to start their own business, focused on the goal of providing uncompromising service to their clients.

◆ Wright Kingdom Realtors founders Stuart Wright (left) and Lew Kingdom

This vision of service proved to be a winning combination with the Boulder community. Many successful real estate agents were drawn to Wright Kingdom due to its philosophy of being an advocate for its clients, both buyers and sellers. With 30 sales associates working for the company now, it does the same amount of business in less than a month than it did in its entire first year.

As a residential brokerage company, Wright Kingdom has always employed a hands-on approach in terms of services to its clients. By participating in city, county and civic organizations, the company maintains an updated sense of the current overall lifestyle in Boulder County. This enables agents to be responsive and sensitive to the ever-changing demands of its clientele, who are usually involved in making a major life decision with their purchase or sale of real estate.

Over the years, Wright Kingdom has emphasized two niches. First, the company strives to represent Boulder County in every way possible. It has full market coverage of Boulder County real estate, with offerings ranging from condominiums to upper-end properties both within the city and in the mountains and plains. Secondly, Wright Kingdom provides Boulder County's only local full-service relocation department and full-time corporate relocation division. For over 10 years this service has relocated companies and employees into Boulder County, making the moving process easier by offering aid in home finding as well as area tours and temporary rentals. This service has been a long time specialty for both corporate and individual moves into Boulder County. Due to Wright Kingdom's combination of local connections and both national and international ties, it is able to represent itself at the same level as any national real estate brokerage.

Wright Kingdom's presence as a local voice in the real estate business has been strengthened by its community activities. Both owners are past presidents of the Boulder Area Board of Realtors, and both are past Realtors of the Year. The company has taken on a sponsorship role on many occasions, with beneficiaries including the Colorado Music Festival and the Boulder Philharmonic Orchestra, among others.

Providing the insight of a local company in the corporate real estate industry comprises one of Wright Kingdom's major long-term goals. Co-owners Wright and Kingdom plan to continue meeting the needs of Boulder County and the surrounding areas for years to come. To this end, both owners remain active in listings and sales, keeping their fingers on the pulse of the ever-changing real estate market. This fierce commitment to providing quality service with independent roots makes up the foundation on which Wright Kingdom's success rests.

◆ The Wright Kingdom staff

Photo by Ron Ruhoff

St. Vrain Valley Credit Union 206

U of C Federal Credit Union 208

Boulder Municipal Employees Federal Credit Union 210

Boulder Valley Credit Union 211

Heritage Bank 212

Premier Members Federal Credit Union 213

Pueblo Bank & Trust Company 214

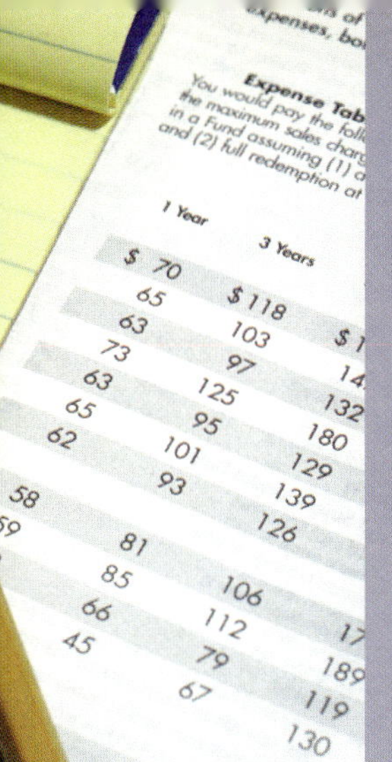

Banks and credit unions, insurance and diversified holding companies provide a financial foundation for all of Boulder County.

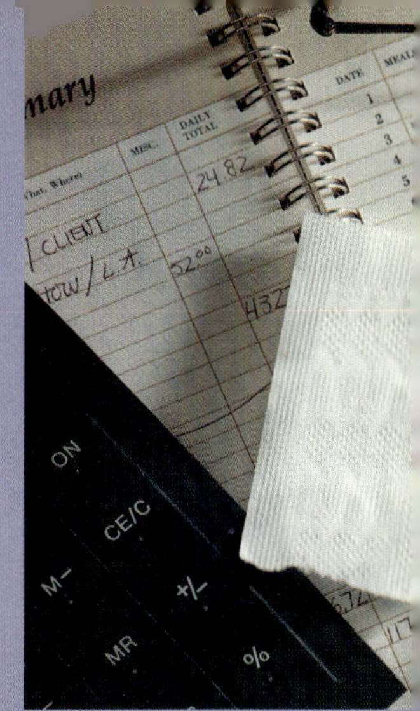

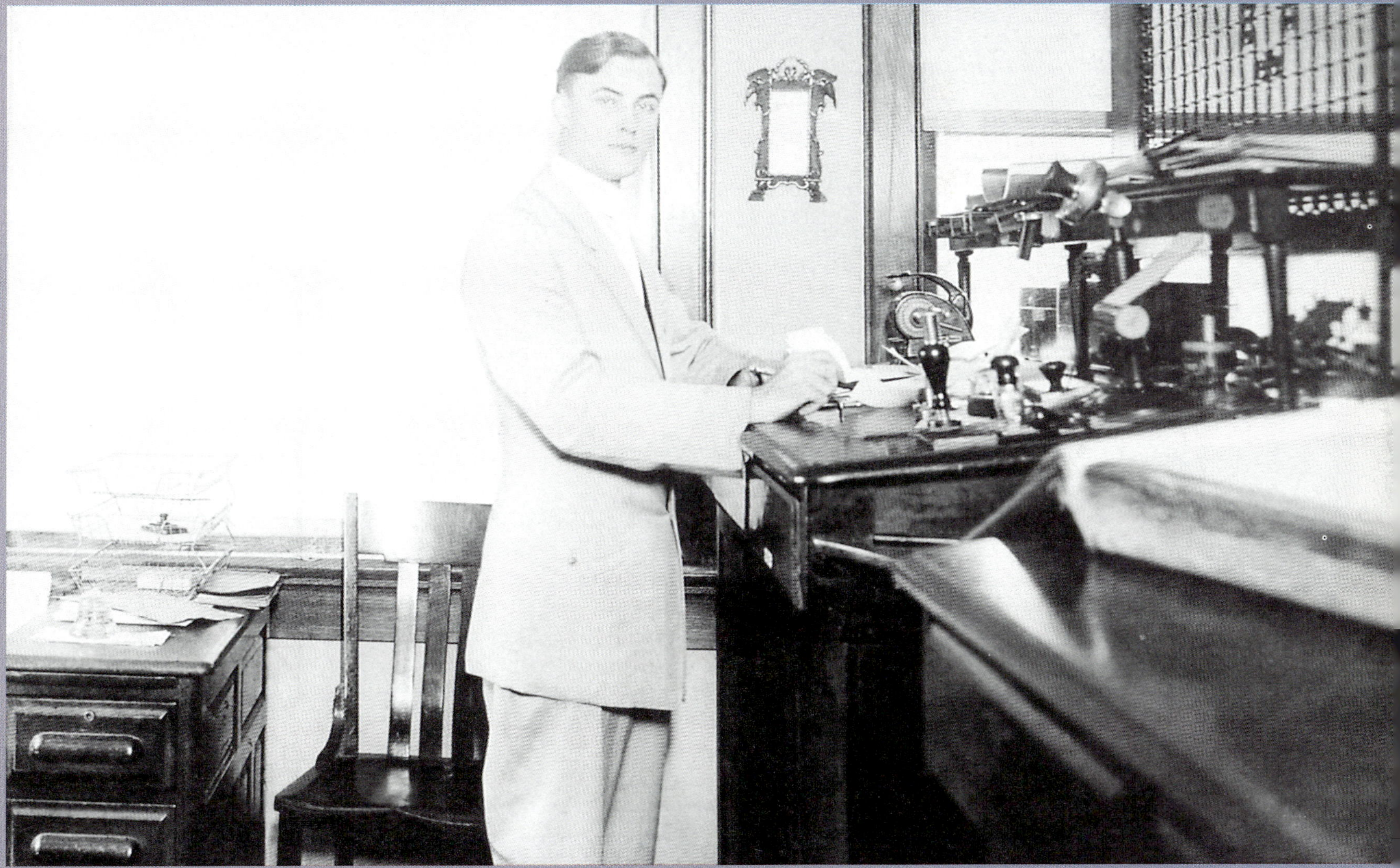

Business & Finance

St. Vrain Valley Credit Union

To say St. Vrain Valley Credit Union (SVVCU) started in a shoebox is more fact than a figure of speech. In the mid-1950s, eight employees of Longmont schools sought a means of making the best of the opportunities and limitations of a teacher's salary — primarily by pooling their savings to provide loans. On November 18, 1954, L.B. Adams, Helen Boyce, Eleanor Trask, Louise Winterburn, Marian Scilley, M.C. Christensen, Kenneth McCauley and Otto Henkel gained a state charter for the Boulder County School Employees Credit Union.

◆ Early growth — SVVCU grew into its first office in the early 1970s, one room in the basement of Osteopath Hospital on Ninth and Kimbark.

For the next several years, they toted a box of records from member's house to member's house — usually the modest Judson Street home of Marian Scilley, a kindergarten teacher. Kitchen tables and school desks served as makeshift "tellers' windows" over which school district employees and their families made deposits and borrowed funds. Early members of the board contributed in all sorts of ways, with William Herring giving his time to keep the records, and Ray Ashbaugh using his own money to fund loans. After the first year in business, the organization was three cents shy of $3,000 in deposits. In the late 1970s, the credit union moved into its first formal office, a one-room basement in the Osteopath Hospital at Ninth and Kimbark, and in 1982 hired its first full-time employee.

◆ From modest beginnings — St. Vrain Valley Credit Union began in 1954 in a modest home on Judson Street.

The organization became the St. Vrain Valley Schools Credit Union when Boulder Valley Teachers Association was allowed to "branch off" and form its own credit union, and evolved to SVVCU in 1985 when Longmont United Hospital employees were welcomed to the fold. The organization now features a diverse mix of member groups, from the Longmont Association of Realtors to the residents of the town of Berthoud.

New Services, Same Great Attitude

St. Vrain Valley Credit Union has come a long way since the pioneering days, and now holds $35 million in assets at a building at 21st and Terry designed especially to serve the needs of nearly 6,500 members. But the best part, the heart of the founders, remains. The credit union provides the full spectrum of current banking services, but still exudes the humility and purpose of the founders. Where banks must respond to the profit motives of stockholders, credit unions focus on the needs of their members.

"We offer about the same range of services you would receive at a bank," explains Eva Gaudio, President/CEO. "Where we try to be different is in how we treat our members. We give personal service. Our members aren't customers; they must qualify to join, and once they join, they are part owners of the credit

union and they have a say in what we do. In banks, the board of directors is paid, where our board of directors is made up of volunteers. We are nonprofit, so profits go back to the members in some way, either through new services, higher dividends or lower loan rates."

SVVCU continually expands services based on members' needs. Members can conduct transactions in the lobby, through the drive-up window or by using TellerTalk, a 24-hour telephone access service. Offerings about to be unveiled include a home banking service that eventually will incorporate electronic bill payment over the Internet.

Building Success for the Members

To better supply all of these services, the 5,600-square-foot building of the SVVCU opened in October of 1995. The architectural design of the building allows for expansion to accommodate the needs of the membership. Considering that the assets have nearly tripled since Gaudio took the reins less than six years ago, SVVCU may come to build on that foresight.

The credit union's growth movement began in 1985 with the admission of the Northern Colorado Education Board of Cooperative Services. The member-

◆ Familiar Surroundings — Most Longmont residents remember the SVVCU's long-time office in the corner shopping center on the north side of Main Street, which opened in 1983

ship diversified with the admission of Longmont United Hospital employees and town of Berthoud residents and employees. Membership continues to grow through the 54 member groups, particularly with employees and students from the St. Vrain Valley School District, and their families. Anyone in an eligible group needs only to walk in and open an account. There is no size limit on member groups, large or small, and one of the fastest growing memberships is in the Prime Times Club for ages 50 and over.

Excellence and Intimacy

The SVVCU is served by 25 employees who earn an "A" average. Combining financial success with excellence in member service, another milestone was reached in 1997 when Callahan and Associates ranked SVVCU in the 97th percentile for providing the best lending and savings programs and member service in the nation. For the past three years, SVVCU also has earned the top rating from state regulators for safety and financial soundness. Such operational excellence is stewarded by a diverse board of directors made up of medical, education, and financial specialists. In addition, a supervisory committee volunteers their time to monitor operations to ensure federal and state compliance.

Credit unions are part of a financial cooperative and work together for community development. In the past few years, the St. Vrain Valley Credit Union and Longs Peak Credit Union helped the members of a cooperative farm near Loveland establish the Sunrise Credit Union.

SVVCU's community outreach is augmented by classroom presentations that teach skills ranging from account reconciliation to loan basics that often begins with the question, "Are any of you students an owner of a financial institution?" The object lesson is further brought home by SVVCU's Skyline High School branch, which is run by students through a dialup computer link.

◆ Supporting the cause — The SVVCU board of directors volunteer their diverse range of skills to ensure the continued success of the credit union.

SVVCU, along with other credit unions throughout Colorado, has spearheaded the Courage Classic Bicycle Tour and Link Up for Children's Hospital, fund-raising campaigns that contributed nearly $3 million to The Children's Hospital over the past nine years. On the local level, the SVVCU is involved in many community projects, such as the Our Center Food Drive, which collected almost 2,400 food items during the 1998 holiday season.

St. Vrain Valley Credit Union strives not only to meet, but to exceed the needs and expectations of its members. With the continued support of its membership, as well as the board of directors, management and staff, SVVCU provides safety, soundness and the latest services with a personal touch.

◆ State-of-the-art facilities — The growing membership can count on the finest services in the building at 21st Avenue and Terry Street, which opened in 1995.

U of C Federal Credit Union

A unique "people helping people" philosophy sets U of C Federal Credit Union (U of C FCU) apart from other financial institutions. Like all credit unions, U of C FCU exists to offer benefits and advantages over other financial providers to help members attain their personal financial goals.

U of C FCU was chartered as a federal credit union in 1953. The personal vision of Ed Pirk, chief clerk in the university business office at the time, was to create a cooperative financial institution for the University of Colorado at Boulder (CU). The original members formed the credit union on the stairs of Macky Auditorium, pooling their shares to make loans to members. One year later, U of C FCU had grown to $35,500 in assets, a strong indication of the university employees' real desire for a member-owned credit union.

Quality service to members exemplified U of C FCU's purpose from the beginning because members have always taken a personal interest in the credit union's success. Members who deposit money in U of C FCU become owners of a democratically controlled financial cooperative. At the annual meeting, members vote for their representation on the volunteer board of directors. The board sets policy and defines the standards of operation, guiding the credit union in a direction that will have the most positive impact on members' lives. Under the guidance of the credit union's second president, M.R. Hellie, the board led U of C FCU into the electronic age, introducing ATMs and becoming one of the first credit unions in the country to offer share draft accounts.

Members entrust the board with charting the long-term direction of the credit union. Key volunteer leaders who have assumed this responsibility for U of C FCU include founding member Ray Johnson, Wray Frieboth, Ed Murrow and Fred Roecker. The board of directors recognized in the early 90s that the credit union needed additional space. In 1996, U of C FCU built and moved into its present headquarters on Diagonal Highway. The move consolidated all departments in one location and enhanced the credit union's technological capabilities to respond to members' future needs.

◆ L.E. Burkey (left), account holder number one, receives his passbook from Ed Pirk (right), the first treasurer and acting manager.

◆ A move into the new headquarters in 1996 allowed the credit union to consolidate many functions in one location.

The credit union now offers new products and services designed for all age groups, such as a children's saving club; a unique package of financial services for university students; expanded mortgage lending; and educational opportunities for seniors. A contract was signed in 1997 between U of C FCU and the university to develop the BuffOne Card. It functions as a student identification card and provides access to diverse credit union and university financial accounts. Such programs demonstrate the credit union's desire to search out quality improvements and product-service enhancements which provide better service to members.

Benefits of the credit union's "people helping people" philosophy extend beyond the doors of its offices. A

◆ Scholarship programs help young adults achieve their educational goals.

◆ Car-buying assistance implemented in the early 90s eases the process of purchasing a vehicle.

community relations program sponsors and contributes to a number of organizations, such as The Children's Hospital, college scholarship programs, The Boulder Food Bank, Toys for Tots and other local Boulder County projects. In 1990, the credit union was awarded the Dora Maxwell Social Responsibility Award, a national credit union award for community involvement.

By focusing on financial empowerment, the credit union has attracted new members who recognize the benefits of the services offered. This continuous growth promotes financial soundness and enables the credit union to respond quickly to the needs of its members. Most importantly, growth indicates the credit union is trusted by its members. In a world where other financial institutions are regularly merged into financial giants, U of C FCU remains locally owned and controlled.

The U of C Federal Credit Union Board of Directors and CEO Jan Hesalroad recognize that technology plays a critical role in supporting the credit union's mission and long-range business strategies. Continuous investment in proven technological advances will provide competitive and convenient services to members. The highest priority for the credit union will always be to fulfill its corporate mission: to anticipate and be responsive to the changing financial services needs of a growing and diverse membership.

◆ As part of its community involvement, "Rags" and other credit union volunteers regularly support local events such as Walk and Bike to work Week.

Boulder Municipal
Employees Federal Credit Union

"Boulder Municipal Employees Federal Credit Union (BME) is a member-owned cooperative established to provide quality financial services and guarantee a safe, sound financial environment." Guided by this powerful mission statement, this credit union, founded in 1965, has grown over the years to incorporate a broad field of satisfied members. Dedicated to the "people helping people" philosophy integral to the credit union movement, BME has consistently provided updated and expanded services to meet member needs.

Orville Hollis was among those city of Boulder employees who attended weekly meetings when the idea arose to form a credit union. With his extensive public service background and previous experience in starting a bank, Hollis proved instrumental in the founding of BME. He guided the original members through the process and became its first treasurer and manager, a job he retained from 1965-1977.

During the early years of BME, Hollis acted as the sole operator of the small institution. He kept the books by hand and did an amazing job in establishing the credit union considering its location: City Yards maintenance building B, in a five-by-eight-foot closet! While the credit union shifted locations many times, the commitment of Hollis and other founding members gave it consistency. Finally, in 1995, the credit union purchased its present building, gaining much-needed space.

With the dedicated guidance of its volunteer board of directors, BME has continued to expand member services. Current president Mark Lau strives to maintain this strong tradition, in part by keeping BME on the leading edge of technological innovation. One way this policy manifests itself is in the credit union's full-service Web site, allowing members access to accounts 24 hours a day.

BME's membership field has increased substantially since its inception. Along with city of Boulder employees, persons eligible for membership today include employees of other surrounding cities and towns, as well as employees and members of a number of local nonprofits and several local businesses. These members also play a huge role in the credit union's community involvement through events such as 1999's BME-sponsored silent auction to benefit KGNU Community Radio, an organization whose members are eligible for membership in the credit union.

The credit union's community service stretches far beyond Boulder. In 1996, 1997 and 1998, BME had the honor to host several Macedonians and Romanians sent by the World Council of Credit Unions (an international organization that helps develop credit unions around the world) to learn about credit union policy, procedures, accounting and marketing. In addition, BME members influenced the historical passing in 1998 of HR1151, the Credit Union Membership Access Act, which ensures consumers a choice in selecting where to conduct financial business. 1998 also brought BME the Credit Union National Association's Bridge Award for excellence in member education (awarded to a credit union of $30 million and under in assets).

From a tiny closet and eight founding members to a growing financial institution of over 5,000 members, BME has stayed true to its original mission. The credit union remains dedicated to member satisfaction, a sentiment that is captured in its vision statement: "Boulder Municipal Employees Federal Credit Union will be proactive in providing member service and education to our expanding member base and in giving members a personalized choice of efficient service delivery."

◆ *Photo by Johnson Photography*

Boulder Valley Credit Union

Credit unions in the United States spawned from a community spirit of "People Helping People" — members sharing their savings for others to borrow. To obtain an alternative to high interest loans and low earnings on savings offered by banks, employer groups such as teachers banded resources to charter their own credit union. Boulder Valley Schools Credit Union was chartered in 1959 by 26 educators who sought accessible low-cost financial services. Membership grew from 119 members and $19,977 in assets after the first year to 13,600 members and $72 million in assets in 1998. In 1987, "Schools" was dropped to reflect the diverse membership.

Boulder Valley Credit Union (BVCU) offers alternative financing to 210 associations and businesses, including public schools, churches and other organizations in Boulder Valley. In 1976, BVCU expanded its membership to include the employees of the Estes Park School District, and in 1978 the employees of the Town of Estes. In 1996, BVCU opened Estes Park's first credit union office to serve every leading employer and 135 organization groups. In 1998, the Boulder Community Hospital Federal Credit Union merged with BVCU. Its office site, located across from the hospital, became BVCU's third location.

In fact, BVCU and Estes Park are closely tied with credit union history. The first Credit Union National Association Conference was held in 1934 in Estes Park. Participants created the Federal Credit Union Act. In 1998, the Independent Banker's Association challenged credit unions, questioning whether they were abiding by the act's membership statutes. Legislators overwhelmingly voted in favor of credit unions, and preserved consumers' choice and the right for credit union expansion.

BVCU's creative signature is its community involvement: Coal Creek Elementary School was curious to see what 1 million pennies looked like and desiring to raise money for playground equipment and the "Make a Wish" Foundation, the children resolved to collect that amount. Although able to build a durable penny case, the school hadn't assessed the many hours required to accurately count the pennies by hand.

After three years, the school had amassed 300,000 pennies. With 700,000 pennies to go, the school agreed to finish at the end of the fourth year regardless of the final count. A "Penny Parent" from Coal Creek called local banks to locate an automatic counter and was unsuccessful. BVCU agreed to assist as the "Official Penny Counter." BVCU offered incentives and rewards to encourage students to redouble their efforts and reach the million penny goal. Perseverance and teamwork paid handsomely when the millionth penny was collected. That day, the principal conducted business from the roof, blowing bubbles and singing songs for the students, and praising them for their hard work.

◆ Boulder Valley Credit Union located on Arapahoe Avenue

The Penny Count community project won BVCU the prestigious credit union State and National Dora Maxwell Awards for prominent community involvement in 1998. This annual award is in memory of Maxwell, honoring her leadership role as a community volunteer, and recognizing credit unions for their unique, results-oriented community efforts. BVCU was the first Colorado credit union to win the national award.

BVCU works hard to strengthen its relations with school districts by providing classroom presentations to all grades, covering all financial topics. In 1998, BVCU placed second among Colorado credit unions and within the top 25 nationally for the number of students reached.

Heritage Bank

Community plays a central role in all aspects of operation for Heritage Bank. Founded as the independently owned Lafayette First Industrial Bank in 1973, the bank converted to a state charter in 1987, recreating its identity as an institution committed to serving the local community's banking needs. Through several name changes and steady growth, Heritage Bank has built a regional reputation for its exceptional staff, personal service and commitment to the communities it serves.

◆ Heritage Bank's flagship office on S. Public Road in Lafayette was known as Lafayette State Bank from 1991 to 1998.

As an independent community bank under local ownership and management, Heritage Bank supports its communities in a number of ways. The bank typically reinvests more than 90 percent of its consumer and business loan dollars in the locales it serves. In addition, it supports local causes as diverse as fund-raising drives for nonprofit agencies, mini-grants for public schools, volunteer firefighter recognition, scholarship programs, scouting leadership events and Habitat for Humanity.

Outside of office hours, many Heritage Bank employees volunteer their talents through a variety of philanthropic organizations and agencies. They have served as guest speakers, board members, sports coaches, festival organizers, chamber of commerce leaders, blood donors, educators, rotary club members, mentors, church elders and Meals on Wheels volunteers, among other things.

Leading this civic-minded staff is chairman and CEO Bob Beauprez, who, with his wife, Claudia, became the majority shareholder of the bank in 1990. A steadfast supporter of community banks and a lifelong resident of Boulder County, Beauprez followed his personal convictions in selling his family farm and assuming a leadership position at Heritage Bank. Beauprez's volunteer activities have included stints on the board of directors for the Independent Bankers of Colorado, the Community Medical Center and the Sister Carmen Community Center. He has also served as a trustee for the Boulder County Advisory Council and the Boulder Community Hospital Foundation; an adviser for the Community Foundation; and chairman of the Colorado State Republican Party.

◆ A well-trained, service-minded staff has been key to the bank's success.

In part because of its community orientation and emphasis on personal service, Heritage Bank has distinguished itself as a small, business-friendly financial institution at a time when fewer and fewer banks are willing to cater to small business owners and operators. A 1997 U.S. Small Business Administration report on credit availability to small businesses ranked Heritage Bank in the top 10 percent of 216 bank locations in Colorado. According to the report, Heritage extended more than $17 million to small businesses in loans of up to $250,000 during 1997.

Heritage Bank plans to continue its mission by offering a community banking alternative, delivering service with personal attention, and reinvesting in the neighborhoods it serves. From an institution with $5.6 million in assets at the end of 1990, the bank topped $125 million in assets by 1998. Such rapid growth attests to a healthy demand for a financial institution committed to personal service and loyalty to the community. With the help of its experienced staff, Heritage Bank will offer consumers viable choices in service-oriented community banking for years to come.

Premier Members Federal Credit Union

To appreciate the story of Premier Members Federal Credit Union, one must first understand credit unions as a whole. The Credit Union National Association (CUNA) defines a credit union as "a non-profit financial cooperative owned and operated by its members. The members pool their assets to provide themselves funds for loans and a wide variety of other financial services." The main difference between credit unions and other financial institutions is that credit unions are nonprofit — any earnings go back to the members. It is upon this premise that Premier Members, originally IBM Rocky Mountain EFCU, was founded in Boulder in 1966.

Products and services range from checking, savings and money market accounts to IRAs, credit cards and loans of all kinds including first mortgage loans.

The history of credit unions begins in Germany in 1864, when a group of farmers combined its money and lent to each other. The idea of consolidating funds to help others in the community soon spread to North America, where the first Canadian credit union was founded in Quebec in 1900, and the first in America was set up in New Hampshire in 1909. Edward Albert Filene played an instrumental role in the credit union movement in the United States. He donated millions of dollars to help credit unions expand westward from New England, and in 1934 became the first president of the CUNA.

Credit unions are traditionally founded by members who share a common bond, such as those few IBM employees who decided to start one in Boulder in the 60s. The original charter members began with a deposit of $5 each and a loan from an IBM credit union in Poughkeepsie, New York. Soon it started making small loans of $50 with volunteers performing transactions during their lunch hour. Eventually, IBM supplied the credit union with a desk to work out of and it was able to pay back the loan to its fellow IBM Poughkeepsie EFCU.

In the early days, the maximum deposit was $2,000 and the maximum loan was $200.

Today there is no limit! Premier Members now employs 66 people, has over 21,000 members and more than $155 million in assets. Members can include both IBM employees and their families throughout the entire Rocky Mountain region, as well as other select high-tech groups. Products and services range from checking, savings and money market accounts to IRAs, credit cards and loans of all kinds including first mortgage loans.

Because of its obvious link to technology, Premier Members was one of the first in the country to offer Internet account access. Members can check all of their accounts via a Web site and can even download account information into their home financial software package. It was also one of the first credit unions in the country to offer financial planning.

◆ A young member of the Premier Members Federal Credit Union makes a deposit.

Premier Members is active and involved in the Boulder community. Each year the employees staff an aid station at the Children's Hospital Courage Classic Bicycle Race. It is also involved with the United Way Pacesetters and the Boulder County Crime Stoppers Annual Golf Tournament.

Although it has grown into a major financial institution, the founding philosophy of Premier Members remains the same — people working together to find innovative ways to help each other.

Pueblo Bank & Trust Company

◆ Alva Adams (1850-1922) was a co-founder of Pueblo Bank & Trust and served as its first president. He also served two terms as Colorado's governor from 1887 to 1889, 1897 to 1899, and in 1905. *Courtesy Pueblo Library District*

When Alva Adams finished his first term as Colorado's governor in 1889, he jumped into business in Pueblo, the industrial capital of the state straddling the Arkansas River. Adams and his partners, W.W. Strait and Christopher Wilson, founded Pueblo Savings Bank on Pueblo's North Union Avenue with $250,000 in capital and solicited deposits from Pueblo's working class by emphasizing the firm's bedrock commitment to personal and commercial trust. In those days, before federally insured deposits, Adams and his fellow bankers touted their adherence to the "virtues of conservatism" — a phrase conveying that "nothing is left undone to assure the depositors that they will receive their principal and interest."

Based on this bedrock of personal and commercial trust, Adams' bank prospered. In ensuing years, it moved several times to better quarters. Its name also evolved. By 1909 it had become Pueblo Savings & Trust Company and, a half-century later, the bank settled on its current name, Pueblo Bank & Trust Company, headquartered at modern facilities at 5th and Court streets.

As the bank completed its first century in business, its directors modified its mission to reflect modern changes. The firm, its officers said, "has evolved from extolling the virtues of conservatism to a philosophy of progressivism and consumerism."

◆ Pueblo Savings Bank moved to the Whitcomb block at Third and Main streets in 1903, one of its several locations in more than a century of service. *Courtesy George Williams*

The ambitions inherent in the bank's outlook since Alva Adams' day were given a boost when, in the 1990s, Colorado's state legislature permitted banks to expand by establishing branches in communities outside their original base. Pueblo Bank & Trust looked outward and, beyond Pueblo, it quickly established its presence in the nearby towns of Canon City, Salida and Colorado Springs.

In 1998 Pueblo Bank & Trust responded to an opportunity to purchase a bank in Boulder. Apropos of its ability to respond swiftly and put its shoulder to the wheel, Pueblo Bank & Trust's acquisition took place on a Friday and, the following Monday, it opened its newest bank under its own name. That day, President and CEO Robert L. Hays opened the doors and greeted his first Boulder customer, a man concerned about his savings account. Hays reassured his client that all was well.

Now an established member of Boulder's financial community, Pueblo Bank & Trust fulfills its role by providing a full range of services to small businesses and individual depositors. Under the direction of its current executive officers, the bank has further redefined its mission for the present and future to include "prudent but aggressive practices that will accommodate the needs of the business community." In contrast to national trends, Pueblo Bank & Trust has remained in local ownership. This has enabled the bank to focus its energies and expertise on the local markets it serves. For instance, the bank will not use voice mail systems on its telephone lines, because it insists that when customers call, they should get a real person on the line.

The bank's principals say they will never consider changing the bank's name, no matter where they do business, because Pueblo Bank & Trust carries more than a century of trust equity with the people it serves.

14,256-feet-high Longs Peak is Boulder County's highest point.
1997 photo by Jim Havey

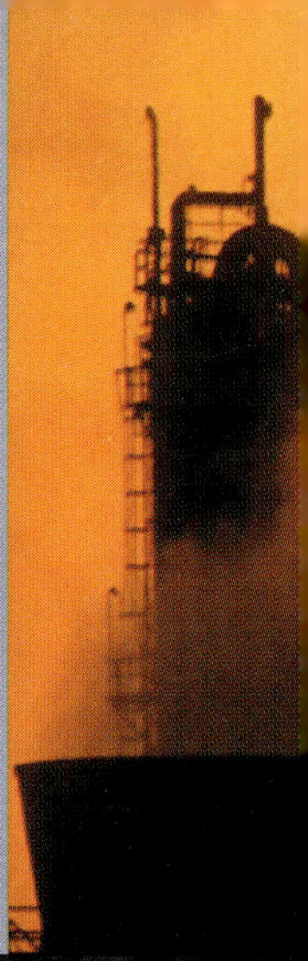

Spyder Active Sports	218
Ball Aerospace & Technologies Corp.	220
Case Logic	221
Celestial Seasonings, Inc.	222
D&K Printing, Inc.	223

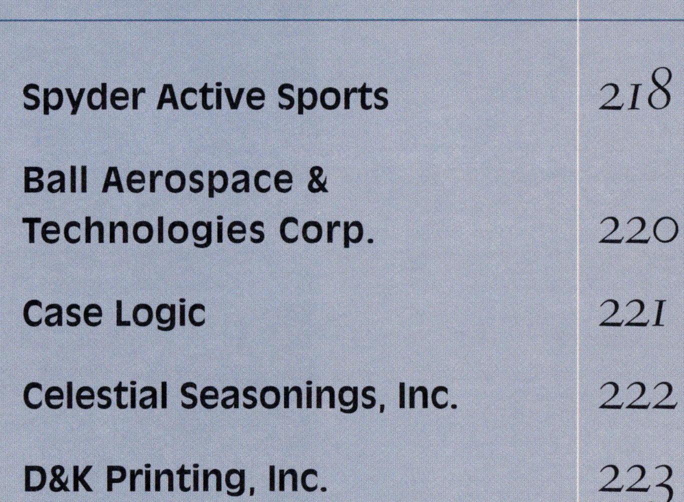

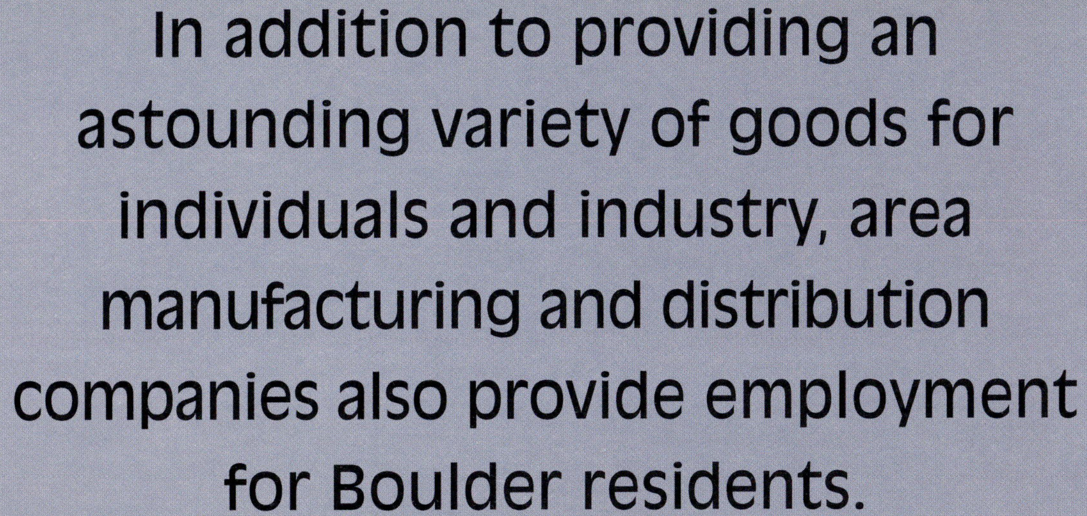

In addition to providing an astounding variety of goods for individuals and industry, area manufacturing and distribution companies also provide employment for Boulder residents.

Manufacturing & Distribution

Spyder Active Sports

In 1978, when his ski-racing sons Jake and Bill were 16 and 14, David Jacobs became aware of their need for padded racing sweaters. With a little research, he discovered an Italian company was the only company manufacturing such a sweater. Convinced he could make a better product, Jacobs designed and produced his own version. He sent a mailer announcing his product to 7,000 ski racers, and received an overwhelming response. Jacobs realized that he had hit upon a market area with an extremely high demand and a low supply.

Thus the Spyder brand was born. The company name emerged when Jacobs' son, Bill, dubbed Spyder's first ski pants "spider pants" due to their striped padding. The owner of a 1964 Ferrari Spyder, Jacobs believed correctly that the name Spyder would stick in people's minds. Henry Beer, currently the president of Communication Arts in Boulder, designed the company's black widow logo. This logo, along with the company's name, would go on to earn international recognition in the skiing world.

Spyder initially featured a one-stop catalogue aimed at the high-profile but numerically small consumer base of serious racers and coaches, as Jacobs wanted to avoid sales representatives, interactions with ski shops, credit and trade shows. After two years, however, he saw that Spyder could not manufacture goods fast enough to keep up with catalogue orders. Realizing that the longer time allowed between orders from ski shops and deliveries to them would solve this problem, Spyder changed gears to become a wholesale business in 1980.

◆ Founder David Jacobs, president and co-owner of Spyder Active Sports

The number of orders overwhelmed Jacobs and his first employee, Jeff Temple, a professional racer who tested some of the first Spyder gear and eventually stayed with the company for 15 years. With the base of operations (his kitchen) overflowing, Jacobs perceived the need for another change. He asked Danny Hanson, the president of Hanson Ski Boots, to warehouse Spyder's products. Hanson agreed and helped Jacobs finance the company's growth, eventually offering to purchase Spyder in 1981. Jacobs sold the company to Hanson for $75,000.

Early in 1982, Hanson informed Jacobs that he was filing for bankruptcy, but was willing to sell Spyder back for $50,000 so that it would not become involved. Eager to reacquire the company, but unable to afford the purchase price himself, Jacobs sent a telex to his clothing manufacturer, Mr. Shimokubo, in Osaka, Japan. He informed Shimokubo that they could buy the Spyder brand for $50,000, but he only had $25,000, hopeful that Shimokubo would be interested in funding the other half. Shimokubo responded that he'd consider the offer.

Two days later, Jacobs' loan officer at First National Bank called to ask what he wanted to do with the $50,000 that had arrived into his account from the Mitsubishi Bank in Japan. Amazingly, Shimokubo had sent the money without signing any sort of agreement. For over 17 years, this remarkably trusting partnership has continued between two businessmen half a world apart. A one-paragraph agreement defines the terms of their co-ownership of the world-renowned Spyder Active Sports.

Spyder's focus has always been on the skiing elite. Since 1989, it has sponsored the U.S. Ski Team, a sponsorship that will continue at least through 2005. Spyder has sponsored national ski teams from Sweden, Australia, Norway, Yugoslavia and Canada. Many of the best skiers

◆ Spyder-sponsored Olympic Gold Medallists Picabo Street and Tommy Moe

in the world race in Spyder clothing, including Picabo Street, who wore the Spyder brand in her 1998 Olympic gold medal performances. Spyder contracts with top skiers like Street and Tommy Moe to build their own signature collections of products.

Always striving to produce the best and most advanced products for its customers, Spyder recently incorporated Speedwyre technology into its racing clothing. This high-tech but remarkably simple redesigned seam reduces aerodynamic drag by as much as 40 percent. In the 1996 World Championship Downhill race, Street, Hillary Lindh and Megan Gerety all posted their best results ever wearing Speedwyre — Street came in first, Lindh third, and Gerety fifth. Wearing Speedwyre, Lindh went on to win a gold medal in the 1997 World Championship. After this race, the third place team protested, which led to the ban of Speedwyre from the skiing events at the 1998 Olympic Games in Nagano. However, other sports picked it up. The U.S. Speed Skating Team posted personal records in Nagano with Speedwyre modified suits. And wearing a Speedwyre suit, downhill rollerblader Pat Naylor won a gold medal at the Extreme Games in 1998.

Spyder's unique role in the ski clothing industry has garnered it recognition in both the business and skiing world. Jacobs and Spyder won the Esprit Entrepreneur of Distinction Award in 1991, and Ernst and Young LLP recognized the company as a finalist for its Rocky Mountain Entrepreneur of the Year Award in 1997. Harvard Business School also selected the company to be used as a case study in two of its courses.

Aside from its powerful role in the business of ski clothing, Spyder finds time to contribute to the Boulder community. Jacobs speaks frequently at entrepreneurial conferences, and the company works with the University of Colorado's entrepreneur internship program. At the end of every year, Spyder gives seconds and product returns to charities such as the Boulder Homeless Shelter. Spyder also donates articles of clothing to silent auctions for schools and other community organizations.

Spyder will continue to have an enduring impact on community life by helping make Boulder the premier address for outdoor sports. Already recognized by much of the industry as the No. 1 technical skiwear brand worldwide, Spyder's long-term plans include aggressive expansion into other athletic clothing markets. By 2000, the Spyder brand should appear in a high-tech clothing line called the Venom Collection, designed for other adrenaline-driven sports such as surfing and wakeboarding. At the Winter Olympic Games in 2002, Spyder hopes to be the strongest high performance multisport company present. By basing its products on the demands of elite athletes and promising the quality of clothing that these athletes have come to expect, the presence of Spyder Active Sports will continue to contribute to Boulder's status as a destination for outdoor sports enthusiasts for years to come.

Ball Aerospace & Technologies Corp.

For more than four decades, Ball Aerospace & Technologies Corp. has been a pioneer in the frontiers of science and space, creating the technologies that expand our knowledge of the universe.

Ball Aerospace's ingenuity, engineering skills and scientific expertise have made it the choice provider of small- to medium-sized spacecraft, civilian and defense payloads, science instruments and a wide range of subsystems, components, software and support services. Its customers include the National Aeronautics and Space Administration (NASA), Department of Defense (DOD), National Oceanic and Atmospheric Administration (NOAA), universities, aerospace prime contractors and international organizations.

◆ By the fourth and final servicing mission, the four-story Hubble Space Telescope, launched in 1990, will have seven Ball Aerospace-built science instruments aboard.

Yet all this grew out of the simple glass jars used for preserving peaches. It began in the late 1880s in Muncie, Indiana, where the five Ball brothers from New York started a business making glass jars for home canning. By 1956 their company was ready to expand. Seeking to inject exciting, new technology into the packaging business, Ball Brothers Company teamed up with scientists at the University of Colorado in Boulder experimenting in sun-oriented pointing control research. Ball Brothers Research Corporation was born.

Today, Ball Aerospace & Technologies Corp. is a wholly owned subsidiary of Ball Corp. In 1959 it won its first contract from the newly created NASA to build a series of satellites to study the sun. Evolving with the aerospace business, Ball quickly gained a reputation for tough problem solving.

Among many accomplishments, Ball Aerospace restored the "vision" for the axial instruments on the Hubble Space Telescope, flew the first Skylab science instruments and created the antenna and electronics for the space shuttle that allowed archaeologists to observe ancient ruins in South American jungles. It also provided the cryogenic hardware that enabled the first direct measurements of the big-bang theory.

Ball Aerospace has developed more than 130 complex instruments and 12 spacecraft for NASA missions, to explore the universe from the entire spectrum of gamma ray, X-ray, ultraviolet, visible, infrared and radio frequency sources. Ball hardware has flown on satellites, the space shuttle, planetary probes, aircraft, balloons and suborbital rockets.

Twenty years ago, Ball cameras sent back pictures of Mars from the Viking Orbiter. When the Mars Pathfinder landed on the Red Planet on July 4, 1997, it relayed back images through a Ball antenna. Ball Aerospace built the GEOSAT Follow-on (GFO) satellite, which transmits precise oceanographic information to ships at sea and Navy facilities on shore. The company's expertise encompasses avionics, simulation and training, electro-optics and cryogenics. Its defense contracts include antenna and video products, star trackers, pointing, acquisition and tracking devices.

Ball Aerospace & Technologies Corp. maintains strong ties with Boulder County. Ball employees are often seen in local classrooms talking about science and space topics such as the Hubble Space Telescope. Health and human services are also a priority for community outreach, both in terms of donations and volunteer involvement.

Commercial space is the frontier of the future. Ball cameras will enable pilots of the giant Boeing 777s to see their landing gear and allow each passenger a panoramic view of the landscape below. New radar technology will make mapping Earth easier and more accurate. Ball spacecraft and optics will also enable us to study the ground at a resolution of about one yard square — invaluable for urban planning, the laying of utility services, studying forest fires, and anything that requires a detailed look at an area of land.

An exciting offshoot from glass jars and aluminum cans, Ball Aerospace & Technologies Corp. changes the way we view the world today.

Case Logic

In 1984, Jamie Temple noticed the absence of quality audiocassette cases on the market, a realization that inspired him to purchase a cassette tray and sew a forest green, soft-sided nylon prototype of a 15-capacity case. Little did he know that this initial effort would end up proudly displayed on the wall of his office, but only after he and the company he created, Case Logic, had spurred a revolution in the field of audio storage products.

From its humble beginnings, Case Logic has grown into a wonderful success story. The company now offers products at over 30,000 locations worldwide and supports in excess of 12 million consumer purchases each year. Four distinct product areas make up the company's sphere of action: audio accessories, photo/video accessories, computer accessories and automotive accessories. In addition to traditional sales, Case Logic offers Case Connect, a service that allows companies such as recent customers Maxell and Panasonic to custom-design bags or accessories for promotional or other needs.

After watching Case Logic prosper, Temple moved on, handing leadership over to Peter Storz in 1995. Storz, who had joined forces with Temple one month after he shipped his first product, believes that the company's success can be traced to a simple but unique formula, captured in Case Logic's mission statement: "To create superior value for all our customers by continually improving and delivering quality, innovative products and flexible services that exceed expectations and assure our mutual growth and prosperity." From Temple's garage in 1984 to Case Logic's current 158,000-square-foot facility, Case Logic has maintained its passion for attending to details and listening to customers' needs.

In addition to its stellar customer service record, ideas and creative energy from the people who make Case Logic happen worldwide have contributed to the company's enduring development. Hagemeyer N.V.'s acquisition of a majority stake in the company in 1991 has supported Case Logic's drive to expand. A positive partnership with this Dutch trading company has given Case Logic the financial resources to further increase its markets while allowing its entrepreneurial spirit to flourish.

◆ Case Logic's headquarters in Longmont, Colorado

Case Logic has expanded its operations to include Hong Kong and the Netherlands, as well as a joint venture in Canada. However, Boulder County is Case Logic's home base. Product assembly and distribution for the United States take place at the headquarters on Diagonal Highway, and Case Logic contracts much of its component manufacturing out to companies in Front Range communities. Another facet of its commitment to the local community is evident in its strong relationship with the United Way.

◆ One of Case Logic's many compact disc organizers

Case Logic's success in the Boulder community and throughout the world lends it the power to dictate its own future. The Case Logic vision statement serves as an inspiring reminder of this to both employees and customers alike: "(Our goal is) to maximize the Case Logic brand by providing exceptional value to a worldwide customer. Strengthened by our shared passion for excellence, we strive to be the premier marketer and distributor of quality, functional products and superior services in our pursued businesses."

Celestial Seasonings, Inc.

What constitutes a healthy mix of ingredients? An extraordinary entrepreneur, a farsighted local community, and a nation in need of healthier habits equals a recipe for success, as Celestial Seasonings, Inc. found in Boulder in 1971.

Founder Mo Siegel began picking herbs on his beloved hikes in Colorado's mountains. First concocting teas for friends as a hobby, they persuaded him to sell it. In need of money, he and a friend found herbs in the hills of Boulder, and picked 19 bales of tea. They packaged it in hand-sewn muslin bags fastened with scrap telephone wire to sell at local health stores. To their great delight, MO's 36 Herb Tea® engendered quite a following! Unlike medicinal-tasting teas on the market, this herbal tea tasted delicious, and Celestial Seasonings was born.

◆ Hand picking teas on the Colorado mountainsides, Siegel's belief in providing products that "nurture people's bodies and uplift their souls" has led Celestial Seasonings to become the premiere tea company in the industry.

Working in an old barn outside of Boulder, Mo and his fellow entrepreneur, John Hay, dreamed of a national herbal tea company, and began creating and selling new teas. John's wife, Beth, an artist, helped create the unique, appealing look that Celestial Seasonings is famous for, including the legendary Sleepytime® bear that marks the tea's celebrated packaging. At a time when the food industry was making negative trends towards using chemicals and less nutritious ingredients, Celestial Seasonings and others went on a crusade to bring health-consciousness into the forefront. "It wasn't just the success or the money," says Siegel, sincerely. "We were on a mission to make the world a healthier place."

◆ As more Americans desire alternatives to increase health and prevent disease, Celestial Seasonings' reputation for excellence is bringing a new standard to the herbal supplements market, and new confidence to consumers.

Working closely with farmers the world over, the company found reliable sources for such exotic ingredients as hibiscus flowers and other nutritious herbs. Its ingenuity attracted food industry giant Kraft Foods, Inc., which bought them in 1984. Kraft's influence broadened Celestial Seasonings' markets while introducing a new line of traditional black teas. In 1988, Kraft sold Celestial Seasonings back to its management, and in 1991, Siegel returned as chairman and CEO to restore the company to it's original mission: exceptional service to the customer, in providing healthy, natural products that "nurture people's bodies and uplift their souls."

Although rather uncommon for a $100 million company, this mission led Celestial Seasonings to become a national industry leader, offering over 40 delicious varieties of herbal, green, black, organic, wellness and chai teas. And that's just the beginning. Celestial Seasonings has broadened its focus to "All Things Herbal." It recently introduced a bold new line of nutritional, herbal supplements and blended medicinal teas that bear the company's famous name, and the quality for which it stands.

Celestial Seasonings always strives to give back to the Boulder community, and attracts 100,000 tourists to the plant and the Celestial Café each year. A well-known advocate of local art, Celestial sponsors an annual teapot design competition. The company is also resuming a popular event called the Red Zinger Cycling Classic, which established a legacy in the 70s and 80s, attracting Tour de France and famous local cyclists to participate in a truly Celestial athletic event. If you talk to Mo Siegel about the company's active sponsorship in these wonderful community events, he'll tell you that Celestial Seasonings is simply a reflection of the environment of the community itself. "I think Celestial and Boulder are a great mix. We couldn't have picked a better place to build a company," says Siegel, smiling.

D&K Printing, Inc.

D&K Printing, Inc., founded in 1964, is a family-run business that focuses on providing customers with high-quality work while treating them with kindness and respect. The printing industry has changed dramatically over the last three decades and D&K has rolled with the changes. With the growth of high-tech companies in the Boulder area, demands on printers have become increasingly sophisticated.

Best of Category Benny Award presented by the Printing Industries of America

Jim Kinkead, owner and founder, was drawn to Boulder to attend the University of Colorado and has remained in the area for over 35 years. During that time, D&K has provided printing services for some of the area's most prominent businesses and organizations: the Denver Nuggets, the Colorado Avalanche, IBM, U S WEST, the University of Colorado, Blue Mountain Arts and the Denver Broncos, along with hundreds of others.

In the early days, printers were more independent. They would tell a customer when a job would be ready, instead of the customer determining the deadline. Today, customer service and meeting deadlines are the keys to success. Fortunately, D&K was ahead of the times. Kinkead founded his business with the idea that treating people in a friendly, courteous manner and providing a quality product would keep them coming back. This philosophy has paid off. D&K has expanded from a small, local printer with two employees in a 1,500-square-foot office, to a nationally known, award-winning business with over 50 employees in a 20,000-square-foot facility. Some employees have been with the company for over 15 years! This focus on both the client and the employee is what sets D&K apart from other printers.

The printing industry has been greatly affected by advances in technology and computers. In the early days, most of D&K's business was simple — newsletters and letterhead printed in one or two colors. Now, the bulk of its work is complex four or eight-color projects made possible by computer-aided graphic design, digital color separations and modernized production equipment. In addition to traditional presses, D&K operates a digital offset press which not only generates complex color jobs, but it can also produce unique, personalized information it receives from a database. Each sheet can be a custom job with different photos and text on it. Because D&K has embraced these new technologies, it has been able to keep pace with the sophisticated demands of Boulder's growing business community.

D&K's presence in the Boulder community can be found predominantly in the arts and recreation arenas. D&K helps to sponsor the popular Memorial Day Boulder Creek Festival, the Open Studios Art Tour, and the YMCA Boulder Dash 5K Run. It also donates printing services to the Boulder County YMCA, Boulder County Hospice, Community Food Share, The Foundation for Boulder Valley Schools and others.

In 1998, D&K was recognized by the Printing Industries of America with a Best of Category Benny Award, named for the premier printer, Benjamin Franklin. Out of nearly 5,000 entries, only 76 Bennys were awarded, with D&K the only Colorado printer to receive one.

With its focus on people, integrity and quality, D&K Printing, Inc. adds a unique touch of color to the Boulder landscape.

High-speed presses help D&K produce top-notch printing jobs.

Mike's Camera 226

Allegro Coffee Company 230

McGuckin Hardware 232

Neptune Mountaineering 234

Peppercorn 236

Art Cleaners 238

Art Mart 239

Beale Fine Art Picture Framing 240

Boulder Cork 241

Boulder Wine Merchant 242

Crossroads Mall 243

Fisher Chevrolet Honda 244

Foot of the Mountain Motel 245

Kinsley & Co. 246

Lafayette Collectables & Flea Market 247

Lighting Plus 248

MacLaren Markowitz Gallery 249

Helping Hands Health Education 250

North Boulder Liquor 251

Pasta Jay's 252

Pearl Street Inn 253

Rocky Mountain Joe's Cafe 254

Sturtz and Copeland 255

Twin Peaks Mall 256

The Village 257

Boulder retail and dining establishments, service industries, arts, leisure and convention facilities offer an impressive variety of choices for Boulder residents and visitors alike.

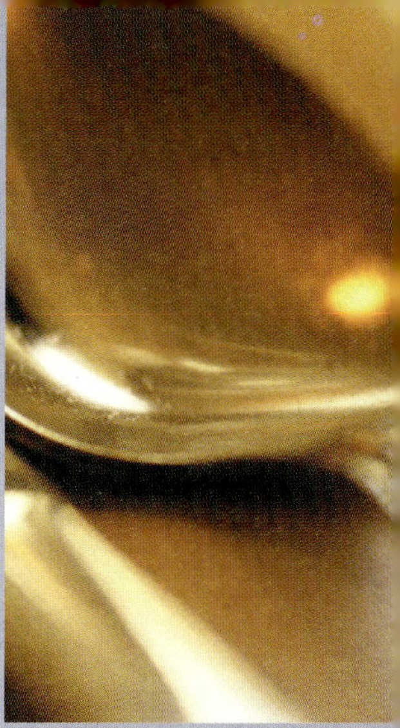

Marketplace

Mike's Camera

Few things in life are as powerful as photographs. A single image printed on paper can evoke forgotten memories or strong emotions. In advertising, it has been proven that carefully chosen images are far more compelling than words. In much the same way, fleeting moments of our own lives become priceless when captured on film. An extraordinary store in Boulder is dedicated to helping customers capture perfect images, and its remarkable service represents a model in the industry that is taking it far beyond the scope of the Boulder area.

Mike's Camera is an award-winning imaging center that has become a focal point for industry professionals and amateur camera buffs alike. With satellite super stores springing up along the Front Range, it offers a plethora of products and services spanning a huge spectrum of imaging needs. Mike's Camera has a 32-year history of outstanding service and record growth, and it all started with a man dedicated to family and unprecedented quality in business.

Kaloust Christianian acquired Mike's Camera from its previous owner in 1980. With a vision of what he knew the store could become, Kaloust began his dream in the 4,500-square-foot facility on Pearl Street, which housed 2,800 square feet of retail space, offices and a warehouse. His absolute insistence on quality and professionalism sparked an unequaled reputation in the area, and the store began to grow rapidly. Kaloust was very pleased when his sons, Jirair, Vahé and Alex joined the staff at Mike's Camera. He was even more pleased to see them apply their passion for photography into a dedication to learning all aspects of the business — from warehousing to the knowledge of imaging equipment and supplies. They prided themselves on becoming knowledgeable of current conditions, future trends and advanced technology in the imaging industry. The family team consists of father Kaloust as president, and sons: Jirair, vice president of finance and administration; Vahé, vice president of sales and marketing of imaging products; and Alex, vice president of sales and marketing of imaging services.

Mike's Camera is an award-winning imaging center that has become a focal point for industry professionals and amateur camera buffs alike.

In November of 1993, the opening of the 22,000-square-foot Boulder super store represented the Christianian's commitment to expanding its focus of the business far beyond its origins to serve the growing needs of the Boulder community. The staff at Mike's Camera worked with the city of Boulder to ensure that the new building would be a source of pride to the community. The super store was designed by Architecturedenver, whose principals, Arpie and Steve Chucovich, are the daughter and son-in-law of Kaloust Christianian. In 1994, the building was awarded the Design Merit Award by the American Institute of Architects. In addition to the

◆ The Boulder superstore at the corner of Folsom and Pearl, a wonderland of products and services

retail facility, the Boulder super store combines a state-of-the-art photo lab, warehouse, industrial/commercial division, corporate offices and rental space. The overall effect is that of a synergistic organization conducive to attracting retail customers and the commercial base that comprises the heart of the business.

With the opening of the new store, the employee base grew from 30 to 70. Mike's Camera is unique in its policy that each employee who has customer contact is required to qualify as a certified photographic consultant and then maintain that status. The program, implemented by the Photo Marketing Association, is a comprehensive examination covering photography and imaging, digital imaging, video and other aspects of photographic technology. It requires the strictest standards in color balance, consistency and overall quality. This training ensures that every customer that enters Mike's Camera is sure to receive the most knowledgeable service of any store around, and that means greater customer satisfaction. It also means high employee satisfaction because the staff feels competent to meet each customer's individual needs, and dramatic results can be seen in the finished product. In the hands of Mike's Camera professionals, who use only the most advanced and highest-quality film processing equipment for both 35mm and APS, the pictures have markedly superior color, quality and consistency.

No other single area retail store processes as much film on a daily basis as Mike's Camera. According to Vahé Christianian, this is the underlying core of every service the store offers. Whether the customer is a novice with film from a family vacation, or the professional hoping for a Pulitzer Prize in photography, he or she can be assured that only the highest-quality materials will be used in this state-of-the-art processing lab. Mike's Camera is then proud to offer a service not found at most other commercial processing labs: staff can critique rolls of film for customers, providing feedback from lighting to composition, etc. that will help its customers take better pictures each time. The photos themselves are printed on Kodak Royal paper — the thickest and highest archival-quality paper in the business. Each print has the negative number printed on the back for easy matching, a service no one else in Colorado offers. Finally, each negative is packaged in stiff, acid-free negative sleeves for optimal protection.

Customers find that all aspects of developing and printing, from one-hour photo finishing to greeting cards, photo business cards, posters and enlargements are available at the Boulder super store. Posters up to 55 inches wide can be produced from a favorite photograph on 24 different materials, from watercolor papers to canvas to Belgium linen and more. Mounting and laminating services are also available, up to 40 inches wide. In addition, Mike's Camera offers a wonderful variety of novelty items made personal with photos, such as T-shirts, coffee mugs and puzzles. Side applications include processing and mounting of slides. The company develops an amazing amount of black-and-white photographs for novices, artist environments and museums.

◆ Mike's Camera boasts the largest selection of binoculars and telescopes in the Colorado region, including quality optics for all ages and all applications.

Mike's Camera carries one of the largest selections of photographic and video equipment in Colorado. Consumer cameras, professional, high-end, medium or large-format cameras, lenses, dark room equipment — traditional and digital — digital cameras, computer and digital printing devices can all be found at the Boulder super store. All imaging needs, from studio lighting to video camcorders, VCRs, binoculars and telescopes are available. The commercial division supplies broadcast cameras and audio-visual equipment to professional studios.

◆ With more cameras and accessories than any other place in Boulder, Mike's Camera is a photo buff's paradise.

Whether one wants to gain experience with photo equipment before buying, or try a specialized piece of equipment for a photo shoot, amateur and professional photographers can rent anything from consumer point-and-shoot cameras to very high-end professional photo equipment at Mike's Camera. A portion of the rental fee may also be applied to the purchase. Corporate customers can find audio-visual equipment and LCD projectors, as well as boardroom systems and screens for special presentations. Production of digital, large-format prints for retail in-store displays, graphics and visuals for trade show applications, and weatherized images for buses are only limited by the imagination of the customer.

The commercial/industrial division meets the needs of the professional community by providing a full range of high-end equipment, from infrared camera systems to video equipment for TV stations, VCRs and editing equipment to electron microscopy film for medical applications.

In a field where change and innovation are constants, classes and literature on the latest imaging techniques and processes are essential for competency. Mike's Camera offers an impressive collection of instructional materials and classes on using the newest photographic and digital imaging equipment. The instructors are well trained on these advance technologies and draw upon first-hand experience.

Mike's Camera offers the longest still-camera repair warranty of any camera repair facility in Colorado: one full year, twice the industry standard. Whether it is a Camcorder, VCR, projector or other imaging equipment, the video and photo technicians at Mike's Camera provide fast, expert repair service to meet customers' immediate and special repair needs. Acquiring the prestigious Rocky Mountain Camera Repair Facility in September 1998, Mike's Camera is now a factory-authorized repair center for most major brands of photographic equipment. A complete line of professional studio and camera equipment will soon be available for rental at the facility.

All major brands of imaging equipment, often double the product selection offered by its competitors, are available at Mike's Camera. By constantly updating inventory and selection, the staff at Mike's Camera is able to provide the best equipment and values to its customers. Year after year, Mike's Camera receives Best of Boulder awards from the *Daily Camera* and the *Boulder Weekly* for extraordinary service and product selection. It is this willingness to meet and exceed customer expectations that has made Mike's Camera the largest independent photographic dealer and reseller in the Rocky Mountain Region.

Year after year, Mike's Camera receives Best of Boulder awards from the Daily Camera and the Boulder Weekly for extraordinary service and product selection.

As the Christianian team watched the overwhelming success of the Boulder super store, it quickly brought about the realization that it was time for expansion, only this time to other locations throughout the front range. September 1998 saw the opening of the new Park Meadows store as a retail resource for customers in the south Denver area. At the Park Meadows location, customers can find answers to all of their photography needs, from traditional to digital imaging; from hardware to supplies to support. Such a full-service concept is an innovation in the industry. With the March 1999 opening of its newest retail location on Colorado Boulevard in Denver, the goal of providing a full range of imaging services to area customers is another step closer to realization.

The Internet will play a big part in customer service in the future of Mike's Camera. Two dramatically different Web sites will serve as online catalogs and information centers. Filling customer orders over the Internet, providing the sophisticated equipment that enables the customer to create, process and produce digital documentation and visuals without leaving the home or office — these are all a part of the foreseeable future for Mike's Camera.

Although the company is growing swiftly, it is still in its infancy. Mike's Camera plans to expand to cities across the United States. The organization's in-depth mission is not to be part of the of the basic evolution of the business, but in the revolution of the industry. This is particularly appropriate at this time of rapidly advancing technology, wherein products and services can change overnight with the introduction of new discoveries in imaging technology. Mike's Camera realizes that the only way to survive each new technology wave is to rise to the top of it. As a result of this philosophy, training and continuing education for both employees and management is critical. Strong roots in the Boulder community combined with the strong ethics instilled by their father have taught them to value growth, changing technology, but above all, people.

That is also the number one reason why Mike's Camera's contributions to the community extend far beyond the professional. The company has a proud history of helping local and national nonprofit organizations, such as promoting the Special Olympics and donating the proceeds of Christmas tree sales to the National Cancer Institute. Other involvement such as active membership in the Boulder Chamber of Commerce proves that giving back to the community is important to both employees and the management of Mike's Camera. No solicitation goes unanswered. The Mike's Camera team feels strongly that success is measured by the number of solicitations it receives and the positive image it projects to the community by being a part of it.

Whether visiting a Mike's Camera in Boulder or in another city in Colorado — or eventually across the nation — there will always be one thing in common that differentiates this store form other imaging stores. This is still a family business, and the passion for photography is felt throughout each store. There is a true desire to cater to each customer and offer the kind of quality that is not provided elsewhere. That core, which has brought Mike's Camera to the forefront of the industry, means not just meeting clients' expectations, but exceeding them. Undoubtedly, that's why customers entrust their precious memories to the staff of Mike's Camera, and why they so often return.

◆ Mike's Camera has the highest-quality photofinishing and film processing services, using Kodak Royal Gold photographic paper for the greatest color and most archival prints available.

Allegro Coffee Company

In an era when virtually every community boasts at least one trendy espresso shop, it is not surprising to learn that Boulder is home to a number of coffee-related businesses. But Boulder's flourishing coffee culture is no mere manifestation of the country's latest gourmet craze. Great coffee was right at home in Boulder before most of us had ever heard the word arabica.

Allegro Coffee Company founder and chairman Jeffrey Cohn opened his first shop, The Brewing Market, in 1977. Three generations of expertise backed Cohn's venture. His grandfather, Harry Cohn, founded Superior Coffee — one of America's original coffee companies and a giant in the field today — in 1908. A gourmet coffee shop and espresso bar, The Brewing Market pioneered the introduction of specialty coffees to the Boulder area. By 1980, the original Brewing Market had expanded to two stores. Soon after, Cohn began roasting his own beans on the premises, exposing Boulder to true gourmet, custom-roast specialty coffee for the first time.

In 1985, increasing demand in the wholesale market prompted Cohn to sell The Brewing Market and launch Allegro Coffee Company, an import, roasting and wholesale distribution venture. Cohn's insistence on using only the purest quality ingredients and traditional, handcrafted roasting methods sparked the interest of local natural foods retailers, just as the natural foods market was beginning a phase of dynamic nationwide expansion. The result was a partnership of shared priorities and ideals which continues to shape and encourage Allegro Coffee's development today.

By 1990, Allegro Coffee had grown to 25 employees. Five years later, Cohn assumed the post of chairman, promoting then Marketing Director Terry Tierney to president. With a full-time staff of 75 and a secure reputation as a national leader in specialty coffees, Allegro continued to enjoy particular success in the natural foods arena. Natural products pioneer Whole Foods Market — one of Allegro Coffee's earliest customers — acquired the coffee company in 1997, bringing to culmination a decade of mutually beneficial business relations. The acquisition united two closely related business which had grown up together to dominate their respective industries. According to Tierney, the companies form a particularly successful union because of their driving passion for quality and a shared commitment to environmental and social issues.

Their passion is evident to anyone who has visited Allegro's "cupping room." Here Master Roaster Kevin Knox brews and samples cup after cup, scrutinizing every nuance of flavor and body in order to achieve the perfect roast. While Allegro produces a number of superb, dark French roasts and espresso blends, the company's ultimate triumph lies in its magnificent lighter-roast, single-origin coffees, which give full expression to the unique characteristics of its premium beans.

Much like the grapes used in winemaking, coffee beans reflect even the subtlest variations of the landscapes and climates in which they grow. To create Allegro coffees, Knox first hand-selects the finest arabica crops from small farms around the world. Once the chosen beans reach Boulder, he roasts, brews and samples a painstaking series of small test batches. Knox strives to coax from every bean its distinctive "Taste of Place," the unique flavor and character that result from a crop's particular microclimate and growing terrain. To

underscore the significance of the "Taste of Place" in its coffee philosophy, Allegro frequently incorporates the names of the small farms where the coffees originate into its retail packaging labels.

Allegro strives to recognize the contribution of small-scale coffee farmers not only through its packaging, but also through direct action in coffee-growing communities. A major contributor to Coffee Kids (a nonprofit organization dedicated to improving the lives of families involved in coffee production), Allegro sponsored the construction of two schools in Jalapa, Mexico, in 1993. Allegro has also taken a leadership role in promoting sustainable agriculture, favoring coffees grown without the pesticides and chemical fertilizers that can harm the people, plants and animals of the world's coffee-growing regions. In short, Allegro is committed to a definition of quality which takes into account not only the characteristics of its coffees, but also the social and environmental integrity of the processes by which they are produced.

Our goal is to be a good neighbor, both locally and internationally," explains Tierney. Closer to home, that means extensive support for the Boulder community. A colorful quilt with an environmental theme hangs in Allegro's conference room, a handmade gift from local school children who visited the company to study the environmental lessons of the coffee industry. Through such educational programs and through financial contributions to dozens of area organizations, Allegro demonstrates that public service is a top priority.

Tierney points out that Allegro's intense commitment to global and local issues is not only good public relations, but also good business. The company's reputation for corporate responsibility and social activism has helped to attract and inspire the top-notch staff upon whom Allegro's success depends. "Maybe it's just the caffeine," Tierney jokes, "but everyone who works here shares an incredible energy and passion for their work and for the company."

Though Allegro Coffee's actions and ideals are far-reaching, even global, in scale, every aspect of the company's identity boils down to the coffee and the community where it all began. "We are in a fortunate position for social activism," says Tierney, "because the people of Boulder are receptive to us. They feel strongly about our coffee, so they take an interest in the causes we support." It's no wonder that the city of Boulder and Allegro Coffee, having grown up together, share a cozy bond of mutual affection and respect.

A unique house blend, custom made by Allegro, will likely be found on a visit to any of Boulder's many, locally owned coffee shops. "We're proud of how we've contributed to Boulder as a community and to the city's distinctive coffee scene," says Tierney.

Allegro Coffee has undoubtedly done much to bring great taste and service to the community, enhancing Boulder's own unmistakable "Taste of Place."

◆ *Photo by Johnson Photography*

◆ *Photo by Johnson Photography*

McGuckin Hardware

From keys to camping goods, power tools to paints, forks to freshly cut flowers, McGuckin Hardware carries it all, in a wide variety of sizes and shapes. It even has the kitchen sink, in many styles and colors, of course. Described as "not your typical hardware store," by owner and manager Dave Hight, McGuckin Hardware has showered its spectacular selection on the Boulder community since opening in 1955.

Original owner and founder Bill McGuckin, an avid fisherman, initially wanted to open a sporting goods store. Noting the slim market for such specialty stores at that time, McGuckin decided to include hardware in his inventory. When McGuckin Hardware and Sporting Goods opened ("Sporting Goods" was later dropped from the name, but not from the inventory), McGuckin was the only employee. Sunny afternoons would sometimes find his customers standing in front of the locked store reading a "Gone fishing, be back later" sign in the window.

McGuckin passed away in 1966, leaving his business to Dave Hight, who is married to McGuckin's daughter, Dee. Hight had joined McGuckin in 1959 as a partner and as the fourth employee, and he still runs the business today. His three sons, Barry, Brent and Robb, as well as his eight grandchildren, all have a hand in the business, guaranteeing its continuation in the family. Hight attributes a significant portion of McGuckin Hardware's success and strength in the community to the fact that since the start, McGuckin's has been a family-owned-and-operated business. Local ownership by a family with roots in Boulder has helped the store retain its focus on serving the local community.

Since becoming a part of the McGuckin's team, Hight has watched and contributed to the store's enormous growth. Through a series of expansions and moves, the current store represents a growth from 3,400 square feet in 1955 to about 100,000 total square feet today, with a main store of 62,000 square feet. In conjunction with the main store, several substores operate nearby. They address specific needs and include the Design Center across the parking lot, the McGuckin Power Equipment Center nearby, and the warehouse. Such growth is reflected also in the large number of employees — more than 320 — and in the fact that the current store probably takes in as much revenue per day as the original store did in its first full year of business.

Entering McGuckin Hardware for the first time will most likely overwhelm the average customer. Nestled in the corner of a bank of smaller stores, the entrance disguises the enormity of the interior space. Luckily, large, helpful signs break up the gigantic interior space into manageable components, pointing the customer in whatever direction necessary, be it toward housewares or one of the 5,000 different kinds of bolts and fasteners in stock. Employees clad in green vests stand ready to direct customers at the slightest hint of confusion. Service and

◆ Dave Hight and Bill McGuckin in front of McGuckin Hardware in the early days

selection emerge as obvious priorities dictating McGuckin Hardware's business plan.

◆ Dave Hight and his son, Barry, in front of McGuckin Hardware *Photo by Johnson Photography*

McGuckin Hardware remains true to its original motive to provide good service, good products and good pricing. More than 200,000 different items comprise the store's impressive depth of inventory. Stretching beyond the normal concept of a hardware store, Hight likens McGuckin's to at least 20 different stores under the same roof. This diversity in product availability, combined with the store's willingness to special order items not in stock from any one of its 5,000 suppliers, carves its own unique niche in the retail industry. Shoppers come not only from Boulder, but also drive from surrounding mountain towns and other nearby communities, as well as from Denver, with the virtual certainty that they will find the products they seek at McGuckin Hardware.

In order to ensure the highest quality of service possible, everyone employed by McGuckin Hardware, from buyers to accounting department staff, works under the same roof. Each buyer abuts his or her department in offices around the perimeter of the store, making knowledgeable sources of product information readily accessible. Ongoing plans for expansion and improvement also reflect McGuckin's commitment to customer service. In fact, the acquisition of the warehouse resulted from a growing concern that items were not always in stock when customers needed them. McGuckin Hardware often accepts new products into its inventory and makes them available to its clientele quickly, striving to remain on the cutting edge of hardware retail for its customers.

Support from customers over the years has been strong, which Hight attributes to McGuckin Hardware's commitment to serve Boulder and the surrounding communities and focus on local needs. Back in 1965, a second location opened in Boulder, but it soon closed when Hight realized that it could not meet customer expectations due to the amazing diversity and enormity of the original store. Since then, McGuckin Hardware has made no plans to open new stores. Whether customers come to purchase items or bring items for repair (McGuckin's also services most of the items it sells), its central Boulder location guarantees easy access to all residents.

Central location notwithstanding, McGuckin Hardware also plays a strong role in the Boulder community by reinvesting virtually all of its earnings into the business and by donating money to community organizations. For example, during the first half of 1999, McGuckin sponsored more than 200 organizations, including scout troops, hospitals, schools and the University of Colorado. McGuckin Hardware sponsors as many community organizations as possible, believing that it best serves the community by diversifying its contributions.

McGuckin Hardware, with deep roots in the community and a firm commitment to selection and service, has established itself as a strong and enduring presence in Boulder. Its prominence, both in location and in its sponsorship of community organizations and events, makes it difficult to miss. The people of Boulder and the surrounding communities will doubtless reap the benefits of shopping in a hardware store that stretches the boundaries of its very definition for years to come.

Neptune Mountaineering

Gary Neptune claims that the opening date for Neptune Mountaineering fell on April Fool's Day in 1973 by sheer coincidence. Despite lack of encouragement from his family and a comment from a prominent climber that he'd be out of business in no time, Neptune forged ahead with his plans. While others may have thought the endeavor foolish, Neptune Mountaineering's enduring success as one of Boulder's premier supply stores for climbers, cross-country skiers, and backpackers would prove them wrong.

Neptune Mountaineering's founding and growth are intricately interwoven with Gary's career as a mountaineer. A biologist and geologist by training, Gary left graduate school in the late 1960s to pursue his dream of somehow marrying his love of climbing with his need to make a living. He moved to Boulder in 1969 to work and climb, with no intention of opening a store, but after a short time, he perceived a need for a mountaineering business.

The original idea became a full-fledged plan during Neptune's 1973 second winter ascent of the Diamond, a 1,000-foot vertical face on 14,000-foot Long's Peak. Even though another local climber had opened a mountaineering store the previous year, Neptune purchased machinery and opened a shop primarily focused on boot repair, selling climbing gear and cross-country skis on the side.

As luck would have it, Neptune Mountaineering's first location was situated in the same shopping center as a competing cross-country ski business, whose owners decided to leave the business in the mid-1970s, selling the business to Gary. Now solidly in the retail business, Gary soon sold the boot repair shop to two of his employees, enabling him to focus on the retail business full time.

Although committed to his business, Gary's unquenchable love of the mountains soon drove him to climb Ama Dablam in the Himalayas. In 1981, he and seven friends, including two employees, traveled to the Himalayas. This trip nearly broke the bank, as the store was still small and had only five staff members. Nonetheless, Neptune Mountaineering managed to survive.

This first Himalayan trip fueled Gary's desire to climb a peak over 8,000 meters. Due to his growing reputation as a mountaineer, Gary found himself with an

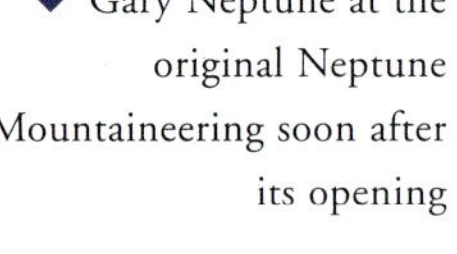

◆ Gary Neptune at the original Neptune Mountaineering soon after its opening

invitation to join a 1983 Everest expedition. The long hours of "tent time" spent talking to other members of his Everest party, in particular Dick Bass and Frank Wells, led Neptune to realize that in order to have ample free time and adequate resources to devote to climbing, he would need to let his business grow. He returned and expanded Neptune Mountaineering, making himself one employee out of 20 rather than one out of five. As a result of this and a subsequent expansion, Neptune Mountaineering is now almost 14 times its original size.

Neptune Mountaineering serves as a hub for the local climbing community for several reasons. It was one of the first climbing stores in the country to hold frequent public slide shows. Only a few people could fit into the tiny original store when the shows began in 1981. As Neptune grew and attracted bigger and bigger names from the climbing community, the shows became weekly events. Neptune hosted the first public slide show in America by Reinhold Messner, who with Peter Habeler made the first ascent of Everest without oxygen in 1978. Other notable speakers have included Peter Habeler, Chris Bonington, Anatoli Boukreev, Catherine Destivelle and Lynn Hill, to mention a few. The shows continue to bring the climbing community together, and the current store can accommodate 400 people at a showing.

Neptune Mountaineering's notoriety stems not only from its slide shows, but also from the fact that it houses a veritable museum of mountaineering history. Climbers, skiers and backpackers come to the store to shop for supplies and to view the vast collection of historical climbing and skiing paraphernalia enclosed in display cases and hanging on the walls. Gary began accumulating materials for the unusual decor in the late 1970s, at which time climbing memorabilia could be purchased quite inexpensively. He has also found himself fortunate enough to be on the receiving end of many generous donations.

Out of this enormous collection, Gary cites three items as his most prized pieces. On one of his trips to the Himalayas, a Sherpa gave him a pair of boots and crampons from Sir Edmund Hillary's Everest expedition (which Hillary later autographed). Another memorable donation came from Anderl Heckmair, who gave Neptune some hardware from the first ascent of the north face of the Eiger. More recently, Peter Habeler donated the down suit he wore on the first ascent of Everest without oxygen.

◆ Gary Neptune with his wife, Bibi, on Gondogoro Peak in Pakistan after Gary's ascent of Gasherbrum II (8,035 meters), July 1997

Gary attributes much of Neptune Mountaineering's success to its focus on serving the climbing and skiing communities to the best of its ability. Gary makes every effort to employ a knowledgeable staff who can answer the questions of his adventurous clientele, as well as sponsoring Eldora Mountain Ski Club, the Access Fund, Colorado Mountain Club, American Alpine Club, and the American Mountaineering Center. Neptune Mountaineering has also upheld this promise by not diversifying into other markets, remaining basically a hardware store for climbers and skiers.

From its humble beginnings as a 1,000-square-foot boot repair shop, Neptune Mountaineering has evolved into a highly respected cornerstone of the Boulder climbing and skiing communities. Neptune takes pride in the fact that his store is not a slick retail operation, but rather a store run by climbers, skiers and backpackers for climbers, skiers and backpackers. He feels privileged to have created such an integral part of the climbing and outdoor communities in Boulder, and Neptune Mountaineering plans to serve them as a valuable resource for years to come.

Peppercorn

Peppercorn is a visual potpourri. Texture and color delight every visitor to the Pearl Street Mall store. Peppercorn's palate includes blue, cerise, silver, turquoise, amber, ruby, chocolate, chartreuse, gold, saffron, alabaster and copper in a wide variety of cut and smooth glass; hand-painted pottery; designer ceramics and fine china; delicate and splashy table linens; imported hutches and cabinets; exquisite shower, bath and bed accessories; delectable jams, sauces and spices; classic and contemporary cookbooks; and of course, top-notch cookware. Peppercorn's selection has earned it the nickname "The Smithsonian of Cookstores" and makes it a necessary stop for Boulder residents and out-of-town visitors alike.

Peppercorn has something for everyone: from Kickin' Cowboy Cookie Mix to Alaskan Smoked Salmon; from omelet pans to pressure cookers and paté knives to Christofle flatware, this store prides itself on its fabulous array of choices. At Peppercorn, selection and customer service come first and the store prides itself on going the extra mile to help each customer feel welcome and satisfied.

◆ Peppercorn's selection creates a visual potpourri and has earned it the nickname "The Smithsonian of Cookstores."

Peppercorn began as a cooking school and small retail store in 1977. The store, then a 1,200-square-foot space located just off the mall, was founded by owner Doris Houghland and her friend and then business partner, Barbara David. While Peppercorn's cooking school, which hosted a variety of classes taught by professional chefs and popular local cooks, closed in 1984, the store has continued to grow and expand, moving several times before coming to rest in its present location on the Pearl Street Mall. Currently, the store boasts a total of 17,000 square feet of merchandise, including the largest cookbook selection in the United States, and is an anchor store for the mall. Many locals stop by for a quick cup of complimentary coffee to see what's new or to enjoy the eclectic displays Doris puts together herself. Additionally, lots of non-Boulder residents make an annual mecca to the store for items they cannot find anywhere else.

What brings customers back to Peppercorn is its beauty and warmth. Owner Doris Houghland believes that coming into the store should be like coming into someone's home. Her attention to every detail — from buying merchandise to creating interesting and colorful displays, grows out of a real interest in supplying customers with not only gifts and merchandise, but an experience that will create a comfortable living and entertaining environment at home, and ultimately add to the customer's quality of life. Her goal for Peppercorn is to sell items people will enjoy, not only on special occasions, but every day.

Peppercorn's determination to serve the community is reflected in the services it provides. Not only will they do special ordering to meet customer needs, but they have an established program to work with corporations customizing gift baskets to supply them with unique gifts for their own clients and customers. The store has ongoing relationships with local decorators to find exactly what they need to successfully fulfill their decorating plans. The result is happy customers, good business relationships, and beautiful homes and offices.

Doris Houghland's commitment to the local community is evident throughout the store. Many items adorn the shelves from local artists and potters, and specialty foods made in Colorado. She is committed to her staff and realizes many of her employees are single mothers. To acknowledge their contributions, and the special challenges of single working mothers, the Peppercorn contributes to and supports many organizations and activities in the community — particularly ones which work to help families, especially women and children. The annual Chocolate Lover's Fling, which raises money for Safehouse, is a popular event Peppercorn regularly supports.

While Doris likes to stay flexible with charitable activities so the store can offer support to those organizations currently involved with activities which uplift the whole community, schools routinely receive support. The prosperity of the community is shared by Peppercorn's donations to fund-raising activities of various local nonprofits. And, as any regular viewer of public television in the Denver metropolitan area is aware, Peppercorn financially supports PBS.

As part of its community involvement, Peppercorn is a member of the Boulder Chamber of Commerce. In 1994 the chamber selected Peppercorn's owners Businesspeople of the Year. Over the years Peppercorn has won numerous awards and is consistently a finalist in *Daily Camera*'s Best of Boulder. It has received recognition for sales excellence and meritorious support by the Junior League of Denver. In 1995 Doris Houghland was selected Entrepreneur of the Year.

Businesses like Peppercorn are part of what makes Boulder and the surrounding environs a wonderfully livable place. Quality, class, selection, community involvement, a customer-focused business philosophy, and being attuned to the needs of the customer all come together in a successful recipe which makes the Peppercorn and its owner, Doris Houghland, valuable members of the community.

Art Cleaners

Art Cleaners, a Boulder old-timer, can trace its history to 1921 when Art Cleaners and Dyers was established at 1110 Pearl Street by George Garrod and H.R. Graf.

Surviving a minor fire in 1936 and a move to 15th Street in 1951, Art Cleaners is still the dry cleaners of choice for discerning Boulder residents. Although the days of dyeing fabrics have disappeared from the title and the business, quality dry cleaning and laundry have not.

There never was an Art in Art Cleaners, but people often ask for him by name. Today, under the ownership of Brian Hansen, Art Cleaners turns dry cleaning into an art form, with its emphasis on quality, service and attention to detail at all three Boulder locations.

Each garment that enters the premises is inspected at least seven times. Missing buttons are replaced and minor repairs made at no extra charge. Pearl buttons are covered to avoid breaking, fuzzy sweaters are de-pilled, a trained spotting technician operates a special spotting area, and everything possible is done to return a garment to its original condition.

The technology has changed since 1921, but Art Cleaners prides itself on continuing to do all the laundry and dry cleaning in-house. Unlike other dry cleaners who often subcontract, the only items to leave the premises are leather garments and drapes. That way they are able to supervise every stage — from receiving inventory, inspecting, sorting out by color and fabric (separating those delicate silks and lace), cleaning, re-inspecting, pressing, finishing, re-assembling and filing each order for easy retrieval.

◆ The ultimate convenience is free pickup and delivery at no extra charge. *Photo by Johnson Photography*

The quest for better cleaning solutions never ends. Dry cleaning solvent is no longer handled openly as in earlier times but regulated by the EPA and air quality standards, and Art Cleaners maintains the highest-quality equipment to meet these changes. The company is increasingly using "wet cleaning," as recommended by Greenpeace, in an effort to keep up with alternative cleaning methods that are environmentally friendly while insisting on the same pristine results.

Art Cleaners also has remedies for dry cleaning nightmares. As a member of the International Fabric Association, they can call on laboratory assistance for solutions to shrinkage, dye loss, size change, wrinkling and stains. A garment someone has already shrunk might be helped by re-seaming and lengthening. Art Cleaners has several experienced seamstresses on the premises to take care of all alterations.

A popular option is the free pickup and delivery service, currently with two routes in operation. Clothes are collected in a special bag left at home or office in a prearranged location. The customer doesn't even need to be present. Today's Boulderites dress more casually than in the Roaring 20s, but they still appreciate their clothes professionally cleaned and finished — and many hate to iron. And the same goes for out of towners. Art Cleaners provides a daily guest valet service to four Boulder hotels.

As an active member of the Boulder Chamber of Commerce, the company does not shrink from giving back to the community — whether it's cleaning gift coats for children's charities at Christmas or providing free cleaning to families in need.

For all these good reasons, and in a tradition of 77 years of cleaning Boulder clothes, Art Cleaners maintains its reputation for artistic merit in dry cleaning excellence and outstanding care. Art Cleaners is simply Boulder's finest cleaners since 1921.

Art Mart

"Your food, drink, and children are welcome here," announces a sign at the entrance of Art Mart, inviting the passerby to enter into a remarkable space filled with the creations of over 300 local and national artists. Paintings, drawings, candles, stained glass, scarves, jewelry, woodwork, baskets, pottery and quilts are only some of the products on display in the colorful interior. A knowledgeable team of employees strives to greet each customer individually and make the customer's experience at Art Mart a pleasant one.

Art Mart came about through the efforts of the husband-and-wife team of Rick Rippberger and Connie Brenton. The couple had observed arts and crafts cooperatives in which artists had to pay an association fee and contribute hours staffing the cooperative. Realizing that most artists would rather spend time creating, Rippberger and Brenton came up with the idea of Art Mart. They believed that with their business skills, they could set up a store where artists could sell their works without sacrificing hours of their time staffing a retail business. As Rippberger and Brenton are both Boulder natives with strong ties to the community, the vibrant Pearl Street Mall seemed a natural choice for the store's location.

In November 1989, Art Mart opened its doors to the Pearl Street Mall, on the same block where Rippberger grew up. The store enjoyed great success over that Christmas season, encouraging Rippberger and Brenton to concentrate on increasing the types of work and the quality of the artists they accepted. The store's success continued to grow over the next few years.

Art Mart provides artists with a unique opportunity to display and sell their works.

Art Mart provides artists with a unique opportunity to display and sell their works. The store is neither a cooperative, nor a gallery. Instead of operating like a gallery, where artwork is often marked up and artists take home only one-third of their work's retail price, Art Mart rents out spaces within the store to individual artists. The artists price their own work and take home 75 percent of the profits. The store takes care of the business end of selling the artwork, charging the artists 25 percent of the profit from each sale. This unique arrangement formed a business in which everyone involved wins.

◆ Inside Art Mart, a world of creativity and color awaits discovery by the passerby.

Art Mart not only offers artists an innovative way to market their works, but also supports the Boulder community. The store contributes to public and private schools in the area, commonly donating gift certificates for fund-raising auctions. Art Mart also sponsors about five community events annually. The store takes its community-oriented philosophy seriously; hence the informative signs posted at the entrance, detailing how the store works to best serve both the artists and the customers.

Art Mart provides a remarkable and innovative way in which people can add more color and creativity to their lives.

Beale Fine Art Picture Framing

Beale Fine Art Picture Framing never turns away a customer. Since he purchased the business in 1987, no matter how unusual the request or unique the item to be displayed, owner Jim Beale ensures solutions are created for them all. And some unusual objets d'art have been brought in, including archaeological artifacts, watches, jewelry, garments, dioramas and other personal treasures. One customer needed to frame a cannonball with a brass plate and certificate of authenticity. Beale was undaunted and constructed a frame and pedestal with a historical appearance that attractively displayed all three.

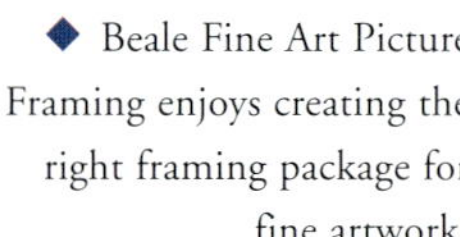

◆ Beale Fine Art Picture Framing enjoys creating the right framing package for fine artwork.

While Beale Fine Art Picture Framing encourages special projects and enjoys creating the right framing package for fine artwork, it can and will frame posters, mirrors, tiles or whatever the customer needs. Many artists who participate in area shows do so with their work in framing from Beale.

Clients are not limited to choosing from the seemingly endless selection displayed. Beale, a woodworker and wood sculpture artist, includes all forms of craftsmanship in the framing process: woodworking, cutting, carving, painting, metalwork, stained glass, cut glass and constructing 3-D displays or pedestals. His creativity expands the selection available and explores unusual and individualized solutions. There is no material Beale Fine Art Picture Framing cannot handle properly, and that gives customers a panorama of original choices.

Customers get fast service, a two-to-three-day turnaround on most orders, and not much longer on complex one-of-a-kind jobs. Jim is a hands-on business owner who enjoys personally serving his customers to be sure a frame is made for them that meets their needs and desires.

Though Beale Fine Arts is not a gallery, works of art by the owner and other artists are on display and for sale. Drawings, tiles, wood sculptures and other beautiful art show not only the talent of the artist but the beautiful frames which can be created in the shop.

The business actively supports the community in a wide variety of ways. The Boulder Museum of Contemporary Art is a primary focus of Beale's generosity. Beale Fine Arts has received BMOCA's BACer Award several years.

But Jim Beale's generosity does not end there. The business donates framing for other organizations and silent auctions. He enjoys supporting art shows that display children's work and give a positive reinforcement to each participant's creativity. Community Food Share, Chocolate Lover's Fling for Safehouse, and the Humane Society of Boulder Valley are all organizations whose activities Beale Fine Art Picture Framing supports through contributions of time, energy and resources. Each year Beale frames the awards for the annual multicultural awards banquet sponsored by the Community Action Program.

Personal service and custom work at affordable prices have been Jim Beale's business philosophy since he purchased The Frame Factory at 9th and Pearl in 1987. In 1997, the store relocated to its present, easily accessible location on Broadway, where the tradition continues. Beale Fine Art Picture Framing reflects the values so highly prized by the Boulder community — creativity, generosity, caring, beauty and accessibility to all.

Boulder Cork

The success of Boulder Cork is a story of consistency. With the same owner, chef and general manager for almost 20 years — a rarity in the restaurant industry — the Cork has created an atmosphere and menu on which Boulderites have come to count.

When it opened in 1969, the restaurant was called The Cork and Cleaver and was part of one of the original steak and salad bar chains. Restaurateur Alan Teran was involved with the parent corporation but left in 1981, bought the Boulder restaurant and renamed it Boulder Cork. Today, locals know it simply as the Cork.

◆ Boulder Cork principals (from left to right) Alan Teran, owner; Jim Smailer, chef; Donna Dooley, general manager; and Gary Silverman, assistant manager *Photo by Johnson Photography*

Teran set out to upscale the place. He diversified the menu by adding seafood and pasta while still offering a few choice beef and steak entrees. He opened up the dining room, changed the décor and stepped up the service. A fine wine list was added, which has grown to over 300 bottles. Now, red wine is a specialty and the Cork has been honored with *Wine Spectator* magazine's Award of Excellence over the last several years.

The Cork is a popular retreat for locals and Boulder's ever-growing business clientele. The relaxed, warm atmosphere keeps people coming back. The tables are spaced far enough apart so patrons are comfortable holding meetings over lunch or dinner. A quick scan of the dining room reflects an eclectic crowd of both businesspeople in suits and locals in casual attire. This wide appeal and repeat business is part of what has kept the Cork so successful over the last 30 years.

Low staff turnover is also a key ingredient in the story of the Cork. Chef Jim Smailer came on board in 1981 and general manager Donna Dooley celebrated her 20th anniversary last year. Smailer makes infrequent changes to the menu, while Dooley cultivates relationships with the Cork's customers. This combination of consistently quality food and outstanding service is the Cork's recipe for success.

Located in North Boulder, a few miles from the center of town and the hub of Pearl Street Mall, the Cork's site has turned out to be a blessing in disguise. While people may be fighting each other for parking spots downtown, the huge parking lot next to the Cork has added to its appeal. The spacious dining rooms can easily accommodate the crowds on the weekends. In addition, three private-party rooms offer ample space for up to 80 people.

The Cork's attitude toward community donations is generous. Organizations are rarely denied a request for a gift certificate or food donation. Though not specifically aligned with any single cause, the restaurant is an avid supporter of many community groups.

The future of the Cork will be similar to its past since Teran took over — minor changes. The wine list will grow and the kitchen will be expanded. The menu will not be altered drastically, nor will the atmosphere or attitude. The Cork will continue to offer Boulder the same quality dining experience it has offered for the last three decades.

◆ *Photo by Johnson Photography*

Boulder Wine Merchant

It seems only right somehow that a place as favored as Boulder should be blessed with a unique wine store like Boulder Wine Merchant.

What makes Boulder Wine Merchant special is the enthusiasm of its owners, Wayne Belding and Sally Mohr, for their product, and its emphasis on excellence of service, not elitism.

◆ Owners and Master Sommeliers Sally Mohr and Wayne Belding
Photo by Johnson Photography

This enthusiasm is reflected in the quality and variety of wines in stock. Boulder Wine Merchant reverses the trend of most liquor stores with 80 percent of sales — and all its focus — on wine. And with the medical benefits now established, even health-obsessed Boulderites feel good about a glass of wine with dinner.

Both Wayne Belding and Sally Mohr started as part-time employees in the original Boulder Wine Merchant store on Broadway and Spruce, shortly after it opened in 1980. Their fascination with wine inspired them to buy the business and, two moves later, expand to 4,000 square feet on Broadway and Alpine.

Anyone unfamiliar with the store might be surprised to learn that in spite of its superior image and offerings of rare and vintage wines with $1,000 price tags, the average price of a bottle sold here is between $6 and $7. The company's philosophy is that good wine doesn't have to be expensive, and with so many countries producing excellent wine at reasonable cost, there's no need to strain the budget.

◆ The favorite shopping place for Boulder's wine enthusiasts
Photo by Johnson Photography

A glance through the monthly newsletter confirms this. An aromatic Coteaux du Languedoc is priced at $6.99 a bottle. A zesty red from the French Corbieres offering a wonderful array of blackberry, black cherry and plum fruit scents enhanced by elements of vanilla, black pepper, violets, leather, herbs and spice is sold for the same paltry $6.99.

Each month the store's newsletter features eight to 12 different exciting wines and contains educational information for the nonconnoisseur. Consistent key words such as crisp, spicy, soft, full- or light-bodied, blackberry, cherry or plum allow the clients to find the elements in their favorite wines and recognize them in other recommendations. Boulder Wine Merchant also conducts classes, tastings and dinners, presenting great food and wine pairings.

It may seem that tasting all these wines — and they do taste everything they sell — is a less than arduous task, but Wayne Belding and Sally Mohr are emphatic that they spit out a lot of bad in the quest for their special offerings. They are, however, uniquely qualified to select the best.

Both are members of that rare breed possessing the Diploma of Master Sommelier, a distinction achieved by only 85 people in the entire world. There are 35 in the United States including the two owners of this Boulder store. The training requires extreme devotion — only one or two people yearly make it through the exacting final exam which includes a blind tasting where applicants must describe and identify a lineup of wines on taste alone.

The same care for detail and service extends to all Boulder Wine Merchant staff members. They spend time with each customer, inquiring about preferences, menu and price range in order to make a selection that will please the client.

The creed at Boulder Wine Merchant is not to intimidate but to educate, showing that wine is fun, fascinating and to be enjoyed — something with which its clients happily concur.

Crossroads Mall

The current Crossroads Mall has changed considerably from the original structure built in 1963. In keeping with this tradition of timely transformation, Crossroads Mall will change again over the next few years.

Originally the brainchild of Denver developer Gerri Von Frellick, Crossroads opened as a regional shopping center in 1963. By 1979, the mall clearly needed renovation and expansion, prompting the Macerich Company, a public Real Estate Investment Trust headquartered in Santa Monica, California, to step in and purchase it. Macerich has remained the sole owner and operator of Crossroads Mall since 1979.

Macerich stands out as a unique company in that it does not build shopping centers from the ground up, but rather specializes in acquiring, renovating and re-leasing existing centers to make them more productive. Macerich orchestrated major renovations at Crossroads, enclosing the mall and adding skylights, a double deck, and a food court during the first renovation and expansion that was completed in 1983. The current store mix is comprised of mid-range merchants, with an emphasis on family apparel retailers. Local, regional and national stores, services and restaurants round out the store lineup at Crossroads Mall.

Ever attentive to the changing needs of the Boulder community, the Macerich Company has decided once again to expand and renovate Crossroads Mall in an effort to create a center that feels "truly Boulder." In 1998, the company took part in a Crossroads Mall Community Consortium, utilizing public input to chart the mall's future. As a result of this process, eight goals were established, including the pursuit of quality retailers for shopping, creating a more community-oriented center where local people will want to spend time, and optimizing energy efficiency, among others. Entertainment additions to the mall include local and regional restaurants, and a 16-screen movie theater, complemented by retailers new to the Boulder market. These changes are being planned in accordance with a shift in the public concept of how a mall should function in the community. This more modern perspective of a mall's role casts it in an urban village setting as a space used not only for shopping, but also as a vibrant community meeting place.

Crossroads Mall's strong community involvement is apparent not only through its dedication to create a new and improved center, but also through its contributions to nonprofit organizations. When Collage Children's Museum needed space to open in 1990, Macerich provided it. Macerich continues to support the museum today. Crossroads also contributes to the Salvation Army, Boulder County Hospice, Habitat for Humanity, The Emergency Family Assistance Association, and the Bolder Boulder. In addition, it sponsors one of the Boulder Philharmonic Orchestra's performances of the Nutcracker Ballet. The mall belongs to the Boulder Chamber of Commerce, Downtown Boulder Incorporated, the Rocky Mountain Shopping Center Association and the Colorado Retail Council.

With so much emphasis on serving the needs of the community, Crossroads Mall's redevelopment will undoubtedly strive to serve in the best interest of the local Boulder community. The Macerich Company hopes that by creating an attractive community gathering place and vibrant shopping complex, the community will find that Crossroads Mall fulfills its shopping and entertainment needs.

◆ Crossroads Mall in 1998

Fisher Chevrolet Honda

Community, customer service and family are the focus of the Fisher family at Fisher Chevrolet Honda. Established on the philosophy that an automobile dealership does not stay in business simply by selling fine automobiles, the Fishers successfully combine the art of customer service with innovation.

Bob Fisher, president of Fisher Chevrolet Honda, began his automotive career as a sales representative in 1947 after serving in the U.S. Navy. His knowledge and enthusiasm led him to become a dealer in 1973 when he bought Russ Lyons Chevrolet, a Boulder dealership originally established in 1919 by J.M. Pike as Pike & King Chevrolet Company. Automobiles, long part of the Fisher family, now became a family business.

Craig, Bob's son, began his career at the age of 16 in the service department and learned all aspects of the business on the job. He attended Fairview High School, Western State College and completed numerous Honda and General Motors colleges and academies. In 1989 he became the dealer. Madelyne Fisher, Bob's wife, is secretary of the corporation. Their daughter, Lynn, who has been the vice president of operations with the dealership for 20 years, oversees compliance with environmental protection programs. Together, they uphold a mission statement of excellence through customer service, employee service and community commitment. In 1991 the business expanded to include a Honda dealership and a modern 55,000-square-foot facility located on nine acres.

One reflection of Fisher's success is its numerous awards, including the coveted Service Supremacy Award won in 1976 and 1994. In 1997 Fisher was given the Honda President's Award, an achievement held in high regard by dealers nationwide. In 1989 it received the TIME Magazine Quality Dealer Award honoring outstanding car dealers in America for exceptional performance combined with distinguished community service. The Fishers quickly acknowledge that their 120 employees are a great foundation for success. Their staff includes longtime employees who have been recognized with numerous awards and certifications from General Motors and Honda for service and training.

◆ Fisher Chevrolet Honda on Arapahoe Road

◆ The Fisher Family: Bob, Madelyne, Lynn, Courtney, Allyson, Valarie and Craig

Commitment to quality is reflected in every aspect of life for the Fishers. Bob and Madelyne are Denver natives, married for over 50 years. They believe one of the best things in life is to spend it doing something you like in a place you love. This dedication and stability serves the community with customers and employees becoming friends and neighbors.

Bob has served as president of the Boulder Chamber of Commerce, Colorado Automobile Dealers Association and State Legislative Director for the American Import Automobile Dealers Association. Craig actively supports numerous organizations in Boulder including the University of Colorado Sports Program. Each year Fisher and its employees contribute to the United Way. Since the early 1980s, the Fishers' innovation and dedication to clean air and the environment have led the way in voluntarily changing waste products disposal methods and adhering to high standards.

With today's technology, business is often done with faceless telephone voices and disembodied e-mail. At Fisher Chevrolet Honda, stability, caring and a sense of community create a welcome place to buy an automobile and make a friend.

Foot Of The Mountain Motel

◆ *Photo by Johnson Photography*

Two towering spruce trees welcome guests to Foot Of The Mountain Motel located at the gateway to Boulder Canyon. The motel's rough-hewn log exteriors with red-scalloped wood trim set against the green foothills make guests feel as if Mother Nature has rolled out the welcome mat. Owners Dave and Carole Nordgren extend Western hospitality to all, even peacocks. A peahen, soon named Penelope, appeared one Christmas Eve a few years ago and stayed until the following May. Though the Nordgrens provided Penelope with shelter and food, she preferred to make her rounds each morning gathering treats left by guests outside their doors. Penelope eventually left Foot Of The Mountain, but lodgers can still enjoy other plentiful birds and wildlife.

When Foot Of The Mountain Motel was built in the early 1930s by Charles and Mary Siebert, Arapahoe Avenue was the only route up Boulder Canyon. The motel consisted of nine cottages and was one of several cottage camps along the road. Shortly after completion, the Sieberts sold it to Walter and Audrey Snair who operated the motel for the next 33 years. The tradition of a family-run business continued when Larry and Maija Fisher bought the property in 1975, and later sold it to the Nordgrens in 1984. Today it is the only motel remaining from that era and has the distinction of being the oldest continuously operating motel in Boulder.

While changes have occurred over the years, each owner has extended the effort to maintain the charm of the original cabins. Each had a kitchen with a coal stove, interior knotty pine paneling, beamed ceilings and hardwood floors. The wood trim and doors remain their original cheery bright red. The kitchens and carports have since been converted to make an additional nine units. Of course the rates of the 30s — $2 for a sleeping room, $5 for a kitchenette — have gone up slightly, but coziness and warmth remain. Situated just minutes from great restaurants, entertainment and fine shopping to the east, and all the natural beauty and solitude of the Rocky Mountains to the west, it is easy to see why motel guests return time and again.

◆ *Photo by Johnson Photography*

Hiking into the adjacent mountain canyon and walking or biking the Boulder Creek Path are two of the activities guests enjoy thanks to the efforts of Dave Nordgren. In the late 1980s, Dave was heavily involved with the Eben G. Fine/West Arapahoe Street project. Upon completion, Foot Of The Mountain was returned to the quiet, park-like setting it enjoyed in the 1930s. For several years, as president and board member of the hotel association, Dave assisted with the Boulder Creek Walk, a popular Christmas festival which was held during the last week of November and the first week of December. The association had a float in the Parade of Lights and sponsored the information bus which sat at the visitor's point off Interstate 36.

As a longtime member of AAA, the Nordgrens assure guests that their lodging facility meets high standards. History, hospitality and nature make Foot Of The Mountain Motel a great place to relax and enjoy the beauty of Boulder.

Kinsley & Co.

Quality Clothiers for 50 Years and Counting

"Haberdashers" might seem a quaint echo from a more genteel era. For those who know Kinsley & Co., haberdashers is a word "worn well" by the apparel sales company on Boulder's historic University Hill. Kinsley & Co. does business the old-fashioned way, with classic fabrics adroitly tailored in timeless styles. Kinsley & Co. combines the best of both worlds: Old World craftsmanship and attention to detail, with stylish labels and contemporary designs.

The shop meshes the ambience of a London Savile Row clothing establishment with the comfort of your favorite den. "It's a place where people can spend a lot of time," owner Court Dixon explains. "They can enjoy the ambience, and sip sherry as they find precisely the right clothing to suit themselves." What has enabled Kinsley & Co. to flourish for 50 years as surrounding storefronts have changed with the seasons is its finest quality merchandise — carefully chosen and expertly fitted to each patron.

The story of Kinsley & Co. begins on March 1, 1949, when Wynn and Faith Kinsley opened the University Shop. The store served Boulder till 1956, when the newly dubbed Kinsley & Co. moved to its current location on 13th Street. Dixon left a career as a custom construction contractor in 1983 to serve as Kinsley's "apprentice clothier," then as minority partner. Dixon has carried on a tradition of leadership as chairman of the University Hill Alliance, and has been active in the renovation of the famous district.

◆ (L-R) Co-owners Do Phan, Edward Kapson and Court Dixon

Wynn Kinsley had aspired to be a philosophy professor, but instead became Boulder's finest clothier. Like his mentor, Dixon began on a quest for diversity and found his life's calling. Dixon and co-owners Edward Kapson and Do Phan took ownership on the final day of 1996, shortly after Wynn Kinsley passed away. Kapson, the primary buyer with roots in the Macys department store executive management program, and Phan, a master tailor, complete the partnership triumvirate that promises to carry the company smartly into the future. A staff of highly skilled associates rounds out the service tour de force.

Wynn Kinsley carried the best domestic makers of British styles, and was the first local purveyor of Ralph Lauren. Today the company provides the world's most distinguished labels, such as Luciano Barbera, Giorgio Armani Le Collezioni, Hugo Boss, Ermenegildo Zegna, Hickey-Freeman, Zanella and Bruno Magli to name a few. Kinsley & Co. also offers custom made-to-measure services for shirts, suits, sportcoats, topcoats, tuxedos and trousers.

The women's shop emphasizes exclusive international lines that cater to the needs of businesswomen, as well as evening wear and distinctive casual designs. The buyers, led by Kapson, evaluate myriad fashions before any one item is selected for sale. Each piece must have fresh, up-to-date fabrics and styling, but also a timeless quality.

The organization has diversified to include one of Dixon's passions. The sister establishment on the north end of the building is Kinsley Outfitters/The Orvis Shop, the full-service, year-round outdoor clothing and fly-fishing source. In addition to supplying the latest travel wear, weekend clothing and fishing gear, Dixon and his staff can lead the novice or expert on guided fly-fishing trips into pristine Colorado trout waters.

In an era of interminable malls and faceless mass market stores, Kinsley's staff and customers have formed relationships. The shop's longtime patrons — some of whom as college students bought their first suit from Wynn Kinsley five decades ago — come from across the nation. Longevity tells its own tale, and Kinsley & Co. is now proud to be the oldest men's clothing shop in the state — 50 years and counting.

Lafayette Collectables & Flea Market

"*Run a* clean store and treat people like you want to be treated" was advice given to Bill and Cheryl Hopkins when they started Lafayette Indoor Flea Market. It has become the store's motto and guiding philosophy. The flea market's friendly, warm, small-town approach to business has been the basis for its success since opening on April 1, 1990. Located in what was originally a bowling alley, this 20,000-square-foot facility on Spaulding, just off South Public Road, has over 500,000 items for sale.

Hopkins was a commercial real estate broker representing a client in lease negotiations for the building that is now home to the market. His client decided not to proceed. Though Bill and Cheryl Hopkins had never been in a flea market, Bill thought it was a great idea and decided to start a business. He had previously owned a photography studio, an experience that taught him the importance of time and opportunity.

Lafayette Indoor Flea Market opened with 17 dealers, an adding machine and a cash box. Two thousand people came through the first day. Business then slowed down, but with persistence, hard work, long days and excellent business skills, Hopkins and his wife, Cheryl, grew the business to its current 116 dealer spaces. In 1995, *Good Housekeeping* rated the flea market 12th in the top 50 biggest and best flea markets in the country.

Ninety different dealers travel from as far away as Kansas and Ohio, lease space and maintain an inventory of various items ranging from secondhand clothing, car parts, collectibles, computers, glass items, books and radios, as well as new antique reproductions and discontinued product lines. Art Deco pottery, household goods, dolls and dishes fill the shelves as far as a customer's eye can see. It is a seven-day-a-week garage sale to beat all garage sales with the convenience of one-stop shopping.

The Lafayette Indoor Flea Market actively supports community participation. Not only does the flea market create jobs in a small community, but the owners hire young people who gain valuable retail experience, while getting a positive start with solid work training. The store has two full-time and seven part-time employees.

Hopkins calls the store "the largest recycling business in the area." It provides a place for quality secondhand items to be bought and sold, and all merchandise leaves the store in recycled packaging.

Hopkins remains active in the community. In addition to being co-founder of Lafayette Old Town, Inc., and Lafayette Merchant's Association, where he served as president for three years, he is also a director on the Lafayette Chamber of Commerce and a director for the Louisville Lafayette Downtown Revitalization. The flea market sponsors floats for local parades and won second place in the State of Colorado VFW Loyalty Day Parade.

Small towns thrive because of businesses like the Lafayette Indoor Flea Market. Customers find good deals at affordable prices. The town and its residents benefit from job opportunities and the positive contribution that a well-run, successful business makes to the whole community.

◆ Owners Bill and Cheryl Hopkins

Lighting Plus

The room darkens. In anticipation, the "audience" quiets. Then, over a hundred lights play across the "stage" before them. Their many colors, intensities and shapes dramatically create moods appropriate to the changing setting. Opening night at the theater? Not quite. This is the innovative lighting laboratory of Lighting Plus, Inc., whose creative owners and staff understand the magical power of light in changing people's lives as well as any theatrical production. Their audience, the customers, will leave the laboratory empowered to select the appropriate lighting to create a particular ambiance for their environment.

◆ (L-R) Rhonda Weiss, Rhonda Jensen, Michael Cortez, Betty Warren, Todd Warren, Lori Warren
Photo by Johnson Photography

Lighting Plus began in 1976 when Keith and Betty Warren sought new professional challenges. Researching the market revealed room for a new lighting store. They began in the same building on Arapahoe Avenue that houses them today. Shortly after, Keith receded to the background as a silent partner for health reasons; Betty put her children to work and hired a manager. His daughter, Lori, joined the business and married Betty's son, Todd. Keith and Betty's daughter, Rhonda Jensen, has worked over the years with creative design of the showroom. Michael Cortez and Rhonda Weiss have worked with the family for years and are familiar faces with Lighting Plus clientele.

The dedication derives from the complexity and creativity inherent in lighting. The business evolved exponentially since the 1970s, when only basic globe fixtures dominated interiors. Now, fixtures fluctuate seasonally like women's fashion, from dramatic to midtown Manhattan, ultra-contemporary and traditional. Changing technology drives these knowledgeable experts to stay current, as their customers demand energy-efficiency, fluorescence, incandescence, track, monorail, low voltage, and other multiplying options.

Each customer is an individual with unique needs and tastes. The dauntless Lighting Plus staff responds warmly, creatively and personally to each need. Projects include not only individual residences but art galleries, restaurants, libraries, a museum in Estes Park, banks in Louisville, health care centers, and hotels, including period lighting for both the Boulderado and the Coburn hotels in Boulder. The rapidly spawning co-housing projects, which allow more than one owner to share private attached housing at affordable costs, demand that Lighting Plus respond to both community areas and individual tastes creatively and cost-effectively. Not confined to Boulder Valley, its customers come from across Colorado and as far away as Montana, Mississippi and Florida. Customers have returned repeatedly over two decades, resulting in a first-name atmosphere with clients who are more like an extended family and friendship circle.

Given that every lighting design is so variable — fixtures, technology, tastes, luminescence, and more — Lighting Plus developed a unique showroom strategy to help customers understand lighting within context, one that is now copied by other businesses. Rather than ceilings packed with lighting fixtures, the showroom features variously themed vignettes. Each one, whether contemporary, rustic or high-tech, displays lighting with furniture and accessories (the store also sells unique antique furniture). Ceiling fans of all sizes and materials compliment the lighting. Finally, the lighting laboratory offers demonstrations of light quality and design including technical variations that affect mood and lifestyle. Nothing about the store is static; customers call it the "fun showroom." Humor, the hallmark of creativity, permeates every aspect of Lighting Plus, making the challenge of lifestyle lighting selection as entertaining and rewarding as attending opening night at the theater.

MacLaren Markowitz Gallery

One of the more vibrant and eclectic areas of Boulder, the west end of the Pearl Street Mall consists of colorful locally owned businesses and restaurants. Here, one can find what Boulder acknowledges as the bookstore and cafe for writers, an antique print shop, hand-crafted jewelry, Tibetan collectibles, and Indian, French, and Mexican cuisine. It seems to be the symbolic heart of Boulder's buoyant, educated lifestyle.

No enterprise typifies this artsy, charming center more than the MacLaren Markowitz Gallery, which regards art as the heart and soul of life, rather than a luxury. Established in 1978, the gallery originally focused on Southwestern art. However, since it changed ownership in 1989, the gallery has shifted its emphasis to an eclectic blend of diverse art and artists, many locally based, others nationally known, with the goal of demystifying art and giving it greater resonance with a broader community. The new owner, Marilyn Reynolds, believes that art is both an accessible and universal treasure — available to everyone, regardless of income or education — and a community affair. The art in the MacLaren Markowitz Gallery, ranging from valuable sculptures and paintings to well-crafted, affordable jewelry, reflects that ethic.

To deconstruct the rarefied reputation that often surrounds art and galleries, MacLaren Markowitz emphasizes educational events. Shows and demonstrations for all aged school groups and for the general public take place regularly. Artists are invited and encouraged to demonstrate their techniques. Most of the very talented staff holds degrees in art or art related fields and are intimately familiar with the special areas for which they are responsible. Informational material is thorough, user friendly for a lay audience, and artfully presented. Simply stated, it is virtually impossible to walk into the well-lit, colorful and uncluttered gallery (which allows one to experience art without feeling overwhelmed) without walking out more knowledgeable about art and, possibly, as a new collector.

Community spirit drives the gallery. Known for its annual benefits, the gallery has housed shows to help causes such as research for breast cancer, the Humane Society of Boulder Valley, and more. Each thematic show presents variously priced art that increases an awareness of the issues intrinsic to the cause at hand. For example, the Humane Society benefit, "A Show of Kindness," incorporated animal imagery; the breast cancer benefit featured photographs by those who had suffered from the disease and which reflected their ensuing insights. That show, "Portraits of Hope," was then assembled into a book.

The exemplary service offered by the gallery becomes visual art itself. The gift-wrapping is so extraordinary that the remarkable gift of art inside doubles the giving. The gallery offers a consulting service, Art Consultants of Colorado, which works with businesses, homeowners, corporations and gift-givers. The gallery will even locate requested artists, regardless of whether their works have been displayed there.

◆ A sample of the treasures available through MacLaren Markowitz Gallery: flower-shaped vase by North River Glass: Kathleen Young and Michael Constantine; bronze bear statue by Gene and Rebecca Tobey; "Pink Iris" oil painting by Julia Jordan; ceramic pot by Bob Smith; Indonesian dowry chest; Persian rug supplied by Megerian's Persian Rug Company
Photo by Johnson Photography

It is the mountain and Mohammed story reborn in art — if, for any reason, the client or the community can't come to the art, then MacLaren Markowitz Gallery will find a way to take the art to them. That kind of spirit and commitment keeps art vital and accessible to everyone in Boulder.

Helping Hands Health Education

Boulder, Colorado, and Khandbari, Nepal, do not have much in common. Yet, they do have a connection — Helping Hands Health Education, a nonprofit organization based in Boulder. Helping Hands sends doctors, nurses and nonmedical volunteers to Nepal to provide free health care and health education. Narayan Shrestha, founder of Helping Hands, immigrated to the United States in 1977 from the village of Khandbari. He has been a Boulder resident and business owner since 1985 and is the local expert for all things Nepalese.

◆ *Photo by Johnson Photography*

Shrestha opened his store, Old Tibet, on Pearl Street Mall in 1986. The store sells clothing, jewelry, Buddhist and Hindu statues and other imported items from Nepal, India and Tibet, Nepal's neighboring countries. The store has remained very successful through the years and is quite popular with tourists. Shrestha also owns a restaurant, Narayan's Nepal Restaurant, located just a few blocks from the store. The restaurant serves traditional Nepalese cuisine, focusing on hearty vegetarian food. In addition, Shrestha is the owner of a travel agency, Narayan's Gateway Travel, and is also the founder of the SANN Research Institute, which organizes semester-abroad programs to Nepal, China and Russia. These Boulder businesses have provided the capital for Shrestha's philanthropic work in Nepal.

◆ Narayan Shrestha and his wife, Sreejana, are pictured in their restaurant, Narayan's. *Photo by Johnson Photography*

When Shrestha visited his homeland in 1986, conditions had deteriorated greatly since the time he had lived there. Poverty was rampant, schools were in disrepair, inflation was up, corruption was widespread and there were few jobs available. Thus, the opportunities for proper health care were also nonexistent, while the rural people of Nepal were experiencing serious health problems associated with Third World countries. Shrestha was determined to help his native country and its people.

He returned in 1988 with a group of health care professionals, who treated almost 3,300 patients on that first visit. Since then, the organization has provided health care for more than 70,000 people in Nepal. There is now a permanent clinic in Kathmandu with full-time staff members. There is also a village relief clinic that rotates through four villages on a monthly basis. Some Nepali people walk for miles or even days through the mountainous terrain to reach the clinics, sometimes carrying their ill and dying family members. The volunteer medical staff treats ailments ranging from toothaches to malnutrition and cancer. They perform operations and attempt to teach rudimentary health care and hygiene.

Helping Hands participants come from all over the United States, and many are from the Denver/Boulder area since the foundation is based in Boulder. Volunteers camp in tents near the clinic and live in a similar fashion to the Nepali people. They work closely with Nepali health professionals, learning of the challenges of providing proper health care in a Third World country. Volunteers work for a term of service ranging from two weeks to six months. Helping Hands also encourages and sponsors Nepali medical students.

Shrestha is devoted to aiding the poor people of Nepal and is committed to educating the Boulder community about Nepalese culture. He is a leader of the local Nepali community and is also recognized nationally as a prominent member of the Nepali-American citizenry. Through his work with Helping Hands, his store, restaurant, travel agency and research institute, Shrestha has broadened the culture of Boulder over the last decade. The Nepalese influence will be palpable for many years to come.

North Boulder Liquor

In a town bloated with rapid new growth and inundated with national chain stores, North Boulder Liquor is an oasis of old-style neighborhood character. Though the modern, brick building and the shopping center it occupies are products of the area's recent building boom, the store's exterior belies its 60 years of rich history.

The store originator, Dick Jones, opened North Boulder Liquor in 1939, selling it three years later to Baldie Maschetti, a Coloradan of rugged mining stock. Another change of ownership occurred in 1959 when Maschetti sold the business to Bill Miller. Current owners Pete and Lynda Conis purchased the business from Miller in 1972. Today, they run the store with the help of their daughter, Stephana. Though each successive owner has updated the building to meet the area's changing needs, North Boulder Liquor has not moved from its original site. The brick exterior we see today actually encases the wooden structure first built by Jones in 1939.

North Boulder's residential settlement dates back to the years following World War II, when a patriotic developer procured large tracts of land in the area with the goal of selling them at low cost to returning soldiers. The close-knit neighborhood bond which characterized the area in its early years has remained North Boulder's defining quality for decades. In the 1960s, the north end of town actually sought to incorporate as a separate community, distinct from the city of Boulder. Though the neighborhood lost to the city in the Colorado Supreme Court, North Boulderites even today take pride in the area's distinctive identity.

Like the rest of the city, North Boulder has seen explosive growth in recent decades. Thanks to business owners like Pete and Lynda Conis, however, the area has preserved a neighborhood character all its own, even through this period of dramatic change. When the Conis family took over North Boulder Liquor in the early 70s, they were struck by the fact that the neighborhood's residential growth was rapidly outstripping its available commercial services. The family built North Boulder Market, a commercial complex which includes a locally owned and operated grocery store and several other Boulder businesses, as well as North Boulder Liquor.

◆ North Broadway Liquor was the store's original name, as shown in this 1959 photograph.

Like North Boulder itself, North Boulder Liquor combines the character and charm of an old-time neighborhood with the style and sophistication of a modern community. The store boasts one of the area's largest selections of California wines, as well as a vast port collection. With over 90 single-malt scotches in stock, North Boulder Liquor is Colorado's leading single-malt scotch retailer. Since Colorado produces more beer than any other state in the nation, no Boulder liquor store would be complete without an expansive inventory of domestic and imported beers. The Conis family is particularly proud to promote beers from the area's many renowned microbreweries.

Patrons of North Boulder Liquor will be impressed not only by the store's outstanding selection of quality products, but also by the courtesy and personal attention which the Conis family shows each customer. For North Boulder residents, the store is a neighborhood gem. For the rest of the city, it is a destination well worth the short drive up Broadway.

◆ Today, North Boulder Liquor is part of the thriving North Boulder Market complex.

Pasta Jay's

◆ *Photo by Johnson Photography*

The history of Pasta Jay's restaurant does not begin in Colorado but in 19th century Italy. This popular Boulder restaurant serves authentic Italian cuisine from recipes passed down through the generations. Its quaint atmosphere, good food and friendly staff help it live up to its motto — a restaurant you can call home.

Owner Jay Elowsky began his career in the restaurant business in San Clemente, California, in 1980. He began washing dishes in his Aunt Kathy and Uncle Sonny's pizza place and eventually worked his way up to cook and manager. Along the way he learned the family recipes passed down to Sonny from his mother, "Mama Genovese," whose grandmother was the cook for the first king of the United Countries of Italy, Victor Emmanuel II, who reigned from 1861 to 1878.

Elowsky introduced Pasta Jay's to Boulder in September of 1988 in a little renovated Victorian house at 9th and Pearl streets. With the help of his parents, the Boulder location became such a success that Elowsky opened two more stores in Breckenridge, Colorado, in 1991 and in Moab, Utah, in 1992. The three stores are thriving today. New locations may spring up eventually in other resort towns.

The Boulder store relocated to 10th and Pearl early in 1999 after a few years at a much larger location at 17th and Pearl. Although the new site seats fewer patrons, the overall feel of the location is much like that of the original restaurant. This location on the Pearl Street Mall brings in a larger lunch crowd and is more accessible to tourists. The brick décor and red-and-white checked tablecloths beckon to the passersby through the large glass windows. A heavy scent of garlic lures hungry shoppers.

The menu, which originally offered only four or five entrees, has about 13 today. Elowsky returns to Uncle Sonny's twice a year to pick up new recipes. The menu offers everything from pizza to traditional Neapolitan Italian dishes, with a strong emphasis on garlic. Catering is also a large part of the business. Pasta Jay's is a popular choice for catered weddings, graduations and parties of any occasion. The restaurant has received four-star ratings in local restaurant guides and many of the regional sports magazines advise their athletes to "carbo-up at Pasta Jay's" when in Boulder for a running race, in Moab for a bike race or in Breckenridge for a day of skiing.

◆ Cyclists, runners, skiers and locals help keep Pasta Jay's a prominent part of the Boulder scene — a restaurant they can call home. *Photo by Johnson Photography*

Pasta Jay's involvement in the Boulder community is magnanimous. A request for a gift certificate donation is never refused. Each September since 1996 it has provided food for the almost 2,000 cyclists in the Boulder Bicycle Classic. It donates food or money to the local homeless shelter, Boulder County Safehouse, the Children's Collage Museum, Mount Hope Lutheran Church, Vineyard Church, the Boulder Fire Department and the Boulder Police Department. It also helps out with fund-raisers for Fairview High, Boulder High and many University of Colorado undergraduate programs.

Pearl Street Inn

Pearl Street Inn, with its flower-filled courtyard, antique treasures and friendly welcome, is an oasis of tranquility in the heart of Boulder. This elegant brick Victorian structure, the first on its Pearl Street block, has a unique history — including a ghost story and a happy ending in its recent renaissance.

When current owner Kate Beeman bought the inn in June 1997, she was fulfilling a long-held dream. A natural caretaker with a master's degree in nursing from the University of Colorado, she had wanted to own a bed-and-breakfast for years.

Originally, the inn had a heaviness to it, almost a feeling of despair. The main building was constructed as a private residence in 1898 — supposedly on ancient Indian burial grounds — by German immigrants George Koehler, an agent for the Pacific and United States Express, and his wife, Doris. It was converted to an inn in 1985 when the two-story addition was built around the courtyard. Strange events followed. Two of the innkeepers claimed to have seen ghosts in the basement, and in an upstairs room people allegedly caught glimpses of a shadow in the mirror just as the rocking chair would start to rock.

Undaunted, Kate called in a spiritual healer who had been initiated in Native American rites. Arriving with her sage stick, she performed a clearing ceremony, assisting the spirits in their departure. Business improved dramatically, with people suddenly commenting on the great atmosphere and remarking that it was better than going home.

Today Pearl Street Inn's European flair and excellent location, only six blocks from the University of Colorado's campus and three blocks from the colorful shops, galleries and street entertainment of Boulder's vibrant pedestrian mall, make it a favorite with out-of-town visitors and business travelers, including Ralph Nader who has been a guest twice.

For Boulder residents, Pearl Street Inn is also a popular setting for weddings, receptions and private parties with a full commercial kitchen and facilities for up to 100 guests. Special seasonal festivities are on the calendar and guest packages are scheduled for weekend retreats. The inn's modern amenities include a fully equipped business office, making it a great venue for small business meetings, with catered meals available. Corporate retreats that include hiking, skiing or horseback riding in the Rockies are also offered.

◆ A friendly welcome awaits at Pearl Street Inn.

Many of the exquisite antiques that furnish the inn date back to the 19th century and possibly belonged to the original owners. There are eight spacious bedrooms, all overlooking the courtyard — four queens, two doubles, one twin and one suite. Each has a cathedral ceiling and its own distinct and charming personality, with fresh flowers, unique decor and comfortable furnishings. The rooms all have log fireplaces (the suite has two), a private bath, TV and telephone. The lavish gourmet breakfast can be eaten in the quiet dining room downstairs or in the flagstone courtyard.

The beautiful garden courtyard with its soothing fountain is a focal point of the inn. One of Kate's aims is to encourage more local people to stop by and enjoy this idyllic setting, perhaps over a relaxing drink. The inn is currently the only bed-and-breakfast in Boulder with its own restaurant and liquor license.

Offering a warm welcome to visitors and residents, Pearl Street Inn is a haven of privacy and peacefulness and a Boulder treasure worth discovering.

Rocky Mountain Joe's Cafe

When Joseph Bevier Sturtevant bought his first photographic equipment in the tiny town of Boulder in 1884, he hoped to preserve the area's beauty and character for future generations. He may never have imagined, however, that his legacy would live on not only in his photographs, but in the wholesome fare and simple charm of the restaurant that would someday bear his name.

Though his life story is rich with Wild West escapades worthy of his sobriquet, Rocky Mountain Joe made his most memorable mark not with a rifle or shotgun, but with a camera. His thousands of striking images provide a priceless record of the daily life of early Boulder County. In his honor, and with his inspiration in mind, original owners Steve LeBlang and Marc Levinson opened Rocky Mountain Joe's Cafe in February of 1982.

Sixteen years later, the restaurant still occupies its original location in a historic downtown building that was spanking new in Joe's day. Steep stairs leading to an airy room walled in worn, exposed brick lend a refreshing, neighborhood quality to the cafe, despite its proximity to the now trendy Pearl Street Mall. Sturtevant's photographs, set off in simple, wooden frames, line the otherwise unadorned walls.

When current owner Darrell Ritchie purchased Joe's in 1997, his minor adjustments to the menu and decor served to enhance, rather than transform, the comfortable, no-frills character that loyal patrons had come to expect. Despite a few decidedly new-age menu options (such as soy-based cheese substitute) and an eye-popping assortment of fashionable blended coffees, the menu overall remains true to the informal, familiar foods that have long been the restaurant's trademark.

As with any genuine neighborhood establishment, every element of the cafe provides a reflection of the community which it serves. A representative mix of professionals, families, students and tourists fills Joe's with a peaceful hum of relaxed chatter. The menu itself makes a point of community, proudly displaying the names of local bakeries, coffee roasters, and other area businesses whose products are served in-house. A peek behind the scenes reveals more evidence of the restaurant's quintessentially Boulder style. A wall-mounted bike rack in the storage area is vivid testimony to the fact that Rocky Mountain Joe's employees, like so many Boulder residents, make top lifestyle priorities of both fitness and the environment.

To owner Darrell Ritchie and his staff, serving the community means more than just hot coffee and clean tables. Support for local educational and cultural resources is a fundamental aspect of Darrell's business practices. The Boulder County Safehouse, Boulder County Humane Society, Community Food Share, and the local library film series are just a few of the groups and events which benefit from Rocky Mountain Joe's contributions. Notes of appreciation from local schools and other organizations crowd a kitchen bulletin board, reminding Darrell and his staff of the greater meaning of service.

Rocky Mountain Joe's Cafe is one of the few places in Boulder where a regular can still order "the usual" and rest assured that the cook knows just what to do. Time has not stood still in this peaceful, uncomplicated cafe. But neither has it surged forward with the aggressive force so typical of communities in rapid growth. Reflecting both the old and the new of its burgeoning neighborhood, Rocky Mountain Joe's Cafe succeeds in preserving a restful simplicity that recalls an earlier era. Perhaps its magic resides in the photos that line the walls.

Sturtz and Copeland

Entering Sturtz and Copeland with its earthy smells and glorious greenery is taking a step into serenity, an escape from the hassles of modern life.

In winter, visitors come to the store just to evade the snowy Boulder weather. They walk the flagstones past giant cacti and verdant trees, take time to talk to the parrot, and enjoy the fountains and the tropical garden feel. In spring, they come for the glory of the bedding plants, to plan out the year's garden or choose a Valentine's bouquet or an Easter present. Sturtz and Copeland products simply make you feel good. Not only that, it's also the best florist and greenhouse in Boulder.

In the front of the store, consultants discuss wedding arrangements and expert designers make up stunning floral bouquets from huge coolers filled with exotic blooms shipped in from all over the world — roses from Ecuador are among the cut flowers that come in daily from California, Europe and South America.

The skilled garden staff assists the customers in the purchase of indoor plants, offering advice on light, pots, fertilizer, watering — everything to make sure the plants stay as healthy as the day they were bought. If a customer's plant is failing, Sturtz and Copeland will diagnose and treat it. It'll even send a pickup and delivery truck if it's too big for the car.

The store changes with the seasons. In winter, the back area is a forest of pine trees and custom wreaths. At planting time, the jewel brilliance of annuals and perennials delights the eye while vegetables and herbs attract organic gardeners and gourmet chefs.

With so many mountain clients from Nederland, Ward, Vail and Aspen, the planting season extends late into the summer. The store carries an unsurpassed variety of perennials, flowers that return year after year, including natives like columbine, monkshood and daisies, tailor-made for the dry Colorado climate and xeriscape plants that need little water. Its suppliers grow selections for Sturtz and Copeland that can't be found anywhere else. One Aspen customer regularly orders a special European geranium for his Swiss-style window boxes.

◆ Carol Riggs with the day's fresh flowers from all over the world
Photo by Johnson Photography

Sturtz and Copeland's custom orders are also famous — whether it's a flower arrangement, a moss basket in pinks and blues, or a customer's redwood tub filled with favorite flowers for sun or shade.

It all began in 1882 when James and Rhoda Hubbard purchased land at 1500 Arapahoe, a humble dirt road on the highway to Denver, to erect five greenhouses. In August 1928 Lloyd Sturtz and his wife Gladys purchased the existing greenhouses of what was by then Fawcett Floral, and in 1929 Lloyd's father-in-law, Albert W. Copeland, moved from Kansas to join the business. The floral choices were roses, carnations, mums and snapdragons, all grown on the premises.

It was a sad day for present owner Carol Riggs, who had worked at Sturtz and Copeland since the 60s when, in 1981, the historic greenhouses on Arapahoe had to make way for expansion of Boulder High School. The new Sturtz and Copeland on Valmont was designed to keep the original feel while benefiting from the latest technology in heating and cooling — a far cry from the old coal-stoked boiler with its pipe taller than Boulder High.

A Web site is currently being designed so that busy customers can place their orders online. But Sturtz and Copeland is a place people will continue to visit and stroll through, enjoying nature's beauty and a return to roots and earth.

Twin Peaks Mall

The idea to construct a mall in the relatively small community of Longmont first took hold when Joslin's Department Store, desiring a presence in the area, approached real estate developer Charles B. Lebovitz. After visiting the area, Lebovitz, owner of the development company CBL and Associates, liked what he saw. Thus, in 1985, CBL and Associates added Twin Peaks Mall to its list of malls across the nation, most of which are located in the Southeast.

At first, it appeared that Longmont might not be able to adequately support a large shopping complex, but years of rapid growth combined with Twin Peaks' continuous efforts to reflect the community's needs have put this worry to rest. To accommodate changes in the economy and the community, the composition of stores within Twin Peaks has shifted over the years. A major renovation in 1996 renewed the mall's commitment to staying current. Following the remodel, Dillard's doubled its size after it purchased Joslin's. United Artists Theatres also moved in, adding a 10-screen, 34,000-square-foot, state-of-the-art complex.

◆ The entrance to Longmont's Twin Peaks Mall invites the visitor in to sample the center's diverse lineup of stores and entertainment.

This added mall footage coincided with an explosion of growth in the community of Longmont. Sporting a new, more modern look, the mall's renovation proved fortuitous, attracting larger crowds as the city began setting building permit records. Residents form the core of the mall's repeat customers, visiting the mall to experience the new and more familiar stores in a brighter setting. While Twin Peaks set records within CBL for growth in sales and volume following the renovation, it also pumped up Longmont's revenue by paying taxes into city funds.

One key reason for the mall's success in Longmont stems from its community orientation. Despite Longmont's rapid growth, the city is still a relatively small town. Recognizing this, Twin Peaks has focused on becoming a hub for local organizations. This approach has proven beneficial in forging strong community ties. The Community Corner, introduced in 1998, includes an events board, a board listing available mall jobs, mall walker news, benches and a gazebo. The walls of the corner come to life with a mural, painted by Boulder-based Artwerks, that depicts the Boulder County skyline and the Front Range. Little League sign-ups, dance performances, blood pressure checks and community meetings all take place in this area of the mall. Twice a year, Twin Peaks puts on Community Days, during which charitable groups and local organizations from all over Boulder County hand out fliers and literature to create community awareness.

One key reason for the mall's success in Longmont stems from its community orientation.

As the community of Longmont continues to grow and change, Twin Peaks Mall plans to remain a flexible and accommodating center of community life by staying attentive to the needs of the local population. This exciting and vibrant mall takes pride in the fact that its presence allows the people of Longmont to fulfill their shopping needs without leaving Boulder County.

The Village

◆ (Far left top and left)
Photos by Johnson Photography

◆ (Far left bottom)
Photo by Ron Forth

How can a place change its location without ever moving? A visit to Boulder's Village reveals the answer. While it now sits in the heart of Boulder, bordered by the major cross streets of Arapahoe, Canyon and Folsom, the original Village was outside the city limits. Developed in the early 1960s, when Boulder was a "dry" town, The Village included several businesses, and a restaurant and bar, the Lamppost.

By the late 60s, Boulder grew to surround The Village and soon incorporated the land into the city limits, as it continued expanding to the north, south and east. The Village, which had once been on the outskirts, was now in the center of town.

◆ *Photo by Ron Forth*

The Village's impressive array of unique stores and restaurants includes more "Best of Boulder" winners than any other location in Boulder. Fifty different places tempt the visitor with fine home furnishings, apparel, services, children's things, sporting goods for every activity imaginable, movie theaters and award-winning restaurants.

One of The Village's prime attractions, McGuckin Hardware, is Boulder's biggest locally owned store. Known for having the "world's largest hardware selection," as well as for its service and expert advice, McGuckin's has something for everyone.

Winner of the city of Boulder's landscaping award for a number of years, The Village's distinctive ambience and special stores have garnered its reputation for "where the locals go." Undeniably Boulder in flavor, historically significant and remarkable for its ability to shift its location without ever moving, The Village offers a special experience for locals and visitors alike.

◆ *Photo by Ron Forth*

Hutchinson Black and Cook, LLC 260

Johnson Photography 262

Leopard Communications 264

architectural manœuvres, p.c. 266

Communication Arts 267

Downing, Thorpe & James 268

Slade Glass Co. 269

Terra Verde Development, LLC 270

Attorneys, accountants, architects, photographers and advertising professionals provide essential services to the Boulder area.

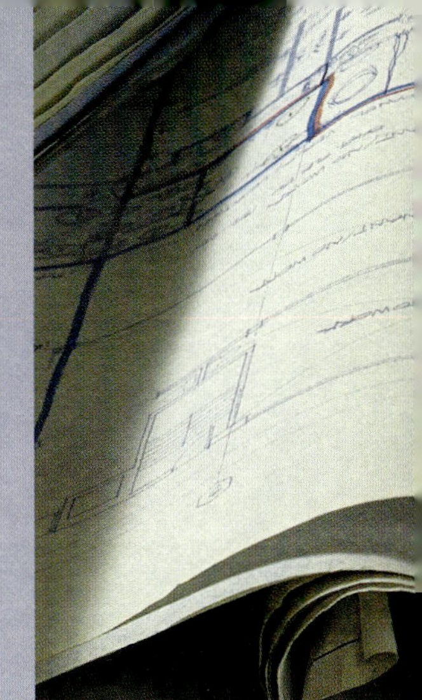

Professional Services

Hutchinson Black and Cook, LLC

The history of Hutchinson Black and Cook, LLC (HBC) in Boulder goes back to 1891. That was the year the firm's founder, attorney Albert A. Reed, arrived in town. At that time, Boulder was a small town of about 6,000 inhabitants, largely catering to the area's gold miners, with only 11 lawyers in the town. From Reed's initial solo practice, the present firm of 21 attorneys grew, adapting to the region's growth and continuing to serve the increasingly sophisticated legal needs of Boulder County and the rest of the Front Range.

◆ Forrest Cook (left) and Stan Black
Photo by Johnson Photography

As the firm has grown from the 19th century into the 21st, it has witnessed and participated in plenty of changes in Boulder. In many ways, the firm's history echoes the history of the community itself. Albert Reed, for example, helped the formation of the local Chautauqua and was a prominent local prohibitionist, largely responsible for the initiation of Boulder's 58-year "dry" period. His wife was an early suffragette, and his daughter one of the first female law students in the state. Dudley Hutchinson Sr., who practiced with the firm from 1918 until his death in 1967, was instrumental in shaping the entire region's water resources for decades as a director of the Northern Colorado Water Conservancy District. Over the years, attorneys in the firm have served as: city attorney; county attorney; members and officers of the Boulder County School Board; presidents of local banks, bar associations, service organizations and the chamber of commerce; church leaders and hospital directors; and members of law school faculties.

While acutely conscious of its unique links to the community's past, the firm manages to combine exceptional stability with deliberate progressivism. Some of its stability can be seen in its deep roots in Boulder. HBC has kept its offices in the heart of downtown Boulder for more than a century. In addition, its stability can be seen in the remarkable lengths of individual attorneys' association with the firm, with four attorneys each practicing there for more than 40 years. (One of the few attorneys who stayed with HBC only a few years was Wiley Rutledge, who was appointed to the U.S. Supreme Court in 1943.) At the same time, the firm was the first in Boulder to have hired a female attorney (1915); one of the first law firms in the nation to computerize its records; and a pioneer in instituting regular sabbaticals for both attorneys and support staff. These sabbaticals have resulted in such diverse experiences as teaching high school math in Brazil; writing a published novel; building a 35-foot cruising sailboat and sailing it to Tahiti; guiding whitewater trips in New Zealand; and working on legal and judicial reform in Bulgaria and Sarajevo. For many consecutive years, Boulder County's legal services organization has recognized the firm as the largest in the county to have every single one of its attorneys contribute pro bono time to the indigent.

For almost three-fourths of a century, the firm included at least one member of the Hutchinson family, either the elder Dudley or his sons Dudley Jr. and T. Henry (Hank), until Hank's retirement in 1991. Today, the firm is made up of a diverse group of attorneys, some of whom are Boulder natives. Other firm members have grown up anywhere from small-town Iowa to New York City. Although many of them attended law school in Boulder or Denver, the firm includes graduates of the Harvard, Yale, Stanford, Cornell and Michigan law schools.

At Hutchinson Black and Cook, the attorneys are aware of the high standards set by their predecessors. Almost a century ago, Albert Reed was described as "faithful to his profession's loftiest purposes." Some 60 years later, at the Boulder courthouse tribute to Dudley Hutchinson Sr. in 1967, the chief judge said simply that his lifetime of legal work "gives us some reasonable basis for calling this building the Hall of Justice."

While acutely conscious of its unique links to the community's past, the firm manages to combine exceptional stability with deliberate progressivism.

Today, the firm represents an exceptional variety of clients and provides them with an unusually wide range of different types of legal services. Its clients include individuals, families, small businesses, nonprofit organizations and larger corporations, and although many live or are based in the Boulder Valley, others come from the rest of the state, the country and the world. From the living room to the boardroom to the courtroom, HBC attorneys help their clients, whether in their happiest times or their worst tragedies. That help can range from: arranging an adoption to finalizing a divorce; writing a simple will to handling a complex estate; forming a two-person partnership to dissolving a large corporation; drafting a contract for the purchase of a house to negotiating an international multi-party software licensing agreement; and negotiating an insurance settlement to litigating a multimillion-dollar intellectual property dispute.

From estate planning to tax advice, employment disputes to domestic relations, corporate mergers to environmental litigation, HBC clients expect and receive comprehensive legal representation. Furthermore, the firm remains committed to providing those services at the highest possible quality in a personalized manner and in the most cost-effective way.

Attesting to the firm's commitment to quality service, the firm received the following tribute from a client in 1918: "When I think back over the past dozen years with your attorneys, it affords me no little pleasure, for I am only glad to know the whole bunch, and unlike some that I have met, they have all been square with me. In every dirty mix-up, they have all been right. When my friend Albert Reed advised me to hire his partners 'because they will take care of you, for there is no more reputable concern in business,' it was a real joy to hear him say it, for it not only put me right there, but explained some other things that go to make life real."

Today, the attorneys and staff at Hutchinson Black and Cook continue to strive to achieve this kind of response from their clients and to always recall with them some of those "other things that go to make life real."

◆ *Photo by Johnson Photography*

Johnson Photography

Juggling a family of six and a free-lance photography business may seem ambitious, but Charlie and Char Johnson of Johnson Photography strike an enviable balance between far-flung adventures in exotic destinations and stable roots in their hometown of Loveland, Colorado. Their work for a stock photography agency takes them to Mexico and Central America several times each year, but photographic commitments in Boulder form the core of the couple's artistic and professional lives.

◆ *(Right and far right) Photo by Johnson Photography*

◆ *Photo by Johnson Photography*

Charlie Johnson came to photography in his 30s after 10 years in the oil and gas industry. When the 80s oil crisis prompted a career shift, Johnson moved to Boulder to study photojournalism and fine art photography at the University of Colorado, rekindling a love of photography that had begun a decade earlier. In 1988, Johnson joined the staff of *The Colorado Daily* as chief photographer, beginning a relationship with the employee-owned newspaper that continued until 1999. When Charlie Johnson joined with Char in marriage, as well as in business partnership a year later, Johnson Photography — the couple's shared free-lance enterprise — began.

Today the Johnsons' projects range from writing stories about and photographing the people and places of Latin America, to documenting the weddings and bar mitzvahs of fellow Boulder residents. Their business is also expanding more and more into the growing commercial world in Boulder. Char Johnson has also managed a successful, nine-year career with Continental Airlines in Denver.

While Charlie and Char cite their work in Latin America as the most exciting aspect of their professional lives, the couple also works extensively in the commercial and editorial realm closer to home. Johnson Photography has created images for the University of Colorado, the city of Boulder, businesses, public relations firms and advertising agencies in the metro area. Charlie has published images in 13 magazines including *Newsweek, U.S. News & World Report, Advertising Age* and *Small Business Opportunities.* Their photographs also appear in greeting cards by Blue Sky Publishing. Charlie has received awards from The Colorado Press Association, the National Press Association and the Society of Professional Journalists.

In addition to their journalism and commercial work, the Johnsons handle a growing schedule of photographing weddings and other events. Building on Charlie's journalistic background, Johnson Photography offers an unconventional, documentary-style approach to wedding pictures. The couple works as a team on every job, offering their clients both Charlie's artistic and technical expertise and Char's business savvy and organizational prowess.

◆ New Orleans Jazz Fest 1996
Photo by Johnson Photography

Johnson Photography has recently moved to Loveland, Colorado, but still maintains their business in Boulder and the metro area. The area's booming economy, combined with its thriving artistic community, makes Boulder and the surrounding area a rich market for the Johnsons' expanding business.

◆ (Far left)
A young girl in Quepos, Costa Rica
Photo by Johnson Photography

◆ Sunset in Quepos, Costa Rica
Photo by Johnson Photography

Leopard Communications

In 1982 when Sherri Leopard decided to dabble in free-lance marketing for Boulder-based companies, she found a niche translating high technology into the language of customer benefits. Leopard soon realized that few people, other than engineers, could discuss the esoterica of computer software and hardware and explain why purchasers of technology should care about one product over another.

At that time in Boulder, as elsewhere, few if any companies were applying classical marketing techniques to the computer industry. To respond to this unmet need, Sherri Leopard founded Leopard Communications, attracting IBM as her first major client. There were few high-tech companies in Boulder then, but the town would soon host numerous start-up companies as individual engineers left large corporations to become entrepreneurs. Today Boulder is often dubbed "Silicon Mountain" in recognition of this industry's expansion.

◆ (L-R) Laurie Taylor, president; Sherri Leopard, CEO; Bettie Boruff, CFO

Over the past 15 years Leopard Communications has played an integral role in this growth. As Boulder's high-tech industry has developed, Leopard has expanded from a one-woman outfit to become a major player in this new marketing field. The company now employs more than 75 people and recently moved into 25,000 square feet of new office space in the Gunbarrel area on Boulder's north end. Annual revenues exceed $7 million, a 30 percent increase from the year before.

Leopard is led by six seasoned executives who bring to the table their experience in strategic marketing and communications, technology and creative services. These executives direct a staff with cutting-edge skills in disciplines ranging from engineering to art, from advertising to information architecture, technical writing to interactive new media.

Today this firm helps its clients develop a strategic direction, as well as the marketing messages and designs that convey that direction. Leopard's strength lies in providing an in-depth review of a client's functions, products and markets before it develops marketing strategies to grow the bottom line.

Once a client's strategic marketing direction is articulated, Leopard provides tangible products that run the gamut from CD-ROMs to content-rich databases to Web sites, from authoritative speeches to attention-getting yet substantive multimedia presentations that create industry buzz. This firm also serves clients whose market requires traditional marketing tools such as printed brochures, posters, advertisements, direct-mail services and similar products.

"Classic brand marketing has transformed the world of high technology," Sherri Leopard explains. "High-tech players are seeking people who can do 'category marketing' of their products. Today the buyer of technology is a corporate executive. Today's CEOs must care about technology because it is so integral to the efficiency and reach of their operations. If they don't leverage technology to change the way they do business, they're going out of business."

If a client seeks to develop a brand identity for its products in a crowded market, it may require a Web site with similarly designed brochures. If a client needs to supply its sales force in the field with up-to-the-second data on product specifications, Leopard will design an Intranet, or customized Internet-based system that makes information available only to employees with passwords. Not all Leopard's products fall into the high-tech category. If an executive needs a speech on his or her company's innovative product for an industry trade show, the company's writers can pen it.

Sophisticated clients often have a strong idea of their needs, but Leopard brings an outside, fresh view. Leopard's success is reflected in the response of the Fortune 500 companies and smaller entrepreneurs it serves, as well as by its own growth.

Sherri Leopard shares the credit for her firm's success with the community where she makes her home. The underlying theme is Boulder's history of progressiveness. She has been lauded for her entrepreneurial success, though she says that people often don't recognize the risk a community takes to support entrepreneurs. She points to the presence of the University of Colorado as a major factor in Boulder's receptiveness to new ideas. Her own success has led to her community involvement with the Boulder Technology Incubator and the board of the University of Colorado's School of Entrepreneurship. Several of Leopard Communications' principal executives also maintain close community ties. President Laurie Taylor serves on the board of the local YWCA, and her firm has contributed pro bono work to help the YWCA communicate its mission. Kathy Simon, vice president for technology, is former chairperson of the Boulder Chamber of Commerce, and sits on the boards of the Colorado Dance Festival and Norwest Bank. Jennifer Constable, vice president for creative services, keeps abreast of developments with her peers through membership in the local chapter of the American Institute of Graphic Artists.

What distinguishes this firm from competitors, its executives say, is that it combines depth in strategic thinking with high-tech tools. Leopard integrates its clients' message, strategy and delivery systems as a natural outgrowth of their business. The process for clients is simple. A project manager at Leopard Communications assembles staff from the creative and technology teams and analyzes a company's business to determine its strategic position. Constable says that appropriate designs flow from understanding this aspect of a client's operation. She says, "Good design does stand out."

Content comes first, agrees Simon. Technology should enhance content, she points out, not overwhelm it.

Taylor says that the firm is dedicated to the personal and professional growth of its employees. In that sense, the firm is very much at home in the progressive Boulder environment. Taylor believes that the firm's success in solving problems and working in the high-tech environment stems from challenging and encouraging its employees. Leopard's management philosophy includes mentoring by seasoned executives for younger workers. Beyond that, she says, five principles are involved: growth of professional skills, integrity, fun, collaboration and excellence at every step prior to the goal-oriented act of producing a product. With this credo, the firm has built a team of people who bring together cutting-edge skills in content, design, technology and client services, a critical balance that fosters a team environment.

Technology has opened the door to a new world and the professionals at Leopard Communications are well-positioned to explore it.

◆ One of Leopard Communications' most effective sales promotions during 1998 was the creation of a mass-marketing communications and awareness-building campaign for IBM Global Services in emerging markets throughout the world.

◆ Leopard Communications built a corporate identity program that reflects BrainPlay.com's business — selling software and other educational products for children.

architectural manœuvres, p.c.

In an age of throw-away architecture scattered indifferently on the landscape, buildings that seemingly grow from their sites herald a rare aesthetic pleasure and environmental ethic. These latter buildings characterize the work of *architectural manœuvres*, which takes cues from the planar landscape and refracted light indigenous to Boulder to create memorable residences and commercial buildings.

Founded by J. Matthew McMullen in 1989, the firm derives its inspiration from Frank Lloyd Wright's use of site materials and forms, from Robert Henri's American Impressionist paintings of blended natural elements which re-create an American landscape, and Charles Haertling's sculptural buildings. McMullen's interpretation results in design by "organic cooking," blending the elements of site and building to create an artistic and functional architecture.

McMullen's residential projects sing with "organic impressionism." Crooked Pine is a 5,100-square-foot home in Boulder, located where flat plains meet the vertical Rocky Mountain slopes. Diverse fragile ecosystems and the fragmented landscape, which included an eroding sandstone formation and subsequent rubble, produced a fractile building geometry fused with organic site materials, sensitively placed to preserve the 100-year-old crooked pine tree that thrives on site. Familiar with Wright's work, the client sought an architect who shared that ethic. The resulting residence was dropped into the hillside to minimize its visual impact and preserve views both for the owners and their neighbors. Vibrant stucco textures and colors reflect those of the surrounding rocks and sky. Rusted metal columns and hammered railings recall the area's mining history.

◆ Private residence — foothills above Boulder ©*1999 architectural manœuvres, p.c.*

◆ Conceptual design for renovation of Pueblo Bank & Trust — 30th & Pearl branch ©*1999 architectural manœuvres, p.c.*

Believing that good design is possible for all budgets, McMullen designed a residence for clients with a modest budget who wanted Mediterranean-type hillside architecture built in Sunshine Canyon in Boulder. Their home sinks into a mountainous site, which required blasting to drop the house into the granite substrate. It echoes with the contextual color, planar surfaces, outdoor rooms and use of natural light typical of Mediterranean design. Vibrant stucco colors reinforce the changing daylight.

Committed to the Boulder Valley community, *architectural manœuvres* has designed a variety of community outreach and commercial projects. The firm has provided architectural consultation to Attention Homes, Inc. in Boulder, a nonprofit that provides residential care and counseling for abused, homeless and delinquent individuals. It donated its design and visualizing capabilities to provide a fund-raising tool for the Colorado Therapeutic Riding Center. Other projects include the redesign of University Hill's retail center to bring life back to the shopping center, a re-design of La Iguana, a Hill restaurant, and the new Pueblo Bank. Holding the client's vision as sacred, architectural manœuvres creates cost-effective, people places that bespeak the soul of what Boulder's landscape and community offer.

Communication Arts

Achieving a sense of place, the genius loci, has historically challenged designers. Even more demanding is incorporating that "spirit" into the social and economic realities of the place. Not all succeed, which makes the internationally known accomplishments of Communication Arts, a firm that excels at re-creating that spirit for each place and each client, unique. Since its founding in 1973, Communication Arts has set the stage for human experiences in diverse locations, with the caveat that the stage mirrors that particular community and environment, rather than the designer.

Founding and managing partners Henry Beer, Richard Foy and Janet Martin point with pride to the Pearl Street Mall, an early project and their office location. Adhering to their beliefs that the client, not the designer, sets the agenda and that projects must be consonant with the users, Communication Arts teamed with Everett-Zeigel and Sasaki Associates, working closely with business and property owners to develop the features, amenities and character that are familiar signatures of the mall. Realizing that what makes Colorado unique is its environment — the mountains, plains, vistas and huge sky — and that Boulder residents love the outdoors, the firm incorporated trees, outdoor terraces for restaurants, play areas, entertainment, and elements of delight and discovery, such as the whimsical-face water fountain.

Viewing themselves as "consummate outsiders" who infuse themselves into a client's needs and locale with fresh perspective, Communication Arts brings its expertise to projects across the world. In 1990, it helped with the renovation of Madison Square Garden in New York City, one of the largest sports-entertainment centers in the nation. Recognizing New Yorkers as self-designated smart people with complicated lives and who value efficiency, convenience, service and speed (the "New York Minute"), the firm designed no-nonsense circulation through a high-tech, sophisticated and colorful center. New Yorkers orient themselves to street intersections, so Garden signage and referents are named for street intersections. The experience vibrates with the vitality that is New York.

Communication Arts' diverse projects and distinctive urban and environmental graphics all attest to its ability to immerse itself in a culture and distill whatever that place and people are. For example, Ontario Mills is a 1.7 million-square-foot entertainment and retail mall in Southern California that not only dissolves the distinction between its two uses but attracts the cultural stew, roughly 26 diverse ethnic groups. Arranging the stores on a race track layout, Communication Arts flooded the interior with brilliant colors, light, water features, and specific plant species that evoke the region's singular environment. The project was nominated to the international Vertigo Exhibition, which will feature utopian solutions to the possibilities and problems in design presented by the messy realities that compose today's cities.

◆ 91-foot stylons proclaim the Founders' program at The Block at Orange. *Photo by Erhard Pfeiffer* *©Communication Arts*

The list attesting to the unique ability to design multicultural solutions to place speaks for itself. Bugis Junction in Singapore re-weaves retail and entertainment into a pulsing center and elicited from its Development Director, Tag Sin Siew, the praise, "Why did I have to go all the way to Boulder, Colorado, to get a design that feels like Singapore?" Other key projects include the Prudential Center, Staples Center, JFK International Arrivals Terminal, Houston Uptown, and The Block at Orange. Worldwide, Communication Arts flourishes an invisible hand connecting people to place.

◆ Children's play area at the Pearl Street Mall *Photo by Thorney Lieberman* *©Communication Arts*

Downing, Thorpe & James

Downing, Thorpe & James (DTJ) is a distinctive architectural firm. Founded in Boulder in 1988, DTJ is firmly committed to the concept of an integrated, multidiscipline design approach. It focuses on creating special "places" — not just building single structures.

This integrated design approach was prevalent in the Planned Unit Developments (PUDs) of the 70s, but lost ground during the 80s due to the poor economy. The partners of DTJ remained focused through this bumpy period and held on to their multidiscipline capabilities. In the 90s, DTJ forged ahead with the "community design" concept, which includes business, residential, institutional and mixed-use. Today, offering multidiscipline design under one roof strengthens the perspective of the individual services.

DTJ projects are also characterized by their gentle integration into the natural landscape. The philosophy of never imposing a solution on the land, but using the site's features to help determine the design, is popular in this day of environmental consciousness. DTJ's flexible style allows it to pursue any number of design approaches when faced with a challenging landscape.

◆ Wonderland Hill in Boulder — a local demonstration of DTJ's national community design specialty

◆ Spruce Street Center in Boulder — a parking structure and retail shops integrated in a context-sensitive design solution

DTJ's trailblazing work in residential community design can be witnessed in the first PUD in Boulder, AppleRidge, which was co-developed by Downing in the early 60s. This led to other noteworthy residential projects in Boulder such as Wonderland Hill, Winding Trail Village and Buckingham Ridge, unique homes clustered in preserved open spaces. Other distinctive residential areas including Wellman Creek, Brookfield and Bridgewalk, a rental neighborhood, are designed to foster a close sense of community.

Influence in the commercial arena is evident in the University of Colorado at Boulder's Research Park and the Interlocken Business Park. DTJ served as the master planner and overall design consultant for both. Interlocken is the corporate headquarters for office supply giant Corporate Express and for the nonprofit international organization Up With People — both designed by DTJ. In Denver, partner Thorpe was involved in the master planning and urban design for the Denver Technological Center, overseeing it through its key development years. Other projects in and around Boulder boast the DTJ signature: the Canyon Center in Boulder, Legacy Ridge Golf Course Community in Westminster and Harvey's Wagon Wheel Hotel and Casino in Central City.

With its early local success and with the advancement of technology, DTJ is also able to serve clients successfully on a national level. It has been recognized by the American Institute of Architects (AIA), Builder's Choice, and Best in American Living Awards (BALA) for places such as: the Fairways at Castle Pines; various projects at Desert Mountain in Scottsdale, Arizona, a high-end residential resort development; the Chop House Restaurant and Brewery in Denver, Colorado, and Washington, D.C.; and Rock Bottom Restaurants nationwide. Other distinguished projects include The Grove and Silverado Springs in Napa, California, and Big Cedar Lodge on Table Rock Lake in Ridgedale, Missouri.

Locally, DTJ has been honored with numerous awards including Historic Boulder's Silver Jubilee Design and Preservation Award for Spruce Street Center. It has also been recognized by three different Colorado chapters of the AIA for the Broadway/College Pedestrian Underpass. The City of Westminster, Colorado, presented DTJ with its Design for Excellence Award for The Pointe at Legacy Ridge, a residential project.

With its passion toward community design through the creation of exceptional places in Boulder and beyond, the future looks promising for DTJ.

Slade Glass Co.

Few substances manifest as many diverse and seemingly contradictory characteristics as glass. At once clear and solid, opaque and reflective, its uses range from practical windows to Steuben sculpture. Nobody mirrors these versatile qualities better than Slade Glass Co., whose own work in Boulder has met the needs of commercial and residential projects with products ranging from prosaic shower stalls to poetic architectural elements.

A rare family-owned business of several decades in a city rampant with newly sprung entrepreneurs, Slade Glass Co. began in 1961 when the Slade family bought an existing glass company. Most of the Slade family members have worked there at some point in their careers. Even their non-family staff tends to stick around, committed to the company's high quality of craftsmanship, diversity of work and intriguing projects, which allow all involved plenty of challenge and camaraderie at work.

Currently run by Terry and his mother, Maxine, the company's projects are equally divided between commercial and residential. Commercial services include storefront framing, exterior glass and interior tenant finishes. Offering different glass products, Slade focuses on two- or three-story buildings with a mix of commercial, retail and industrial clients. Among its many more impressive projects are the Lakeshore Building in the Flatirons Business Park, which demanded, among other things, filling 102 window openings with six panes of glass each! Green-tinted windows with an internal heat mirror sandwiched in between allowed for high energy-efficient performance. Slade Glass Co. makes every effort to seek out energy-efficient solutions for a new millennium that demands sustainable design. Artistry also colors its commercial work, with windows that wrap corners, a clock placed in a round window in a commercial building at 20th and Pearl streets, and an impressive glass atrium at the Bank One Building in the Table Mesa Shopping Center.

Its residential work ranges from the expected repairs and installation of energy-efficient windows to more creative interior details: mirrors, shower enclosures, tables, counters and almost every imaginable fixture re-created in glass. Given a market composed of a large number of high-end builders and residences, Slade Glass Co. has built an impressive palette of European glass enclosures and elegantly designed mirrors and counters. The most unusual residential challenge consisted of a home constructed on a rock outcropping with one of Boulder's stunning mountain views. The owner wished to emphasize the setting — glass perfectly revealed the setting while providing shelter and definition. A glass hand railing ethereally slips up the stairs and points a magical line to the mountains. A glass-enclosed heated bridge suspended over moss-covered rocks connects two parts of the building while allowing a view beyond; a glass awning over the patio provides protection and visual access to the mountains and stars. The interior offers even more visual delight — suspended glass cabinets overhang stainless steel sinks, fancifully revealing function. One-inch-thick glass triangular shower stall seats turn bathing into an art form. Clear glass vanity tops, frosted glass interior doors, diverse mirrors, and heavy, frameless glass doors allow a mystical connection between outside and inside, solid and space.

The Boulder community historically prides itself on living sensitively, gracefully, and now, sustainably, in an exotic mountain setting. "Clearly," few companies re-create that ethic as aesthetically as Slade Glass Co.

Terra Verde Development, LLC

Serendipity gambled with sweet success the day Mark Queripel and Rick Oswald met. Until then, Mark partnered in a Denver-based architectural firm and Rick led design services for a Boulder builder. Both longed to offer superior design/build services by maintaining in-house quality control and accountability throughout the entire architectural and construction processes. With the financial help of a silent partner, the two founded Terra Verde in 1996, and now thrive on delivering sensitively conceived, highly detailed and sustainable single and multi-family homes.

◆ Custom residence at Somerset Estates in Niwot, Colorado (exterior)

Terra Verde designs homes for all settings, from mountains to prairies (particularly high-end luxury homes), with the caveat that the specific site dictates the building's manifestation. Building from the ground up creates not only a timeless indigenous architecture that appears to have almost grown on site, but allows the incorporation of "green" building principles, such as solar orientation, use of native materials, ambient lighting and opening to views, that ground the foundations of Terra Verde's philosophy. Cognizant of the growing client demand for environmentally friendly homes, the partners participate in the Green Builder Program of Colorado and incorporate water and energy efficiency, recycled materials and indoor air quality into all of their projects. Equally aware of client insistence on financial accountability, the firm delivers all its award-winning homes within budgeted costs.

◆ Custom residence at Somerset Estates in Niwot, Colorado (interior)

Terra Verde regards architecture as art and, like architect Ludwig Mies van der Rohe, recognizes that "God is in the details." Meticulously crafted details of varying woods, such as cherry or birch, evolve from the design, rather than springing superfluously as add-ons, and draw people around corners and into the character of each interior space. Its prairie-style Bellflower home in Boulder County sings with simple elegance. An arc forms a uniting motif; equally proportioned arcs of different sizes and materials echo throughout the interior, creating a collective balance and homogeneity. The ceiling arcs in wood, hundreds of tiny maple inlays accent the arcs and a congruent home theater offers entertainment. Native materials and craftsmanship proliferate throughout, in stained glass patterning, individually designed lighting fixtures, a Colorado slate floor and stair rails built by a Boulder artisan. Sited for views and fit to the terrain's contours, it uses the same Colorado buff sandstone detailing inside and outside. "Green" and sustainable achievements include an extraordinary efficiency rating, state-of-the-art heating and cooling systems, roof tiles designed to last for 75 years, stonework recycled from fly-ash waste and materials chosen for low toxicity and recycled content.

Mark and Rick credit their diverse office staff with their ability to design flexible client-pleasing spaces. Hailing from across the United States, the employees excel in all aspects of design, from construction to interiors, and technical ability, such as 3-D computer imaging. Widely recognized in the community, Terra Verde consistently wins design awards, publishes widely in professional journals and belongs to a plethora of organizations, including the American Institute of Architects, the National Association of Home Builders and various chambers of commerce. From attention to detail to maintaining a broad knowledge of its field, Terra Verde exudes a design excellence sought by a knowledgeable discriminating clientele who seek exquisitely liveable homes.

Indian Peaks hiking,
1999 photo by Tom Noel

Boulder Community Hospital 274

Community Medical Center 276

Boulder Chamber of Commerce 277

The Academy 278

Colorado Chautauqua Association 280

Colorado Music Festival 282

Boulder Theater 283

Downtown Management Commission and Downtown Boulder Inc. 284

University of Colorado at Boulder 286

Haystack Mountain Golf Course 288

Historic Boulder, Inc. 289

Longmont United Hospital 290

The Daily Times-Call 291

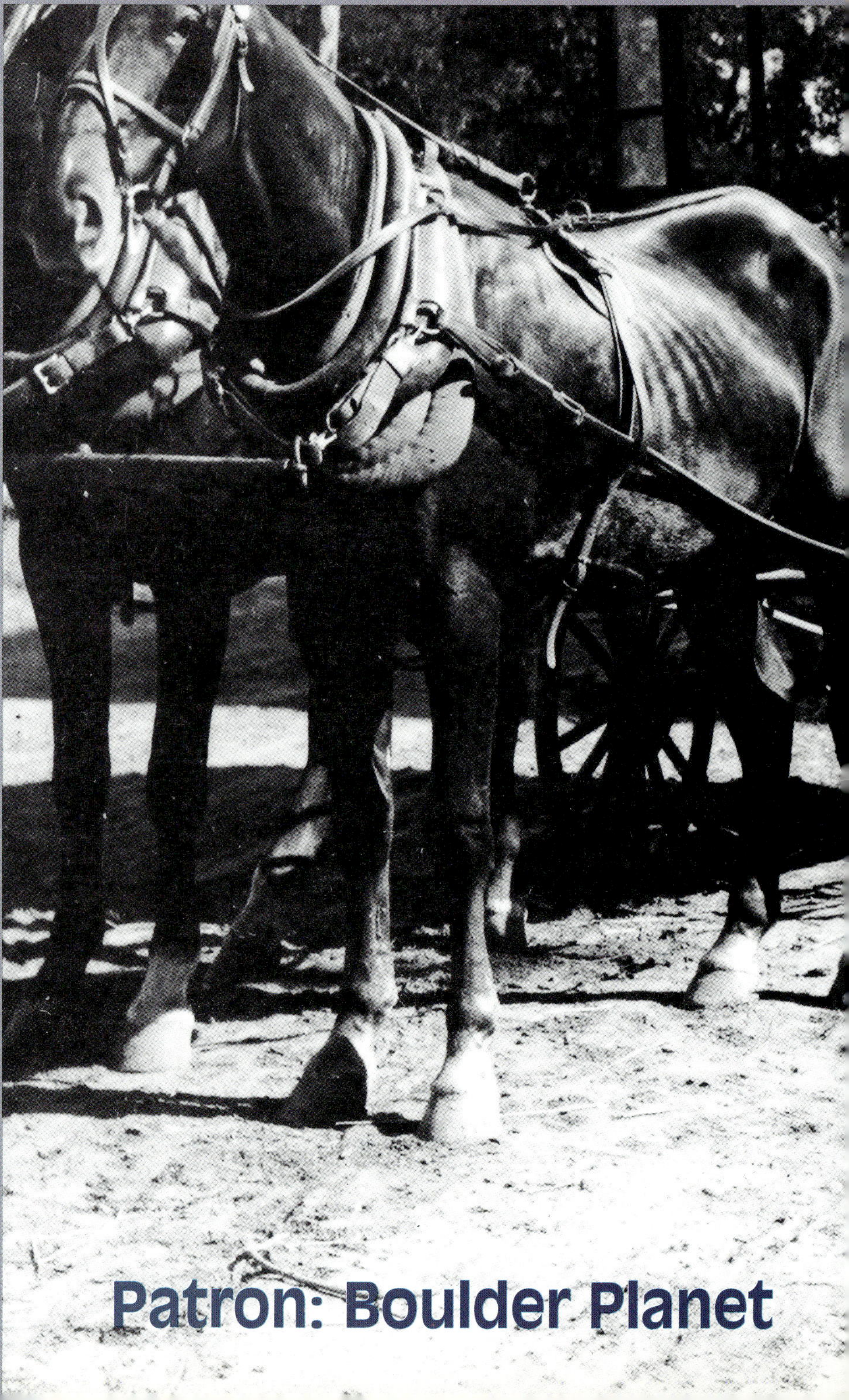

Patron: Boulder Planet

Medical, educational and civic institutions as well as culture and recreation contribute to the quality of life enjoyed by Boulder residents and visitors.

Quality *of* Life

Boulder Community Hospital

When Boulder Community Hospital was dedicated in April of 1926, those who took part in the ceremony could not have known that their modest community hospital would grow in size and stature to become a nationally recognized acute care facility.

The University Hospital, established in 1889, was Boulder's first health care facility. Located on the University of Colorado campus, it served as a teaching hospital for medical and nursing students until 1920, when the CU Regents decided to move the medical school to Denver. A group of local physicians, seeing that Boulder was about to lose its only hospital, bought the Hagman residence on North 12th Street (Broadway) in 1921 and converted it into the 15-bed Boulder Hospital. Early in 1922, the Regents offered to lease the University Hospital building to the town for three years on the condition that Boulder would establish its own hospital within that time. Realizing that the two hospitals were in direct competition, the physicians deeded their hospital to the community in 1922, and in April of that year the two facilities were consolidated under the Community Hospital Association as a not-for-profit hospital.

In October of 1924, a community-wide fund-raiser, dubbed "The Battle of Boulder," absorbed the population in the struggle to raise money for the new facility. Donations flooded in from citizens, churches and civic groups. Even summer visitors donated to the swelling fund. The new Boulder Community Hospital, dedicated on April 4, 1926, was established as a locally owned and operated not-for-profit hospital, governed by a local board. To this day, the hospital relies on community involvement to maintain its independent status.

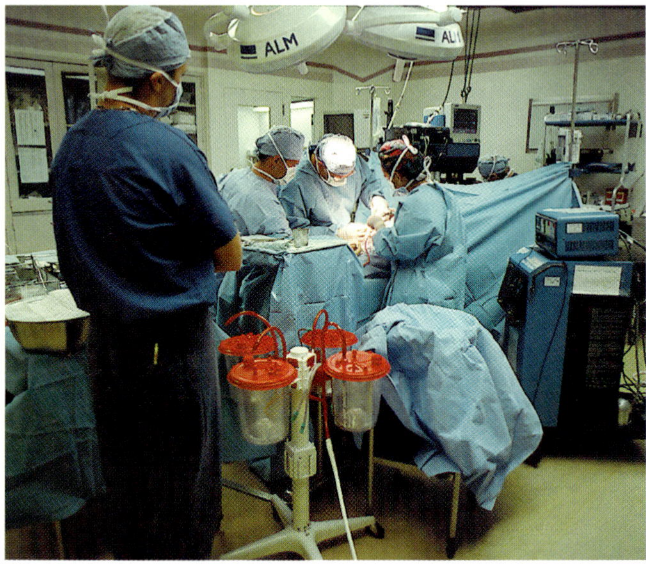

◆ The hospital has grown into a 265-bed acute care facility and has an outstanding reputation for its capabilities in surgery, cancer care, cardiology, orthopedics and maternity care. *Photo by Johnson Photograpahy*

◆ Boulder Community Hospital, circa 1928

After World War II, the baby boom hit Boulder County and the occupancy rate at BCH soared to 90 percent. The hospital was bursting at the seams. Financed by capital campaigns chaired by board member Frank G. Jamison, two expansions were approved during the 1950s. Expansion and modernization went hand in hand. Each room was wired for installation of TV sets. A central oxygen supply which fed into each patient's room, hydraulic-lift operating tables in surgery and a two-way intercom nurse call system combined to make the hospital a state-of-the-art facility.

Accelerated expansion and incorporation of the latest advances in medicine and technology were hallmarks of the 80s and 90s.

The Mapleton Center was added to the hospital complex in 1989. The center's earliest predecessor was the Boulder Colorado Sanitarium, which was opened in 1895 by the Seventh Day Adventist Church. The convalescent center was noted for helping patients recuperate from devastating illnesses (such as tuberculosis) and promoting wholesome lifestyles. Over the years, the sanitarium expanded its facilities and opened a professional nursing school. In 1962, it was renamed Boulder

Memorial Hospital. In the 1970s, the institution was extensively remodeled into a modern hospital which was purchased by Boulder Community Hospital in 1989 and renamed the Mapleton Center. Today, the Mapleton Center enjoys an excellent reputation for its comprehensive inpatient and outpatient rehabilitation services.

BCH has grown over the years into a 265-bed acute care facility. More than 425 physicians in 40 medical specialties have privileges at BCH. The staff of 1,700 includes registered nurses and technologists, many of whom have earned national certification in their specialties. These highly qualified professionals see over 30,000 emergency patients, 9,600 inpatients, 8,400 surgical patients and 150,000 outpatients annually. Boulder Community has always seen its mission as a provider of compassion and the human touch, as well as the highest quality medical services. The hospital's 450 indispensable volunteers, who assist staff and patients alike, also help to put a friendly face on BCH.

BCH's ongoing commitment to provide local access to the latest medical advances has been demonstrated repeatedly. Boulder Community was the first hospital in Colorado to offer the revolutionary Bispectral Index technology that analyzes a patient's brain wave pattern, enabling anesthesiologists to administer the optimal amounts of anesthetic drugs and virtually eliminating the possibility of regaining consciousness during surgery.

The hospital's Boulder Center for Sports Medicine, a part of the U.S. Olympic Committee's Sports Medicine Rehabilitation Network, provides world class treatment, rehabilitation, performance enhancement and injury prevention services to recreational athletes and Olympians alike.

In 1998, an independent study ranked Boulder Community Hospital best in the state for treatment of heart attacks. The hospital has also earned recognition for its capabilities in surgery, cancer care, cardiology, orthopedics and maternity.

The hospital's unwavering commitment to maintaining its status as a locally governed, not-for-profit facility makes it exceptional in an era when so many communities have lost control of their medical facilities. At BCH, the true "bottom line" is meeting needs throughout Boulder County. The physicians of Community Medical Associates provide a full range of medical care at their offices in Boulder, Gunbarrel, Lafayette and Louisville. Health screenings and other services are provided to residents aged 55 and older through eight wellness sites scattered across the county. The Community Medical Center in Lafayette, established in 1985 as a satellite facility, provides convenient access to urgent care for thousands of residents of eastern Boulder County.

Boulder Community's compassion extends beyond national boundaries. In 1995, BCH joined 25 other U.S. hospitals in forming a partnership with the federal government to assist the devastated hospitals in the former Soviet Union. BCH formed a partnership with City Medical Center in Boulder's sister city, Dushanbe, Tajikistan, agreeing to concentrate on improving care for women and children and to provide training, supplies and equipment to the hospital.

Indigent workers and their families in Mante, Mexico, also have reason to be grateful to the generous and compassionate staff at Boulder Community. For eight consecutive years, volunteers from the hospital and First Presbyterian Church have repaired cleft palates, removed cataracts and provided scores of life-transforming surgeries for people who have no other access to medical care. The mission also transports medical supplies, drugs and used equipment to the Mante hospital. Why does plastic surgeon Claude Burrow volunteer year after year to return to Mante? "Because it's pure medicine," he says. "You do what you were trained to do, without expectation of reward, but simply for the joy of doing it." That sums up the spirit of Boulder Community Hospital.

◆ One of many 1990 improvements was a new main entrance. *Photo by Johnson Photography*

Community Medical Center

When the Community Medical Center in Lafayette opened its doors in April of 1985, its staff extended an invitation to the residents of eastern Boulder County to "come see us before you need us!" The medical facility, located on South Boulder Road west of Highway 287, represents the commitment of Boulder Community Hospital to provide convenient access to quality medical services to the growing populations of Lafayette, Louisville, Broomfield and Erie. Over the years, CMC has become an integral part of the community, offering the expertise of a staff of family practice physicians and specialists to complement the Center's urgent care and rehabilitative services.

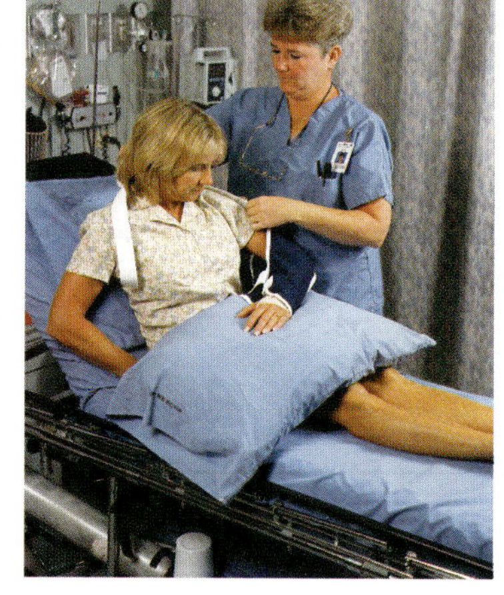

◆ The Center's Urgent Care facility handles a comprehensive range of health problems, from simple sore throats to broken bones. *Photo by Johnson Photography*

Open 16 hours a day, seven days a week throughout the year, Community Medical Center's Urgent Care facility provides immediate attention for a wide variety of medical problems, from broken arms and deep cuts to sore throats and ear infections. The Urgent Care Center's reputation for excellence attracts 16,000 patients annually. Community Medical Associates of Lafayette, the CMC's board-certified family practice physicians, provide scores of area families with the feeling of security that comes from having a long-term relationship with physicians who can treat the entire family's medical needs. The Center's association with Boulder Community Hospital means that CMC patients have ready access to a comprehensive health care network.

Community Medical Center provides some special services to area businesses as part of Boulder Community Hospital's overall Occupational Health Services network. Workers suffering on-the-job injuries at companies in Lafayette, Louisville, Broomfield and Erie regularly use the Urgent Care Center for quick treatment. Urgent Care staff also provide non-emergency services like physical examinations and drug screening. CMC's physical therapists are available to provide comprehensive rehabilitation for workers who need extended assistance in getting back to the workplace.

The board of directors at Boulder Community Hospital — a locally governed not-for-profit hospital — understand very well how feedback from local residents can improve the provision of health care. That's why they established a separate advisory board for CMC. This advisory board, comprised of residents of eastern Boulder County chosen for their dedication to the community and their vision for the future of CMC, provides valued input into determining both the range and cost of services at the facility.

Not all of Community Medical Center's interactions with area residents involve medical emergencies. Center staff regularly participate in local health fairs and civic celebrations, providing complimentary services like blood pressure and cholesterol screenings. The Center has also played an important role in the Quaker Oats "Smart Heart Challenge," a cholesterol reduction program that has helped make Lafayette's annual oatmeal festival a nationally known event.

Recent years have witnessed a population explosion in eastern Boulder County. Boulder Community Hospital planners are developing plans to ensure that Community Medical Center maintains its ability to meet the changing needs of its rapidly growing community in a cost-effective manner. However Community Medical Center eventually evolves, area residents can rest assured that their medical needs will be well met.

◆ Community Medical Center on W. South Boulder Road, Lafayette, Colorado *Photo by Johnson Photography*

Boulder Chamber of Commerce

Colorado's majestic Boulder Valley is found nestled in the Rocky Mountains amongst blue skies, wildflowers and a history of growth and prosperity. Founded on August 4, 1905, the Boulder Chamber of Commerce has been serving the Boulder business community as a resource for supporting the local economy, building powerful partnerships and supporting its diverse membership.

In the 50 years before the chamber was created, gold seekers established the first non-native settlement in Boulder County on October 17, 1858. Less than a year later, the Boulder City Town Company was organized by A.A. Brookfield and 56 shareholders. At an original purchase price of $1,000 each, 4,044 lots were laid out to attract residents. Growing slowly, Boulder developed as a supply base for silver and gold mining by providing equipment, agricultural products, housing and transport services, and gambling and drinking establishments. It also encouraged the creation of railroad service, hospital and school buildings, and a stable town government to support the mining trade.

In 1874 the University of Colorado was established in Boulder, and the first bank was built. In 1910 the Boulder Chamber of Commerce launched its first membership campaign. And by 1919, the Boulder Chamber's most requested information from visitors and potential residents was about tourism in the mountains, its health resort amenities, business openings and schools. Meanwhile, Boulder's 1920 census showed 11,006 residents.

The Boulder Chamber worked to raise $2,100 in 1927 to keep the hospital open and coordinated the planting of 3,000 pine tree saplings over five acres of burned mountain area. In the 1930s, cleaner and more well-marked streets, reforestation of city park land, cooperation with farmers, and development of a golf course and airport for tourists were Boulder's priorities.

By 1940, the census count was 12,958, and Hotel Boulderado dedicated office space for the Boulder Chamber of Commerce. After the first influx of new residents, the population soared to 20,000 in 1950 while parking and transportation become challenging problems for the bustling Boulder community.

A decade later, Boulder business leaders were actively recruiting new "clean" industry and improved transportation, securing a new highway and funding a site for the National Bureau of Standards in 1952. Other research and development industries soon followed. Boulder continued to expand and from 1950-1972 grew from 20,000 to 72,000 residents. In 1962 the average median family income in Boulder County was $6,114.

◆ Boulder, Colorado

With the purchase of thousands of acres of open space beginning in 1967, adoption of the Boulder Valley Comprehensive Plan in 1970, passage of both the building height restriction ordinance in 1972, and the residential growth management ordinance in 1977, Boulder began a period of in-fill and re-use of its past architectural development that continues today. By the mid 1980s, the Boulder Chamber had relocated its offices to its current location on Pearl Street and boosted its tourism efforts while the Boulder community made growth management one of its highest priorities.

And as the 1990s come to a close, the Boulder Chamber of Commerce celebrates its membership, reaching an all-time high with more than 2,100 businesses; follows Boulder's residential housing growth, slowing to one percent; manages Boulder City Council's decision to implement a moratorium on commercial growth; watches Boulder jobs reach over 90,000; and sees Boulder's average home price reach over $260,000.

Source: Boulder Landmarks Preservation Advisory Board

The Academy

More than 100 years ago on the hills overlooking Boulder, a Catholic nun dying from tuberculosis had a dream. Sent by the Sisters of Charity of the Blessed Virgin Mary in Dubuque, Sister Mary Theodore O'Connor and two companions envisioned a school to provide chronically ill children with opportunities to heal both the mind and body. O'Connor believed this was the place for such a holistic institution, and knew it would be blessed by the brisk, invigorating winds of the Boulder hills.

◆ The Sisters of Charity chose an inspiring location in the Boulder Hills to build Mt. St. Gertrude Academy.

In 1892, Mt. St. Gertrude Academy was born in a stately yet beautiful, $30,000 brick structure standing four stories high, with a lofty bell tower reaching towards the heavens. Most importantly, it was founded on "fresh air and sunlight, wholesome and nutritious food, regular hours for rising and retiring and an abundance of healthful recreation and outdoor exercise," to promote the good health of the students, as defined in a later school catalog. Unfortunately, Sister Mary did not live to see the opening of the school as she succumbed to her illness. Her wake was held in the building just one week before the building was finished, but her dream lived on in what became a holistic school for girls.

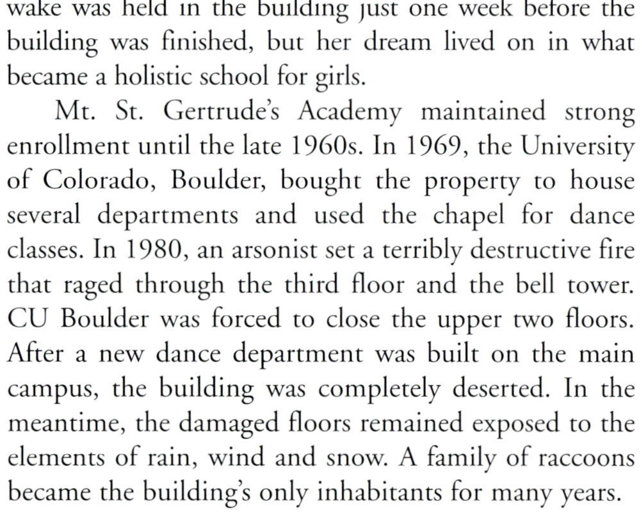

Mt. St. Gertrude's Academy maintained strong enrollment until the late 1960s. In 1969, the University of Colorado, Boulder, bought the property to house several departments and used the chapel for dance classes. In 1980, an arsonist set a terribly destructive fire that raged through the third floor and the bell tower. CU Boulder was forced to close the upper two floors. After a new dance department was built on the main campus, the building was completely deserted. In the meantime, the damaged floors remained exposed to the elements of rain, wind and snow. A family of raccoons became the building's only inhabitants for many years.

Between 1983 and 1989, CU tried unsuccessfully to sell the property. It finally decided to lease it to developers and sent out requests for proposals. Bruce Eckstrand, the vice chancellor of the board of regents, acknowledged the need for a retirement community in Boulder, adding it to the list of recommended Requests For Proposals (RFPs). That's when The Academy Group, L.P. became involved. Initially composed of Tom Surguine, an investor, and Gary Berg, a business attorney, The Group spent a year negotiating a long-term land lease with CU during the RFP process. They were later joined by Karen McMurry, another local attorney, and two other partners. All of The Academy Group partners are CU Boulder alumni with strong ties to the Boulder community. Their vision entailed a community where residents 62 and better could receive the level of care and independence they desired in a beautiful environment rich in art, community events, residential activities, wellness and fitness programs, and continuing education opportunities.

◆ For more than 100 years, the building has stood for holistic health and well-being.

◆ A view of the Flatirons can be seen from The Academy.

The group proposed a variety of living options. Restoring the original Academy building and constructing an adjoining structure and a series of one-story dwellings, the entire project would include 41 apartments and nine bungalows. The Academy Group's proposal was accepted, but the next seven years was spent overcoming neighborhood objections, red tape and litigation. They were finally able to begin construction in 1996.

Before crews could begin working, however, all 75 raccoons had to be removed from the premises and relocated. Then came the most difficult aspect of the project. Local and national historic agencies had strict stipulations regarding the restoration of the original Academy building (such as continuity in wood trim from the original body of the 1893 building to the changes in the portion added on in 1921). In addition, workers found that because of the tremendous damage the upper floors had sustained, not a single door, frame or piece of wood was straight! After salvaging what they could, crews re-created the rest in the spirit of the original building. In the meantime, Karen teamed up with interior designer Jane Bartlett to hand pick every piece of furniture and artwork. They shopped seven galleries in Boulder, buying almost exclusively from Colorado artists.

The end result was magnificent: historical architecture, luxurious decor, and comfortable convenience. In preparation for opening, the team realized many people had played very critical roles in the completion of the project. The group held a special black tie "Academy Awards" to honor more than 150 people, and many personal experiences were shared.

In July 1998, the doors opened to residents in the Academy building, and in November of the same year, the Flatirons building opened. Residents began coming from all over the nation. From state senators to artists, librarians to housewives, each resident has added character and culture to the new community.

Residents choose to enter a new era in their lives at The Academy for many important reasons. Life there offers an inviting atmosphere where friends and family truly feel welcome. A great example is the Piñons Dining Room with its luxurious setting and unique offerings of healthy, delicious food and beverages, with amenities perfect for entertaining in a relaxed atmosphere.

The proximity to cultural, educational and community events is another major attraction. Nearby CU welcomes residents to classes, and the Naropa Institute offers such educational opportunities as gerontology courses, memoir writing workshops, and intergenerational dance classes. The Academy itself hosts intriguing forums and special events which take place in the beautifully renovated chapel. The Wellness Center offers exercise programs such as Tai Chi and Yoga, along with personalized nutrition counseling. Residents enjoy walking the beautifully landscaped grounds and the nature paths that traverse the nearby hills. All services at The Academy are based on individual needs and desires of each resident, from near autonomy to home health care services when needed. One thing is certain — The Academy is a wonderful place to start a new life.

Though lost for a number of years, the stately, red brick structure of The Academy is once more a beautiful testament to living well in Boulder. Many believe that Sister Mary Theodore O'Connor would be pleased with the holistic vision being carried out in The Academy. In fact, there have been claims made of seeing Sister Mary's ghost three times during the renovations by different work crews who knew nothing about her history. Those who saw her did say she was smiling. And because she hasn't been seen since the grand opening, she has in effect, conveyed all that needs to be said. From a historic past to a promising future, The Academy is a place where very real dreams come true.

◆ The dining room at The Academy is equivalent to a four-star restaurant.

Colorado Chautauqua Association

When Colorado's Chautauqua opened its doors over 100 years ago on July 4, 1898, the entire city of Boulder was decorated with flags and bunting. More than 4,000 people packed the newly constructed auditorium to listen to several hours of speeches by the day's greatest orators, climaxing in what was described as a "blaze of glory with the most elaborate and grandest pyrotechnic display of fireworks in the West."

◆ The Flatirons backdrop for the Colorado Chautauqua *Courtesy of Chautauqua Archives*

An unforgettable day for the city of Boulder, that Independence Day was also a landmark in a unique stage in American history — part of a stirring movement Theodore Roosevelt once called "the most American thing in America."

The name Chautauqua was originally a Seneca Indian word meaning "two moccasins tied together with a piece of string" or "place where fish jump." For Americans, it has come to mean a place where people come together to learn and share ideas in a beautiful surrounding. A rare survivor of a great ideal, the Colorado Chautauqua retains the same mission and philosophy as it did in 1898.

Today, more than 1 million visitors annually enjoy Chautauqua Park, hiking its wooded trails or climbing near the massive faces of the Flatirons. They still crowd the original auditorium for cultural events and the Community House for dance classes, poetry readings and photography exhibits. They discuss provocative topics in the annual Summer Forum series, occupy the Chautauqua's 60 guest cottages and two historic lodges, and eat in the original dining hall. But few can conceive of the impact the Chautauqua made to millions of lives 100 years before.

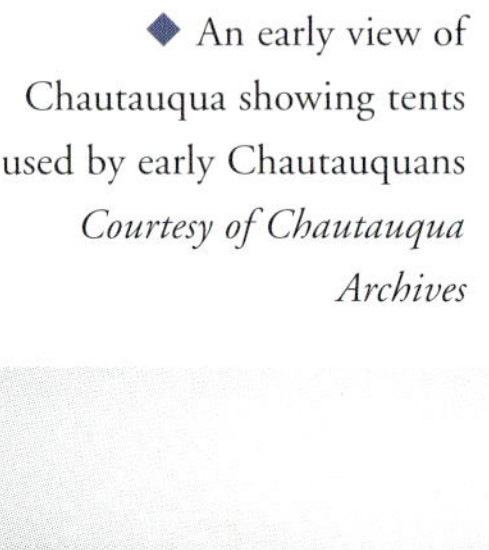

◆ An early view of Chautauqua showing tents used by early Chautauquans *Courtesy of Chautauqua Archives*

It was 1874, less than a decade since the end of the Civil War. Approximately three percent of Americans graduated from high school. People were desperate for education. John Heyle Vincent, a Sunday school director, and Lewis Miller, businessman and inventor, envisioned a series of summer educational courses in a natural setting where one could also hike, swim and boat — fulfilling the ancient Greek ideal of a balance between body and mind.

The New York Chautauqua Assembly was created and the concept spread like wildfire. There were no radios, televisions or telephones, and even newspapers could be hard to obtain. The Chautauquas answered an urgent need in rural America. By 1898 there were more than 150 Chautauquas across the country, each with an auditorium or pavilion, tents or cottages for long-term guests, vespers, campfires and a whole range of cultural and academic programs.

Boulder won its Chautauqua against fierce competition from other Colorado cities. The Texas Board of Education wanted to send teachers to the "cool and colorful Rocky Mountains" during the scorching Texas summers. Also, the Gulf and Southern Railroad companies wanted to increase their ridership. The Texas-Colorado Chautauqua Association was created, and campaigning began to become the chosen site.

Boulder seized the prize, its merchants and citizens fired by the prospect of tens of thousands of visitors every summer, a railway link down Broadway to the rest of America and appearances by the most distinguished people of the day.

Within 11 weeks from start of construction, the city built a 1,200-seat auditorium and a dining hall to seat 300, both of which are still in operation. In exchange, the Texans offered a full summer program of education and entertainment at no cost to Boulder.

Although Boulder's Chautauqua had been described as the most perfect campground, all too soon it had to face competition from dozens of others in the West. Two years after opening, the Chautauqua was $32,000 in debt to its railroad underwriters.

Once again Boulder merchants took action, the *Daily Camera* proclaiming that loyalty to the Chautauqua was the most immediate duty of Boulder's citizenry. The railroad was offered incentives to forgive the debt and a successful subscription drive began. On December 20, 1900, the Texas-Colorado Chautauqua became the Colorado Chautauqua Association.

Attending the Chautauqua was an exciting experience for a visitor from one of the isolated rural communities. Great orators filled the auditorium to overflowing, thrilling the audience with their exhortations against big business, the railroads and utility companies, Standard Oil, Wall Street and the sins of alcohol.

Between the speakers were a variety of musical acts — Swiss yodelers and Russian Cossack choruses, Gospel ('Jubilee') singers, harp quintets, a virtuoso mandolinist, dueling grand pianos and a marching band. The occasional 'educational' silent film also became a part of the programming.

The American Chautauqua flourished between 1905 and 1928. By 1923 there were thousands of permanent Chautauquas as well as 10,000 circuit Chautauquas that sprang up each summer.

But it was not to last. By 1932 many of the permanent Chautauquas and all the circuit ones had vanished. Movies, radio and automobiles ruled the day. There was no need to travel to a Chautauqua to hear music or new ideas.

Yet Boulder's Chautauqua survived. With the automobile's popularity, it became a summer base for family motor excursions in the Rockies. Cottage owners and renters were a source of income from 1933 on. In 1946 the cottages were rented as winter housing for University of Colorado graduate students and visiting professors. By 1953, Boulder residents were coming to the auditorium to watch motion pictures, which then made up 98 percent of its summer programming.

◆ Historic photo of early Chautauquans
Courtesy of Chautauqua Archives

In the early 70s the Chautauqua seemed doomed. A city-commissioned study suggested razing the decaying structures for a new year-round resort. However, in 1974, Laurence T. Paddock, then publisher of the *Daily Camera* and president of the Boulder Historical Society, joined forces with local citizens and Chautauqua cottage owners to have the auditorium declared a National Historic Landmark.

Under the leadership of new members of the board of directors, the Colorado Chautauqua Association began developing new visions for the Chautauqua. By summer of 1978, a multiyear historic preservation program had begun. Cultural programs returned, with a summer concert series and a resident orchestra in the auditorium.

Boulder's love for its Chautauqua was evidenced when Boulder City Council extended its lease to 2017. The Colorado Chautauqua celebrated its grand centennial on July 4, 1998, looking back to the community and Chautauqua's historic past and forward to an exciting future.

◆ The Colorado Chautauqua Auditorium
Photo by Mark Sherman

The winterization of the Community House makes it the only Chautauqua to offer performing arts and educational programs throughout the entire year. The new era heralds a return to the great orator focus in the auditorium, with a roster of speakers such as Jesse Jackson, Middle East hostages, Tom Sutherland, Terry Anderson, Tom Wolfe and Ray Bradbury.

As new programs blossom and the historic preservation of the past moves towards completion, the Colorado Chautauqua continues to play a vital role in the Boulder community, delighting residents and visitors as a special place where the educational, cultural and recreational aspects of their lives merge into a balanced whole — just as its creators envisioned 100 years before.

Colorado Music Festival

◆ (Right and Bottom) Conductor Giora Bernstein directs the full Colorado Music Festival Orchestra.

More than 20 years ago, no quality orchestral music graced the ears of Boulder residents during the summer, and an elegant historic building nestled at the base of the Flatirons sat falling gradually into disrepair. These two facts struck a chord in Giora Bernstein, who had recently arrived as a professor of conducting at the University of Colorado at Boulder. Guided by his skillful hand, the Colorado Music Festival successfully debuted in the summer of 1976.

Maestro Bernstein, a world-renowned conductor, had earlier founded both the Boston Chamber Orchestra and the Claremont Music Festival, which he had directed for seven years. Upon his move to Boulder, Maestro Bernstein discovered that virtually no professional music was available in Colorado during the summer, except in Aspen. People encouraged him to follow up on his success in Claremont and found a summer music festival in Boulder. Inspired, Maestro Bernstein began piecing together the necessary components to create a welcome summer tradition for the Boulder community.

Funding and organization for the Colorado Music Festival initially came from private donors. Chris Brauchli, a local lawyer, and David Stainton, a local real estate broker, provided instrumental support. Alan Shapley served on the board of directors and as the president of the festival for several years. With the generous aid of these and other individuals, the festival opened its inaugural five-week season hosting one chamber music concert a week at the First Presbyterian Church in downtown Boulder.

By its second year, the Colorado Music Festival began holding the chamber music concerts in the elegant,

rustic setting that would become its permanent home, the Chautauqua Auditorium. The auditorium's acoustics needed only minor fine tuning, providing a perfect location for the concerts. Maestro Bernstein attained his goal of conducting a full symphony orchestra by the third season, and ever since, audiences have enjoyed the offerings of both full orchestral and chamber music concerts.

The growth and success of the festival spurred the creation of several annual special events. Caryl Kassoy, who has been active in the festival since its inception, started the tradition of young people's concerts in 1987, giving children ages four to 10 a unique opportunity to appreciate the festival twice each summer. In recognition of the Boulder community's support, the festival hosts a free outdoor concert at Chautauqua every Independence Day, with 5,000-6,000 people in attendance.

The Colorado Music Festival has gained recognition for its excellence in both musicians and in music performed. Every year 85 selected orchestra members converge in Boulder from all over the United States, with a few coming from Europe and Asia. To accompany the orchestra, the festival hosts many solo artists before they achieve careers as well-known performers. In addition to inviting high-quality musicians, the festival has received six prestigious ASCAP awards for adventuresome programming of contemporary music. This success can be attributed to Maestro Bernstein's desire to expose audiences to 20th-century music.

From the direction of Maestro Bernstein and the festival staff to the high caliber of artists and musical works, the Colorado Music Festival celebrates the value of quality orchestral music in a distinctive Colorado setting.

Boulder Theater

Boulder Theater bears its city's name yet is an anomaly in venue and architecture, attesting to its enduring charm. Since its grand opening on January 9, 1936, which featured Claudette Colbert and Fred MacMurray movies, Mickey Mouse and the University of Colorado, Boulder's "crooning quarterback," it has experienced enough owners to staff several theaters and enough closures to throw its fate into public question frequently. Now owned by New Hope Entertainment, headed by Doug Greene, it has given the enterprise its legacy — new hope. Boulder Theater attracts a stunning diversity of talent that draws audiences through its doors nightly.

Located on 14th Street facing the courthouse on the Pearl Street Mall, Boulder Theater is the second theater to stand in its location. Built from the bricks of the 1906 Curran Theater, the refurbished building is the only example of Art Deco style in the city. Art Deco derives from the large, flat surface forms of Egyptian and Mayan architecture, the geometric forms of the Cubists, the rich color usage of the Fauves, and the subjective forms of the Expressionists. Designed by architect Robert Boller, who had 92 theaters under his belt, the building displays the characteristic flat terra-cotta facade with upper-story panels in terra-cotta, blue-green, red and yellow signature Art Deco colors. Modernistic, 25-foot-tall circular murals with designs that are interpretations of Western flora — columbine, mariposa, lily, mountain poppy, alpine-aster, Western pine cone, and a wind-blown pine tree — decorate the auditorium. Silver and gold tones and rich drapes accent the lobby and the foyer, which is flanked by six-foot-wide staircases. The building received its name in a contest held by the *Daily Camera.*

Through the 40s and into the 50s, the theater thrived until the advent of television. Declining admissions led to some design alterations, including a marquee, box office and display cases. The mix of movies and live entertainment broadened to include artistic films, but the theater could not compete with the two, four, six and eightplex cracker-box theaters opening in the suburbs. Beginning with the Fox Company, the theater endured a succession of owners. In 1979, local investors called Boulder Theater Associates bought the building and leased it to Historic Boulder Inc. in a last effort to save it as part of a city arts complex. Historic Boulder obtained local landmark designation for the exterior, and the theater had another grand opening, but the public defeated the funding that would have supported the new arts center in 1980.

◆ Boulder Theater facade, 1938

The next decade and a half heralded another revolving door of ownership, coupled with some redesign and an enticing offering of talent. In keeping with the growing "cabaret style," a bar, tables and detached seating replaced seating rows in the back of the auditorium. The theater featured Ricky Lee Jones, James Taylor, Willie Nelson, B.B. King and nascent stars, Shawn Colvin, David Wilcox and Leo Kotke. Too little to compete with big theaters and too big to be a bar, the theater's unique intimacy allowed talent to interact with ecstatic audiences. These performances and the building's historic character — it is one of only three historic Boulder theaters — drew Doug Greene as a new owner and continue to draw the Boulder community to its box office.

◆ Boulder Theater interior

Downtown Management Commission and Downtown Boulder Inc.

Historic Downtown Boulder is the heart and soul of the city. The gathering place for the community, it centers in the Downtown Boulder Mall. The pedestrian mall, which covers four brick-paved blocks on Pearl Street between 11th and 15th streets, achieved national attention after its completion on August 7, 1977. Crowded with tourists and popular with residents year-round, the mall offers a mix of unusual stores, many of which are locally based; talented street performers; festivals; an attractive planted streetscape; and public art, including a water-face fountain and animals that double as climbing toys. Even the playground is unique, comprised of boulders taken from the nearby mountains. The mall sits in a nationally landmarked historic district with locally and nationally landmarked buildings, many dating back to Boulder's birth in 1859.

◆ A gift from Boulder's Russian sister city, the beautiful Boulder-Dushanbe teahouse houses a restaurant for tea or dining. ©*Anne Krause Photography*

No less intrinsic to the mall than the historic buildings and unique atmosphere, are the citizens that envisioned it since the 1960s, when the area was a disparate mix of buildings covered with false aluminum siding and sliced by traffic. In 1988, those entities coalesced into Downtown Boulder Inc. (DBI), a consortium of property owners and retailers and the Downtown Management Commission (DMC), which represents the city of Boulder. This smoothly functioning partnership attests to the level of cooperation achieved among the notoriously vocal Boulder citizenry to work together to ensure the mall's continuing success.

◆ Three small children enjoy a treat downtown amid the annual spring tulips. ©*Anne Krause Photography*

The cooperation evolved with the citizens' groups who acknowledged that everybody benefited from a cooperative effort for a revitalized downtown. New outlying malls surrounded by parking lots were attracting customers away from downtown. The first downtown organization formed in 1966, long before the bricks and benches saw fruition. Consisting of city officials and property owners who recognized citizen participation as vital in their planning process, the group began a two-phase downtown improvement plan. Phase One, planning and fund-raising, facilitated Phase Two, an actual plan for the mall.

The current mall design surfaced from a series of proposed plans. The Gruen Associates plan called for off-street parking structures, a civic center, improved traffic circulation, and a superblock/pedestrian mall. The Carl Worthington Partnership scaled back the pedestrian core to four blocks on Pearl Street. With the passage of bonds to build the mall and Governor John Love's signature on the 1970 Public Mall Act, which allowed Colorado towns to shut down traffic circulation to create pedestrian malls, the public and private sectors invited proposals and selected the plan submitted by Everett-Zeigel, Trumpes and Hand Architects, with Sasaki Associates, Communication Arts and Larry Smith & Company. This team designed today's nationally acclaimed Downtown Boulder Mall.

The mall players had transformed into several new organizations over this period. Finally, in 1988, the Downtown Business Association, primarily retailers and restaurant owners, and the Downtown Boulder Partnership merged their often-overlapping efforts into the existing Downtown Boulder Inc. This nonprofit entity coordinates all mall activities with the DMC. Their successes have been numerous. Festivals held throughout the year on the mall include the Art Fair, which draws artists and visitors nationally and internationally; the Fall Festival; the Out to Lunch entertainment program for downtown workers; the holiday family activities; and the Lights of December parade. The last proved to be the most challenging, demanding the involvement of entities from all over Boulder to sponsor floats and costs for the parade. The event is now one of the most eagerly anticipated in Boulder.

Throughout this process, the private sector has played an equal hand with the city and taken a heavy burden financially. The mall was built through a special mall assessment of downtown property owners who raised more than $1.2 million and received a $650,000 Federal Block Grant in 1976 to build the mall. This assessment continued until 1992. As part of the plan to revitalize the downtown area with the building of the pedestrian mall, another assessment enabled the formation of the Central Area General Improvement District (CAGID) to provide parking. This assessment is accredited for the purchase of parking lots and the building of parking structures. Mill levy increases and bonds allow this to continue today.

Mall maintenance is provided by the City Parks and Recreation Department and downtown meter revenues. The mall's popularity has far exceeded what the original design team anticipated. Capital improvements and maintenance ensure that it will be an attractive place to visit. Because parking is such a complicated issue, downtown has creatively initiated alternative transportation modes for its employees and visitors. One particularly innovative success of the DBI and DMC was the Downtown Bus Pass program, which allows employees to receive a bus pass paid for by the CAGID funds. This program grew into the Regional Transportation District's Eco-Pass program, now available to businesses in the entire Denver Metro region. Encouraging employees to leave their automobiles at home and take a free bus ride to central Boulder, the bus program resulted in 41 percent of downtown employees now using alternative modes of transportation to work.

Another achievement was the formation of the Downtown Alliance, a coalition of nonprofit and city stakeholders in downtown Boulder. The DMC and DBI joined Historic Boulder Inc., the Downtown Design Advisory Board, Landmarks Board, Planning Board and representatives from the three surrounding residential neighborhoods to plan for one future vision of downtown. City Council had mandated that the entire city be rezoned. The Alliance achieved a unified, viable proposal.

The partnership attributes its success to two factors. First, the planning approach is proactive and participatory. Given the high level of education, involvement and willingness to articulate opinions on which Boulder citizenry prides itself, this is no small accomplishment. Secondly, the entities maintain a high level of mutual trust. Respecting each other's different roles, the two welcome advice on all mall issues. Recognizing an environment of constant change at the city and state levels, and realizing that predicting future trends and necessities is nebulous at best, the DBI and DMC outline their goal as "how to make what works work even better and maintain the strong sense of community vitality" prevalent in the mall.

◆ The historic Hotel Boulderado — A Boulder landmark since 1909, this premier hotel offers Victorian elegance in the heart of downtown.
©*Anne Krause Photography*

◆ Shopping in the fall sunshine
©*Anne Krause Photography*

The future and physical manifestation of downtown growth are unpredictable, but accomplishments like the building of The Dushanbe Teahouse on 13th Street, a gift from Boulder's sister city, and the continued investment of property owners in redeveloping and enhancing their holdings, are ensured by the zoning regulations adopted in May 1997 by City Council. Challenges include future improvements east and west of the mall and the endless parking and transportation dilemma. But what Downtown Boulder Inc. and Downtown Management Commission do best — actively monitor the pulse of Boulder's citizenry and manage its vital and viable city heart, the Downtown Mall — bespeaks their flexible success in maintaining the exuberant core of Boulder.

University of Colorado at Boulder

Before the first pioneers came, the site for the University of Colorado was grazing land for wild game and the hunting ground of the Arapaho. In 1858, a wagon train brought the first settlers to Boulder Valley, most of them looking for gold. It was not long before they became concerned about the education of their children and contributed their money and labor to construct the first school building in Colorado.

Their interest in education did not stop there. As early as 1861, a group of Boulder citizens started working to establish a university in Boulder. In 1874, The Territorial Legislature appropriated $15,000 for a university to be located in Boulder on the condition that the citizens of the city raise the same amount. The money was raised through the hard work and sacrifice of many people who wanted to see a university established in Boulder. When Old Main was completed in 1876, it housed the entire university and also provided living quarters for the first president, Dr. Joseph Sewall, and his family, as well as the building's caretaker and his wife. One of the first graduates commented that it was an "imposing structure... its head above a barren, wind-swept plain... a monument of patience looking down upon the frontier village... removed from any sidewalk by nearly a mile of mud."

A sidewalk connecting the university and the town of Boulder was one of many improvements made over time to the property. Sewall's wife, Ann, had grass and trees planted. Sewall worked to recruit the first faculty and succeeded in hiring Mary Rippon, the first woman in the United States to teach at a state university. The first graduating class celebrated commencement in spring of 1882 and numbered six, all men.

◆ Its Tuscan Vernacular architecture and mountain backdrop combine to earn the campus recognition as one of the most beautiful in the United States. *Courtesy CU-Boulder Public Relations Photography*

◆ Today, CU-Boulder, with an enrollment of over 25,000 students, has gained top rankings as one of the best public institutions of higher education in the country. *Courtesy CU-Boulder Public Relations Photography*

The growth of the campus and the faculty and staff was slow but steady in these early years. Cottages and a three-story building with running water and electricity were constructed as student dormitories. A house was built for the president, and the establishment of a department of medicine led to the construction of a hospital building. The first football coach, F.G. Folsom, had his team practice on a rocky, wind-swept field and then run a mile back to campus.

By the university's 25th anniversary in 1902, there were 105 faculty members, 550 students, and 575 degrees had been granted. A building was constructed for the library, and the school of medicine moved to Denver. In 1904 a Phi Beta Kappa charter was granted for a society to be formed at CU. This was a great honor and recognition of CU's early academic excellence, as very few charters had been granted west of the Mississippi River.

In 1914, when World War I began in Europe, the student body numbered 1,300, and the 20 buildings on campus were crowded to capacity. CU was one of the first institutions in the United States to have an ROTC unit, and the campus was turned into an armed camp with barracks built on campus and instruction provided in airplane maintenance and military mapping. At the end of the war, there arose an interest in the appearance of the buildings on campus, which had been designed in a hodgepodge of different architectural styles. Then President Dr. George Norlin hired the Philadelphia firm of Day and Klauder to come up with a single architectural style for the campus. They settled on a style called Rural Italian or Tuscan Vernacular, characterized by native flagstone walls and red-tile roofs. Almost all the buildings since that time have been constructed in this style.

During the Depression, the university faced financial hardship but was able to complete construction of Macky Auditorium and build a larger library, named Norlin Library, in honor of the president. During World War II, a Navy ROTC unit was established on campus and a Japanese language school was set up in the Faculty Club. Many students on campus attended classes in uniform.

The end of war heralded a new era for CU. Enrollment doubled from 5,483 students in 1946 to 10,421 students in 1947. Several dorms were built to deal with the influx of students. The newly constructed University Memorial Center replaced the old student center. It was dedicated by the governor as the official state memorial to those who had died in the two great wars in order "to preserve our democratic freedom."

The baby boom of the 1940s kept pushing up enrollment projections at a dramatic rate: 15,000 by 1970 and 20,000 by 1980. Many new facilities continued to be built to accommodate the influx of students, and CU extension centers in Denver and Colorado Springs were made into full degree-granting institutions. The university during this era also grew in stature as a national leader in scientific research. CU attracted many major scientific research centers to Boulder including the Bureau of Standards (now known as the National Institute of Standards and Technology or NIST), the National Oceanic and Atmospheric Administration (NOAA), and the National Center for Atmospheric Research (NCAR). In recognition of CU's rise in academic and research prominence, it was admitted to the American Association of Universities (AAU) in 1967. The Boulder campus was cited in 1976 as one of America's most significant works of architecture.

Today, the University of Colorado system includes the main campus at Boulder (CU-Boulder) and campuses at Colorado Springs (CU-Colorado Springs), Denver (CU-Denver), and the Health Sciences Center in Denver (CU-Health Sciences Center) with a combined enrollment of about 44,500 students. The Boulder campus enrolls more than 25,000 students and has graduated more than 210,000 students. The campus includes about 200 rural Italian-style buildings and complexes. In addition, the Norlin Quadrangle, including the original Old Main building, is listed in the State and National Register of Historic Places. The campus continues to be noted as one of the most beautiful in the country.

CU-Boulder's new $11 million Integrated Teaching and Learning Laboratory, unique in the world, is representative of the university's Total Learning Environment Initiative, which is transforming the university to meet the needs of the 21st century. The 34,400-square-foot engineering center provides hands-on, real-world learning experience to engineering students and also to teachers and school-aged children in the community. Just a few of CU-Boulder's recent research efforts have helped to measure chemicals associated with ozone depletion using a student-built satellite; establish a link between RNA and the evolutionary chain; develop new ways to deal with natural hazards; and create a new form of matter just a few hundred billionths of a degree above absolute zero. Undergraduate students have the opportunity to work on research projects with faculty through the Undergraduate Research Opportunities Program.

From a lone building on a wind-swept plain, CU-Boulder has grown into a comprehensive research institution of national prominence and earned top rankings as one of the best public institutions of higher education in the country.

◆ When Old Main was completed in 1876, it sat upon a hill above Boulder and housed the entire university.

◆ Colleges

Architecture and Planning
Arts and Sciences
Business and Administration
Engineering and Applied Science
Music

◆ Schools

Graduate School
Graduate School of Business Administration
School of Education
School of Journalism and Mass Communication
School of Law

Haystack Mountain Golf Course

Haystack Mountain Golf Course and the surrounding land are entrenched in Native American history and legend. Many years ago, Chief Niwot claimed the property as a winter home for his Arapahoe tribe. The mountain itself was a lookout for small herds of buffalo, or to locate straying cattle. Tepee rings — the original stones used to hold down the tepees — were visible until the 1970s. Today this land is a unique and popular golf course where people come from miles around to enjoy the bucolic surroundings and to improve their golf game in a relaxed, down-to-earth environment.

◆ Everyone learns to play golf at Haystack.

Bud and Lois Ebel purchased the 240-acre tract in 1963 with help from family and their household savings. For 25 years before 1963, the land was owned by a ranching family and operated as a farm and cattle ranch. Previously, the land was part of a government land grant in the settling of the West in the early 1900s. The original deed is rumored to have Theodore Roosevelt's signature.

The Haystack property itself is rich with history. West of the fifth hole stood Boulder County's oldest log cabin, built by Jacob Affolter. The cabin has since been moved to Old Mill Park by the Longmont Historical Society. The original settler's cabin is still intact with a modern house built up around it. By the first tee, a row of pig houses now stores wood, and an old farm equipment shed holds golf equipment.

In 1966, the golf course opened to a skeptical community. The Niwot location, seven miles north of Boulder, was considered too far from town. However, who could have predicted that Boulder County would eventually grow up around it? Today, the course is known as one of the few privately owned public courses in the region. It is a favorite for beginners, families, and those who prefer a laid-back mood to the formal, serious atmosphere of most courses. At Haystack, all levels and ages are welcome and encouraged. Electric carts are not allowed and there is no course rider waving players along. Advance tee times are not taken.

◆ Haystack Mountain Golf Course, "a timeless place to be"

The layout and arrangement of Haystack was conceived with an emphasis on nature and a respect for the land. The nine-hole, par 32 course wraps around Left Hand Creek through old cottonwood trees. The course was designed to fit in with the surrounding landscape, to stay in tune with nature. The greens are meant to use the raw qualities of the land without changing it artificially. It is a flat course, known as "links style," based on the original Scottish courses.

Today, Haystack is building its reputation as a teaching course. C.J. Ebel, son of the owner, is the Haystack golf professional and instructor. He is also a master club fitter and began Haystack's "No Embarrassment Golf School". The course is being improved to enhance the emphasis on instruction. The practice tee is three times its original size. Seven target greens, a complete short game facility, and an all-weather instruction/practice building are now being created. Tees are being enlarged and holes lengthened to add challenge for every level of golfer.

Haystack Mountain Golf Course is a place where golfers of all ages and abilities can play in a relaxed, natural and historical setting.

Historic Boulder, Inc.

A cartoon hangs in the Arnett-Fullen house, Historic Boulder, Inc.'s headquarters, depicting a large developer holding the "crackerbox luxury apartments" looming over the 1891 Highland School. A tiny preservationist stops him with, "If it's all right with you, we'd rather you put that thing somewhere else." Published in Boulder's *Daily Camera*, the cartoon encapsulates community recognition of Historic Boulder's preservation of historical, architectural, visual and environmental heritage in Boulder County through advocacy, education, intervention and alliance building.

Catapulted into being by a wrecking ball, Historic Boulder first fought for Central School (1871), which was slated for demolition and replacement by a parking lot. Simultaneously, a developer proposed leveling Highland School, using the building's bricks to build a wall around his proposed apartments. Enraged preservationists rallied and, although unable to save Central, they rescued Highland by persuading seven banks to guarantee loans for $20,000 each for investors to rehabilitate it into what are now elegant offices that retain historic structural integrity.

Boulder's rapid growth threatened domino-like demolition of historic structures, prompting founders, including Joyce Davies, Phyllis Olsen, Margaret Hanson, Prissy and Bob Bowron and Betty Chronic, into incorporating and holding the organization's first meeting in the Boulderado Hotel in 1972. Preservation advocacy required a literal rolling up of sleeves and digging into heavy physical and political work. Boulder Depot, the city's original railroad station, was saved from demolition in 1972 by relocation farther east. The building's stone structure required careful dismantling and reassembling on its new site. Restoration of the "ROAR" (Renovate Our Architectural Resources) House in 1983 elicited intensive volunteer renovation for eventual reselling. Historic Boulder enticed fascinated community members, who wielded hammers and brushes while learning the exacting skill of using original materials to restore a building according to standards set by the Department of the Interior for historic preservation. The project earned Historic Boulder the 1986 "Preservation Honor Award" from the National Trust for Historic Preservation for restoration and education efforts.

Even its offices attest to the organization's ethic. The Woodward-Baird House ("Little Grey House") at 1733 Canyon, which once housed Historic Boulder's headquarters, was locally landmarked, rehabilitated and resold and continues to function as an office while representing Boulder's historic working-class residential architecture. In the 1990s, Historic Boulder locally landmarked and bought the gothic 1877 Arnett-Fullen House, Boulder's Victorian "Gingerbread House." Extensive rehabilitation of the house and grounds will return it to its original splendor and educate the community on proper preservation methods.

Efforts extend beyond city limits and individual structures. A county preservation program spearheaded in 1996 has successfully landmarked and rehabilitated post offices, residences, barns, schools, and other buildings and turned them into museums and interpretive sites throughout the county. Historic Boulder wrote and helped enact both the city of Boulder's 1974 Landmark Preservation Ordinance, which protects city historic properties, and Boulder County's Landmarks Preservation Ordinance, which protects county historic properties. They have helped designate several national and local historic districts, including the national Downtown Boulder Historic District, the national and local Chautauqua Historic District, and the Mapleton Hill, Floral Park, and West Pearl Historic Districts (all local).

◆ The Arnett-Fullen House (1877)

Preservation successes too numerous to list will keep pace with the development that threatens Boulder's unique heritage. Historic Boulder welcomes the challenge of recycling Boulder's heritage to build its future.

Longmont United Hospital

Personalizing, humanizing and demystifying the world of medicine characterizes the mission of Longmont United Hospital (LUH). As a nonprofit hospital flourishing during a time when more and more hospitals are functioning as for-profit corporations, LUH takes its mission seriously. Under the guidance of a volunteer board of directors, LUH has historically worked to serve Longmont and the surrounding area by listening and responding to community needs.

As Longmont's only hospital, LUH's commitment to excellence has been highly valued by local residents since its inception. Back in 1954, a group of business people and doctors recognized the need for a new hospital. Not long after, the Longmont Community Hospital Association was formed to aid in building, maintaining and operating the new facility. In order to receive nonprofit status and apply for funds from the federal government, the community had to raise $570,000. A massive community effort ensued. With the hard work of individuals in the community who believed strongly in the importance of establishing a nonprofit community hospital, the necessary funds were collected.

The original 50-bed hospital was dedicated in 1959. After several expansions, Longs Peak Osteopathic Hospital and Longmont Community Hospital merged in 1971 to form Longmont United Hospital. Expansions and improvements have continued over the years, both in order to stay current with ever-changing medical technologies and in response to community demands. Key improvements stimulated by community interest include the Therapy Pool, which opened in 1985, and the Hope Cancer Center, which opened in 1996. Both of these community efforts received financial backing and guidance from the LUH Foundation, a separate organization that raises and manages donated money and assets for the hospital.

The foundation has been instrumental in helping to fund LUH's latest expansion, a patient tower. Upon the tower's initial opening, the hospital will accommodate 122 beds. Ultimately, the space available will allow for growth to approximately 200 beds, reflecting LUH's responsiveness to the rapid growth of the community it serves.

Such responsiveness can also be seen in the evolution of LUH's services. The hospital sponsors a number of educational outreach programs, including exercise classes, support groups, family education and PrestigePLUS, a wellness program designed to meet the needs of people 55 years of age and older. LUH also offers the Homestead Adult Day Program and Alzheimer Program, giving caregivers of adults a dependable, safe place to take their loved ones for adult day care. In addition, LUH recognizes the value of complementary medicine and has incorporated such services into its repertoire.

Still in its original location, though greatly expanded in both size and services, LUH represents a remarkable blend of old and new. While it continues its tradition of incorporating state-of-the-art medical technology as it becomes available, the hospital always remains focused on its original mission. This mission includes educating patients to take part in their treatment and care, and creating a comfortable atmosphere where patients feel that they are ultimately in control of medical decisions. In this age of rapid technological advancement, LUH is committed to its role in the community — to be an institution devoted to the wellness of the mind, body and spirit.

◆ Architectural rendering of the expanded LUH facility, to be completed in winter 1999

The Daily Times-Call

The Daily Times-Call, the newspaper serving Longmont and the greater St. Vrain Valley for more than 125 years, publishes with an emphasis on local news and information.

The newspaper reaches more than 22,000 subscribing families each weekday and more than 24,000 households on Sundays.

In addition to Longmont, the *Times-Call* serves readers and advertisers in a wide area in Boulder, Weld and Larimer counties. Community news, features, sports, photography and advertising from area communities are a part of the daily package. *Times-Call* readers are also served by writers and photographers from throughout the world through the work of the Associated Press and other news wire services.

The *Times-Call*'s roots date to the days of the *Burlington Free Press* established near Longmont in 1871. The newspaper has had different names and owners over the years as early publishers bought, sold and merged with one another. The newspaper has been produced on a daily schedule since 1893 when the *Weekly Times* became the *Longmont Times. The Longmont Call* started as a weekly newspaper in 1898 by William Forgey. It was then sold to George W. Johnson. The *Call* began publishing six days a week in 1905. In 1931, the *Times* and the *Call* merged and installed a new flatbed roll-fed press at the Fourth Avenue plant. Dr. J.A. Matlack and Ray Lanyon joined forces and assumed joint publisher roles.

"To Build a Better World, Start in Your Own Community."

In 1957, Ed and Ruth Lehman bought a major interest in the *Times-Call*. Circulation at that time was 4,000 copies. Ten years later, the company bought the *Loveland Daily Reporter-Herald*. The *Canon City Daily Record* became a part of the company in 1978.

In 1997, other Boulder County newspapers, including the *Louisville Times*, with roots to 1913, and the *Lafayette News*, which started in 1974, and the *Erie Review*, all became a part of the Times-Call family of newspapers. The company has nearly 500 employees and its newspapers have a combined paid circulation of more than 50,000 copies. In addition to newspaper publishing, the company does commercial printing.

◆ The Daily Times-Call expanded into this building in 1988.

Through the years, the Times-Call has provided editorial leadership to help develop a high quality of life for the community. The Times-Call's motto is: "To Build a Better World, Start in Your Own Community."

The Times-Call has had a variety of locations over the decades, including on Main Street. The newspaper constructed the foundation of its current facility on Terry Street in 1964. The offices and printing plant were expanded in 1973 and 1987 to a present size of more than 45,000 square feet. There is an additional location of more than 14,000 square feet for newsprint storage and advertising insert handling at the company's warehouse two blocks south of the main building.

The *Times-Call* was published in the evenings for decades before switching to seven-day-a-week morning delivery in 1998.

The *Times-Call* is part of Lehman Communications Corp. — operated by Edward Lehman, chairman of the board and *Times-Call* publisher; Ruth G. Lehman, associate publisher; Dean G. Lehman, company president and *Times-Call* editor; and Lauren Lehman, member of the board of directors.

The Daily Times-Call can be found on the World Wide Web.

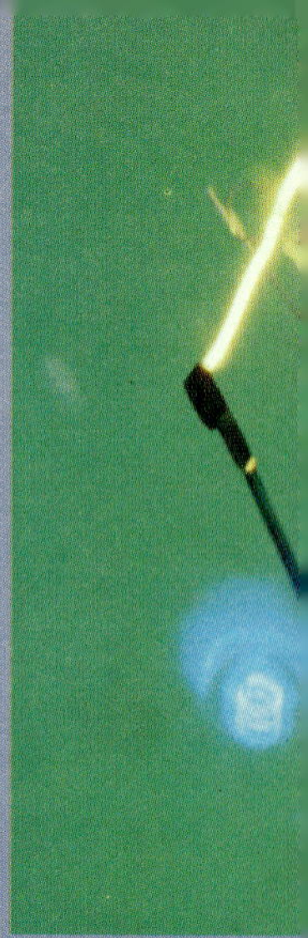

Access Graphics 294

EDS Centrobe Corporation 296

Exabyte 298

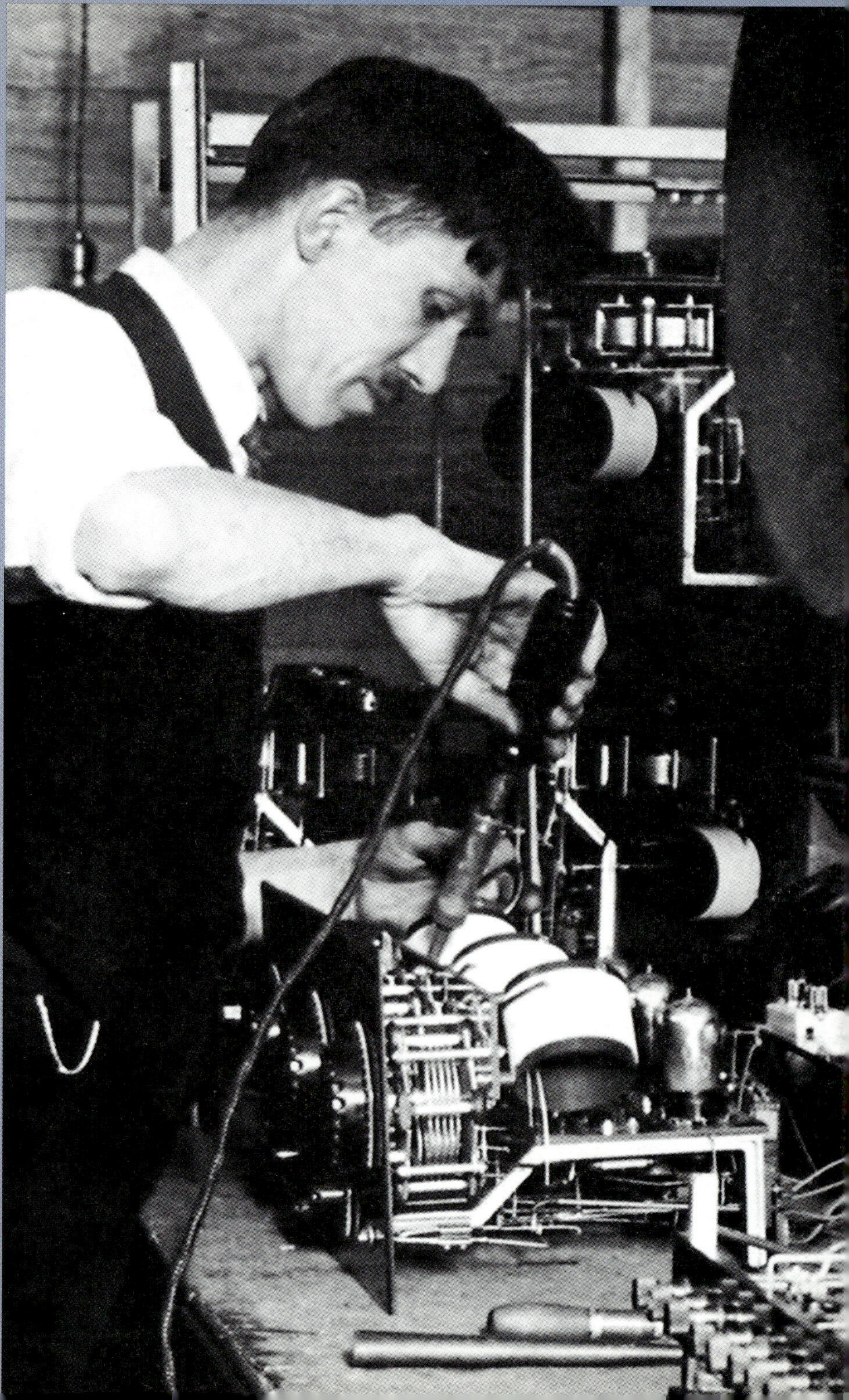

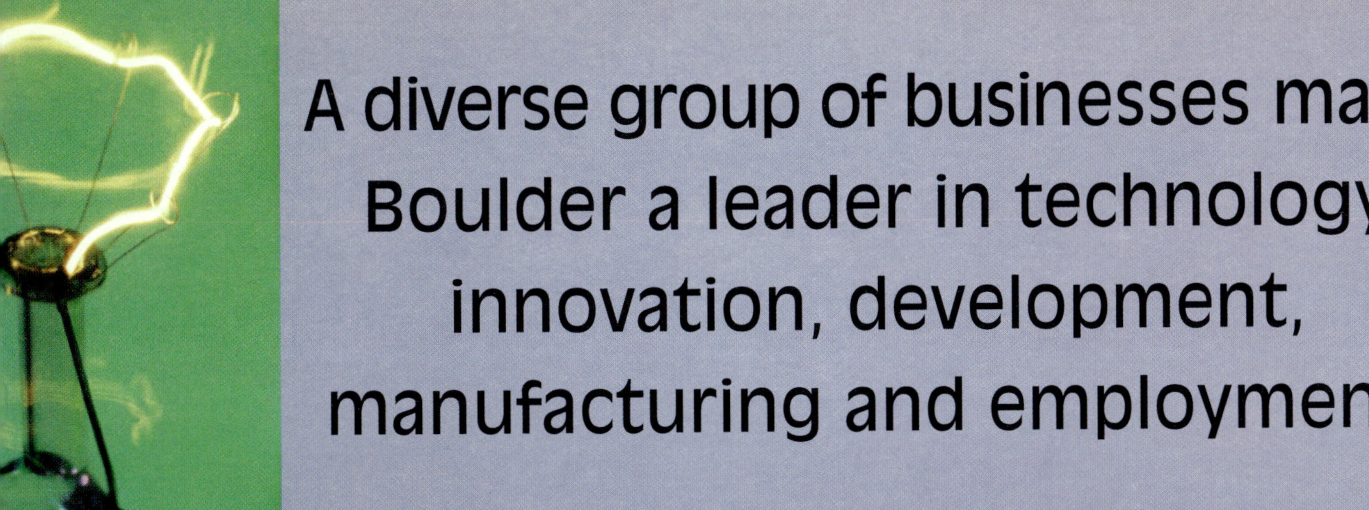

A diverse group of businesses make Boulder a leader in technology innovation, development, manufacturing and employment.

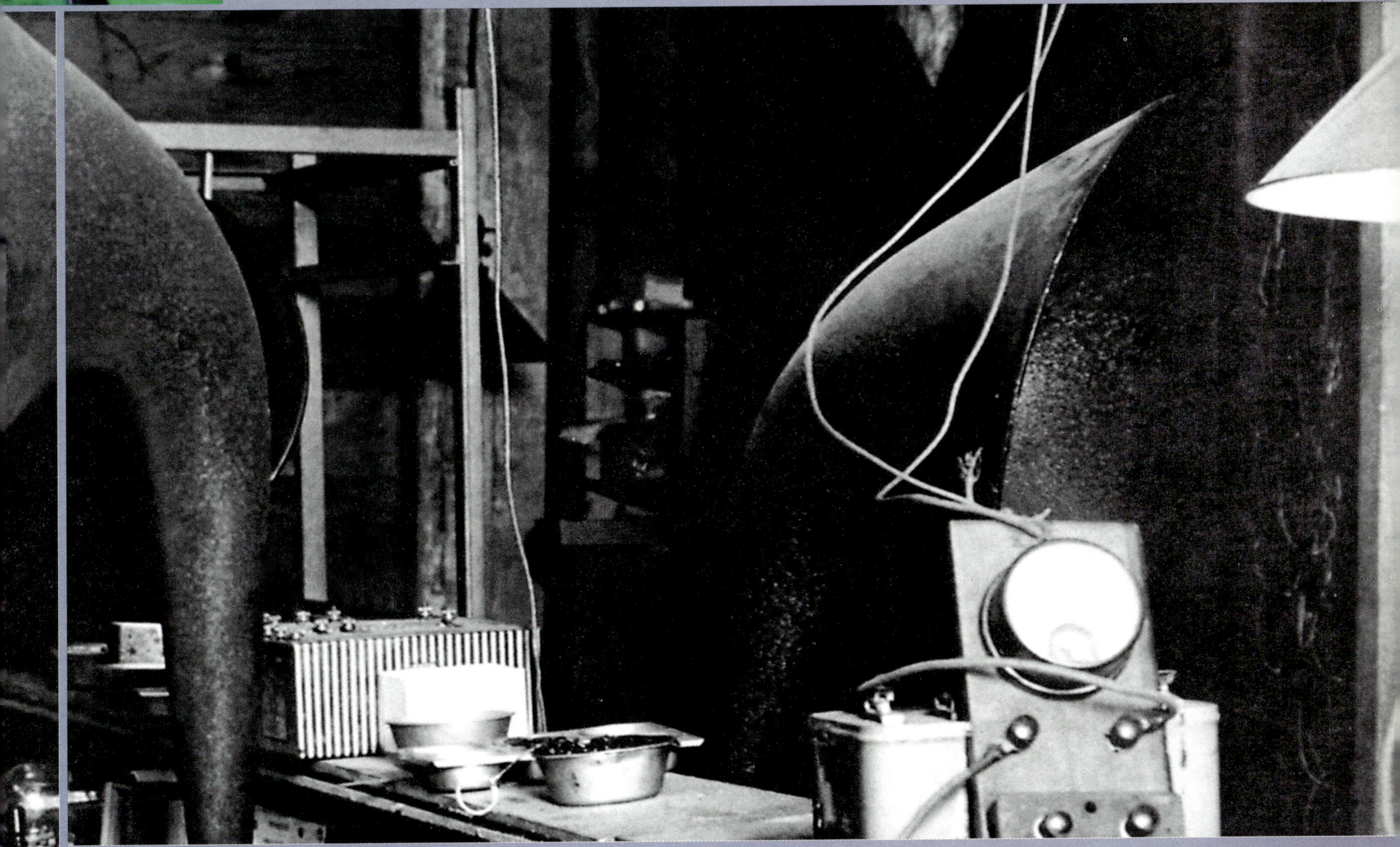

Technology

Access Graphics

◆ Over 10 years on the mall — Access Graphics has occupied this space on the 14th block of Pearl Street Mall since its beginning in 1988.

In the technological revolution of the last decade, Access Graphics has carved its niche, distributing for and servicing the leading manufacturers for the high-end computer market.

Access Graphics was founded in 1988 through the merger of three CAD (computer-aided design) distributors, based respectively in Boulder, Atlanta and New Jersey. The three founders, Jim Hudson in Boulder, John Ramsey in Atlanta and J.A. Alexander in New Jersey came together to form a national distribution business. The new company focused on the graphics and CAD market, which were booming in the late 80s. Hewlett Packard and CalComp were two of the large vendors whose products it distributed at that time.

Located at the Pearl Street Mall, Access Graphics has expanded to occupy two entire buildings as well as the second and third floor of the building where the original Boulder company was situated.

In 1997, Access Graphics was purchased by General Electric and became part of the GE Information Technology (IT) Distribution Group™, which represents all of General Electric's computer distribution businesses and employs 850 people worldwide.

Quickly growing to become an industry leader in high-end complex computer product distribution and services, Access Graphics underwent big changes in 1991. First, it was purchased by Lockheed Martin. That same year it obtained the rights to distribute the Sun Microsystems product line, and it is currently the largest Sun Microsystems master reseller. Access Graphics is also the largest Unix distributor in the world, representing a huge and fast-growing market in the enterprise business environment. Access Graphics does not distribute directly to end-users. Instead Access distributes products and services through a base of worldwide high-end computer resellers who focus primarily on the commercial marketplace.

Sun Microsystems is still its largest vendor, but in 1994 Access Graphics also entered into a distribution relationship with another major vendor, Silicon Graphics. This was the first time that Silicon Graphics had moved its products through the two-tier or indirect channel, the industry term for the sales chain which moves products from manufacturer to distributor to reseller and, finally, to the end-user, the business customer. One of Access Graphics' strengths is teaching new vendors, unfamiliar with the process, how to work in the channel and help them to realize the full benefits it can bring to their business and sales.

Access Graphics is a value-added distributor. It warehouses the manufacturer's product and manages the inventory, in addition to offering a wide array of professional services, including technical support, and educational, consulting and financial services to its customers.

Over the years, Access Graphics has differentiated itself in the marketplace by the innovative products and services it offers the computer reselling community. As a customer-intimate company, Access Graphics focuses on understanding its customers' business issues and needs and developing innovative solutions to meet those needs.

Many Access Graphics initiatives have become industry standards. It was the first distributor to offer overnight shipments and an outside field sales organization. Access Graphics still possesses the most robust outside field sales organization in the industry.

Another of its innovations is the Consulting Partner Network, wherein Access Graphics partners up with consulting firms to provide their resellers with temporary staffing resources to help them win and implement larger deals. In today's environment where there is a shortage of highly skilled IT professionals, this program has been particularly successful in helping resellers grow their businesses. Resellers often bid on large deals that would require additional staffing resources to properly implement. Without the Consulting Partner Network, many of these deals would be out of reach. This program allows resellers to get the temporary resources they need to help them win the deal and manage the workflow without adding to their overhead.

Access Graphics is also blazing a trail in new directions. It aims to be the industry leader in offering integrated or pre-engineered solutions to its resellers. A pre-engineered solution allows the resellers to offer their customers a system that can be delivered, integrated and ready to be implemented to meet their business needs. Although it may sound simple, it is actually a very complicated procedure. Pre-integrating extremely complex computer software onto a hardware platform and having it ready to use in an end-user environment involves not only the necessary software and hardware, but requires a thorough understanding of the customer's business operations and the services of highly-skilled, technical support engineers. By investing in new technology and methods, Access Graphics makes it possible for its customers to enter these markets by leveraging Access Graphics' knowledge, resources and investments.

Under the GE IT Distribution Group, Access Graphics is organized into vertical lines of business supporting focused sales and marketing efforts for the Sun Microsystems and Silicon Graphics product lines. Furthermore, these vertical business units are supported by horizontal GE IT Distribution lines of business, including the Enterprise Solutions Group, which manages relationships with high-end software companies; AlliancePoint, which offers pre-integrated, ready-to-implement solutions; and the Professional Services Group.

The Professional Services Group includes technical support, consulting services, service programs (maintenance contracts and warranties), education services and a program called System Engineering Services, which places regional systems engineers in the field to be closer to their customers. Also included in this group is the Net Technologies Group, which oversees the networking and storage management products.

◆ Tom Wyman, Access Graphics Sun sales operations manager, Eastern region, has been an employee with Access Graphics for six years.

Business is growing rapidly — not surprising considering the computer's escalation in power and capability, and its impact on all industries. In 1999, the GE IT Distribution Group's revenue exceeded $2.3 billion.

Access Graphics also gives back to the community. The company focuses much of its charitable contributions on educational programs for children, the University of Colorado, and family assistance programs such as the Boulder County Safehouse and the Emergency Family Assistance Agency. It also has a major global campaign every year to benefit the United Way. (Its parent company, General Electric, is the United Way's largest corporate contributor.) In addition, it actively supports its employees' personal involvement in the community and charity events.

Matching creative solutions to complex needs, Access Graphics stands out as a leader and innovator in the high-tech arena, serving its vital role in today's fastest-growing industry with proficiency and flair.

EDS Centrobe Corporation

In the age of the Internet, companies are struggling to recapture intimacy with their customers. With a multitude of customer contact points, the typical company can lose focus on its individual customers — and lose track of even the best customers. Centrobe is out to change that.

The company has undertaken an aggressive program to focus on Enterprise Customer Management (ECM) — managing all interactions between a company and its customers to establish relationships resulting in increased loyalty and value.

While the Centrobe name is new, the Boulder community is familiar with one of the component companies, Neodata, which emerged in 1963 after starting in 1949 as a fulfillment house for *Esquire* magazine. That fledgling organization relocated to 13th and Portland Place with its 13 magazine accounts. In time, the company outgrew that facility, establishing headquarters in Louisville, with customer service centers occupying half a dozen buildings in Boulder County alone. Over its 50 years, Neodata has operated under the auspices of A.C. Nielsen Company, and Dun and Bradstreet, growing to become the nation's largest magazine subscription fulfillment company. Magazine subscribers became accustomed to seeing the familiar Boulder, Colorado, return address on subscription cards for publications such as *The New Yorker*, *Newsweek*, and *Road & Track*.

◆ EDS Centrobe has facilities in Louisville, Longmont and Gunbarrel and maintains a presence across the United States and in 19 countries worldwide.

In 1990, Hicks, Muse, Tate & Furst combined the efforts of Neodata and TMI, a telemarketing, fulfillment and distribution services company. EDS soon entered the picture. In 1997 the Plano, Texas-based company merged four successful international operations — Neodata, dbINTELLECT, The Lacek Group, Inc. and Customer-Solutions — under the $16.9 billion EDS umbrella. By the time Neodata became an EDS subsidiary and was rechristened as Centrobe, it was ranked among Boulder County's largest employers, with more than 2,700 employees in Boulder, Louisville and Longmont, and some 14,000 employees worldwide. In 1999, the company was expanding its headquarters offices again.

By 2005, Centrobe is predicted by some industry insiders to be leading the field in the rapidly growing ECM marketplace. The Yankee Group, a leading industry analyst, called Centrobe "a significant value-based services offering that has the added value of 'one-stop shopping' across the entire range of customer management needs."

What distinguishes Centrobe from its primary competitors in the burgeoning ECM market space is the unparalleled breadth of its service offerings, which encompass: ECM consulting, database services, analytics, customer care, fulfillment services, and distribution and electronic commerce.

What distinguishes Centrobe from its primary competitors in the burgeoning ECM market space is the unparalleled breadth of its service offerings...

◆ Centrobe operates 60 call centers on behalf of its clients, with more than 6,000 call center seats.

Centrobe flourishes by being the voice to the customer for large corporations. The company completes millions of individual customer transactions per year on behalf of its clients. Sixty Centrobe customer care centers annually handle 100 million telephone transactions and more than 3 million Internet communications. On the physical side, Centrobe has more than 1.4 million square feet of warehouse space and operates in 19 countries. The company annually sends 609 million pieces of mail, receives 227 million pieces and ships 66 million packages, making it the U.S. Postal Service's fourth-largest customer. Such huge volumes benefit Centrobe's clients with dramatic efficiencies and economies of scale.

Centrobe flourishes by being the voice to the customer for large corporations.

While Centrobe is an international force, it has dedicated considerable energy to having a positive impact in Boulder County. The company established Community Involvement Teams as a way of ingraining volunteerism into the corporate culture, fostering employee participation in events such as food drives, clothing drives, walk-a-thons and bike-a-thons. Centrobe employees have consistently been among the leading contributors to Boulder County causes such as Community Food Share, March of Dimes, United Way and Boulder Shelter for the Homeless. The company is a local sponsor of Boulder's own E-Town radio program and has contributed to Hospice of Boulder County. Executives at Centrobe demonstrate their commitment to the children of the community by contributing their leadership skills to the YMCA, Collage Children's Museum, Boulder Valley Schools and other causes. Since 1997, Centrobe volunteers have joined EDS co-workers around the world for the annual Global Volunteer Day, donating their time to a variety of community improvement projects in Boulder County. Following through on the promise of "corporate intimacy," Centrobe combines a global presence with a commitment to the community.

◆ With roots reaching back to 1949 as a fulfillment house for *Esquire* magazine, Boulder's Neodata Corp. evolved to become one of the main components of EDS Centrobe and its Enterprise Customer Management approach.

Exabyte

All of the information recorded on the paper made from 50 billion trees would equate to 10,000 times the amount of written information in the Library of Congress — or one exabyte (1,018 bytes). Imagining a future in which such vast amounts of information increasingly find themselves discussed in everyday conversation required creativity and foresight, qualities possessed by the founders of Exabyte. Exabyte's founders, led by Juan Rodriquez, were inspired by a belief that video camcorder technology could break new ground among data storage devices by vastly improving the amount of information contained on a single tape cartridge. This vision led to the formation of Exabyte.

After successfully finding investors to fund the venture, Exabyte opened its doors in 1985, and by the early 1990s was recognized as one of the fastest growing companies in the United States. This success stemmed from the innovative nature of Exabyte's products. The company introduced the first low-cost, high-capacity tape drive in 1987, the EXB-8200, for backing up data stored on computer hard drives. A derivative of consumer 8mm camcorder technology, the revolutionary EXB-8200 offered more than 10 times the storage capacity of anything else in existence at the time. In addition, this tape drive boasted a smaller size, which translated into lower power requirements and a significant reduction in the price per gigabyte of data stored. Previously, secondary data storage systems had required the presence of a human operator to swap data cartridges in and out, as the tape drive capacities had been too small to store all of the required information. With its high-capacity tape drive, Exabyte broke this paradigm. The introduction of open systems with unattended backup launched Exabyte into a position of industry leadership.

> *Upholding its reputation for creating high-capacity, high-performance tape drives, the company has successfully launched mammoth-2.*

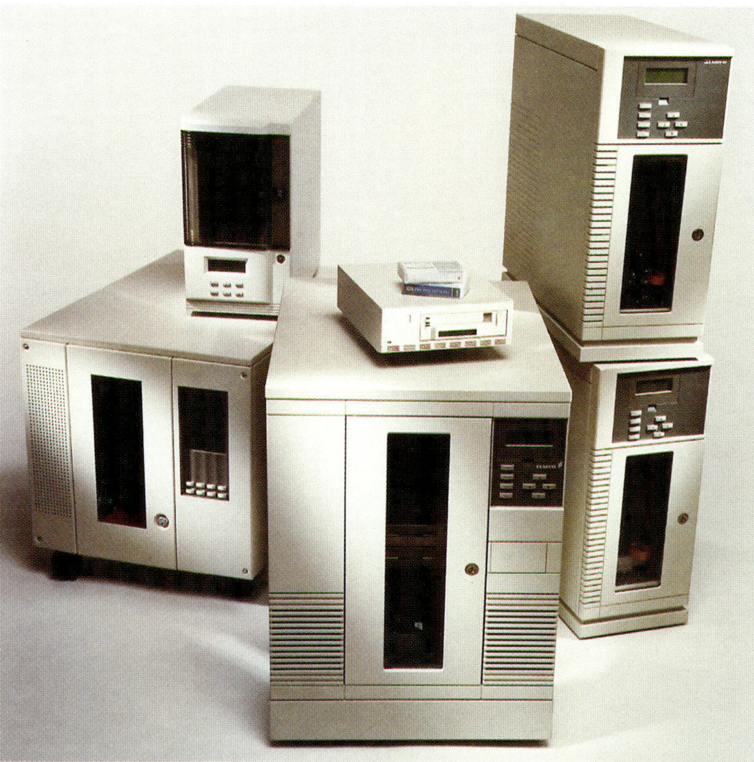

◆ Exabyte tape drives and automated tape libraries

Upholding its early reputation for creating high-capacity, high-performance tape drives, the company has continued to develop innovative products. Exabyte went public in 1989, and soon after expanded its base of business by introducing the industry's first automated tape library for the open systems marketplace. An automated tape library integrates one or more tape drives, many tape cartridges and intelligent robotics to efficiently manage unattended backup. Demonstrating a continued dedication to improved storage capacity, both the high-capacity tape drive and tape library have undergone remarkable progress since their inceptions. While Exabyte's first high-capacity tape drive placed 2.2 gigabytes of data on a cartridge, mammoth-2 for 1999 will store up to 150 gigabytes, comparable to 100,000 floppy disks or one to two floors of academic journals.

Similarly, Exabyte's initial library in 1989 held 600 gigabytes, while an m2 library will hold up to 30 terabytes, comparable to five times the printed collection of the Library of Congress, or 2,500,000 trees made into paper and printed.

Customers trust the company to constantly enhance capacity and product performance while maintaining backward compatibility to protect their prior investments. Additionally, the cost reduction in storage technologies and the resultant explosion in the information industry have aided Exabyte in fulfilling its commitment to continually reduce the price of its products to its customers.

◆ Exabyte's mammoth-2 stores up to 150 gigabytes.

Exabyte is also recognized for its award-winning customer service. Available worldwide, Exabyte's services help customers integrate products and protect their investments in the company's technology. In addition, the company's worldwide services promise minimal downtime and high data availability. Spanning entire product lifecycles, the company provides a full range of data storage, migration, recovery and storage automation services, ensuring ongoing data protection.

The company's customer base continues to expand due to recent technological innovations. Currently, Exabyte has shipped more than 1.5 million tape drives and over 60,000 libraries. With the advent of client server computing, in which the data from personal computers is aggregated onto a server, the amount of data requiring backup has expanded rapidly. New applications and information technology in the audio and video fields, including such scientific applications as medical imaging, have also led to an explosion of information digitization, creating tremendous opportunities for the storage technology industry. Exabyte stands ready to take on the opportunities of the digital information age.

The 1,250 employees worldwide, including nearly 900 employees in Boulder, are committed to providing industry leadership and to making a positive contribution to the local community. As one of the largest employers in the city, the company has a significant impact on the local economy. Exabyte works hard to ensure that it impacts Boulder positively by giving back to the community in three main areas: arts, education and social services. Among the dozens of groups benefiting from Exabyte are the YMCA, Boulder Valley School District, E-Town, Boulder Philharmonic Orchestra, United Way and Community Food Shares. Individual employee volunteerism is encouraged as well through such events as The March of Dimes WalkAmerica.

Clearly, Exabyte's story has been one of success for both the company and for the community. Exabyte has garnered numerous awards and recognition within both the industry and the general business world. The company looks to the future with plans to innovate, evolving from its role as a component supplier into a network backup systems and solutions provider. Recognized within the industry as a leader, the company's goal is to create long-term growth for shareholders, employees, customers and suppliers through the development and production of higher capacity and performance products, as well as data storage solutions, at lower costs.

◆ Bill Marriner, chairman, president and CEO of Exabyte Corporation

Bibliography

Books:

Bailey, Delores S. *Boulder County Miners: A Tribute to those Who Left their Mark in Colorado History.* Boulder: Self-published, 1995. Vol. I, 800 p., illus, photos, 12" x 9" spiral bound, Vol II, 250 p, illus, photos, 12" x 9"

Bailey, Delores S. *God's Country U.S.A. Wall Street, Colorado: The Life and History of Milling, Mining and Families Along the Switzerland Trail.* Fort Collins: Robinson Press, Inc., 1982. 150 p., maps, photos, drawings, 11" x 9" hardback

Barker, Jane Valentine and Sybil Downing. *Martha Maxwell: Pioneer Naturalist.* Boulder: Pruett Pub. Co., 1982. 138 p., bib, photos, 6" x 9" paperback (Women of the West Series)

Benson, Maxine. *Martha Maxwell: Rocky Mountain Naturalist.* Lincoln: University of Nebraska Press, 1986. 335 p., index, bibliography, endnotes, photos, 6" x 9" hardback

Boulder Commercial Association. *Outdoor Life in Boulder County.* Boulder: 1907 32 p. illus.

Boulder County, Colorado, *Yearbook-Directory,* 1935. Seibert: National Directory Co., 1935. 116 p. illus. map

Boulder County Directory. Boulder: Boulder Pub. Co. 1896 1v. plates

Boulder County Directory: Containing the Names and Addresses of the Voters of Every Precinct in Boulder County, with a Classified Business Directory... a Complete Church and Lodge Directory of the Cities of Boulder and Longmont. Denver: Interstate Advertising and Investment Co., 1898. 190 p.

Boulder Daily Camera. Souvenir Industrial Edition of the *Daily Camera,* Descriptive of Boulder County and the Achievements of the Year 1902. Boulder: 1902. 96 p. illus. ports

Cobb, Bertha B. and Anita Ernest,: *A Story of the Rocky Mountains.* Boston: The Arlo Publishing Company, 1927? 285 p. photos, illus, NW 5" x 7" hardback (1988).

Cobb, Harrison S. *Prospecting Our Past: Gold, Silver and Tungsten Mills of Boulder Country.* Boulder: The Book Lode, 1988. 153 p., index, bib., glossary, maps, photos

Coel, Margaret. *Chief Left Hand: Southern Arapaho.* Norman: University of Oklahoma Press, 1981. 339 p., index, bib., footnotes, illus.

Collins, Mary. *Pioneering in the Rockies.* Denver?: Self Published, 1909? 99 p.

Crossen, Forest. *The Switzerland Trail of America* with an Added Chapter. Fort Collins: Robinson Press, Inc., 1962, 1978. 422 p., index, photos, endpaper, maps

Cushman, Ruth Carol & Glenn Cushman. *Boulder Hiking Trails: The Best of the Plains, Foothills & Mountains.* Boulder: Pruett Publishing Co., 1995. 212 p., index, bib., maps, photos by Glenn Cushman

De Haan, Vici. *Hiking Trails of the Boulder Mountain Area.* Boulder: Pruett Publishing Co., 1979. 116 p., maps. photos, 9" x 6"

Dunning, Harold Marion. *Over Hill and Vale: In the Evening Shadows of Colorado's Longs Peak.* Boulder, CO: Johnson Pub. Co., 1956-1971. 3 vols.. photos, index

Dyni, Anne Quinby. *Back to the Basics: The Frontier Schools of Boulder County, Colorado, 1860-1960.* Boulder: The Book Lode, 1991. 153 p., index, photos, 2 appendices, 11" x 9" paperback

Dyni, Anne Quinby. *Pioneer Voices of the Boulder Valley: An Oral History.* Boulder: Boulder Country Parks and Open Space Department, 1989. 116 p., index, bib., 5 appendices, photos, 9" x 12" paperback

Ellis, Russell, Jr. *Boulder Colorado: Home of the Switzerland Trail.* Boulder: Boulder Motel Association, 1960?, 30 p., maps, photos, 9" x 6"

Fritz, Percy Stanley. *The Mining Districts of Boulder, County, Colorado.* Boulder, CO: University of Colorado, 1933. 639 p. Thesis (Ph.D)-University of Colorado

Hallowell, John K. *Boulder County As It Is.* Denver: Colorado Museum of Applied Geology and Mineralogy, 1882. 19 p.

History of Clear Creek and Boulder Valleys, Colorado. Containing a Brief History of the State of Colorado... A History of Gilpin, Clear Creek, Boulder and Jefferson Counties, and biographical sketches. Chicago: O.L. Baskin and Co. 1880. 713 p. illus. Index comp. by Sanford Charles Gladden, printed by Empire Reproduction and Print, Boulder: 1970.

Kemp, Donald C. *Silver, Gold and Black Iron: A Story of the Grand Island Mining District of Boulder, Colorado.* Denver: Sage Books, 1960. 230 p., index, bib., photos, endpaper maps, 6" x 9" hardback

Meier, Thomas J. *The Early Settlement of Boulder... It Ain't Necessarily So.* Boulder: Boulder Creek Press, 1993. 24 p., endnotes, drawings, photos, 9" x 11" paperback

Meier, Thomas J. and Ed Tangen, *The Pictureman: A Photographic History of the Boulder Region, Early Twentieth Century.* Boulder: Boulder Creek Press, 1994., 384 p., index, bib., photos, 9" x 11" hardback

Montgomery, Frances. *Castle O'Montgomery.* Nashville, TN: Parthenon Press, 1974. 228 p., bib., illus., 6" x 9" hardback

Murray, John A. *The Indian Peaks Wilderness Area: A Hiking and Field Guide.* Foreword by Tim Wirth. Boulder: Pruett Publishing Co., 1985. 181 p., index, bib., maps, photos, 9" x 6"

Ochs, S. Alice. *Water: Basis for Success: Left Hand Ditch Company History, The First 130 Years.* Longmont: The Author, 1966. 126 p., 9" x 6"

Pettem, Silvia. *Excursions from Peak to Peak Beginning in Boulder.* Boulder: The Book Lode, 1987. 31 p., photos, maps, 6" x 9"

Pettem, Silvia. *Excursions from Peak to Peak, Then and Now.* Boulder: The Book Lode, 1997. 130 p., photos, maps, 6" x 9"

Pettem, Silvia. *Gold Mining in Boulder County, Then and Now: Red Rocks to Riches.* Boulder: Stonehenge Books, 1980. 123 p., maps, glossary, photos

Pettem, Silvia. *Guide to Historic Western Boulder County.* Evergreen: Cordillera Press, 1989. 48 p., photos, maps, 9" x 8"

Roach, Gerry. *Colorado's Indian Peaks: Classic Hikes and Climbs.* Golden: Fulcrum Publishing, 1998. 180 p., maps, photos, 9" x 6"

Rodeck, Hugo G., ed. *Natural History of the Boulder Area.* Boulder: University of Colorado Museum, 1964. 100 p. illus. (University of Colorado Museum. Leaflet no. 13). 6" x 9"

Rogers, Maria M. *In Other Words: Oral Histories of the Colorado Frontier.* Intro. by Patricia Nelson Limerick. Golden: Fulcrum Pub. Co., 1995. 192 p., index, illus.

Schlender, Shelley D. & Reed Glenn. *The Insiders' Guide to Boulder & Rocky Mountain National Park.* Boulder: Boulder Pub. Co., 1994. 427 p., index, map, photos, ads, 6" x 8"

Schmaltz, David Alan. *Nobodie: Homeless in Paradise [Boulder, Colorado]*: Boulder: University of Colorado, Ph.D. dissertation Sociology, 1992

Smith, Phyllis. *Once a Coal Miner... The Story of Colorado's Northern Coal Field.* Boulder: Pruett Pub. Co., 1989. 249 p., index, bib., notes, appendices, illus., 7" x 10" hardback 1989.

Spitler, Laura L. & Lou Walther. *Gem of the Mountain Valley: A History of Broomfield.* Boulder: Mathis Printing & Broomfield Centennial-Bicentennial Committee, 1975. 85 p., bib., maps, photos, 9" x 11" paperback

Stepping Out: A Colorado Living History. Boulder County Vol. 2 Boulder: KR Publishing, 1982. 39 p., photos, 11" x 9" paperback

Toll, Oliver W. *Arapahoe Names and Trails.* Tolland: Oliver W. Toll, 1962. 43 p., photos, 6" x 9" paperback

Waldrop, Henry Arthur. *Arapaho Glacier: A Sixty-Year History.* Boulder: University of Colorado, 1964. (Univ. of Colorado Studies, Series in Geology, No. 3). 37 p., bib., maps, charts, photos, 10" x 7" paperback

Walther, Lou. *Old Names and Golden Splendors.* Boulder: Johnson Publishing Company, 1983. 106 p., maps, illus., photos, bib. 10" x 7" paperback

West, Elliott. *The Contested Plains: Indians, Goldseekers and the Rush to Colorado.* Topeka: University Press of Kansas, 1998. 442 p., index, bib., endnotes, illus., maps., cloth

Articles, Reports, etc:

Holleran, Michael, and Carmela Canzonieri. "Boulder Valley Ditches: A Landscape Preservation and Design Study." Denver: University of Colorado at Denver, 1994

McCoy, Earl. "Adventures of Ivy Baldwin, Aerialist," The Denver Westerners Roundup Magazine, XLIX (March-April, 1993), pp. 3-12

O'Dell, John. Caribou, Eldora, *Nederland & the Middle Boulder Valley.* Denver: University of Colorado at Denver M.A. Thesis, 1999. 110 p.

Paddock, Laurence T. "The Peripatetic Press or How the Good News Came to Boulder," The Denver Westerners Roundup Magazine, XL (May-June, 1984), pp. 3-14

Stewart, Jennie E. *Boulder County Pioneers.* Boulder: Arapahoe Chapter, D.A.R. Boulder: 1945-48. 219 p.

Weiss, Manuel, ed. *Boulder County Historical Site Survey.* Boulder: Carnegie Library for Local History, 1981. 4 vols.

Allenspark

Durning, Mabel Downer. *Historical Reminiscing in the Allenspark Mountain Area.* Longmont: Sharer Books, 1975. 40 p. illus. 9" x 11" paperback

Durning, Mabel Downer. *St. James on the Mount — Allenspark, Colorado.* Allenspark: St. James on the Mount, 1976, 9 p., 9" x 7" paperback

Boulder City

Allen, Frederick S., Ernest Andrade, Jr., Mark S. Foster, Philip I. Mittering, H. and Lee Scamehorn. *The University of Colorado, 1876-1976.* N.Y.: Harcourt Brace Jovanovich, Inc., 1976. 319 p., index, endnotes, 9" x 6" hardback

Barker, Jane Valentine. *Historic Homes of Boulder County.* Boulder: Pruett Publishing Co., 1979. 200 p., index, photos by Jerry Cleveland, 12" x 9" hardback

Barker, Jane Valentine. *76 Historic Homes of Boulder, Colorado.* Boulder: Pruett Publishing Co., 1976. 200 p., index, photos, 12" x 9" hardback

Boulder and Surroundings: The Romantic Situation, Enterprising People, Beautiful Scenery, and Points of Interest... Boulder: Daily Herald Steam Print., n.d. 18 p. illus.

Boulder, Colo. Chamber of Commerce. *Boulder in Cool, Colorful Colorado.* Boulder: 195? 12 p. illus. Later printings pub. under title *History of Boulder in Cool Colorful Colorado*

Boulder, Colo. Chamber of Commerce. *The Boulder of Yesterday and Today: A Brief History of Boulder, Colorado.* With a Thumbnail Sketch of the Present Community. Boulder: 1956. 16 p. illus.

Boulder, Colo. Chamber of Commerce. *Maybe This Will Show It: Being a Compilation of Facts and Figures on Boulder, Boulder County and the State of Colorado.* Boulder: 1943. 12 p. illus. map

Boulder Commercial Association. *Boulder:* "The Place to Live." Boulder: 1905. 20 p. illus.

Boulder Commercial Association. *Boulder, Colorado.* Boulder: 1916 20 p. illus.

Boulder Commercial Association. *Boulder County, Colorado: The County of Opportunities.* Boulder: 1911. 32 p. illus. maps

Boulder Garden Club. Roadside Committee. *Boulder Arboretum.* Boulder: 1951. 17 p.

Boulder Post-Office Souvenir. Colorado Springs: McMaster, 1898. 28 p. illus.

Brace, Mabel (Maxwell). *Thanks to Abigail: A Family Chronicle.* n.p.: 1948. 192 p. illus. ports

Bradley, Ruth. *Dellie, A Lotus in the Dust: From Bangkok to Boulder.* Berkeley, California: Ber-Cal Pub. Co., 1967. 192 p., illus., endpaper map, 7" x 10" hardback

Carrigan, Beverly H. "Frederick Law Olmstead, Jr.: Maker of Parks, Planner of Cities." Unpublished article, 1992

Casotti, Fred. *Football CU Style Casotti Uncensored.* Boulder: Pruett Publishing Co., 1972. 281 p., photos. 9" x 6" hardback

Castellino, Robert L. Boulder: *Heart & Soul, People & Place.* Story & Photographs by R.L. Castellino. Boulder: Whispering River, LLC, 1998. 112 p., color photos, 10.5" x 10.5" hardback

Collins, Mary. *Pioneering in the Rockies.* Place? pub?, 1909, 99 p., 7" x 9" hardback (1989). NW

Corson Dan W. "The Black Community in Boulder, Colorado." CU-Denver History Research Paper, 1996

Corson, Dan W. "Boulder's First Zoning Ordinance." CU-Denver History Research paper, 1997

Crossen, Forest. *Boulder By-ways.* Boulder: Boulder Savings and Loan Association, n.d. 68 p.

Darley, Ward. *The University of Colorado: Eighty Years Young!* 1876-1956. N.Y.: The Newcomer Society in North America, 1956. 24 p., drawings, 6" x 9" paperback

Daughters of the American Revolution. Colorado. Arapahoe Chapter, Boulder. Green Mountain Cemetery Records, Boulder, Colorado. Boulder?: 1939? 90 lv.

Davis, William E. Glory *Colorado: A History of the University of* Colorado, 158-1963. Boulder: Pruett Press. Inc., 1965. 798 p., bib., endnotes, photos, maps, appendices, 11" x 8"

Deane, J.W. *Come to Our Mountains, Beautiful Boulder.* Denver: H.J. Mayham Investment Co., 1898? 12 p.

Deno, William R. *Body & Soul: Architectural Style at the University of Colorado at Boulder.* Boulder: University of Colorado, 1994. 46 p., maps, photos, drawings, definitions, chronology

de Raismes, Joseph N. III. "From Lefthand to Cole Creek: Boulder's Open Space Program." Unpublished article, 1999

Fetter, Richard. *Frontier Boulder.* Boulder: Johnson Books, 1983. 100 p. index, photos, sources, notes, 6" x 9" paperback

Fine, Eben G. *Boulder, Colorado, and Her Mountain Wonderland:* A Travelog... Boulder: Chamber of Commerce, 1940? 20 p. illus.

Fine, Eben G. *Remembered Yesterdays.* Pub. under auspices of the Boulder Historical Society. Boulder: Johnson Pub. Co., 1957. 108 p. illus., 7" x 10" hardback

Frink, Maurice. *The Boulder Story: Historical Portrait of a Colorado Town.* Boulder: Pruett Press, 1965. 90 p., photos, drawings, 7" x 10" hardback (1985)

Galey, Mary. *The Grand Assembly: The Story of Life at the Colorado Chautauqua.* Boulder: First Flatiron Press, 1981. 154 p., index, endnotes, photos, 12" x 9" hardback

Geological Society of America Headquarters Building: *A Guide for Visitors.* Boulder: The Geological Society of America, Inc., 1988. 84 p., bib., photos, 6" x 9" paperback

Eckel, Edwin B. Geological Society of America Headquarters Building: *Life History of A Learned Society.* Boulder: The Geological Society of America, Inc., 1982. Foreword by Robert F. Leggert. 167 p., bibliography, photos, 12" x 9" hardback

Gladden, Sanford Charles. *Animal Tales from Boulder Newspapers.* Boulder: The Author, 1975. 23 p. (Tales of Boulder for Young Folks, no. 2)

Gladden, Sanford Charles. *The Beginnings of Boulder.* Boulder: The Author, 1975. 24 p. illus. (Tales of Boulder for Young Folks, no. 1). 6" x 9" paperback

Gladden, Sanford Charles. *Education: Public Schools.* Boulder: The Author, 1974. 112 p. illus. (Early Boulder Series, no. 3A). 6" x 9" paperback

Gladden, Sanford Charles. *Fire Protection.* Boulder: The Author, 1974. 106 p. illus. (Early Boulder Series, no. 2). 6" x 9" paperback

Gladden, Sanford Charles. *Hotels of Boulder, Colorado from 1860.* Boulder: Johnson Pub Co., 1970. 152 p., illus., map, photos, 11" x 8" hardback

Gladden, Sanford Charles. *Ladies of The Night.* Boulder: The Author, 1979. 47 p. illus. (Early Boulder Series, No. 5). 6" x 9" paperback

Goodykoontz, Colin B. *A Short History of the Congregational Church of Boulder, Colorado.* Boulder: The First Congregational Church, 1954. 31 p., photos, 6" x 9" paperback

Graf, Nelly Dawson. *No Vacancy.* Denver: University of Denver Press, 1951. 223 p., hardback

Historic Boulder. *Walking Tours of Boulder.* Boulder: Historic Boulder, Inc., 199?. 7 vols.(Chautauqua Park, Columbia Cemetery, Downtown, Mapleton Hill, University Hill, University of Colorado Campus, Whittier Neighborhood, illus., maps, glossary, 4" x 9", set of seven.

James, Ronald A. *Our Own Generation: The Tumultuous Years, University of Colorado, 1963-1976.* Boulder: University of Colorado, 1979. 189 p., index, appendices, photos, 11" x 8"

League of Women Voters. Boulder, Colo. *This is Boulder.* Boulder: 1962. 21 p. illus.

Lovelace, Walter B. *Boulder in Its Centennial Year, 1859-1959.* Boulder: Johnson Pub. Co., 1959. 44 p. illus., ads

Mackey, Sampson B. *Picturesque Boulder: Gems of Boulder County.* Boulder: The Author, 1901. 4 p. illus.

MacRoberts, Mary. *Boulder County, Colorado: Deaths and the Insane,* 1859-1900, Newspaper Abstracts. 1991

Mandel, Siegfried and Margaret Shipley. *Proud Past... Bright Future: A History of the College of Engineering at the University of Colorado,* 1893-1966. Boulder: Univ. of Colorado College of Engineering, 1966. 331 p., index, bib., appendices, photos, drawings, 7" x 10" hardback

Nichols, Lynn Wayne. *The Evolution of the Colorado Shakespeare Festival.* Boulder: Univ. of Colorado, Ph.D. diss. Theater, 1992

Norlin, George. *A Voice from Colorado's Past for the Present: Selected Writings of George Norlin.* Ed. by Ralph E. Ellsworth. Boulder: Colorado Associated University Press, 1985. 106 p., bib., 6" x 10" hardback

Of Valmont Vintage: A Celebration of Valmont Church and Its People. Boulder: Valmont Community United Presbyterian Church, 1981. 83 p., illus., bib., recipes

Olmsted, Frederick Law. *The Improvement of Boulder, Colorado: Report to the City Improvement Association.* Boulder: 1910 viii, 106 p.

Perrigo, Lynn Irwin. *A Municipal History of Boulder, Colorado 1871-1946.* Boulder: Boulder County Historical Society and the City of Boulder, 1946. x, 330 p.

Pettem, Silvia. Boulder: *Evolution of A City.* Niwot: University Press of Colorado, 1994. Foreword by Liston Leyendecker. 216 p., index, bib., hardback

Pettem, Silvia. *Chautauqua Centennial Boulder, Colorado: A Hundred Years of Progress.* Foreword by Leslie Durgin. Longmont: The Book Lode, 1998. 126 p., index, photos. paperback

Pettem, Silvia. *Legend of a Landmark: A History of the Hotel Boulderado.* Boulder: The Book Lode, 1986. 109 p., index, illus, photos, 7" x 9" paperback, 1986

Pettem, Silvia. *Seperate Lives: The Story of Mary Rippon.* Longmont: The Book Lode, 1999. viii + 280 p., index, bibliography, endnotes, 30 photos, 9.5" x 6.5" hardback and softcover

Repplier, Frederick Oakleigh. *As a Town Grows: The Schools of Boulder, Colorado, 1860-1959.* Boulder: Boulder School District, No. 3, 1959. 236 p. illus. ports. 9" x 6" hardback, (1986)

Ricaby, Sanford B., ed. *Look Boulder Over: Its Worth Your While to Visit Boulder, Colorado.* Boulder: The Commercial Association, 1901. 32 p. illus.

Runnells, Donald D. *Boulder: A Sight to Behold Guidebook.* Boulder: Estey Printing Company, 1976. maps, diagrams, photos, 6" x 9" paperback

Schoolland, John Bernard. *A Pioneer Church: Being a Reverently Realistic Account of the First Presbyterian Church of Boulder, Colorado, in its Total Pioneer Origin, 1872-1972.* Boulder: First Presbyterian Church, 1972. vi, 182 p. illus. 1985

Schoolland, John Bernard. *Boulder in Perspective: From Search for Gold to the Gold of Research.* Boulder: Johnson Pub. Co., 1980. 421 p., index, bib., photos, 12" x 9" hardback

Schoolland, John Bernard. *Boulder Then and Now: Picturesque Boulder and Gems of Boulder County.* Boulder: Pruett Press, 1967, 1987 new updated edition. 268 p., index, bib., maps, illus., 11" x 7" hardback

Schureman, William H. *Historical Sketch of the Presbytery of Boulder, Colorado and Its Enrolled Churches, 1883 to 1933.* Fort Collins: Robinson's, c. 1933. 69 p., photos, 6" x 9" paperback

Sewall, Jane. Jane, *Dear Child.* With a Foreword by Robert L. Stearns. Boulder: Univ. of Colorado Press, 1957. 198 p.

Sketch of Boulder, Colorado: Its Resources and Advantages. Together with map and business directory. From Blake & Willett's Hand-book of Colorado for 1873. Denver: Blake & Willett, 1873. 15 p. illus.

Smith, Phyllis. *History of Mapleton School.* Boulder: Boulder Valley Schools, 1975, revised ed. 1986. 29 p. bib., endnotes, photos

Smith, Phyllis. *A Look at Boulder: From Settlement to City.* Boulder: Pruett Publishing Company, 1981. 263 p., index, bib., endnotes, photos, endpaper maps, 8 appendices, 11" x 9" hardback

Steele, Edward Dunsha. *Edward Dunsha Steele, 1829-1865: Pioneer, Schoolteacher, Cabinetmaker, and Musician. A Diary of His Journey from Lodi, Wisconsin, across the Plains to Boulder, Colorado, in the Year 1859.* Ed. by Nolie Mumey. Boulder: Johnson Pub. Co., 1960. 90 p. map, Limited ed. of 500 copies, 7" x 11" hardback

Stewart, Jennie E. *Boulder County Pioneers.* Comp. and ed. by Jennie E. Stewart for Arapahoe Chapter Daughters of the American Revolution. Boulder: 1946-1948. 219 p.

Sturtevant, Joseph Bevier. *Views of Boulder and Vicinity.* n.p.: 1880. 26 p. chiefly illus.

Wellington Association. *Wellington Gardens: Prosperous Homes for Thrifty People.* Boulder: Wellington Association, 1909? 32 p. illus.

Whitacre, Christine and R. Laurie Simmons. *Goss-Grove Neighborhood History and Survey Results.* Boulder: 1985/1986 Boulder Survey of Historic Places, 1986

Wilson, Thomas V. Boulder: *A City of Pretty Homes and a County of Vast Natural Resources.* Denver: Press of Irrigation Era, n.d. 16 p. illus.

Yale, D.B. *Boulder and Vicinity: The Beauty Spot of Colorado.* Souvenir ed. Boulder: Camera Press, 1891. 28 p. chiefly illus.

Caribou

Buchanan, John W and Doris G. Buchanan. *The Story of A Ghost Town,* Caribou. Boulder: Boulder Pub. Co., 1957. 36 p. illus.

Smith, Duane A. *Silver Saga: The Story of Caribou, Colorado.* Foreword by Robert G. Athearn. Boulder: Pruett Publishing Co., 1974. 269 p. index, bib., illus. 6" x 9" hardback

Eldora

Kemp, Donald Campbell and John R. Langley. *Happy Valley: A Promoter's Paradise; Being an Historic Sketch of Eldora, Colorado and Its Environs.* With an intro. by Clyde Robertson. Denver: Smith-Brooks Print. Co., 1945. 59 p. illus. map. 9" x 6"

Eldorado Springs

Sampson, Joanna. *A Glimpse at Eldorado's Colorful Past: High-Wire Aerialist, Rancher, and Ballrooms.* Denver: Eldorado State Park, Colorado Historical Society and Great Outdoors Colorado, c. 1995. 26 p., illus, 7 x 9" paperback

Gold Hill

Balsley, Robert. *Early Gold Hill.* Boulder: The Author, 1971, 1992 revised reprint by Storyteller Images. 52 p., bib., endnotes, drawings, 7" x 9" paperback

Courtney, Chellee, Lynne Walter & Rebecca Waugh. *Gold Hill, Colorado, 1859-1952.* Boulder: Historic Boulder, Inc., 1999. 28 p., bibliography, photos, 8.5" x 11" paperback

Montgomery, Mabel Guise. *A Story of Gold Hill, Colorado: Seventy-Odd years in the Heart of the Rockies.* Boulder: The Book Lode, 1987 reprint of 1930 original. 37 p. illus., map, Preface by Silvia Pettem. 5" x 7" paperback, $4, endpaper map

Mumey, Nolie. *History of Gold Hill & Gold Hill District Laws of 1859.* Boulder: Johnson Publishing Co., 1960 reprint of original 1859 mining district laws. ("A Rare Keepsake Accompanying the Diary of Edward Dunsha Steele") 24 p., 6" x 8" hardback

Regnier, Richard James Dussart. *Gold Hill is Where You Find It.* Boulder: Dussart Art Studio, 1995. 4 books (vols)., photos, poems, 7" x 9" paperbacks

Stepanek, Joseph Edward. *Gunug Mas Ranch: First Half Century,* 1941-1991. Boulder: Gold Hill Publications, 1996

Lafayette

Hutchison, James D. *Lafayette, Colorado History: Treeless Plain to Thriving City,* 1889-1989. Dallas, Texas: Curtis Media Corp.& The Lafayette Historical Society, 1990. 382 p., index, map, photos. 13" x 10" hardback

Hutchinson, James D. *Survey and Settlement: Lafayette, Colorado.* Lafayette: Morrell Graphics, 1994. 177 p., bib. photos, 13" x 10" hardback

Phillips, Eleanor Fullerton, ed.. *A Living History: Times of Crisis.* By Fifth Grade Students at Ryan Elementary School, Lafayette. Boulder: Boulder Valley Schools, 1987. 287 p., illus., 10" x 12" spiral in bound paperback

Longmont

Baber, Daisy F. as told By Bill Walker. *Injun Summer: An Old Cowhand Rides the Ghost Trails.* Caldwell, Idaho: The Caxton Printers, Ltd., 1952. 223 p., photos, 10" x 7" hardback, NW

Boyles, Berlyn L. (Billy). *The St. Vrain Valley: Its Early History.* Longmont, CO: Times-Call Pub. Co., 1967. 124 p. index, illus, map, 6" x 9" paperback (1988)

Boyles, Berlyn L. (Billy). *The St. Vrain Valley: Its History. 1900-1910.* Longmont: St. Vrain Valley Press, 1976. 156 p. illus.

Boyles, Berlyn L. (Billy). *Tales (Some Pretty Tall) of the St. Vrain Valley.* Longmont: St. Vrain Valley Press, c.1968. 79 p.

Brown, Seletha, ed. *They Came to Stay.* Longmont: St. Vrain Valley Historical Association, 1971. 276 p. illus., 7" x 10" hardback

Bullard, Charles & Sally Vecchio-Martin. *Longmont's History in Architecture Today.* Boulder: Johnson Pub. Co., 1986. 94 p., illus.

Chicago Colorado Colony. Chicago: Republican Print and Engraving Co., 1871 16 p. illus. map

Chicago Colorado Colony. *Chicago Colorado Colony: Constitution and By-laws.* With Comprehensive Chapters on Agriculture, Irrigation, Climate, the New Town of Longmont, Schools, Societies, Churches, etc. Longmont, Colorado. July 1st, 1871. Denver: Rocky Mountain News Print. House, 1871. 32 p.

The Church of St. John the Baptist. *Longmont: Daily Call Press, 1921.* 68 p., index, illus., ads, 10" x 7" paperback

Durning, Mabel Downer. *The Chicago-Colorado Colony Founding of Longmont.* Longmont: City of Longmont Centennial, 1976. bib., 34 p., drawings, map, 7" x 9" paperback

Gehlert, Vera. *Longmont Architectural Heritage.* Denver: The Author, 1976. 46 p. photos, drawings, maps, bib., paperback

Hastings-Greenly, Melissa & E. D Greenly. *So Long Longmont: A Critical Look at Longmont as it Was and as It Is.* Longmont CQG Ltd. Publishing, 1996. 290 p., photos, 6" x 9" paperback

Hickman, H. *Longmont, 1870-1970.* Longmont, CO: 1971 1v. illus.

Large, Dorothy. *As We Were: Life in Early Longmont, 1871-1900 As Reflected in the Newspapers of the Day.* Longmont: Sharer Books, 1977. 63 p., drawings, 8.5" x 11" paperback

Large, Dorothy. *Old Burlington: First Town on the St. Vrain, 1860-1871.* Longmont: St. Vrain Publishing Co., 1984. 174 p., index, endnotes, maps, drawings, 6" x 9" hardback

Large, Marjorie E. *The Appropriation to Private Use of Land Water in the St. Vrain Valley before the Founding of the Chicago-Colorado Colony (1871).* Boulder: Univ. of Colorado, 1932. M.A. Thesis

Longmont, Colo. Board of Trade. *The Pride of the Rockies:* Longmont, Colorado. Longmont?, CO: 1905. 39 p. illus.

Longmont, Colo. Board of Trade. *Sketch of Longmont, Colorado.* Longmont, CO: 1887 52 p. illus. maps

Longmont, Colo. Commercial Association. *Longmont, Boulder County, Colorado: Prosperous, Progressive, on the Lincoln Highway.* Longmont: 1911 11 p. illus.

Longmont, Colo. Commercial Association. *Longmont, Under the Shadow of Old Long's Peak.* n.p.: 1909? 20 p. illus.

Longmont's 75th Anniversary Official Souvenir Program, 1871-1946

Longmont: N.P., 1946? 24 p., drawings, photos, 6" x 8" paperback

Morgan, Gary. *Sugar Tramp: Colorado's Great Western Railway.* Fort Collins: Centennial Publications, 1975. 97 p., index, bibliography

Newby, Betty Ann. *The Longmont Album: History and Folklore of the St. Vrain Valley.* Virginia Beach, VA.: The Donning Company Publishers, 1995. 208 p., index, bib., map, photos, 9" x 12"

Puffer, Rodney Arthur. *The Organization and Early History of Longmont.* (The Chicago-Colorado Colony). Boulder: University of Colorado, 1915? 25, 9 lv. illus. map. M.A. Thesis

Sekich, *Vera. A Coal Miner's Daugher Who Became a Farmer's Wife.* Longmont: CQG Books Ltd., 1993. 11 p., photos, 8" x 6" paperback

Sheppard, Mary Louise, *Longmont, Colorado: An Urban Development in an Agricultural Situation.* Boulder: University of Colorado, 1947. 65 p. illus. M.A. Thesis

Louisville

Conarroe, Carolyn. *The Louisville Story.* Louisville: The Louisville Times, 1978. 74 p., bib., endnotes, maps, photos, 7" x 10" hardback, (1986)

Liscum, Gina. *Louisville: On Main Street, A Collection of Memories.* Louisville: The Author, 1985. 90 p., endnotes, map, illus., 11" x 9" spiral-bound paperback

Lyons

Lyons and Surrounding Area: Double Gateway to the Rockies. Text by the Lyons Historical Society, photos by Olga Seybert. Lyons: Lyons Centennial-Bicentennial Committee, 1977 (printed by Johnson Pub. Co. of Boulder). 80 p., photos, 6" x 9" paperback

Wallin, Ivan E. *The Professors' Ranch: Montani Semper Liberi.* Boulder: Johnson Pub. Co., 1964. 112 p, illus., map, 6" x 9" hardback, (1991)

Weaver, Frank D. *A History of the Old Stone Congregational Church/United Church of Christ Lyons, Colorado, 1889-1974.* Lyons: The Congregational Church, 1974?. 58 p., photos, 9" x 6" paperback

Weaver, Frank D. *'That Beautiful Valley:' E.S. Lyon: A Man with a Dream.* Lyons: The New Lyons Recorder, 1978. 45 p., photos, 5 x 7 paperback

Nederland

Amen, Don F. *History of Nederland, Colorado, 1870-1920.* Denver: University of Denver, 1960. 884 p. Thesis (M.A.)

Becker, Isabel M. *Nederland: A Trip to Cloudland.* Denver: Scott Becker Press, 1989. 171 p., index, bib., drawings, photos, maps, 8" x 7" paperback

Meyring, Geneva (Todd). *Nederland, Then and Now.* Boulder, CO: Boulder Pub. Co., 1941. 32 p.

Pettem, Silvia. *Inn and Around Nederland, Accommodating the Traveler Then and Now.* Longmont: The Book Lode, 1998. 130 p., index, photos, paperback

Marshall

Mernitz, Scott. *The Impact of Coal Mining on Marshall, Colorado, and Vicinity: An Historical Geography of Environmental Change.* Boulder: Univ. of Colorado, 1971. 82 p., illus. maps. M.A. Thesis

Sampson, Joanna. *Walking Through History on the Marshall Mesa.* Boulder: City of Boulder Open Space Department, 1995

Niwot

Dyni, Anne Quinby. *Niwot Colorado: Echoes for a Railroad Town.* Boulder: The Book Lode, 1994. 49 p., bib., 6" x 9" paperback

Peaceful Valley

Pettem, Silvia. *The Peaceful Valley Story: Fulfillment of a Dream.* Boulder: The Book Lode, 1994. 58 p., bib., photos, 9" x 6" paperback

Sunshine

Howard, June Peterson. *Stories of Sunshine: Life in A Mining Camp.* Longmont: The Book Lode, 1994. 85 p., index, bib., map, photos, appendices, 11" x 9" paperback

1997 photo by Jim Hutley

Index

Adams, A.B. 19
Adams, Governor Alva 51,74,136
Affolter Cabin 161
Affolter, Jacob 119
African Methodist Episcopal Church 54, 55
African-Americans 54
Aikins Party 26
Aikins, Thomas A. 25,30,121
Allen Hotel 84
Allen, Alonzo H. 85
Allen, Alonzo N. 70,71,84
Allen, Charles F. 86
Allen, Judge Alonzo P. 33,71,121
Allenspark 59,71,159,168
Altona Grange 121
Ambler Realty Company 143
American Forestry Association 125
Ammons, Governor Elias M. 113
Anderson Ditch 51
Anderson, Marti 75
Anthony, Scott 21
Antlers Hotel 66
Apollo Theater 19
Arapaho 14,26
Arapaho Glacier 14,53,140
Arapaho Indians 16, 18, 26
Arapaho Pass 16
Armas, Jocy Ann 125
Arnett Hotel 50,159
Arnett, Anthony 32,43,60
Arnett, Willamette 50
Aspen 176
Aspen Grove Inn 75
Atkinson, Peggy 131
Atomic Energy Commission 145
Bachelder Ranch 135
Bader School 121
Bailey, Delores S. 75
Bailey, Deputy Sheriff Raymond 110
Baker, James H. 43
Baldwin, Ivy 76
Ball Brothers Research Corporation 145
Baptist Catholic Church 87
Barker Dam 66
Barker Lake 66
Barker, Hannah 68
Barth, Kathryn 144
Bartlett, Albert 146
Bartlett, Mayor J. Perry 145
Baseline Road 108,118,135,163
Baskin, Oliver L. 25
Bastille Point 78
Bathke, Ed 63,137
Battle Creek 31,48
Bean, Trafton H. 146
Beasley School 120
Beatrice Hover Personal Care Unit 95
Beech Aircraft 145
Benedict, Jacques 72
Benedict, James B. 16
Benedictine Order 47
Bent Brothers 17
Bent, William 18
Bergheim, Milton 51
Berkeley, Judge Granville 121
Bernard, Dale 92
Better Boulder Party 56
Bevier, Joseph 134
Big Elk Ranch 169
Big Five Mines 74
Billings Cabin 161
Bird, Isabella 41,83
Bixby, Amos 25,63,160
Black Diamond Mine 100
Black Hawk 59,152
Black Hills 17
Bloomerville 52,74
Blue Birds 62
Blue Mountain Quarry 126, 152
Blue Ribbon Mine 110
Bluebird Hotel 62
Bluebird Lodge 60,62
Bonai Shalom 55
Booth, Vella 168
Bosetti, Monsignor Joseph J. 71
Boswick, David 118
Boulder Arts Commission 176
Boulder Canyon 30,41,60,119,138
Boulder City Brewing Company 35
Boulder City Council 136
Boulder City Improvement Association 140
Boulder City Open Space 100,170
Boulder City Planning Department 147
Boulder City Town Company 30
Boulder County Agricultural Society 121
Boulder County Bee 34
Boulder County Courier 34
Boulder County Fair 82,121
Boulder County Herald 57
Boulder County News, The 26,50,121
Boulder County Open Space 167
Boulder County Social Services 110
Boulder Creek 14,26,43,59,118,141,157,177
Boulder Cultural Plan 176
Boulder Depot Museum 116
Boulder Dinner Theater 56
Boulder Industrial Park 145
Boulder Landmarks Board 157
Boulder Municipal Complex 51
Boulder Museum of Contemporary Art 176
Boulder News-Courier 99,102
Boulder Valley Comprehensive Plan 147
Boulder Valley Grange Hall 120
Boulder Valley League of Women 172
Boulder Valley Railroad 33,51,99
Boulder-Longmont Diagonal Highway 171
Bowman, Lorenzo 54
Boyd Smelter 30,51
Boyd, James H. 51
Boze, R. Franklin 87
Brainard Lake 74
Breath, Samuel 72
Breed Smelter 63
Breed, Abel D. 63
Brierley, John 119
Brodie, John 152
Brookfield, Alfred A. ....
....22,18,26,27,53,98,121,129,168
Broomfield 52,98,128,168
Broomfield County 176
Broomfield Heights 129
Broomfield Lumber Company 130
Bross, William 81
Brown, Abner Roe 31
Brown, Kent 93
Brown, Nathan 65
Brunner Farmhouse 180
Bryan, William Jennings 136
Buchanan, Frank 176
Buchanan, John W. 62
Buckingham, Charles 139
Buckout, Pam 68
Buechner, John C. 149
Bug Town 34

Bunce School...72,159
Burlington Free Press, The 85
Butsch, Valentine 34
Byers, William N. 19,81
Callahan House......................................93,160
Callahan, Thomas M.................................161
Callahan, Tom 161
Camp St. Malo Chapel.................................71
Campbell, Ida..57
Canfield 30,51,154
Canfield General Store 101
Canfield, Isaac 100
Capp, M.P. 113
Cardinal City 64
Cariboo House 63
Cariboo Mining District...............................63
Caribou Lake 16
Caribou Mill..63
Caribou Mine..63
Caribou Park 79
Caribou Post 63
Caribou School House 64
Caribou Silver Coronet Band 64
Caribou Silver Mine 79
Carlisle, Sam...110
Carpenter, Scott 177
Carter Museum 44
Casey Middle School 30
Catlin, George 14
Caywood, William 125
Cech, Thomas 149
Chaffee, Jerome 64
Chalmers, Archie 99
Chautauqua Board of Directors 136
Chautauqua Meadow 136
Cheney, Louise 136
Cherry Creek 26
Chicago Tribune 81
Chicago-Colorado Colony........................81,82
Chief Buckskin 53
Chief Left Hand.......................................19,26
Chief Niwot 14,117
Chivington, John Milton 20
Chronic, Betty.....................................159,162
Church, Sarah...128
City Bakery 85
Clay, James 54
Clear Creek County 63
Coal Creek Valley 105
Coburn Development.................................174
Coel, Margaret...21,26
Coffield, Dana 163
Coffintop Dam..185
Coffman, Enoch J. 86
Collins, Susan 23
Collyer Park 82
Colonial Revival 160
Colorado Chautauqua Association........134,136
Colorado Department of Highways 130
Colorado Department of Transportation 111
Colorado History Museum 15,88
Colorado Music Festival 136
Colorado State Penitentiary 69
Colorado Supreme Court Justice 176
Columbia Cemetery 51
Columbia Hotel 72,163
Cominco Smelter 79
Con-Agra Conglomerate...............................95
Conarroe, Carolyn...............................105,164
Conarroe, Douglas 163
Coney Creek...16
Conger, Samuel P. 62
Consolidated Mining Company 64
Convery, William J. 87
Coon Track Creek 64
Correll, Ruth 176
Corson, William 43
Coulson, Druella 128
Cowell, George 61
Cramer, William...160
Crawford, Dana.....................................94,159
Crawford, Miles 128
Crescent Grange Hall 129
Crisman 52,59
Crossen, Forest 177
Crossroads Mall 141
Crystal Springs Brewery 36
Culver-Bixby-Woodward-Baird House 159,160
Culver Brothers 60
Curran Opera House 38
Daily Camera.............................34,41,135,186
Daily Times-Call 186
Dance-A-Lot Hall..71
Danish Plan 144
Danish, Councilman Paul...........................144
Dartt, Amy 48
Davidson Mesa 119
Davidson, William 72,118,119
Davies, Joyce...157
Davis, Adeline Beckett 110
Davis, Jefferson 42
Day, Frank Miles 44
De Longchamps, Pete.................................131
Deardorff, Cyrus...72
DeBacker, John 122,166
DeBoer, Saco R. 143
DeLong, Ira M. 57
Deno, William 149
Denver Art Museum.....................................12
Denver Boulder Turnpike...........................130
Denver Grain Elevator 164
Denver Museum of Natural History......18,98,186
Denver Pacific Railway 51,81
Denver Post 186
Denver Public Library 12,55,58,80,140
Denver, Boulder &
Northwestern Railroad 52,167
Denver-Boulder Turnpike................98,129,177
Dickens Opera House 85
Dickens, William H. 85
Dimick, Erastus H. 43,47
Dodd, Ruth 117
Dollar, Erna 110
Donnelly, Edward.......................................122
Donnelly, Leo 63
Dow, John 43
Downing, Roderick L..........................130,144
Downtown Business Association
of Louisville 164
Dubofsky, Jean 176
Dunkard Church 124
Dunn, John 166
Durgin, Leslie..136
Dutch 64
Dwight, Jason L...160
Dyni, Anne 117,163
Edbrooke, Frank...32
Eisenhower, Mamie 78,129
Eldora 52,166
Eldora Ski Area...70
Eldorado Canyon State Park..........................79
Eldorado Springs 52,60,78
Elliott, George 103
Elmore, Dr. R.D. 129
Elmwood Stock Farm 128
Empson Cannery.....................................88,89
Empson, John H. 88
Empson, Lida 88,89
Enchanted Mesa 144
Ensor, K.C...129
Epstein, Richard 173
Erie-Canfield Independent 100
Estes Park 88,152
Eugene Field...62
Evans, Griff 153
Ewing, John 119
Farmers Ditch..51
Ferrard, Dr. F. 36
Finn, Brian 62
Finn, Frank...62
Fitzpatrick, Thomas 18
FitzSimmons, Ann 164
Flagstaff Mountain 54,141
FlatIron Crossing regional mall 98,172
Flory, Reverend Jacob S. 119,124
Ford, Henry... 114
Fort Lupton 17
Fort Lyon...21,152
Fort Pella 124
Fort St. Vrain...17,26
Fort Vasquez 17

Fort Wise Treaty 19
Fowler, Frank D. 77
Fowler, Jack 79
Fox Theater 92
Francis, William 55
Frietchie, Barbara 32
Frost, Robert 148
Fuller, Tim 174,176
Gardens, Elitch 76
Gardner, Alexander 21
Gay, Sidney H. 81
Gerstle, Eva 146
Gillaspie House 68
Gillaspie, Dr. Carbon 68,159
Gilpin County 54,59
Gilpin, Governor William 42
Ginacci House 164
Gladstone Mine 111
Gold Hill 20,30,51,117,154
Gold Hill Miners 61
Gold Hill Mining District 60
Gold Hill Organization 154
Gold Miner Hotel 166
Gold Run Creek 60
Golden West Flour Mill 93
Good Templar Lodge 120
Goodall, Stephen 107
Gould, Emma 33
Gould, Jerome 117
Gove, Aaron M. 45
Graham, Thomas J. 30
Great American Desert 82
Great Western Railway 86
Great Western Sugar Beet Company 90
Greeley, Horace 27
Green Mountain Cemetery 99
Gregory Canyon 138
Grigsby, Harriette 84,160
Gunbarrel Hill 114
Gunter, Carole 122
Haertling, Charles 157
Haertling, Joel 158
Hake, William C. 111
Hale, Horace M. 43,44
Hall, Jessie 85
Hansen, Margaret 157,162
Har HaShem,Congregation 55
Harbeck, J.H. 51
Harbeck, Kate 51
Hartronft, Eric 164
Hauck, Robert 20,86
Havel, Vaclav 125
Havey, Jim 82
Hawkins, David 148
Hayden, Dr. Ferdinand V. 114
Hecla Mine 106
Hellems, Dean F.B.R. 158
Hendricks, Tom 78,167
Hercules, Michael 78
Hetherington, Thompson D. 46
Hetzer House 66
Hetzer, County Commissioner Elmer 159
Hewlett Packard 90
Hitzel, J. 119
Holmberg, Carolyn 168
Horsfal Hill 61
Horsfal Lode 30,60
Horsfal, David 30,60
Hotel Boulderado 141
Housel, Peter 122
Hover Company 94
Hover Manor 95
Hover, Katherine 95
Hoverhome Farmstead District 162
Hugh Murphy Quarry 152
Hunter, James 143, 160
Hutchison, Beth 111
Hygiene Cheese Factory 125
IBM 92,147,171
Immaculate Conception Cathedral 72
Imperial Hotel 86
Indian Peaks Wilderness Area 16,179
Indiana Female College 31
Ingenito, Father Benedict 105
International Order of Good Templars 35
Irwin, Jessie 111
Isabelle Glacier 140
Jackson, Helen Hunt 140
Jackson, J.W. 18,98
Jackson, Oliver Toussaint 55
Jacobs, Wesley 105
James Creek 75
Japanese 90
Jaramillo, Joseph 97
Jefferson, Thomas 16
Johnson Pub 140
Johnson, Ed 114
Johnson, LaVern 151,186
Joint Institute 149
Jones, Tommy 121
Jones, William 137
Judd, Morris 147
Kanemoto, Goroku 90
Kellogg, Dr. John Harvey 48
Kemp, John 69
Kerr, David 102
King, George 50
Kinney, Mary 85
Klauder, Charles 44,148
Klein, Dick 92
Knecht, Mayor Robert 157
Koenig Alumni Center 43
Koopmann, Richard W. 169
Kremmling 16
Ku Klux Klan 54,55,88,105,147
Kuner Pickle Company 89
Kupfner, Daniel 112
Lafayette 30,32,52,107,108,110,111,184
Lafayette High School 184
Lafayette Historical Society 111
Lafayette Leader 110
Lafayette Volunteer Fire Crew 164
Lafayette-Louisville Downtown Revitalization 183
LaFollette, Senator Robert 136
Lake Isabelle 179
Lake Park 82
Lake, Henry H. 65
Lake, Terry 85
Lakeview Cemetery 128
Lakewood 147
Lakota Sioux 14
Lamont, Bill 157
Lampert, Julia 14
Langford, Augustine 99
Larimer County 47
LaVern Johnson of Lyons 151
Leavenworth Times 26
Lefferdink, Allen J. 147
Lennon, Florence Becker 133
Leslie, Frank 26
Lewis, Alisa 66
Lewis, Oscar 111
Lewis, William 111
Lilly, John 70
Lindberg, Andrew 127
Long Gold Mine 184
Long, J.D. 50
Longmont 83,85,89,92,93
Longmont City Council 154
Longmont Sentinel 83
Longmont Sugar Company 90
Louisville Beer Hall 103
Louisville Historical Museum 164
Louisville Inn 102
Louisville Miner, The 106
Louisville Times, The 106,164
Lousiville Historical Commission 164
Lundeen, George 148
Lyon, Ed 151
Lyons Historical Society 153,185
Lyons Redstone Museum 152
Lytle, George 63
Machebeuf, Joseph P. 47
Macky Auditorium 43,44
Macky, Andrew J. 38,43,44, 46
Malo, Oscar 71
Marshall 30,52,77
Marshall Mesa 100
Marshall, Joseph W. 99
Martin, William 63
Martinek, Ed 77
Maxwell, Martha Dartt 48
Maxwell, James P. 42
McAllister Saloon 153

McCaslin, Matthew 60,117
McCaslin, Miranda 61,117
McClure, Louis C. 58
McConnell, LaVern 151
McGinty, Hugh 24
McKelvey, Mavis....146
McKelvey, Robert 146
Meadow Brook Farm 165
Means, U.S. Senator Rice 55
Meeker Park 168
Mehls, Steven 163
Meier, Thomas....26,51
Methodists 84,105,122
Miller, Mary 108
Miller, Ralph 108
Miller, Thomas Meagher....14
Mills, Enos 88
Miners Hotel 62
Miners Inn 60
Miners Museum 159
Miss Broomfield Heights 131
Mitchell, Scott 143
Moffat Lakes Resort Company 77
Moffat, David....64
Mogul Tunnel....70
Monarch High School 99
Monarch Mine 97
Moore, Hugh 155
Morley, Governor Clarence F. 55
Mother Jones 113
Mother Superior Mary Thomas 48
Mount Alto Park 52,74
Mount Sanitas 141
Mount St. Gertrude Academy 48
Mullen, Catherine Smith 71
Mullen, John Kernan 87
Murata Outland Associates....180
Muriel Sibell Wolle 64,166
Murphy, Jack.... 160
National Bureau of Standards 144
National Center for Atmospheric Research........
....144,145,148,156,157,176
National Land Company 82
National Trust for Historic Preservation ....
....136,158,174
Native Americans....16,98,166,170
Natvig, J. Martin 40
Nawatny, Kathinka 103
Nawatny, Louis....102
Nebraska City Times 27
Nebraska Territory 27
Nederland....52,152,184
Nederland Meadows 140
Nederland Mining Company 65
Nelson, Andrew J. 35
Neodata 144
New Nederland House 66
New Urbanism 173,174
Newton, CU President Quigg 149
Ni Wot Mining Company 72
Nichols, David H. 22,42
Nielsen, Aksel 129
Nishida Family 90
Niwot 26,53,110,163
Niwot Mountain 22
Niwot Tribune....126
Nomad Playhouse....160
Nomad Theater 173
Nomads Housing 173
Norgren, Carl 129
Norlin, George 44,147
North Longmont 82
North Park 14
Northern Coal Fields 98
Northern Colorado Agricultural Society......121
Oasis Brewery....36
Ohline Quarry 152
Olander, August 127
Old Louisville Inn 102,183
Old Mill Park 86,161
Old Mill Site Inn 75
Old Prague Inn....125
Old Stone Garage 159
Old Town Niwot 163
Old Whiterock 114
Olmsted, Frederick Law....41,140
Olson Park 153
Olson, Charles 127
Omni International Resort 184,185
Orodelfan (Orodell) 59,59,60,163
Otto, Robert....158
Owens, Governor Bill....186
Paddock, Laurence 157
Paddock, Lucius C.....34
Paddock, Lucius G. 34,35,41,135
Paget, Karen 176
Paris Dry Cleaning Parlor 54
Park, Bohn 153
Parkhill, Forbes....62
Patrons of Husbandry (Grange) 87
Patterson, D.C.....60
Pawnee 14
Peaceful Valley 60
Peak Inn 88
Peak Milling Company....87
Peak to Peak Highway 74
Pearl Street 23,35,48,119,144,155,178
Peerless Mine 100
Pei, I.M. 148,157
Pella 124
Penfield Tate....174
Penney, J.C. 161
People's Republic of Boulder....176
Pettem, Silvia 43,144,177
Pikes Peak Library District 119
Pillar of Fire 108
Pine Brook Hills....158
Pine Street Junction 103
Pine Street School....32
PLAN-Boulder 146,154
Platte River 16,17,26,82
Pleasantview Grange 120
Poe, Edgar Allen 79
Poisal, John....17
Poisal, Margaret 18
Pollock, Peter....47,132
Polzin, Frank 122
Potosi Boarding House 65
Potosi Mine Boarding House 65
Potpourri Players 93
Pratt, N.C. 81
Pride of the Rockies Flour Mill....88
Priester, Sandy 159
Prohibition 36,100
Pruett Publishing 64
Prussian Mine....86
Public Road 110,183
Public Service Company 68
Pudim, Rob 172
Pumpkin Pie Day 89
Red Rocks 27
Reese, John 151
Rettger, Father Cyril 105
Richmond Homes 112,182
Rippon, Mary....43
Rob Roy Mine 100
Roberts, Dr. Walter Orr 148
Roberts, Janet 176
Roche, Josephine 106
Rock Creek....112,168,177
Rock Creek Farm 168
Rocky Flats....145
Rocky Mountain American....55
Rocky Mountain Eagle 34
Rocky Mountain Joe....134
Rocky Mountain National Park....16,70
Rocky Mountain News 60,81
Roeschlaub, Robert....94
Rogers, Maria 50,97,108
Romano, Celeste....104
Roose, Mary 66
Roper, Laura....21
Rothstein, Arthur 95
Ryland, Charles S. 128
Ryssby 127
Sacred Heart of Jesus Catholic Church....47
Sacred Heart of Mary Catholic Church 47
Salina 52, 59
Sampson, Joanna 98
Sampson, June 146
Sand Creek Massacre 20,119

Sands, Emil 110
Sandstone Ranch 182
Schofield, Arlene 111
Scott, Malcolm 149
Seawalk, Millie 92
Second Baptist Church 54
Settlers Park 27
Seventh Day Adventist Church 48
Sewall, Dr. Joseph A. 43,147
Shakespeare Festival 43
Sharp Nose 20
Sheep Mountain 16,166
Sherman House 63
Sherwood, Jean 62
Shoo Fly Saloon 64
Shoup, Governor Oliver H. 44
Silver Lake 53
Simpson, John 107
Sisters of Charity 48
Skaggs, Congressman David 176
Slack, Walter Orr 176
Smith, Duane A. 64
Smith, George Edward 23
Smith, Jack 23,51
Smith, Marinus 22,42,119
Smith, Phyllis 57
South Arapahoe Peak 77
South Boulder Creek 44,77,140,165
South Boulder Peak 140
South Platte River 17,28,51,87
South St. Vrain Trail 153
Southern Arapaho 14,26
Southern Cheyenne 18
Squires, Frederick A. 48
Squires-Tourtellot House 22,50
St. Catherine Chapel 71
St. James Chapel 159
St. James-on-the-Mount 71
St. John, William 107
St. Joseph School 87
St. Louis Church and School 105
St. Stephen Episcopal Church 84,161,162
St. Vitus Episcopal Church 71
St. Vrain Creek 14,17,26,28,81,87,
....117,151,152,170,177,182,185
St. Vrain Historical Society 86,119,160,170
St. Walburga Benedictines 48
St. Walburga Monastery 47
Stanley Steamer Mountain Wagons 68
Star Mine 101
Stearns, Robert L. 148
Steinbaugh Hardware 164
Stevens, Henry 54
Stevens, Mary Ann 85,138
Storage Technology Corp. 107
Strathmore Mine 110
Strawberry Festival 83
Sturdevant, Jill 74
Sturtevant, Joseph B. 35,55,60,70
Sugar Loaf 59
Sulfide Flats 66
Sullivan, John 129
Sullivan, Mary 33
Sun Dance Ceremony 18
Sunset 52,59
Sunshine Canyon 53,61,140
Sunshine Creek 30
Sunshine Girls 89
Superior 30,48,159,172,182
Swan, Balmore 129
Swedish 53,127
Swiss 119
Switzerland Trail 52,60,137,155
Table Mesa 145
Tallman, Kenny 168
Talmadge, Carl 70
Tanaka Family 90
Tangen, Ed 32,44,66,116,142,153
Tate, Mayor Penfield 174
Taylor, William 126
Tego Drug Store 106,164
Teller House 63
Terry, Jane 82
Terry, Seth 81
Terry, William H. 83
Texas-Colorado Chautauqua Association 134
Thomas, Harlan 46
Thomas, Miss Mary L. 31
Thompson Library 83
Thompson Park 82
Thompson, Thomas 83
Toll, Oliver 16
Tommy Jones Stage Station 33
Tourtellot, Jonathan 47
Trevarton, Lillian 168
Tull, William 32
Turner, Susie Sunshine 60
Turnpike Land Company 129
Union Pacific Railroad ....
....52,73,86,125,152,155,185
United Mine Workers of America 106
United Nations 174
United States Forest Service 184
United States Supreme Court 143
University Heritage Center 42
University Memorial Center 149
University of Colorado 40,55,60,85,141,174
Utes 14,17,53,61
Valmont 33,47,74
Valmont Bulletin 33
Valmont Butte 33,122
Valmont House 121
Valmont Presbyterian Church 53,120,121
Van Vleet, Lynn 165
Varian, Ernest Philip 32,43
Varra, Louis 97
Varsity Lake 43
Vasquez, Pierre Louis 17
Viele, Albert 165
Viney, Benjamin 181
Voegtle, August 36
Wagoner, Hobart D. 46,148
Walker Ranch 167
Walker, James 167
Wall Street 52,59
Wall Street Gold Extraction Company Mill ..75
Walsh, Thomas F. 45
Walter, Lynne 61
Walter, Tim 155
Waneka Greenlee Thomas House 163
Waneka, Adolph 163
Waneka, Anna 120
Wangelin, O.H. 57
Ward 16,52,75,118,154
Ward, Calvin 72
Waschak, Mayor John 164
Waugh, Rebecca 68,159
Weisenhorn Lake 122
Weisenhorn, Frank S. 36
Welch Mine 107
Welch, Charles Clark 102
Weld County 17,55,100,129,171
Wentworth House 60
Wentworth, Charles 62
West, Elliott 17
Westcor 172
Wharton, Editor Junius E. 31
White Rock Flour Mill 122
White, Alma 108
White, Lily 51
White, Oscar 54
Whiteley, Richard 158
Whiteley-Hellems House 158
Widner, Amos 120
Williams Village 148
Wise Elevator 100
Wise Family Homestead 101,102
Wise Farmhouse 159
Wise, Dr. Sarah 102
Wise, Oliver E. 100
Wolf Tongue Mill 66
Wolff, Joseph 119
Woman's Christian Temperance Union 35
Woodland Flats 69
Wright, Alphonse 28
Wright, Ken 176
Wright, Mary Merkle 128
Wright, Ruth 146
Wurl, Leon 164
Wynkoop, Major Edward 21
Zang Investment Company 129
Zang, Adolph 128
Zweck Hotel 86
Zweck, George 86,125

Partners Index

The Academy 278
Access Graphics 294
Allegro Coffee Company 230
architectural manœuvres, p.c. 266
Art Cleaners 238
Art Mart 239
Ball Aerospace & Technologies Corp. 220
Beale Fine Art Picture Framing 240
Boulder Chamber of Commerce 277
Boulder Community Hospital 274
Boulder Cork 241
Boulder Municipal Employees Federal Credit Union 210
Boulder Theater 283
Boulder Valley Credit Union 211
Boulder Wine Merchant 242
Case Logic 221
Celestial Seasonings, Inc. 222
Chrisman Construction 190
Coburn Development, Inc. 198
Colorado Chautauqua Association 280
Colorado Music Festival 282
Communication Arts 267
Community Medical Center 276
Crossroads Mall 243
The Daily Times-Call 291
D&K Printing, Inc. 223
Dean Callan & Company 199
Downing, Thorpe & James 268
Downtown Management Commission and Downtown Boulder Inc. 284
EDS Centrobe Corporation 296
Exabyte 298
Fisher Chevrolet Honda 244
Flatiron Companies 192
Foot of the Mountain Motel 245
Haystack Mountain Golf Course 288
Helping Hands Health Education 250
Heritage Bank 212
Historic Boulder, Inc. 289
Hutchinson Black and Cook, LLC 260
Johnson Photography 262
Kinsley & Co. 246
Lafayette Collectables & Flea Market 247
Leopard Communications 264
Lighting Plus 248
Longmont United Hospital 290
MacLaren Markowitz Gallery 249
McGuckin Hardware 232
Mike's Camera 226
Mock Realty and Mock Property Management Companies 200
Neptune Mountaineering 234
North Boulder Liquor 251
Pasta Jay's 252
Pearl Street Inn 253
Peppercorn 236
Premier Members Federal Credit Union 213
Prudential Wise-McIntire Realtors 194
Pueblo Bank & Trust Company 214
RE/MAX of Boulder, Inc. 201
Rocky Mountain Joe's Cafe 254
Slade Glass Co. 269
Spyder Active Sports 218
St. Vrain Valley Credit Union 206
Sturtz and Copeland 255
Terra Verde Development, LLC 270
The W.W. Reynolds Companies 196
Twin Peaks Mall 256
U of C Federal Credit Union 208
University of Colorado at Boulder 286
The Village 257
Wright Kingdom Realtors, Inc. 202